Communications in Computer and Information Science   1053

Commenced Publication in 2007
Founding and Former Series Editors:
Phoebe Chen, Alfredo Cuzzocrea, Xiaoyong Du, Orhun Kara, Ting Liu,
Krishna M. Sivalingam, Dominik Ślęzak, Takashi Washio, Xiaokang Yang,
and Junsong Yuan

More information about this series at http://www.springer.com/series/7899

Miguel Felix Mata-Rivera · Roberto Zagal-Flores ·
Cristian Barría-Huidobro (Eds.)

Telematics and Computing

8th International Congress, WITCOM 2019
Merida, Mexico, November 4–8, 2019
Proceedings

Editors
Miguel Felix Mata-Rivera ⓘ
Instituto Politécnico Nacional
Mexico City, Mexico

Roberto Zagal-Flores ⓘ
Instituto Politécnico Nacional
Mexico City, Mexico

Cristian Barría-Huidobro ⓘ
Universidad Mayor
Santiago, Chile

ISSN 1865-0929   ISSN 1865-0937 (electronic)
Communications in Computer and Information Science
ISBN 978-3-030-33228-0   ISBN 978-3-030-33229-7 (eBook)
https://doi.org/10.1007/978-3-030-33229-7

This Springer imprint is published by the registered company Springer Nature Switzerland AG
The registered company address is: Gewerbestrasse 11, 6330 Cham, Switzerland

Preface

Nowadays, interest in telematics is increasing, especially as the field continues to be immersed in various lines of research and converges with areas such as artificial intelligence and data science. Without neglecting the high interest in climate change and environmental issues, which cannot be alienated from the geospatial revolution, high-quality jobs with a wide range of approaches were unarguably received, including computer security and the Internet of Things. During WITCOM 2019, all these topics were incorporated and reflected upon. This year, the research papers included machine learning, augmented reality, and education in different cases studies.

The WITCOM conference attracts a large number of students, researchers, and industrialists; in this edition, the GIS community had a broad participation providing an opportunity for meeting and interaction between attendants. The current proceedings contain the selected research papers. In total, 78 research papers were submitted and all submissions underwent a thorough peer-review process. Three members of the Program Committee reviewed each, and 31 were accepted (an acceptance rate of 40%).

Together, the documents presented here represent a set of high-quality contributions to the literature on GIS, computing, and telematics that addresses a wide range of contemporary issues. The conference program presented a broad set of session topics that extend beyond the documents contained in these minutes. The materials for all sessions are available on the conference website at www.witcom.upiita.ipn.mx and www.witcom.org.mx.

More than 78 presentations were received on all the tracks and workshops of WITCOM 2019, and it was a great effort to review them and join them into a consistent program. We want to thank God and all those who contributed to this effort, especially to the Laboratory of Geospatial Intelligence and Mobile Computing of UPIITA-IPN, ANTACOM A.C., CENTROGEO, Parque Científico y Tecnológico de Yucatán, article authors, session presenters, coordinators, members of the Program Committee, UPIITA staff, and sponsors. Without them, the event would not have been so successful.

November 2019

Miguel Felix Mata-Rivera
Roberto Zagal-Flores
Cristian Barría-Huidobro

Organization

Organizing Committee

General Chair

Miguel Félix Mata-Rivera   UPIITA-IPN, Mexico

Workshop Chair in Spatial Intelligence

Miriam Olivares   Yale University, USA

Academic Chair

Roberto Zagal-Flores   ESCOM-IPN, Mexico

Informatics Security Track

Cristian Barria-Huidobro   Universidad Mayor, Chile

Local Manager

Jairo Zagal-Flores   UNADM, Mexico

Posters Chair

Noe Sierra   UPIITA-IPN, Mexico

Program Committee (Research Papers)

Christophe Claramunt	Naval Academy Research Institute, France
Cristian Barria	Universidad Mayor, Chile
Lorena Galeazzi	Universidad Mayor, Chile
Claudio Casasolo	Universidad Mayor, Chile
Alejandra Acuña Villalobos	Universidad Mayor, Chile
Clara Burbano	Unicomfacauca, Colombia
Gerardo Rubino	Inria, France
Cesar Viho	Irisa, France
Jose E. Gomez	Université de Grenoble, France
Ken Arroyo Ohori	Delft University of Technology, The Netherlands
Mario Aldape Perez	CIDETEC-IPN, Mexico
Anzueto Rios Alvaro	UPIITA-IPN, Mexico
Ludovic Moncla	LIUPPA - UFR S&T de PAU (UPPA), France
Jose M. Lopez Becerra	Hochschule Furtwangen University, Germany
Shoko Wakamiya	Kyoto Sangyo University, Japan
Patrick Laube	ZAUW, Switzerland
Sergio Ilarri	University of Zaragoza, Spain

Sisi Zlatanova	TU Delft, The Netherlands
Stephan Winter	University of Melbourne, Australia
Stephen Hirtle	University of Pittsburg, USA
Steve Liang	University of Calgary, Canada
Tao Cheng	University College London, UK
Willington Siabato	Universidad Nacional, Colombia
Xiang Li	East Normal China University, China
Andrea Ballatore	University of London, UK
Carlos Di Bella	INTA, Argentina
Haosheng Huang	University of Zurich, Switzerland
Hassan Karimi	University of Pittsburgh, USA
Luis Manuel Vilches	CIC-IPN, Mexico
Victor Barrera Figueroa	UPIITA-IPN, Mexico
Adrián Castañeda Galván	UPIITA-IPN, Mexico
Thomaz Eduardo Figueiredo Oliveira	CINVESTAV-IPN, Mexico
Hiram Galeana Zapién	Laboratorio de TI, Cinvestav Tamaulipas, Mexico
Laura Ivoone Garay Jiménez	SEPI-UPIITA, Mexico
Domingo Lara	CINVESTAV-IPN, Mexico
Aldo Gustavo Orozco Lugo	CINVESTAV-IPN, Mexico
Giovanni Guzman Lugo	CIC-IPN, Mexico
Vladimir Luna	CIC-IPN, Mexico
Omar Juarez Gambino	ESCOM-IPN, Mexico
Itzama Lopez Yañez	CIDETEC-IPN, Mexico
Miguel Ángel León Chávez	BUAP-Facultad de Ciencias de la Computación, Mexico
Alberto Luviano Juarez	UPIITA-IPN, Mexico
Marco Antonio Moreno Ibarra	CIC-IPN, Mexico
Mario H. Ramírez Díaz	CICATA-IPN, Mexico
Mario Eduardo Rivero Angeles	Communication Networks Laboratory, CIC-IPN, Mexico
Francisco Rodríguez Henríquez	CINVESTAV-IPN, Mexico
Patricio Ordaz Oliver	Universidad Politécnica de Pachuca
Izlian Orea	UPIITA-IPN, Mexico
Rolando Quintero Tellez	CIC-IPN, Mexico
Grigori Sidorov	CIC-IPN, Mexico
Miguel Jesus Torres Ruiz	CIC-IPN, Mexico
Rosa Mercado	ESIME UC, Mexico
Blanca Rico	UPIITA-IPN, Mexico
Blanca Tovar	UPIITA-IPN, Mexico
Chadwick Carreto	ESCOM-IPN, Mexico
Ana Herrera	UAQ, Mexico
Hugo Jimenez	CIDESI, Mexico

José-Antonio León-Borges	UQROO, Mexico
Alejandro Molina-Villegas	CENTROGEO, Mexico
Néstor Darío Duque Méndez	UNAL, Colombia
Diego Muñoz	Universidad Mayor, Chile
David Cordero	Universidad Mayor, Chile
Jacobo Gonzalez-Leon	UPIITA-IPN, Mexico
Saul Ortega	Universidad Mayor, Chile
Robinson Osses	Universidad Mayor, Chile
Hugo Lazcano	ECOSUR, Mexico
Daniel Soto	Universidad Mayor, Chile
Gomez-Balderas Jose	GIPSA LAB, France
René Rodríguez-Zamora	UAS, Mexico
Carolina Tripp Barba	UAS, Mexico
Iliana Amabely	UPSIN, Mexico
Leonor Espinoza	UAS, Mexico
Diana López-Mesa	Unicomfacauca, Colombia
Diana Castro	ENCB-IPN, Mexico

Sponsors

ANTACOM A.C.
UPIITA-IPN
GIS LATAM

Collaborators

Alldatum Systems
Samani

Contents

Artificial Intelligence and Machine Learning

Software Engineering and Education

Internet of Things

Informatics Security

GIS and Climate Change

Real Geographies in Virtual Space: A Practical Workflow for Geovisualization with Immersive VR

Florian Hruby[1,2]([envelope]) [ORCID], Rainer Ressl[1],
Genghis De la Borbolla del Valle[1], Oscar Rodríguez Paz[1],
Verónica Aguilar Sierra[1], and Jorge Humberto Muñoa Coutiño[1]

[1] National Commission for the Knowledge and Use of Biodiversity
(CONABIO), Mexico City, Mexico
{fhruby, rressl, gborbolla, orodriguez,
vaguilar, jmunoa}@conabio.gob.mx
[2] Department of Geography and Regional Research, University of Vienna,
Vienna, Austria
florian.hruby@univie.ac.at

Abstract. Propelled by the video game industries, virtual reality (VR) systems are on the verge of entering the electronic mass media market. VR not just allows generating imaginary worlds, but also visualizing real geographies and possible past and future scenarios of real-world environments. However, VR capabilities of current geographic information systems (GIS) are limited as yet, thus challenging the transport of geodata into VR applications. Given the shortcomings of GIS, the present article proposes a practical workflow for the visualization of geographic information with immersive environments. Principal work steps are 3D-modeling, composition, performance optimization and the final dissemination on VR platforms. We will illustrate all elements of our workflow using the example of an immersive VR application of a coral reef in the Mexican Caribbean, thus providing both theoretical and practical background on the visualization of real-world data in VR space.

Keywords: Virtual reality · Immersion · Computer graphics · Game engine · Geographic information system

1 Introduction

1.1 Immersive VR

Recent literature on geographic information science (GIScience) documents an increasing interest in the application of immersive virtual reality (VR) technologies for geovisualization matters [1–3]. This interest is based upon the assumption that immersive VR stimulates understanding through the formation of spatial presence, defined as the sense of "being there" in a virtually mediated environment [4]. In line with current research [4, 5], immersion can be considered a technological quality of media that describes the extent to which an illusion of reality is delivered to the user.

© Springer Nature Switzerland AG 2019
M. F. Mata-Rivera et al. (Eds.): WITCOM 2019, CCIS 1053, pp. 3–15, 2019.
https://doi.org/10.1007/978-3-030-33229-7_1

To create such an illusion, highly immersive VR relies on stereo head-mounted displays (HMD) and 6 degrees of freedom (DoF) tracking systems. Moreover, a high-performance graphics processing unit (GPU) is required to render stereo images onto the HMD at a suitable frame rate in order to sustain the experience of presence and to avoid motion sickness.

Regarding the case of geovisualization, we can define several criteria an immersive VR system needs to meet in order to deliver an illusion of geographic realities [2]: (a) interactive and stereoscopic explorability; (b) 1:1 scale level, where users perceive a VR representation of a real place as they would do being physically there [6]; (c) realistic visualization of the geographic environment and all relevant agents regarding both appearance and behavior.

1.2   From GIS to Immersive VR Environments

Considering the aforementioned definitions and criteria, immersive VR is challenging geographic information systems (GIS) - a standard tool of GIScience - in several ways. Firstly, direct compatibility between GIS and HMD is as yet limited. Secondly, GIS data usually lacks resolution and information necessary to visualize geographic space in a realistic manner (e.g. 1:1 scale level, 3D models of fauna and flora). Thirdly, environmental characteristics such as atmospheric conditions (e.g. wind) or lighting can be visualized just indirectly and in an abstract manner with GIS. Given these shortcomings, the present article presents a practical workflow for the visualization of GIS-based data in immersive VR environments. This workflow is built upon four main steps of (a) 3D-modeling, (b) ecosystem composition, (c) performance optimization and (d) publication in VR-capable formats.

Figure 1 summarizes these steps, which will be discussed in further detail in the following sections. In parallel, we will illustrate each element of our workflow using the example of an immersive VR application of a coral reef in the Mexican Caribbean, which has been developed as part of the Mexico VR (MXVR) project.

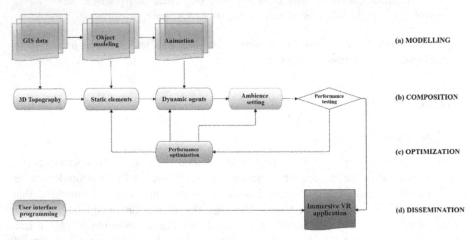

Fig. 1. Workflow for geovisualization with immersive VR - principal work steps: (a) modelling, (b) composition, (c) performance optimization and (d) dissemination

We cannot fail to mention that parts of the workflow shown in Fig. 1 have been already discussed by other authors (e.g. [7]). However, given the spatial extension and complexity of the underlying coral reef, this text will complement former work by several fundamental elements (e.g. ecosystem composition, collective movement, performance optimization).

2   3D-Object Modelling

2.1   GIS Base Data

Using basic features of points, lines and polygons, GIS data represents real-world phenomena in a categorized manner and from a bird's eye perspective. To generate meaning, GIS users have to interpret these features, e.g. in accordance with the map legend. However, in real space we rather see 3D objects than 2D features. Hence, in order to visualize GIS-based data within an immersive VR environment, points, lines and polygons need to be translated into the most important and (proto)typical objects of the real-world environment being represented.

Moreover, these objects are not distributed in a neutral and flat map space, but rather integrated into physical world's topography – information typically managed within digital terrain models (DTM) by GIS. In the present case of a Caribbean coral reef, high resolution bathymetry information, derived from WorldView-2 data, was available [8] (Fig. 2, left).

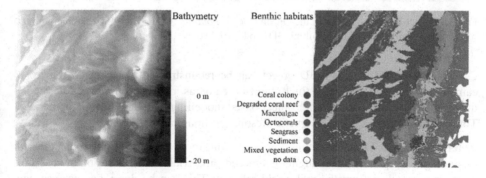

Fig. 2. GIS base data used for the MXVR project

More arbitrary is the disaggregation of points, lines and areas into 3D models of real-world elements. In our model case, classes of benthic habits (Fig. 2, right) were translated into lists of species documented by the Mexican National Biodiversity Information System [9] for each habitat within the study area shown in Fig. 2. Based on both ecosystemic and aesthetic criteria, the most important species of these listings were then selected for further 3D modelling (cf. Sect. 2.2).

2.2   Object Modelling

Object-Based Modelling. The probably most genuine approach of rebuilding a realworld object in digital space is measuring the object itself. Structure from motion (SfM), for instance, is a widely applied method of 3D modelling, where 3D structures are being estimated from a set of partly overlapping 2D photos taken from the original object [10].

Under appropriate conditions, SfM based modelling results not only in a detailed 3D replica of the object's form, but also provides high resolution textures of the object's surface. The Digital Life Project gives a series of examples on how SfM can be applied to model even living animals in a realistic manner [11, 12]. An application of SfM-based modelling within our coral reef VR visualization is given in Fig. 3.

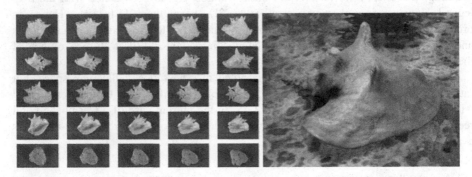

Fig. 3. Object-based modelling of the Queen Conch (*Lobatus gigas*) with SfM - sample of input scenes (left) and render of the resulting 3D model (right)

To achieve 2D images a 3D object can be reconstructed from, any commercial camera system can be used (incl. built-in cameras of smartphones). Alternative methods to generate input data for object-based modelling include X-ray Computerized Tomography (X-ray CT) or Magnetic Resonance Imaging (MRI) [13].

Reference-Based Modelling. Less genuine but more common than object-based modelling is the generation of digital geometries, materials and textures on the basis of guide images taken from the real-world referent. This can be done, for instance, via box-modelling techniques, where a geometric primitive (e.g. a cube) is iteratively modified and subdivided.

A different approach is followed by sculpting, where a polygon- or voxel-based mesh is digitally molded in analogy to clay in the physical world [14]. Regardless of the particular technique applied, guide images (ideally taken in a systematic way from side-, back-/front- and top-/bottom views) are used to realistically approximate the referent with adequate detail.

Sculpting allows representing organic shapes in a very fine detail, while box-modelling facilitates visualizations at a high geometric precision level (cf. Fig. 4).

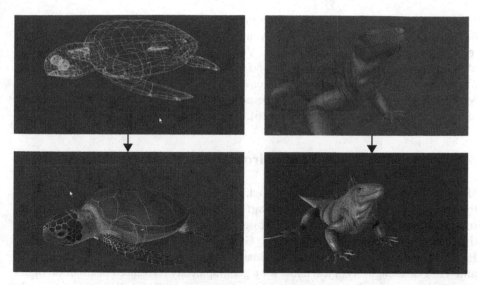

Fig. 4. Box-modelling (left) vs. sculpting (right) – exemplified by models of loggerhead sea turtle (*Caretta caretta*) and black iguana (*Ctenosaura similis*)

2.3   Animation

In Sect. 1.1 we argued that – in order to generate an illusion of geographic reality in VR space – users must perceive the virtual representation of a real place at a level of detail as they would do being physically there. This means not just realistically modelling all objects and agents (i.e. the computed objects that represent the real-world creature) of a geographic environment but also to simulate their motion sequences, that is to animate the 3D models created in the previous step (Sect. 2.2).

Skeletal Animation. Skeletal animation is a commonly used approach to convert static into dynamic 3D objects [15]. As indicated by the technique's name, a skeleton-like structure is defined for each object, representing its main parts (e.g. head, legs, and arms of a sea turtle) by so-called bones. Transforming position, scale and orientation of each bone in a systematic, frequent and hierarchical manner, motion patterns of the real-world referent can be represented (Fig. 5).

Fig. 5. Animation of the loggerhead sea turtle (*Caretta caretta*): Skeleton of the 3D model (left) and scenes from a resulting animation sequence (right)

Vertex Animation. Directly controlling the movement of vertices rather than bones, the vertex animation is another widely applied 3D computer animation technique relevant to immersive VR environments. Vertex positions are stored for typical stages of a motion sequence (e.g. the left- and rightmost position of a fish's caudal fin movement) and then interpolated between these stages during the animation process. Morph animation and pose animation (especially used to animate facial expressions) are two subtypes of vertex animation [16].

3   Composition of the VR Environment

Having defined relevant GIS data sets (incl. a high-resolution DTM) and disaggregated them into 3D models (Sect. 2), we can start blending these basic elements into a highly immersive and realistic environment. While this blending process cannot be done with the limited VR capabilities of current GIS, computer game engines (e.g. Unreal Engine® or Unity 3D®) provide an alternative approach to close the gap between GIS and VR. Game engines not just allow for a geographically referenced distribution of 3D models, but also a realistic setting of ambience parameters. We shall discuss these main steps at the composition stage of our workflow subsequently in further detail.

3.1   Topography

Since DTM contain 3D information (x/y position + z height) by definition, their visualization in VR systems is a straightforward process whose results depend on horizontal and vertical DTM resolution. Game engines can interpret topographical information in several vector and raster formats. In the present project, a grayscaled heightmap of the reef bathymetry (Fig. 2) was converted into a 3D mesh in Unreal Engine (cf. Fig. 6).

Fig. 6. GeoIVE before (left) and after (right) ambience setting.

3.2   Static Elements

Flora, inanimate nature and built-up areas, for instance, can be considered as static elements of geographic environments for conserving their position in space. Just as topography data, we can import information on the distribution of static elements directly (i.e. as georeferenced raster files) from GIS into game engine software. These distribution maps can, then, be used as a reference for allocating all 3D-models correctly.

We can exemplify the process of static element distribution relying once again on the model case of a VR coral reef. In a first step, information on the benthic habitats shown in Fig. 2 was (temporarily) mapped onto the bathymetry mesh. Since each habitat/color on the reference map had been already translated into 3D models of the most typical species (Sect. 2), we now distributed these models upon the bathymetry mesh by assigning each model to the accordant habitats/colors of the reference map.

Figure 6 illustrates a result of this process: Areas shown in red in Fig. 2 refer to coral colonies. Since Elkhorn corals (*acropora palmata*) are typical of our study area, they had been modelled in 3D and were then assigned to all areas labelled in red on the reference map.

3.3 Dynamic Agents

While static elements (e.g. seagrass, algae or corals within a reef) can be easily distributed in a realistic (i.e. georeferenced) manner, a different approach needs to be adopted for the simulation of dynamic agents (e.g. fish). In the simplest case, solitary agents have to avoid collision with other members of VR space. More complex is the modelling of collective movements (e.g. of animal swarms). Here the individual agent not just has to avoid collision, but also needs to polarize (i.e. to align with the average heading of neighbors) and aggregate towards the average position of the collective.

A common way of visualizing dynamic agents in VR space is path animation, where the 3D model is being attached to a predefined motion path (Fig. 7). Programming of ruled based motion patterns is an alternative and more realistic, yet computationally demanding approach, which allows to simulate not just movement but also behavior (foraging; relations of predator vs. prey; etc.) [17].

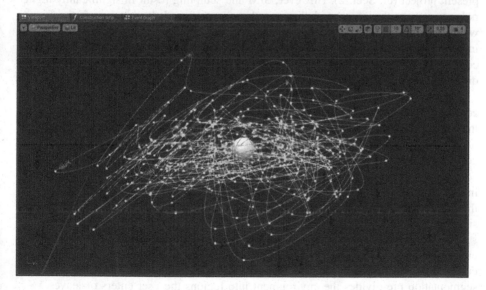

Fig. 7. Path network used to animate fish swarms in VR.

3.4   Ambience

The Oxford English Dictionary defines ambience as "[t]he character and atmosphere of a place." [18]. Character and atmosphere of a geographic place depend, for instance, on lighting conditions, ambient sound and atmospheric parameters. Including these elements into an immersive environment will strongly affect whether a given VR scene is perceived as realistic or not (cf. Fig. 6: left vs. right). Computer game engines provide a rich set of tools to simulate ambience by land and sea, and even underwater.

In our model case, we simulated color and visibility range of Caribbean waters by post-process-volume and exponential height fog functions in Unreal Engine. Underwater caustics were visualized with an animated material of the principal VR light source, while the effect of waves, e.g. on seagrass, was simulated by a virtual wind function. Suspended solids and air bubbles were represented by particle systems. Moreover, non-visual ambience settings were implemented via stereo scuba sounds [19].

4   Performance Optimization

Complex immersive geovisualizations, e.g. the VR coral reef discussed throughout this paper, are often constructed with millions of static objects and thousands of dynamic agents. All these elements have to be rendered in real time and at a high frame rate onto the HMD to sustain an illusion of reality. To guarantee these frame rates not just on highly specialized VR systems, but also on consumer-level gaming PCs or even mobile VR devices, several improvement measures can be implemented along the whole workflow.

At the stage of object modelling, different techniques have been tested within the present project (cf. Sect. 2). However, SfM and sculpting result in significantly higher polygon counts than box-modelling, so that we preferred the latter over the former where possible. In the case of objects rich in detail (Fig. 4), the 3D mesh was sculpted in a first step, and retopologized afterwards in order to reduce the sculpted model's complexity while conserving its details. Additionally, all objects were generated at different levels of detail (LOD) both regarding their polygon mesh and textures.

At the stage of dynamic agents, skeletal animation techniques provide higher control of motion patterns but require considerable amounts of processing power, since three parameters (rotation, translation and scale) need to be calculated per bone, per object and per frame. Texture based vertex animations, on the other hand, are more complex to define, but more flexible to integrate into advanced processes of ecosystem composition. For instance, vertex animated models can be used as hierarchically instanced static mesh components, where just a single object needs to be processed by the GPU while several instances of this object can be rendered. We use this method to simulate the shoaling behavior of fish.

A final step of optimization is the relative and/or absolute segmentation of the VR environment. In the case of relative segmentation, only objects visible from the user's current position in VR space will be rendered at different levels of detail. Absolute segmentation pre-divides the environment into regions the user enters or leaves.

Figure 8 illustrates this approach, which we adopted for the MXVR project: Suppose that Fig. 8 represents VR space in a map-like manner. Suppose further, a given user is virtually located in the central hexagon 1 (H1). Only within this hexagon, both static and dynamic elements are rendered, while neighboring hexagons (H1a-f) and hexagon spots (H2 and H3) remain empty, since they are beyond the user's range of vision. Imagine the user now moving from H1 towards H1c: As soon as the user leaves H1, all objects of H1 will be eliminated from the PC's working memory, and all objects of H1c will be loaded and rendered as soon as this hexagon is entered. The interspace between neighboring hexagons shown in Fig. 8 corresponds with the visibility range within the VR environment to avoid abrupt (dis)appearance of 3D objects. For the areas between hexagon spots (e.g. between 1a-f and 2a-f) only static elements are rendered. Users can traverse these areas or switch between different hexagon spots via teleports.

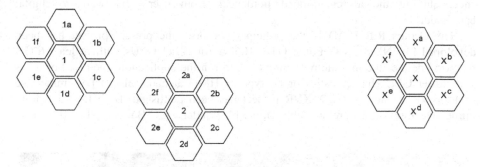

Fig. 8. Absolute segmentation of geographic VR environments

5 Dissemination

5.1 User Interface

Interactive and stereoscopic explorability at a 6DoF level is a defining criteria of immersive VR (cf. Sect. 1). To comply with this requirement, VR hardware relies on positional tracking systems in order to register and translate the user's position and movement in physical space into congruent views and actions in VR space. To make this translation between physical and virtual space as intuitive as possible, different approaches of user interaction and interface have been discussed by human–computer interaction (HCI) research (cf. [20]). This research focuses not just on possible techniques of user input (e.g. gestures, voice), but also on effective metaphors on how to map the user's perception and position in VR (e.g. avatars, embodiment) [21].

Since the MXVR project is tailored for the Oculus Rift headset, we use a wireless game controller as standard input device. Based on the flying vehicle control model metaphor [22], we programmed the controller for surging (x-), swaying (y-) and heaving (z-), as well as yawing, all at a constant speed. Rolling and pitching is only enabled by movement of the head(set) to simplify navigation.

Moreover, a small information dashboard advises the users on their position, diving depth and direction in VR space. Additional information on the species modelled is provided via 3D icons giving access to fact sheets in audio and text format.

5.2 Release

Consumer analysis on VR systems indicates a still small but constantly growing market, which is clearly dominated by the Oculus Rift® and HTC Vive ® platforms [23]. Both HMD systems are broadly supported by game engine software. However, when it comes about rendering stereo images on the fly, the actual bottleneck of immersive VR is not so much the availability of a suitable HMD, but rather the performance limits of current gaming GPUs. While these limits might be overcome – in accordance with Moore's law [24] – during the next years, streaming platforms provide an alternative approach to deliver high resolution VR environments to a broad audience, shifting the aforementioned bottleneck from user's hardware to digital bandwidth.

The Oculus Rift HMD is the principal platform, the present project has been developed for. NVidia's GeForce GTX 1060® (or equal GPUs with at least 6 GB memory) defines the minimum requirements to run the application fluently. For users with lower GPU characteristics or no type of HMD at hand, also a low-immersive desktop VR version of the MXVR project has been published. Both full- and low-immersive applications are available online [25] under a CC BY-NC-ND 4.0 license.

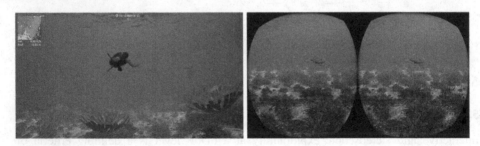

Fig. 9. Non-stereoscopic (left: desktop) and stereoscopic (right: Oculus Rift®) renders from the MXVR project (release candidate)

6 Conclusion

In this paper, we presented a practical workflow on how to convert GIS data into a realistic immersive VR application. This workflow is just an early and only one possible way of bridging geographic and virtual reality. However, paths are made by walking, and during this text we tried to take a few steps further to make this path. These steps have proven feasible and effective (Fig. 9), but future improvements on our workflow are foreseeable at all stages.

At the stage of geographic base data, next generation GIS may already provide significantly higher VR capabilities, thus speeding up the information transport between real and virtual space. ESRI's CityEngine®, for instance, already offers plug-ins to support GIS integration with game engines [26], indicating that GIScience may – in line with our workflow – rather opt for an indirect connection between GIS and VR via game engines than trying to make GIS directly compatible with HMDs.

At the stage of object modelling, currently common but time-consuming reference-based techniques may be displaced by semi- and full-automated approaches like SfM. Recently presented mobile devices with (stereo) pairs of cameras could convert SfM based modelling into a common form of 3D data acquisition and communication.

At the stage of ecosystem composition, we mapped interactions between flora and fauna of the MXVR project only at a very coarse level, e.g. in terms of path animations. Implementing artificially intelligent (AI) behavior will allow us to realistically simulate even higher order relationships, e.g. food chains or predator-prey-relationships, as well as future or past environmental (e.g. climate change) scenarios [17].

At the stage of dissemination, increasingly powerful and affordable hardware could further broaden the application range of VR technologies. For example, wireless HMDs and also mixed-reality headsets (e.g. Microsoft Hololens®) may facilitate new forms of interaction and interfaces between real and virtual space [27, 28], that is: between human and computer.

References

1. Çöltekin, A., Oprean, D., Wallgrün, J.O., Klippel, A.: Where are we now? Re-visiting the digital earth through human-centered virtual and augmented reality geovisualization environments, 119–122 (2019). https://doi.org/10.1080/17538947.2018.1560986
2. Hruby, F., Ressl, R., De la Borbolla del Valle, G.: Geovisualization with immersive virtual environments in theory and practice. Int. J. Digit. Earth 12(2), 123–136 (2019). https://doi.org/10.1080/17538947.2018.1501106
3. Klippel, A., et al.: Transforming earth science education through immersive experiences: delivering on a long held promise. J. Educ. Comput. Res. (2019). https://doi.org/10.1177/0735633119854025
4. Skarbez, R., Brooks Jr., F.P., Whitton, M.C.: A survey of presence and related concepts. ACM Comput. Surv. (CSUR) 50(6), 96 (2017). https://doi.org/10.1145/3134301
5. Cummings, J.J., Bailenson, J.N.: How immersive is enough? A meta-analysis of the effect of immersive technology on user presence. Media Psychol. 19(2), 272–309 (2016). https://doi.org/10.1080/15213269.2015.1015740
6. Hruby, F.: From third-person to first-person cartographies with immersive virtual environments. Proc. Int. Cartogr. Assoc. 2, 44 (2019). https://doi.org/10.5194/ica-proc-2-44-2019
7. Edler, D., Husar, A., Keil, J., Vetter, M., Dickmann, F.: Virtual Reality (VR) and open source software: a workflow for constructing an interactive cartographic VR environment to explore urban landscapes. Kartographische Nachrichten 68(1), 3–11 (2018)
8. Cerdeira-Estrada, et al.: Benthic habitat and bathymetry mapping of shallow waters in Puerto Morelos reefs using remote sensing with a physics based data processing. In: IEEE International Geoscience and Remote Sensing Symposium, pp. 4383–4386. IEEE, Munich (2012). https://doi.org/10.1109/igarss.2012.6350402

9. Sarukhán, J., Jiménez, R.: Generating intelligence for decision making and sustainable use of natural capital in Mexico. Curr. Opin. Environ. Sustain. **19**, 153–159 (2016). https://doi.org/10.1016/j.cosust.2016.02.002

10. Carrivick, J.L., Smith, M.W., Quincey, D.J.: Structure from Motion in the Geosciences. Wiley, Chichester (2016)

11. Digital Life. http://digitallife3d.org. Accessed 11 June 2019

12. Bot, J.A., Irschick, D.J.: Using 3D photogrammetry to create open-access models of live animals: 2D and 3D software solutions. In: Grayburn, J., Lischer-Katz, Z., Golubiewski-Davis, K., Ikeshoji-Orlati, V. (eds.) 3D/VR in the Academic Library: Emerging Practices and Trends, pp. 54–72. Council on Library and Information Resources, Arlington (2019)

13. Tran, M.H., Vu, H.M.Q.: A research on 3D model construction from 2D DICOM. In: International Conference on Advanced Computing and Applications (ACOMP), pp. 158–163. IEEE, Can Tho City (2016). https://doi.org/10.1109/acomp.2016.031

14. Knopf, G.K., Igwe, P.C.: Deformable mesh for virtual shape sculpting. Robot. Comput.-Integr. Manuf. **21**(4–5), 302–311 (2005). https://doi.org/10.1016/j.rcim.2004.11.002

15. Jensen, J.A., Burton, R.P.: Fourveo: integration of 4D animation into conventional 3D animation workflows. Comput. Animat. Virtual Worlds **29**(3–4), e1816 (2018). https://doi.org/10.1002/cav.1816

16. Basori, A.H., Al Jahdali, H.M.A.: Emotional facial expression based on action units and facial muscle. Int. J. Electr. Comput. Eng. **6**(5), 2478–2487 (2016). https://doi.org/10.11591/ijece.v6i5.12135

17. Magallanes Guijón, G., Hruby, F., Ressl, R., Aguilar Sierra, V., De la Borbolla del Valle, G., Rodríguez Paz, O.: Modelling of collective movement in immersive environments. In: International Archives of the Photogrammetry, Remote Sensing & Spatial Information Sciences, vol. XLII–4, pp. 397–402 (2018). https://doi.org/10.5194/isprs-archives-xlii-4-397-2018

18. OED: The New Oxford Dictionary of English. Oxford University Press, Oxford (2001)

19. Hruby, F.: The sound of being there: audiovisual cartography with immersive virtual environments. KN-J. Cartogr. Geogr. Inf. **69**(1), 19–28 (2019). https://doi.org/10.1007/s42489-019-00003-5

20. Wilk, M.P., Torres-Sanchez, J., Tedesco, S., O'Flynn, B.: Wearable human computer interface for control within immersive VAMR gaming environments using data glove and hand gestures. In: 2018 IEEE Games, Entertainment, Media Conference (GEM), pp. 1–9. IEEE (2018). https://doi.org/10.1109/gem.2018.8516521

21. Ahn, S.J.G., Bostick, J., Ogle, E., Nowak, K.L., McGillicuddy, K.T., Bailenson, J.N.: Experiencing nature: embodying animals in immersive virtual environments increases inclusion of nature in self and involvement with nature. J. Comput.-Mediat. Commun. **21**(6), 399–419 (2016). https://doi.org/10.1111/jcc4.12173

22. Duan, Q., Gong, J., Li, W., Shen, S., Li, R.: Improved cubemap model for 3D navigation in geo-virtual reality. Int. J. Digit. Earth **8**(11), 877–900 (2015). https://doi.org/10.1080/17538947.2014.947339

23. Steam Hardware & Software Survey. https://store.steampowered.com/hwsurvey/Steam-Hardware-Software-Survey-Welcome-to-Steam. Accessed 11 June 2019

24. Moore, G.E.: Progress in digital integrated electronics. Electron Devices Meet. **21**, 11–13 (1975). https://doi.org/10.1109/N-SSC.2006.4804410

25. CONABIO Geovisualization. https://www.biodiversidad.gob.mx/v_ingles/region/geoviz.html. Accessed 11 June 2019

26. Boulos, M., Lu, Z., Guerrero, P., Jennett, C., Steed, A.: From urban planning and emergency training to Pokémon Go: applications of virtual reality GIS (VRGIS) and augmented reality GIS (ARGIS) in personal, public and environmental health. Int. J. Health Geogr. **16**, 7 (2017). https://doi.org/10.1186/s12942-017-0081-0
27. Keil, J., Edler, D., Dickmann, F.: Preparing the HoloLens for user studies: an augmented reality interface for the spatial adjustment of holographic objects in 3D indoor environments. KN-J. Cartogr. Geogr. Inf. **69**, 1–11 (2019). https://doi.org/10.1007/s42489-019-00025-z
28. Satriadi, K.A., Ens, B., Cordeil, M., Czauderna, T., Willett, W.J., Jenny, B.: Augmented reality map navigation with freehand gestures. In: IEEE Virtual Reality (2019, forthcoming)

Cross-Layer Architecture Applied to Geospatial Information Communication in Embedded Systems

Luis Angel Camacho Campos$^{(\boxtimes)}$ (iD), David Araujo Diaz,
and Jesus Alfredo Martinez Nuño

ESCOM-IPN, Juan de Dios Bátiz, Lindavista, 07738 Mexico City, Mexico
lcamachocl600@alumno.ipn.mx

Abstract. This paper presents a high-level design for cross-layer architecture, it was implemented using an embedded system, which aims an effective communication for Geospatial Information through Wi-Fi technology, in order to emulate an Automatic Dependent Surveillance Broadcasting (ADS-B) system. This system shares geospatial information gathered from one or more Global Navigation Satellite System (GNSS) through another communication mechanism onboard. Since one module of ADS-B was proposed to be necessary for the future for most of the controlled airspace. Therefore, the proposed system presents the main advantage of providing a low-cost solution in low-performance hardware. Also, it brings the capability of increment situational awareness through a graphic interface. In this study a real-world deployment was simulated in order to know the viability for development and node's location accuracy; results showed that ADS-B functionalities were attained successfully by proposed implementation in mobile devices and it turned into a location aid that could be useful in several scenarios.

Keywords: Communication · Embedded systems · Geospatial information

1 Introduction

Currently, air navigation is mostly supported by satellite systems; among these systems are the Global Positioning System (GPS), the European Geostationary Navigation Overlay Service (EGNOS), Galileo and others [1]. However, data gathered from these systems are useful for final users such as pilots and drivers, above is caused by the lack of proper communication systems that allow sharing information in order to know nearby vehicles position.

According to [2], communication is one of the most important aspects to get success in an operation where many vehicles participate. Therefore, different mechanisms, systems, and approaches have been studied to provide an effective data link between vehicles. In [3] for software reconfigurable is proposed in order to rearrange logically communications devices on board when one or more of these systems fail. On the other hand, in [4] an additional communication system based on WiMAX Technology was proposed, in order to attain a decentralized and unstructured mechanism

M. F. Mata-Rivera et al. (Eds.): WITCOM 2019, CCIS 1053, pp. 16–24, 2019.
https://doi.org/10.1007/978-3-030-33229-7_2

called ait-to-air Communication (A2A Comm), through an Ad Hoc network configuration. Also, the use of microsatellite terminals was proposed in [5], this solution brings a centralized solution with a long-range operation but it has a high operational cost due to the L-band congestion, which is the operating band for this kind of devices. Following, in [6] a theoretical concept about Wi-Fi Technology was proposed as an alternative for the ADS-B system and according to the Federal Aviation Administration (FAA), an ADS-B OUT module will be necessary for most controlled airspace [7] in 2020, therefore this work describes the development of a communication protocol based on a cross-layer architecture to share geospatial information on a Mobile Ad Hoc Network (MANET) using mobile low-performance devices.

ADS-B is a single-hop communication; i.e., the sent data is acquired by an ADS-B IN module and the data is treated, however, ADS-B data flow is not considered as a multi-hop communication, Oluwatosin, *et al.* [8] mention the challenges of this kind of architecture, that they name device-to-device (D2D) communication. Hence, ADS-B functionality could be extended and improved using MANET's approach for multi-hop communication.

Next section describes the development of proposed architecture, following by a section that shows the results and their discussion, then a section of conclusions and references.

2   Development of the Vehicle Location System (VLS)

ADS-B is divided mainly in two modules ADS-B OUT and ADS-B IN [9], first module gathers information from GNSS or other Geospatial Information provider and then transmit that information even if there are not nearby receivers; the second module receives data and process it to be interpreted by a final user, in Fig. 1 general data flow between vehicles is depicted, vehicles are going to be named nodes henceforth.

The Wi-Fi technology selection was based on the study presented in [10] where a data link of 279 km was established as a result of this research, thence, in a smaller area Wi-Fi turns into a more suitable alternative.

2.1   Cross-Layer Architecture Design

Traditionally, the Open System Interconnection (OSI) model is referred to explain how communication is carried out through layers, for this reason, a comparison using this model is depicted in Fig. 2, in order to explain how the proposed cross-layer architecture works.

Proposed VLS moves data from application, presentation and session layer to transport layer where User Datagram Protocol (UDP) is used, then, due to Ad Hoc configuration, a package is carried out from the transport layer to network layer, finally, the standard 802.11 [11] that works in the data link and physical layers is responsible for transmitting message. Thence, the receiver does the same action inversely.

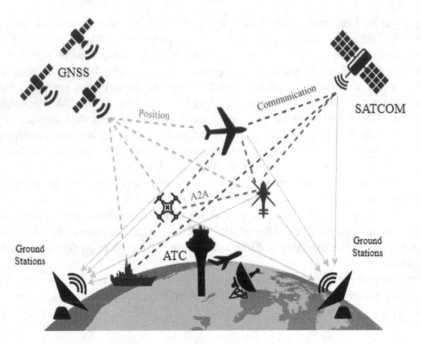

Fig. 1. Data Flow in an ADS-B system. A2A Comm does not need a centralized point forward gathered data from GNSS.

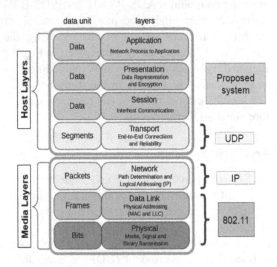

Fig. 2. Cross-layer comparison with the OSI model.

2.2   Communication Protocol Design

Designed VLS implements a software approach protocol and it defines rules to transmit and receive data but it is supported by designed protocols and standards on each layer. i.e., the software manages lower layers to make transmission possible. In Fig. 3 ADS-B OUT data flow diagram is depicted. A GNSS receptor is necessary and the most common protocol used to get geospatial data from receptors such as GNSS is NMEA [12] protocol that provides a text string with positioning data, visible satellites and other information, predefined GGA and RMC strings from NMEA protocol, were used to get positioning data, after, software concatenates battery state and node state to form the message, then, a security standard cipher this message, finally an identifier is added for transmission. UDP sockets are used in order to increase performance due to it does not need verification or response messages, avoiding bandwidth consumption in comparison with TCP sockets.

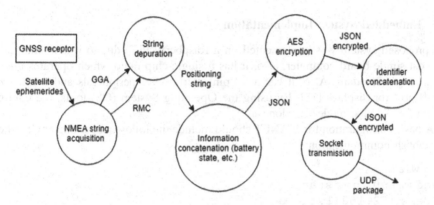

Fig. 3. ADS-B OUT data flow diagram.

For the ADS-B IN module, Wi-Fi adapter receives packages and the standard 802.11 treats them to the upper layer, socket listeners trigger the process to recognize the received package and if it is not repeated security standard decipher the message. At this point, and in the sender counterpart, the Advanced Encryption Standard (AES) [13] is used for this purpose due to it belongs to symmetric key authentication mechanisms, i.e., the receiver needs to have the same transmitter's key (e.g., passphrase, shared token or others), the above pursues bringing data privacy due to simple Ad Hoc configuration does not provide authentication mechanisms such as WPA [14]. After that, the actual information is obtained and finally, the software provides data as a service that web application consumes to show on a web browser where digital cartography is deployed from a Geographic Information System (GIS). In Fig. 4 this process is depicted.

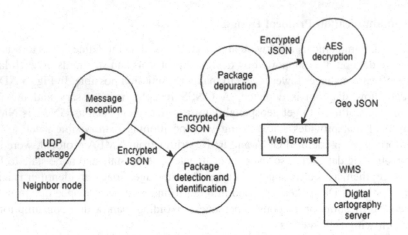

Fig. 4. ADS-B IN data flow diagram.

2.3 Embedded System Implementation

The proposed system was implemented on a Raspberry Pi 3, due to it is a small and low-cost single-board computer, also, it has a single-chip radio which operates under 802.11 b/g/n standard, Also, it has a 40 pin interface for peripherals and a full-size HDMI port for displays [15]. By using the Operating System (OS) tools, the configuration for Ad Hoc mode was done.

A basic configuration for MANET should include the following parameters in order to establish communication:

```
auto wlan0
iface wlan0 inet static
address 192.168.1.1
netmask 255.255.255.0
wireless-channel 1
wireless-essid MYADHOCNET
wireless-mode ad-hoc
```

Where address refers to static IP address and it has to be different for each node while wireless-essid has to be the same for nodes in that network. After MANET was setting up, the system was embedded using nodejs wrapper, giving the advantage of deploying the system on any OS. Although this configuration works, it would be better if this configuration occurs automatically since there could exist a large number of nodes connected and due to its dynamism they can leave or join the MANET several times, in [16] a prophet address allocation is proposed and it is a suitable option for scale this system application.

Digital cartography was served by a Java-based GIS called GeoServer which manages raster resources using Web Map Service (WMS) and serves them to the web browser using HyperText Transfer Protocol (HTTP) [17]. There, all data is gathered, and it is shown on different data layers. The final integration of all data layers is depicted in Fig. 5, where a display allows an understandable data interpretation, thence,

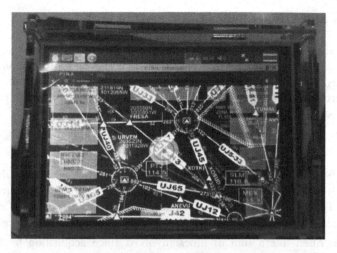

Fig. 5. Actual photo of the deployed full system.

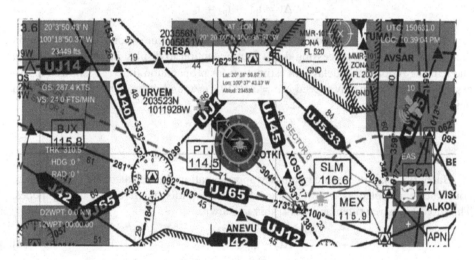

Fig. 6. Graphic interface with gathered geospatial data displayed.

it provides a georeferenced graphic way for providing situational awareness. Above is due to the graphic way is the most used Human-Computer Interaction (HCI).

Consequently, graphic interface is composed by useful preprocessed data such as latitude, longitude, altitude, vertical and horizontal speed, Universal Time Coordinated (UTC), a number of visible satellite and zoom in and zoom out gadget. Also, according to the pointer position a context menu shows neighbor nodes coordinates (Fig. 6).

3 Results and Discussion

After implementation, for avoiding possible collisions, accuracy test was simulated, above due to there is a delay between position acquisition and information displaying which derives in position difference, one aspect to consider for avoiding crashes. Although there are many variables to take into account such as reflected signals [18], a time-based accuracy factor is described starting in (1).

$$\Delta t = t_f - t_i \tag{1}$$

Where t_f is the time where data is displayed and t_i is the time where GNSS data is received, both actions take place in different nodes. For (1), clock synchronization is needed, so UTC could be used but its accuracy is 1 s, thence, Δt could take a value of 0, in small areas or high dynamic scenarios. In order to obtain a difference estimation $\widetilde{\Delta t}$, (1) is rewritten like a sum of times involved since acquisition to display, (2) describe this sum.

$$\widetilde{\Delta t} = t_{p1} + t_{p2} + t_e \tag{2}$$

Where t_{p1} is processing delay from positioning data acquisition to transmission in the source node, t_{p2} is processing delay from reception to display in the receiver node, and t_e is the propagation delay. An estimation for propagation time $\widetilde{t}_e$ is showed in (3), assuming that known wave speed is $c = 3 \times (10^8)$ m/s, and distance average d_e between neighbor nodes.

$$\widetilde{t}_e = \frac{d_e}{c} \tag{3}$$

Based on (3), now distance accuracy approximation can be calculated, this distance could be represented as a geofencing which alert pilots or drivers of nearby nodes. Therefore (2) is rewritten and in (4) this is shown.

$$\widetilde{\Delta t} = t_{p1} + t_{p2} + \widetilde{t}_e \tag{4}$$

Up to now, $\widetilde{t}_e$ described in (3) allows obtaining a radius, i.e. it is the position accuracy calculated from the time difference between the source and destination nodes.

Table 1. Radius estimation in different scenarios.

Vehicle	d_e	$\widetilde{t}_e$	$\widetilde{\Delta t}$	s	Φd
Car (populated city)	1	3.3×10^{-9}	0.223035	2.77	**0.61**
Plane (Boeing 787)	500	1.6×10^{-6}	0.223037	222.22	**49.56**
Fighter aircraft (Northrop F-5)	2.5	8.3×10^{-9}	0.223035	277.77	**61.95**
Helicopter (Bell 412)	250	8.3×10^{-7}	0.223036	62.77	**13.99**

With (5) is possible to get radius estimation Φd, where s is the speed of the node. Also, taking into account data described in Table 1 some estimation is given [4, 19, 20].

$$\Phi d \approx (\widetilde{\Delta t})(s) \qquad (5)$$

Using JavaScript tools the average of t_{p1} and t_{p1} were settled in 0.012858 and 0.210177 respectively after 10 simulations from data gathering to displaying. Distance is showed in meters and time in seconds, so Φd is shown in meters.

Based on Table 1, radius Φd is different for each vehicle, while speed increments a major geofencing radius is necessary in order to increase accuracy. According to related work, this paper presents an augmented fencing solution which increases avoidance for possible collisions; also, this work provides a low-cost solution, unlike satellite terminals proposed in [5], on the other hand, proposed system is added on, however, proposed solution in [3] could be used jointly thought different communication interfaces.

Despite using the same principle of Ad Hoc network, this work offers an easy and cheap implementation alternative and proposed solution augments traditional ADS-B single-hop communication, due to nodes relay the received package, becoming in a multi-hop communication system, and it gives wider area coverage than the traditional one. The accuracy is a stochastic value because many factors impact it, however, the presented time-based accuracy bias is lower than their WiMax counterparts presented in the results of [4].

4 Conclusions

Results obtained show a suitable alternative for new requirements in an increasing aerospatial industry, although there are systems with similar capabilities, this work approach allows a non invasive implementation and a low-cost alternative that can be applied not only in rotary-wing aircrafts or planes with small dimensions, but also in drones or Unmanned Aircraft Vehicles (UAV), cars, ships, and other dynamic element.

Safety could be the most important aspect in trends for unmanned transportation since human mistakes are avoided but technology inherits those responsibilities, improvements presented show aid for manned vehicles, therefore, it could be scalable, in order to provide automatic navigation.

As part of future work, optimization is needed to accomplish international standards that prove this system can be used in commercial flight, highly populated controlled airspace, as well as, vehicular control according to safety protocols for autonomous cars. Application scenarios are not limited, and above describe just a few ones; people tracking, location aid for vehicles, and traffic assistance for smart cities, node networks, pervasive computing and more. Also, this VLS could be provided with video streaming capabilities, since bandwidth constraints are manageable from each node (e.g. in [21], a Cross-Layer Technic is mentioned in order to allow video streaming).

Acknowledgment. We would like to express our gratitude to *Consejo Nacional de Ciencia y Tecnología (CONACYT), Instituto Politécnico Nacional (IPN)* and, especially to *Escuela Superior de Cómputo (ESCOM)*, for supporting this research.

References

1. Groves, P.D.: Principles of GNSS, Inertial, and Multisensor Integrated Navigation System, 2nd edn. A. H, Boston (2013)
2. Mexican Air Force: private interview (2018)
3. Jayachandran, M., Manikandan, J.: Software reconfigurable state-of-the-art communication suite for fighter aircraft. In: 2011 International Conference on Communication Systems and Network Technologies, pp. 729–733 (2011)
4. Vengadesh, A., Gunasekaran, P.: Design and development of aircraft to aircraft communication by ad-hoc networks. In: 2015 International Conference on Circuit, Power and Computing Technologies (2015)
5. Lee, L.-N., et al.: Micro satellite terminal-based high data rate communication for rotary wing aircraft. In: 2014 IEEE Military Communications Conference, pp. 1698–1703 (2014)
6. Deepu, G.K. Sethuraman, N.R.: A study of various aircraft communication technologies. In: International Conference on Communication and Electronics Systems (2017)
7. Federal Aviation Administration ADS Page. https://www.faa.gov/nextgen/programs/adsb/. Accessed 15 Mar 2019
8. Amodu, O.A., Othman, M., Noordin, N.K., Idawaty, A.: A primer on design aspects, recent advances, and challenges in cellular device-to-device communication. Ad Hoc Netw. **94**, 101938 (2019)
9. Busyairah, S.A.: ADS-B system failure modes and model. J. Navig. **27**, 995–1017 (2014)
10. Flickenger, R.: Very long-distance Wi-Fi networks. In: ACM SIGCOMM Workshop on Networked Systems for Developing Regions (2008)
11. IEEE Standard for Information Technology. IEEE Standard 802.11 (2012)
12. NMEA data. https://www.gpsinformation.org/dale/nmea.htm. Accessed 02 Apr 2019
13. Crypto. https://nodejs.org/api/crypto.html. Accessed 20 Mar 2019
14. Kaur, R., Singh, T.P., Khajuria, V.: Security issues in vehicular ad-hoc network (VANET). In: 2nd International Conference on Trends in Electronics and Informatics, pp. 884–889 (2018)
15. RPI 3 Model B Product. https://www.raspberrypi.org/products/raspberry-pi-3-model-b. Accessed 10 Feb 2019
16. Zhou, H., Ni, L.M., Mutka, M.W.: Prophet address allocation for large scale MANETs. Ad Hoc Netw. J. **1**, 423–434 (2003)
17. GeoServer. http://geoserver.org. Accessed 01 Feb 2019
18. Yu, P., Yao, Y., Lou, M., Zhang, L.: Analysis and research of GNSS near ground signal based on the dilution of precision. In: IEEE ICCC, pp. 1790–1794 (2016)
19. Excelsior. https://www.excelsior.com.mx/comunidad/2016/11/14/1128068. Accessed 29 Apr 2019
20. FAA. https://www.faa.gov/air_traffic/separation_standards/. Accessed 01 May 2019
21. Rathod, N., Dongre, N.: MANET routing protocol performance for video streaming. In: 2017 International Conference on Nascent Technologies in the Engineering Field (2017)

Methodology to Create Geospatial MODIS Dataset

Geraldine Álvarez-Carranza[1] and Hugo E. Lazcano-Hernández[2(✉)]

[1] El Colegio de la Frontera Sur, Estación para la Recepción de Información Satelital ERIS-Chetumal, Av. Centenario Km 5.5, 77014 Chetumal, Quintana Roo, Mexico
[2] Cátedras CONACYT-El Colegio de la Frontera Sur, Chetumal, Quintana Roo, Mexico
hlazcanoh@ecosur.mx

Abstract. Training and testing of algorithms used in computing for application in several studies, require datasets previously validated and labeled. In the case of satellite remote sensing, there are several platforms with large volumes of open source data. Aqua and Terra satellite platforms have available the sensor MODIS (Moderate-Resolution Imaging Spectroradiometer) which has available open access data for earth observation. Despite the facilities offered by the MODIS data platform, extracting data from a particular region for the construction of useful dataset requires an arduous work that includes manual, semi-automatic and automatic stages. The present study proposes a methodology for the construction of a geospatial dataset using MODIS sensor data. This methodology has been successfully implemented in the construction of dataset for the analysis of physical and biological variables in the Caribbean Sea, highlighting its application in the monitoring of Sargasso along the coastline of the state of Quintana Roo. Its application can be extended to any of the data and products offered by the MODIS sensor.

Keywords: MODIS dataset · Geospatial dataset · Sargasso · MODIS processor

1 Introduction

Studies of earth observation are carried out with open-access optical satellite data, highlighting the sensors AQUA-MODIS, TERRA-MODIS, and Landsat-OLI [1–5]. Spectral and radiometric resolutions of MODIS sensor have been sub-used since a few bands have been limited to the use of RGB images and some indexes. For example, the MODIS sensor allows 38 bands with 12 bits of radiometric resolution [6], which in principle mean 155648 possible values for every pixel. Therefore, it is advisable to work with the data that composes every band. Therefore, this study propose to build a dataset with the spectral and radiometric MODIS data, to training, testing, and validate data science algorithms. As a very first stage, to build the data set, it is necessary to define:

© Springer Nature Switzerland AG 2019
M. F. Mata-Rivera et al. (Eds.): WITCOM 2019, CCIS 1053, pp. 25–33, 2019.
https://doi.org/10.1007/978-3-030-33229-7_3

study region, analysis time, physical or biological variables according to the characteristics of the study and the spatial, temporal, radiometric and spectral resolutions useful for the analysis. All the above will allow to know which satellite platform and which sensor is suitable for the study. The methodology explained below can be applied to all data compatible with the SeaDAS [7] software.

2   Materials and Methods

As an example of this methodology, we show the construction of the data set that was used for the quantitative analysis of the presence/absence of Sargasso along the coastline of Quintana Roo. However, the methodology is useful to any other study that uses data that can be processed with SeaDAS.

2.1   Example Region

The example requires pixels from the coastal zone of the state of Quintana Roo, which has an irregular perimeter, therefore the clipping tool does not work for this case, therefore, select each pixel manually is necessary. Additionally, the study requires only pixels within the aquatic zone. Figure 1 shows the study area.

2.2   Dataset Construction

As an example, Aqua-MODIS sensor dataset was chosen. MODIS allows high quality of spectral and radiometric resolution. Once the type of study and the files to be used are designed, the creation of the dataset can be divided into three main tasks: (1) Selection and download of files, (2) Selection and labeling of pixels and (3) Processing. Both lists of data generated in stages one and two feed the processing stage. Below some details of each stage are described.

2.3   Selection and Download of Files

According to dates and specific features of the study, at this stage, a list with names of every files used for the study was created. In the case of MODIS files, the Julian day and the universal time coordinated (UTC) was used to select accurately the file to be used. To get the information and download the files the lance-modis [8] and ocean-data [9] websites were used.

To automate the download of files, a software developed at home was used (Simple web crawler for MODIS data ver 1.0)[1], which was fed with the names of the files. Based on the study case [10], 80 PDS files of the Aqua-MODIS sensor [11], were selected and grouped in two different classes: 42 files of the years 2015 and 2018 corresponding to presence of Sargasso and 38 files to 2014 and 2017 corresponding to the absence of Sargasso [12,13]. Only the files that correspond to the study dates without clouds were selected, therefore, in total only 80 files were used.

---

[1] INDAUTOR registry number: 03-2018-092011022400-01.

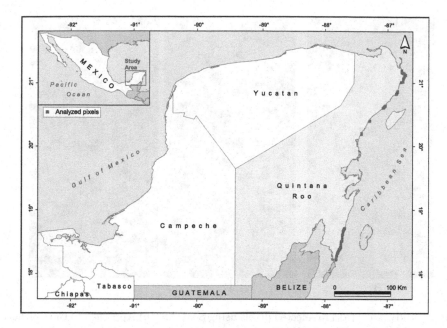

Fig. 1. Study Area: Represent by 115 pixels of $1\,km^2$ (red squares) along some sections of the coastal zone of Quintana Roo. The challenge is to extract the data from the different MODIS bands for the pixels of interest. (Figure credit: Holger Weissenberger). (Color figure online)

2.4   Selection and Labeling of the Pixels

In this stage, a list of latitude and longitude of every study pixels was built. The list built in this stage allows knowing which data will be extracted from the files in the processing stage. The visualization, selection, and ordering of the data were done with SeaDAS. To validate the pixels position, Google Earth Pro [14] software was used. Once the pixels have been selected and validated the file was converted into a ".csv" format and finally downloaded. Figure 2 shows the pixel selection and validation stage.

3   Results and Discussion

3.1   Data Processing

The file and pixel information generated in the previous stages feeds processing stage. To automate the processing for the study, a software tool developed at home was used (L2-JEP-MODIS-Processor)[2], which uses the SeaDAS software as CORE. During this stage, the raw files go through several levels of processing. The original raw data is re-projected, radiometric and atmospheric

---

[2] INDAUTOR registry number: 03-2019-032810002000-01.

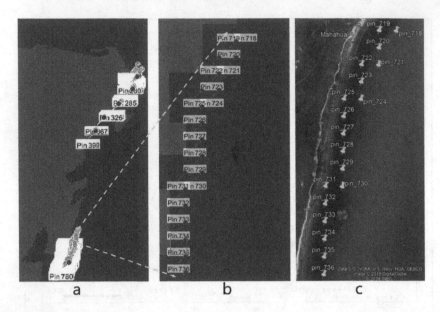

Fig. 2. Study Area: (a) 115 selected pixels using SeaDAS. (b) Approach to the southern area close Mahahual using SeaDAS. (c) Approach to the southern area close Mahahual using Google Earth.

corrected to finally obtain 36 differents reflectances corresponding to the wavelengths offered by MODIS sensor. Finally, it is possible to select the products to be used in the study. For the present example, the surface reflectance (rhos) and top atmosphere reflectance (rhot) products were used, which correspond to the reflectances with atmospheric corrections. In summary all rhos and rhot values are atmospherically corrected reflectances in two different situations: presence and absence of Sargassum. MODIS-Aqua was the data source to calculate all reflectances values. Figure 3 shows some examples of rhos imagery used for this example.

To developed this study the differences between the values of the reflectances with the presence and absence of Sargassum was compared. The latitude and longitude values allow located the corresponding reflectance value on the earth's surface. The area of study is the same but the values could be different for every file. As an example, in Fig. 4 pixels from 718 to 728 were shown, every pixel is related to a specific area. For every file, the values related to every pixel (area), could be different. The pixel values for different files feed the dataset.

As an example of presence and absence of Sargasso along the coast line is depicted in Fig. 5a and b respectively. The difference in the color between the sea with presence and with the absence of Sargasso is indeed the difference in reflectance between both conditions and that's just what the satellite sensor measures.

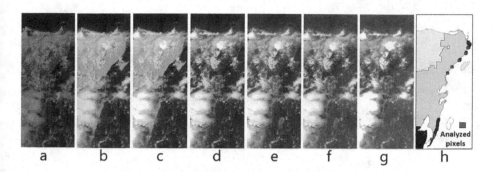

Fig. 3. Sample of Aqua-MODIS imagery used to build the dataset. rhos product at different wavelengths: (a) 412 nm. (b) 469 nm. (c) 555 nm. (d) 645 nm. (e) 859 nm. (f) 1240 nm. (g) 2130 nm and (h) Reference map.

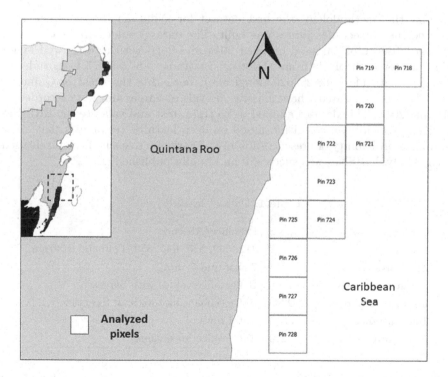

Fig. 4. Pixels from 718 to 728 were shown, every pixel is related to a specific area. For every file, the values related to every pixel could be different. The pixel values for different files (dates) feed the dataset.

a   b

Fig. 5. Presence and absence of Sargasso along the coast line is depicted in a and b respectively. The difference in the color between the sea with presence and with the absence of Sargasso is indeed the difference in reflectance between both conditions and that's just what the sensor measures. (Photographs credit: Hugo Lazcano) (Color figure online)

Using this methodology, the first dataset for Quintana Roo coastline with rhos and rhot reflectance values was built. The dataset values are labeled with presence/absence of Sargasso between 2014 and 2018 with latitude and longitude data for each pixel (from 21.496124 Latitude, −87.546677 Longitude, to 18.477211 Latitude, −88.293625 Longitude), bordering the coast of Quintana Roo. The area is located where massive arrivals of Sargassum were recorded in 2015 and 2018. This dataset allowed us to train, test and validate the ERISNet algorithm, which is an algorithm based on deep learning techniques that allow assigning a probability of presence/absence of Sargasso to each of the pixels used for the study. ERISNet was successful and finally published [10].

Table 1. Dataset features.

Clases	2	Presence/Absence
Wavelengths	7	412, 469, 555, 645, 859, 1240 and 2130 nm
Attributes	14	7 rhos and 7 rhot
Instance with Sargasso	2306	Reflectance values with Sargasso
Instance no Sargasso	2209	Reflectance values without Sargasso
Total instance	4515	Total rows
Total data	63210	Total reflectance values

The Dataset[3] is available for download and can be used for training and testing other types of algorithms. The dataset is a multivariable one, real and useful for classification. Additional features are shown in Table 1.

---

[3] DOI: 10.7717/peerj.6842/supp-1.

No.	rhos_412	rhos_469	rhos_555	rhos_645	rhos_859	rhos_1240	rhos_2130	class
1	0.052152324	0.052924864	0.078956269	0.059047472	0.313017517	0.221179157	0.055592567	sargasso
2	0.071715146	0.07867194	0.105367005	0.09423589	0.312823981	0.239947498	0.055137292	sargasso
3	0.093492866	0.10366448	0.130337417	0.125553533	0.298490912	0.258938372	0.109737001	sargasso
4	0.116701886	0.132209212	0.161379695	0.137303367	0.256019771	0.209399059	0.107257076	sargasso
5	0.180689469	0.212102711	0.230555534	0.184178293	0.181868449	0.180037439	0.167549506	sargasso
6	0.198726386	0.239959747	0.244443953	0.165482953	0.162698612	0.164480999	0.15228337	sargasso
7	0.198726386	0.239959747	0.244443953	0.165482953	0.162698612	0.164480999	0.15228337	sargasso
8	0.145068794	0.169581518	0.213087574	0.181584254	0.18303977	0.188654929	0.13669683	sargasso
9	0.136557832	0.161865592	0.205120787	0.173587158	0.168291375	0.154429734	0.120287903	sargasso
10	0.147212878	0.175906926	0.223769039	0.188709438	0.172622785	0.160727993	0.126777232	sargasso
*								
*								
*								
4506	0.100795411	0.09297581	0.104628555	0.077412575	0.1807293	0.115392119	0.032929752	no sargasso
4507	0.08891055	0.088557221	0.097570471	0.051598925	0.129012987	0.070378661	0.018634548	no sargasso
4508	0.08891055	0.088557221	0.097570471	0.051598925	0.129012987	0.070378661	0.018634548	no sargasso
4509	0.083234534	0.078605145	0.077768646	0.043270942	0.072734974	0.043083854	0.01292566	no sargasso
4510	0.087852933	0.082776748	0.075534701	0.044971626	0.049547803	0.035988212	0.022290619	no sargasso
4511	0.143806383	0.143241793	0.164001077	0.124509245	0.264211565	0.176976666	0.053056546	no sargasso
4512	0.143806383	0.143241793	0.164001077	0.124509245	0.264211565	0.176976666	0.053056546	no sargasso
4513	0.123276174	0.117157415	0.119024001	0.094687805	0.121894434	0.066987023	0.034441635	no sargasso
4514	0.104469262	0.101257265	0.117801137	0.095885374	0.142424852	0.115805306	0.048878536	no sargasso
4515	0	0.897335172	0.859892905	0.852634668	0.80787456	0.643370211	0.213192061	no sargasso

Fig. 6. Dataset example, some values corresponding to rhos reflectance at different wavelengths (412, 469, 555, 645, 859, 1240, 2130 nm). The columns correspond to the wavelengths, the rows to the instances and the cells to the reflectance values.

The built dataset was used successfully in the training, testing, and validation of ERISNet, an algorithm based on convolutional and recurrent neural networks to classify pixels with presence/absence of Sargasso [10]. Figure 6 shows a dataset example of some values corresponding to rhos.

As summary Fig. 7 shows some details of every stage of the proposal methodology: (1) selection and download of files (stages with light yellow fill), (2) selection and labeling of pixels (stages with light rose fill) and (3) processing (white). The software "Simple web crawler for MODIS data ver 1.0" and L2-JEP MODIS-Processor were developed at home using batch and python (Anaconda 3) languages. Lenovo Workstation (with Intel Xeon EP processor, 64 GB of RAM and Ubuntu 18.04 64 bits) was used for software developed.

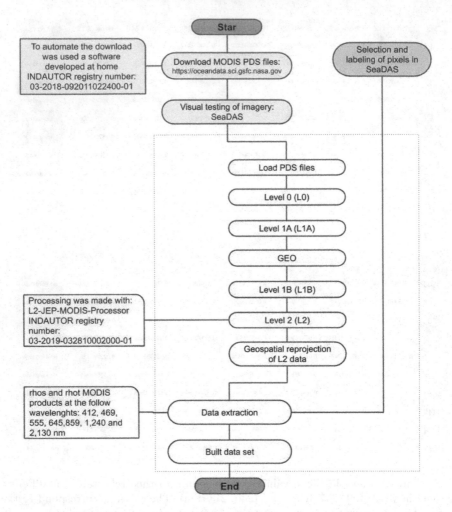

Fig. 7. Process Flow Diagram: Selection and download of files (light yellow), selection and labeling of pixels (light rose) and processing (white) (Color figure online)

4   Conclusions

This study shows the methodology to build a geospatial dataset using as input Aqua-MODIS data. The dataset it is valuable in itself. Therefore was registered in INDAUTOR with the name of CaribeMX-Dataset[4]. The dataset is composed of reflectance values at seven different wavelengths (412, 469, 555, 645, 859, 1,240 and 2,130 nm.) from two different MODIS products (rhos and rhot). According to fieldwork the dataset values was labeled as Sargasso or No Sargasso (2306 rows related to presence of Sargasso and 2209 rows related to absence of Sargasso). Finally the dataset has 63210 values.

---

[4] INDAUTOR registry number:03-2019-010810340300-01.

The built dataset was used successfully in the training, testing, and validation of ERISNet algorithm. The data set is available for their download and can be applied to other studies. The proposed methodology can be used in the construction of different dataset from other areas and for other objectives.

According to the data source and the final application, the method to build geospatial dataset could be different. There is no better method than another, the study emphasizes the use of open-source data and tools.

Acknowledgments. Geraldine Álvarez thanks ECOSUR for her research assistant fellowship. We thank the NASA Ocean Biology Processing Group (OBPG) for providing all MODIS raw data used in this study. Finally the authors are grateful to the reviewers for their contribution to improve this manuscript.

References

1. Nathan, F.: Simulating transport pathways of pelagic Sargasso from the Equatorial Atlantic into the Caribbean Sea. Prog. Ocean. **165**, 205–214 (2018). https://doi.org/10.1016/j.pocean.2018.06.009
2. Schell, J.M., Goodwin, D.S., Siuda, A.N.: Recent Sargassum inundation events in the Caribbean: shipboard observations reveal dominance of a previously rare form. Oceanography **28**(3), 8–11 (2015)
3. Gower, J.: Satellite images suggest a new Sargassum source region in 2011. Remote Sens. Lett. **4**(8), 764–73 (2013)
4. Wang, M.: Mapping and quantifying Sargassum distribution and coverage in the Central West Atlantic using MODIS observations. Remote Sens. Environ. **15**(183), 350–67 (2016)
5. Wang, M.: Predicting Sargassum blooms in the Caribbean Sea from MODIS observations. Geophys. Res. Lett. **44**(7), 3265–73 (2017)
6. García-Mora, T., Jean-Francois, M.: Aplicaciones del sensor MODIS para el monitoreo del territorio, 1st edn. Secretaría de Medio Ambiente y Recursos Naturales (Semarnat), México (2011)
7. SeaDAS. https://seadas.gsfc.nasa.gov/. Accessed June 2019
8. Lance MODIS. https://lance-modis.eosdis.nasa.gov/. Accessed June 2019
9. Ocean Color. https://oceandata.sci.gsfc.nasa.gov/MODIS-Aqua. Accessed June 2019
10. Arellano-Verdejo, J.: ERISNet: deep neural network for Sargasso detection along the coastline of the Mexican Caribbean. PeerJ, **7**, e6842, 1–19. (2019). https://doi.org/10.7717/peerj.6842
11. MODIS-Aqua, M.-A.O.C.: NASA goddard space flight center, ocean ecology laboratory, ocean biology processing group. Moderate-resolution imaging spectroradiometer (MODIS) Aqua l0 Data; NASA OB.DAAC, Greenbelt, MD, USA (2018). Accessed 01 Nov 2018
12. Van Tussenbroek, B.: Severe impacts of brown tides caused by Sargasso spp. On near-shore caribbean seagrass communities. Mar. Pollut. Bull. **122**(1–2), 272 281 (2017)
13. Rodríguez-Martínez, R.E.: Afluencia masiva de sargazo pelágico a la costa del Caribe mexicano (2014–2015). In: Florecimientos algales nocivos en México, CICESE, Ensenada, Mexico, pp. 352–365 (2016)
14. Google earth. https://www.google.com/intl/es/earth/. Accessed June 2019

Data Acquisition System for Solar Panel Analysis

Hernán De la Rosa[1(✉)], Margarita Mondragón[2],
and Bernardino Benito Salmerón-Quiroz[1(✉)]

[1] ESIME Azcapotzalco, Instituto Politécnico Nacional,
Avenida de las Granjas No. 682, 02250 Mexico City, Mexico
dlrgh@hotmail.com, bsalmeron@ipn.mx
[2] CIIDIR Oaxaca, Instituto Politécnico Nacional, Hornos 1003,
Santa Cruz Xoxocotlán, 71230 Oaxaca, Mexico

Abstract. This project introduces a data acquisition system for solar panel technologies, mainly for analysis and report purposes. The measured variables are the current and voltage generated by the panel so that the power and voltage curve can be plotted to analyze. The system is made up of two parts, the hardware that will be designed using an Arduino circuit board with a voltage sensor, a current sensor and a temperature sensor that feedback the modeled circuit based on Matlab and Simscape platforms. As an addition to the hardware system, an embedded system is designed using operational amplifiers to simulate a solar panel, this emulation is based on the mathematical model that gives our values for variables generated by solar technologies. For simulation of the modeling and plotting of the generated data, we propose the use of Wahba's method, for smoothing noisy data using spline function. This model will serve as a research/experimentation tool for technologies that improve the efficiency range of a solar cell.

Keywords: Solar energy · Embedded system · Matlab/Simscape · DATA network · Validation parameters · Autoregressive model · Wahba's problem

1 Introduction

In the last 15 years, there has been an unprecedented change in the consumption of energy resources. The high growth in the renewable energy market, in terms of investment, new capacities and high growth rates in developing countries, has changed the landscape for the energy sector. We have seen the growth of unconventional resources and improvements in the evolution of technology for all forms of energy resources [1]. In particular, solar energy has proven to meet up this energy scenario [2].

Solar cells, also called photovoltaic (PV) cells, convert solar radiation directly into electricity. They capture photons by exciting electrons through the band gap of a semiconductor, which creates electron pairs and holes that are then separated by charge, usually by PN junctions introduced by doping. The bonding interface conducts the electrons in one direction and the holes in the other, which creates a potential difference in the external electrodes equal to the band gap.

M. F. Mata-Rivera et al. (Eds.): WITCOM 2019, CCIS 1053, pp. 34–44, 2019.
https://doi.org/10.1007/978-3-030-33229-7_4

The concept and configuration are similar to those of a semiconductor diode, except that the electrons and holes are introduced into the junction by the excitation of the photon and are removed at the electrodes [3]. Currently solar cells reach a wide variety of applications and contribute to the massive or isolated generation of electrical energy. Crystalline silicon is a well-studied material and its technology is mature, it is the most common material used in Photo Voltaic (PV) technologies, the global production of solar cells increases rapidly and the amount of silicon used exceeds the set of semiconductor devices such as diodes, transistors and circuits.

The huge gap between the potential of solar energy and its use is due to the cost and conversion capacity. Fossil fuels satisfy our energy demands at lower cost than solar alternatives, in part because fossil fuel deposits are concentrated sources of energy, while the sun distributes photons quite evenly on Earth at a more modest energy density. The use of biomass as a fuel is limited by the production capacity of the available land and water. The limitations of cost and capacity in the use of solar energy are addressed more effectively with a single research objective: to increase conversion efficiency in a cost-effective manner.

Several mathematical models have been developed that describe the behavior of a solar cell. All the models are based on the current-voltage ratio resulting from a diode, whose manufacture represents the n-type and p-type doped semiconductors, used in the manufacture of a solar cell [4]. These models can be used in the design and development of data acquisition (DAQ) systems which measure physical phenomenon such as voltage, current, temperature, pressure, or sound converting them into digital signals. These signals in turn, are processed and conditioned by a computer with programmable software to allow their easy analysis and visualization.

In this work a circuit is designed in Simscape to simulate the behavior of a real PV panel. A sensor board was constructed to collect the current, voltage and power values generated by the photovoltaic panel. The DAQ system was completed by a computer code programed to process and smooth the signals into a format that could be used for analysis purposes.

2   Process and Development

2.1   Mathematical Modeling of a Solar Panel

A solar cell is the building block of a solar panel. A photovoltaic module is formed by connecting many solar cells in series and parallel. Generally, the equivalent electrical

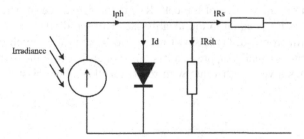

Fig. 1. Electrical representation of a solar cell

circuit of a solar cell consists of a photo-current source generated by the action of solar radiation, a diode, a resistance in parallel and a shunt resistance (representing the internal resistance of the material to the flow of the current), as shown in Fig. 1.

Applying Kirchhoff's law to the representation of a solar cell as seen in Fig. 1. The next equation can be obtained.

$$I = I_{PH} - I_D - I_{SH} \tag{1}$$

Where I_{PH} is the photo-generated current, I_D is the current of the diode, I_{SH} is the shunt resistance loss in parallel and I is the output current of the cell. The first term can be determined from next equation and depends on the irradiance, area and temperature in which the cell is being exposed.

$$I_{PH} = \frac{G}{G_{STC}} [A \cdot J_{SC} + \alpha J_{SC}(T - T_{STC})] \tag{2}$$

where G is the irradiance value under given conditions, G_{STC} is the irradiance value under standard conditions, A is the area of the cell, J_{SC} is the short-circuit current density of the cell, αJ_{SC} is the temperature coefficient of the short-circuit current density, T is the temperature under given conditions, T_{STC} is the temperature under standard conditions.

The second term from Eq. (1) is the current of the diode which can be determined from the Shockley equation.

$$I_D = I_0 \left(e^{\frac{V_D}{nV_T}} - 1 \right) \tag{3}$$

Where I_0 is the saturation current, V_D is the voltage of the diode, n is equal to the ideality factor of the diode and V_T is the thermal voltage. From Eq. (3) the diode saturation current is obtained, which is that part of the reverse current in a semiconductor diode caused by diffusion of minority carriers from the neutral regions to the depletion region

$$I_0 = \frac{J_{SC} \cdot A - \frac{V_{OC}}{R_{SH}}}{\left(e^{\frac{V_{OC}}{nV_T}} - 1 \right)} \tag{4}$$

Where J_{SC} is the short-circuit current density of the cell, A is the area of the cell, V_{OC} is the open circuit voltage of the cell, R_{SH} is the resistance in parallel, V_T is the thermal voltage and n is equal to the ideality factor of the diode.

The third term from Eq. (1) is shunt resistance loss current which corresponds to the current leakage is usually suppressed in some models because the parallel resistance (RSH) usually has a very high value with respect to the series resistance.

$$I_{RSH} = \frac{V + R_S I}{R_{SH}} \tag{5}$$

Where V is the output voltage of the solar cell, RS is the series resistance, RSH is the parallel resistance and I is the resistance current in parallel.

Equations 2, 3 and 4 are substituted in Eq. 1, so the general modeling equation for a solar cell is obtained.

$$I = I_{PH} - I_O \left(e^{\frac{V + R_S I}{nV_T}} - 1 \right) - \frac{V + R_S I}{R_{SH}} \tag{6}$$

A solar panel is formed by grouping cells in series, in order to obtain the output current (I) of a solar panel the output voltage (V) in the Eq. 6 is divided by the number of cells (Ns) [5, 6].

$$I = I_{PH} - I_O \left(e^{\frac{\frac{V}{N_S} + R_S I}{nV_T}} - 1 \right) - \frac{\frac{V}{N_S} + R_S I}{R_{SH}} \tag{7}$$

3 Data Validation

To represent the mathematical equation and to model a solar panel, the Matlab and Simulink platform tools are used, this model is visualized as a set of subsystems connected and configured to calculate the variables needed to be analyzed.

3.1 Cell Modeling

Using the tools from Matlab and the mathematical equations, a model is built for the PV cell; this model represents the circuit equations of a PV cell taking into account the effects of physical and environmental parameters such as the solar radiation and cell temperature, as shown in Fig. 2.

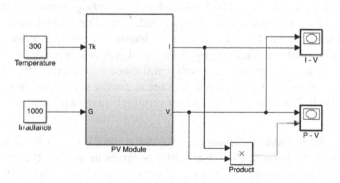

Fig. 2. Simulink model designed to represent a PV module.

Inside the block that represents the PV module, the values and elements from Eq. 7 are modeled in subsystems Fig. 3.

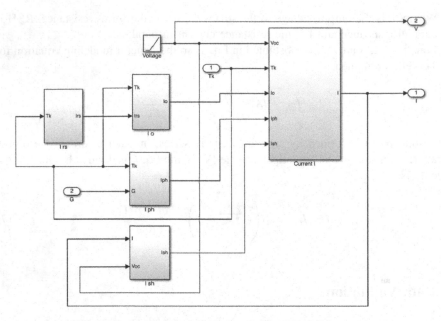

Fig. 3. The subsystems within the designed Simulink model.

The fundamental parameters related to solar cell are short circuit current (I_{sc}), open circuit voltage (V_{oc}), efficiency of solar cell and fill factor. These values are measured using the hardware circuit built in an arduino board using voltage, current and temperature sensors. Short Circuit Current is the condition when the impedance is low and it is calculated when the voltage equals to zero.

I_{sc} occurs at the beginning of the forward-bias sweep and is the maximum current value in the power quadrant. For an ideal cell, this maximum current value is the total current produced in the solar cell by photon excitation. I_{sc} is the short-circuit current of cell at 25 °C and an Irradiance 1000 W/m^2, I_{ph} is the light generated current directly proportional to the solar irradiation, Io is the diode saturation current of the cell varies with the cell temperature, Irs is the reverse saturation current of a cell at a reference temperature and a solar irradiation, Eg is the band gap energy of the semiconductor used in the cell and I_{sh} stands for Parallel resistance loss current, this term of the equation that corresponds to the current leakage is usually suppressed in some models because the parallel resistance usually has a very high value with respect to the series resistance [6].

Modeling the Solar Panel in Simscape. To Model the PV cell in Simscape involves the estimation of the I-V and P-V characteristics curves to emulate the real cell under various environmental conditions. The most popular approach is to utilize the electrical equivalent circuit, which is primarily based on diode. The Solar Cell block in

SimElectronics Fig. 4. represents a single solar cell as a parallel current source, I_{ph}, an exponential diode, D and a shunt resistance, R_{sh} that are connected in series with a resistance R_s.

Fig. 4. Solar cell element in Simscape.

The Solar panel circuit is modeled using elements from Simscape and Simulink. Solar cell was connected with blocks such as current sensor and voltage sensor to measure the current and voltage across solar cell. Blocks for varying Irradiance level and Temperature, were also connected in the above model. Rest of the blocks were the interface between major blocks and used for plotting I-V characteristics (Fig. 5).

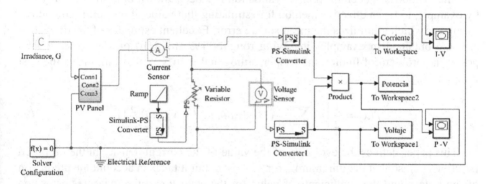

Fig. 5. Simscape array for a solar panel

This model circuit works with the data we acquired from the readings of our experimental solar cell at a lab.

Parameter Estimation Methodology. Smoothing splines are well known to provide nice curves which smooth discrete, noisy data, in this case it is proposed a system based on parameter estimation theory which will allow the system to filter measurements which can be considered error. In signal processing, an autoregressive (AR) model is a representation of a type of random process; as such, it is used to describe certain time-varying processes, the model specifies that the output variable depends linearly on its own previous values and on a stochastic term.

The AR model is a widely used model to understand time series data. Traditionally, the innovation noise of the AR is modeled as Gaussian. However, many time series applications, for example, situations arising in applications of signal processing where the time series are non-Gaussian and heavy-tailed, either due to intrinsic data generation mechanism or existence of outliers, the AR model with more general heavy tailed innovations is preferred.

Another issue that frequently occurs in time series is missing values, due to system data record failure or unexpected data loss. In the recent era of data deluge, many applications collect and process time series data for inference, learning, parameter estimation, and decision making. The AR model is a commonly used model to analyze time series data, where observations taken closely in time are statistically dependent on others. In an AR time series, each sample is a linear combination of some previous observations with a stochastic innovation.

An AR model of order p, AR(p), is defined as.

$$y_t = \varphi_0 + \sum_{i=1}^{p} \varphi_i y_{t-i} + \varepsilon_t \tag{8}$$

Where y_t is the t-th observation, φ_0 is a constant, φ_i are autoregressive coefficients, and ε_t is the innovation associated with the t-th observation, which is assumed to be Gaussian distributed, as a result of the linearity of the AR model, means that the observations are also Gaussian distributed.

The method of generalized cross validation has been shown both theoretically and by example, to be an effective method for estimating that value of the spline smoothing parameter which minimizes the mean square error. Excellent estimates of the derivative are also obtained in examples involving roughly 1% and 1/10 of 1% noise, Wahba posed the problem of finding the proper orthogonal matrix A that minimizes the cost function [6, 7].

$$f(x) = \frac{1}{2} \left[\mu \left(\sum_{j=1}^{n} (MesEstimated - v_{mes}(j))^2 \right) \right] \tag{9}$$

This paper defines the evolution of the value of the current density in the proposed function $f(x)$, so that the minimum error is chosen, but it takes in account the prediction of the state x and the coefficients of value for the state μ and the measures estimated (MesEstimated = MS) at the instant k.

The motivation for this cost function is that if the vectors are error-free and the true matrix $f(x)true$, is assumed to be the same for all the measurements, then *MesEstimated* is equal to $v_{mes}true(j)$ for all j and the cost function is equal to zero, which is clearly the minimum value, for $f(x)$ equal to $f(x)true$.

So for this method we define $f(x)$ as our current density I_x and adapted it to get the next formula.

$$I_x = \frac{1}{2} \left[\mu \left(\sum_{j=1}^{n} (I_{est} - I_{mes}(j))^2 \right) \right] \tag{10}$$

Where I_X stands for the parameter estimation in which the optimal values considered for each test are, I_{est} for the estimated current values, I_{mes} is for the current date measured and n will stand for the number of readings we get each in a minute [8].

4 Results

In this section, part of the simulation and results are represented in order to show the performance of the proposed system, from our readings captured by our circuit, this data is inserted in the Simscape modeling.

The readings obtained from the test are fluctuating and represent a certain percent of noise and error; we must determine the optimal value to get the plot needed to analyze Fig. 6.

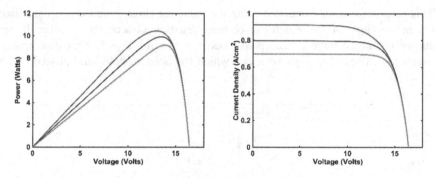

Fig. 6. 1-V and power curve plotted from variable sample reading in the laboratory

Applying the Eq. 10 in each of the sampling readings from our test the optimal value can be determined with the minimum range of error.

As presented in the Table 1 the values obtained for I_{SC} are calculated as the optimal and with less percentage of error.

Table 1. Data obtained from readings

Variable	Magnitude	Measuring Unit
Short-circuit current, ISC	00.796	A
Open-circuit voltage, V_{OC}	0.457	V
Irradiance used for measurements, G	1000	W/m^2
Quality factor, n	1.2	N/A
Series resistance, R_S	0.0056	OhmΩ

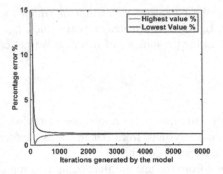

Fig. 7. Percentage error obtained by our optimal value compared to the highest and lowest values of variation in the test.

This percentage error calculated using the value for short circuit current stabilizes rapidly in the range of 1% which can be interpreted as an acceptable range; the test results we registered have an acceptable percentage error Fig. 7. This data reading represents the values of a single solar cell which has been modeled and plotted Fig. 8.

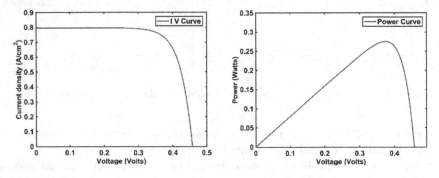

Fig. 8. Plotting for the I-V and power curve obtained from experimentation data for a single solar cell.

To get the power curve we have programed a code that calculates the value using Watt's law, so when the plotting process in Matlab starts both curves are sent to us to analyze.

The simscape model we designed can be modified to represent a complete solar panel, the element we configured with our readings can be connected in series or parallel to represent the model of Solar panel we desire Fig. 9.

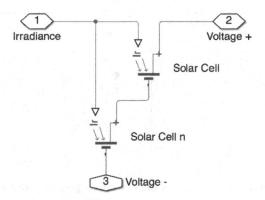

Fig. 9. Solar cell series connection

Depending of the number and connection type of the solar panel, a subsystem configuration can be created to represent the PV module needed to analyze Fig. 10.

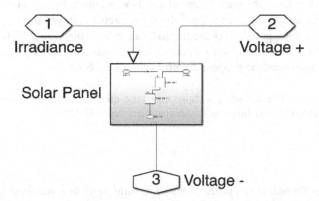

Fig. 10. Solar panel created in a subsystem

This way, the PV panel designed can be analyzed in solitary, or add more panels to represent a PV array, the curves obtained from the readings in this solar panel can be saved for report or analysis Fig. 11.

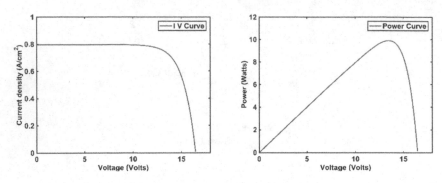

Fig. 11. I-V curve and power curve for a photovoltaic panel.

5 Conclusion

This paper has analyzed the development of a method for the mathematical modeling of PV arrays, using a simulation platform and an embedded system which simulates these systems.

The method obtains the parameters of the I–V equation by measuring the values generated by our solar panel, which are the open circuit voltage, short-circuit current, and maximum output power. To accomplish our main objective which is to reduce error and represent a clean and smooth curve for analysis and report purposes, we used the cross validation method proposed with Wahba's problem.

Acknowledgements. The authors gratefully thank the financial support of the Secretaria de Investigación y Posgrado del Instituto Politécnico Nacional (SIP-IPN).

References

1. World Energy Council Home page. https://www.worldenergy.org. Accessed 2019
2. Kirmani, S., Jamil, M., Akhtar, I.: Effective low cost grid-connected solar photovoltaic system to electrify the small scale industry/commercial building. Int. J. Renew. Energy Res. 7(2), 797–806 (2017)
3. Matsumoto, Y.: Celdas Solares De Silicio: Fundamento y Tendencia. Caos Conciencia 5, 32–44 (2011)
4. Crabtree, G.W., Lewis, N.S.: Solar energy conversion. Phys. Today 60, 37–42 (2007)
5. Villalva, M., Gazoli, J., Filho, E.: Comprehensive approach to modeling and simulation of photovoltaic arrays. IEEE Trans. Power Electron. 24, 1198–1208 (2009)
6. Granda-Gutiérrez, E.: Modelado y simulación de celdas y paneles solares (2013)
7. Craven, P., Wahba, G.: Smoothing noisy data with spline functions. Numer. Math. 31, 377–403 (1978)
8. Salmerón-Quiroz, B.B., Villegas-Medina, G., Guerrero-Castellanos, J., Milhacea, E.O., Villalobos-Martinez, R.: A quaternion approach in the estimation of the attitude of an industrial robot (2017)

Pattern Recognition Through Empirical Mode Decomposition for Temperature Time Series Between 1986 and 2019 in Mexico City Downtown for Global Warming Assessment

Mauricio Gabriel Orozco-del-Castillo[1,2], Jorge J. Hernández-Gómez[2,3(✉)],
Gabriela Aurora Yañez-Casas[4], Mario Renán Moreno-Sabido[1],
Carlos Couder-Castañeda[3], Isaac Medina[3], Raúl Novelo-Cruz[1,2],
and Mauro Alberto Enciso-Aguilar[4]

[1] Departamento de Sistemas y Computación,
Tecnológico Nacional de México/I.T. Mérida, Mérida, Mexico
{mauricio.orozco,e17081430}@itmerida.edu.mx, mario@itmerida.mx
[2] AAAI Student Chapter at Yucatán, México (AAAIMX),
Association for the Advancement of Artificial Intelligence, Mérida, Mexico
[3] Centro de Desarrollo Aeroespacial, Instituto Politécnico Nacional,
Mexico City, Mexico
{jjhernandezgo,ccouder,imedinas}@ipn.mx
[4] Escuela Superior de Ingeniería Mecánica y Eléctrica Unidad Zacatenco,
Sección de Estudios de Posgrado e Investigación, Instituto Politécnico Nacional,
Mexico City, Mexico
g.yanezcasas@gmail.com, mencisoa@ipn.mx

Abstract. Global warming is a real threat for the survival of life on Earth in the following 80 years. The effects of Global Warming are particularly harmful for inhabitants of very saturated urban settlements, which is the case of Mexico City. In this work, we analyse temperature time series from Mexico City Downtown, taken hourly between 1986 and 2019. The gaps in the time series were interpolated through the kriging method. Then, temporal tendencies and main frequencies were obtained through Empirical Mode Decomposition. The first frequency mode reveals a clear increasing tendency driven by Global Warming, which for 2019 was of $0.72\,°C$ above a 30-year baseline period mean between 1986 and 2016. Furthermore, the shorter periods identified in the first intrinsic mode functions are likely driven by the solar activity periods. It remains to find the origin of the smallest identified periods in the time series (<0.36 years).

Keywords: Empirical Mode Decomposition · Climate Change · Global Warming · Time series · Artificial Intelligence · Pattern recognition · Temperature increase · Mexico City · AI · EMD

© Springer Nature Switzerland AG 2019
M. F. Mata-Rivera et al. (Eds.): WITCOM 2019, CCIS 1053, pp. 45–60, 2019.
https://doi.org/10.1007/978-3-030-33229-7_5

1   Introduction

Nowadays, we constantly face dread events due to Climate Change (CC), like glacier melting and intensification of drought and precipitation episodes [1,2]. Since the middle of the 20th century, scientists detected a clearly increasing tendency in the temperature records all around the world. This information along with paleoclimatic records during the Holocene constitute an unfailing proof of Global Warming (GW) [3,4].

GW is defined as the increment in the global mean temperature over land and ocean, and it has a direct effect over the whole Earth's ecosystem [4]. In its last report, the International Panel on Climate Change (IPCC) remarks that for the year 2100, a rise in the mean global temperature of 2.5 °C (with respect to the mean temperature in the 1961–1980 period) is expected, driving severe consequences for mankind as well as for nature, which threatens the survival of life at Earth in the nearby future [4,5].

GW has unleashed a very intense research activity in CC since the second half of the 20th century. Most of the research in the field focuses on both the study of the anthopogenic causes and consequences of related physicochemical processes, and on providing projections or predictions of the global mean temperature behaviour in diverse scenarios [3].

From the point of view of natural phenomena, some of the most remarkable investigated effects of GW are on droughts [1,6], floods [2,7], permafrost/glacier alterations [8,9], ENSO phenomenon [10,11], hurricane activity [12,13], sea level rise [14,15], biodiversity affectations [16,17], as well as the temperature increment itself [18,19], etc. Of special importance are the impacts of GW on human socioeconomics. There are clear indications that GW already has importantly affected agriculture [20,21], wine production [22,23], cattle farming [24,25], wood assets [26,27], fishing [28,29], textile industry [30,31], transportation [32,33], manufacturing [34,35], energy [36,37], among many others.

In 2018, an estimated 55.3% of the world's population lived in urban settlements [38], in contrast to the value of 33.616% in 1960 [39]. Moreover, by 2050 it is expected to rise to 68% (up to two thirds of mankind) [40]. Therefore, the effects of GW on urban settlements and on their dwellers are of the greatest concern to scientists and governments. In this sense, several hazards for urban environments have been detected/forecast, for instance in interurban transportation [41], urban-based pollution [42,43], health issues in inhabitants, [44,45], urban design plans and policies [46,47], urban growth and land use [48,49], natural hazards in city environments [50,51], poverty and gender aspects of population [52,53], adaptation of current urban infrastructure [54,55], governance, policies, resilience and adaptation [56,57], feeding challenges, [58,59], sustainability under population growth [32,60], forced migration/mobility [61,62], as well as pronounced temperature increments yielding to heat waves (heat islands) [63,64],

In this sense, it is very important to focus efforts to mitigate the effects of GW in big cities. This is the case of Mexico City, the fifth most populated in the world in 2018 according to United Nations [38] (and the second in America, just below Sao Paulo, Brazil), which in the last years has faced serious events of heat waves, precipitations, as well as forest fires and pollution peaks [65]. In this work, we tackle the rise temperature in Mexico City Downtown by means of computational science techniques which have proved to be successful to interpret and forecast data arisen from both natural and social sciences, particularly those in the field of Artificial Intelligence (AI) [66]. Artificial intelligence is a collection of methods dealing with *the simulation of human intelligence on a machine, so as to make the machine efficient to identify and use the right piece of "Knowledge" at a given step of solving a problem* [66, section 1.2]. Despite its proved capacity to analyse data and to solve problems, AI has been barely used in GW and CC with respect to the huge amount of research in the area. In this sense, relevant AI techniques to assess CC and WG have been applied, like [67], fuzzy theory [68,69], agent-based modeling [68,70], swarm optimization [71], genetic algoritmhs [72,73], pattern recognition [74], machine learning [75,76], cellular automata [68,77], and artificial neural networks (ANNs) [78,79].

In this paper, currently a work in progress, we implement a pattern recognition system to analyse temperature time series measured near Mexico City Downtown. The purpose is to identify periodicities and tendencies in the data that might suggest that temperature is being driven by GW, as well as to build local indicators to accurately guide local strategic decision-makers to design and implement adequate policies and actions to mitigate and counteract CC. This work is presented as follows: In Sect. 2 we present details about the region under study and about the analysed data, while in Sect. 3 we present the applied theoretical background. The obtained results are presented in Sect. 4 along with an enriching discussion, while finally in Sects. 5 and 6 we present some final remarks, as well as future work, respectively.

2   Region Under Study

The region under study is located in the south-central part of Mexico, in the geographically-northern part of Mexico City, which is located in the previously called Distrito Federal state, which lies in the Valley of Mexico/Anahuac Valley. Orographically, it is limited at north, east, west and south by Guadalupe, Santa Catarina, de las Cruces and Ajusco mountain ranges respectively. Pollitically, it adjoins at south with the State of Morelos and at north, east and west with the State of Mexico.

From the 71 weather stations operated by SIMAT (SIstema de Monitoreo ATmosférico, an state agency operated by the Mexican government) in the Metropolitan Zone of the Valley of Mexico (MZVM), we chose the Merced (MER) Station, the closest one to Mexico City Downtown (1.71 km from Zocalo square). The selection of the station was based on its centricity with respect to the urban spot (considering the metropolitan area of the City), the time of service (length of records), the fact that the atmosphere of the north-east of the city is more commonly polluted [80], the consistency of its records as well as its completeness. The characteristics of MER station can be observed in Table 1, while its location can be observed in Fig. 1.

The temperature records taken by SIMAT with the version and key numbers DT001-IAD-20190523-163843 and M-K5Y2N-6THR8-KMZJ2-FYVNE respectively, consist of data taken between January 1st, 1986 and April 30th, 2019,

Table 1. Features of the selected station.

Name	Keyword	Long (°)	Lat (°)	Alt (m)	Station ID
Merced	MER	−99.119594	19.42461	2245	484090170127

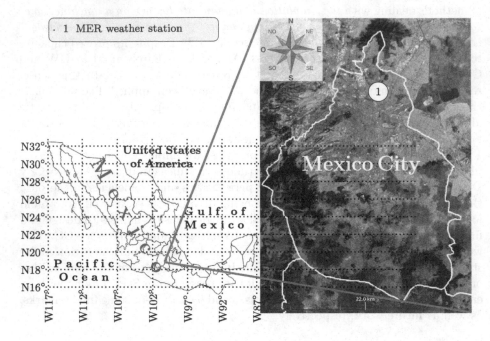

Fig. 1. Location of the region under study.

with a sample interval of 1 h. In this way, the time series is constituted by 292,152 records, each of which consists of the following instances: date, hour, station, parameter (temperature in this case), value and unit (Celsius). It ought to be remarked that the obtained temperature time series has some data gaps, which were originated when the temperature sensor at the station is under maintenance or when it presents failures. Thus, data gaps are interpolated through the kriging method [81,82], which is explained in what follows. Interpolated temperature time series in the referred station and sample period can be observed in Fig. 2.

3   Methodology

In this section, we briefly describe the methods used in this paper.

3.1   Kriging Method

Kriging method is an advanced interpolation procedure that is aimed to generate an estimated surface from a set of scattered points. The method fits a

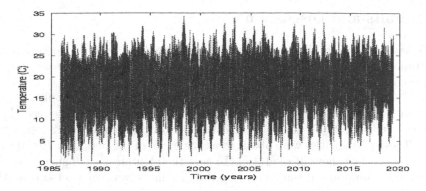

Fig. 2. Temperature time series obtained from MER station, where the values gaps have been interpolated through the kriging method.

mathematical function to the specified points, or to the points within an specific radius to determine the output value for each location. This algorithm assumes that the distance or direction between the sample points indicates an spatial correlation which can be used to generate a surface with adequate variations. Thus, kriging is suitable when there is a directional influence in the spatially correlated distance within the data.

In order for kriging method to weigh measured surrounding values so to calculate a prediction of a location with no measurements, a geostatistical estimator is used [3].

Kriging method has been extensively used in both natural sciences as well as in applied mathematics and computational sciences [83, 84]. The interpolated temperature data in MER station can be observed in Fig. 2, along with the original temperature time series. Once the data has been interpolated, we determine tendencies and main mode components of the time series through Empirical Mode Decomposition (EMD).

3.2   Empirical Mode Descomposition

EMD algorithm, first presented by Huang in 1998 [85], produces smooth envelopes defined by local extrema of a sequence and subsequent subtraction of the mean of these envelopes from an initial sequence. It requires to identify all the local extrema connected by cubic spline lines to produce the upper and lower envelopes [86].

This adaptive analysis method is adequate to process non-steady and non-linear time series. The final purpose of EMD is to divide the series in modes, the so called Intrinsic Mode Functions (IMFs) in the time domain, which is the main difference between EMD and other analysis methods for time series such as Fourier transform, and wavelet decomposition. As EMD always stays in the time domain, it has the advantage of taking less processing time to yield results. For further information on EMD, the reader is referred to [87].

4   Results and Discussion

EMD has been widely used in different science fields to perform operations as recognition [88], analysis [89], filtering [90], prediction [91], etc. From the 22 computed IMFs, the first six ones can be observed in Fig. 3.

In Fig. 3, the behaviour of the first six IMFs obtained by the application of EMD to the original temperature time series of Fig. 2, can be observed. Furthermore, in Table 2 we report the identified periods in each of the 22 computed IMFs. These periodicities were obtained as the mean of the periods between consecutive peaks or valleys of the IMFs. To ease the identification of such peaks or valleys, the temporal tendency given by the first mode was subtracted from the rest of the mode functions.

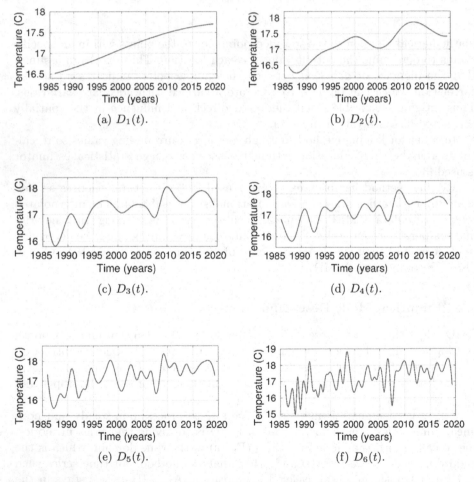

(a) $D_1(t)$.   (b) $D_2(t)$.

(c) $D_3(t)$.   (d) $D_4(t)$.

(e) $D_5(t)$.   (f) $D_6(t)$.

Fig. 3. Individual view of the first six Intrinsic Mode Functions (IMFs) obtained through the application of EMD to the temperature time series in Fig. 2.

Table 2. Identified periodicities in the 22 computed IMFs through EMD.

IMF	Mean period (year)	IMF	Mean period (year)
$D_2(t)$	12.9960	$D_{13}(t)$	0.0598
$D_3(t)$	6.5174	$D_{14}(t)$	0.0353
$D_4(t)$	3.8167	$D_{15}(t)$	0.0207
$D_5(t)$	2.5956	$D_{16}(t)$	0.0123
$D_6(t)$	1.4766	$D_{17}(t)$	0.0073
$D_7(t)$	1.2312	$D_{18}(t)$	0.0042
$D_8(t)$	0.9818	$D_{19}(t)$	0.0026
$D_9(t)$	0.5864	$D_{20}(t)$	0.0018
$D_{10}(t)$	0.336	$D_{21}(t)$	0.0013
$D_{11}(t)$	0.1785	$D_{22}(t)$	0.0009
$D_{12}(t)$	0.0986		

The first extremely notable result that ought to be remarked is the very first IMF, $D_1(t)$, which is observed in Fig. 3a. The lowest frequency mode, $D_1(t)$, reveals a clear increasing tendency in the temperature from 1986 to April, 2019. In order to have a better acquaintance of how representative is this increment, we take the mean of the temperature records in the time series with a 30 years baseline, i.e. splitting the data and taking the first set of records between January 1st, 1986 and January 1st, 2016. The baseline mean temperature is 16.98 °C. Actually, the tendency shown by the first mode function ($D_1(t)$) reached such value in August 29th, 1997, at 10:40:59.56, so there is a clear increasing tendency above the baseline mean temperature since mid 1997. In this sense, we can confirm that GW has been noticeable since such date.

Furthermore, by the end of the baseline period, the temperature increase was 0.67 °C while by April 30th, 2019, it was 0.72 °C above the baseline mean. In order to try to assess the future impact of GW in the region under study, we extrapolated the data for the first frequency function ($D_1(t)$) in order to try to forecast the tendency which is present in the dataset. The extrapolation is performed by a linear algorithm. The temperatures in the meteorological station

Table 3. Forecasted values of temperature at MER station in Mexico City downtown through the extrapolation of the first Intrinsic Mode Function ($D_1(t)$) in Fig. 3a through a linear algorithm, for three key years in Climate Change according to IPCC [92].

Key year	Forecast temperature (°C)	Temperature above baseline (°C)
2030	17.8328	0.8491
2050	18.0709	1.0872
2100	18.6663	1.6826

under study (MER) as well as their values above the baseline mean temperature were forecast for three key years according to IPCC: 2030, 2050 and 2100 [92]. Such predicted values can be observed in Table 3.

As it can be observed from the data shown in Table 3, the current tendency expects an increment of 1.09 °C above the baseline temperature for 2050, which could increment to 1.68 °C for 2100. Although this simple tendency is within the SR15 GW scenario which considers as a goal to limit the temperature to reach 1.5 °C by 2050 [93] it entails disastrous consequences to the urban spot at Mexico City as well as to its dwellers.

As for the periodicities identified in the following EMD modes in Fig. 3, and which are shown in Table 2, we can make the following observations.

The second IMF, $D_2(t)$ (see Fig. 3b) reveals a coarse frequency that corresponds to a mean period of 12.9960 years, which is almost two years above the typical mean duration of the solar cycle, so it is possible the solar cycle to partially drive this IMF. Furthermore, it is interesting to note that the first minimum in such time series occurred at August 23th, 1987 (see Fig. 3b), while the closest minimum of solar activity was reported almost one year before, at August 28th, 1986 [94], which reinforces this hypothesis.

Table 4. Periods T of the thirty harmonics obtained from [94]. The periods are given in years.

Harmonic	Period	Harmonic	Period	Harmonic	Period
1	10.83	11	0.98	21	0.52
2	5.42	12	0.90	22	0.49
3	3.61	13	0.83	23	0.47
4	2.71	14	0.77	24	0.45
5	2.17	15	0.72	25	0.43
6	1.81	16	0.68	26	0.42
7	1.55	17	0.64	27	0.40
8	1.35	18	0.60	28	0.39
9	1.20	19	0.57	29	0.37
10	1.08	20	0.54	30	0.36

In order to identify if the periodicities found in the subsequent Intrinsic Mode Functions $(D_i(t) \; \forall i = 3, \cdots, 22)$ are probably driven by solar activity, they are compared with those reported by [94, 95]. The later records, which are obtained from different sun activity indicators as Ground Level Enhancements (GLEs), number of sunspots, etc., are a set of short term periods within the solar activity, and can be observed in Table 4.

In this sense, it is important to note that the last EMD frequency components, $D_i(t) \; \forall \; i > 10$, have shorter periods than those reported by [94, 95], so

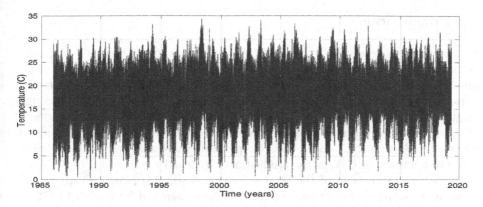

Fig. 4. IMF 22 ($D_{22}(t)$) of the EMD applied to the original temperature time series in Fig. 2. It can be observed that due to its small enough periodicity (1.33 days), it reproduces qualitatively well the original time series by itself.

Table 5. Comparison of the obtained periods through the application of EMD with those reported in the literature for the solar activity [94,95] for the coincident IMFs, along with the relative error between both.

IMF	EMD period (year)	Measured period (year)	Relative error (%)
$D_2(t)$	12.9960	10.83	20.00
$D_3(t)$	6.5174	5.42	20.25
$D_4(t)$	3.8167	3.61	5.73
$D_5(t)$	2.5956	2.71	4.22
$D_6(t)$	1.4766	1.55	4.74
$D_7(t)$	1.2312	1.20	2.60
$D_8(t)$	0.9818	0.98	0.18
$D_9(t)$	0.5864	0.57	2.88
$D_{10}(t)$	0.336	0.36	6.67

no match can be made. Nevertheless, they constitute themselves a good hint for researches to investigate the existence of such very short periods in the solar activity.

Finally, it is important to observe that the highest frequency IMF, $D_{22}(t)$, has a really small period of 0.0009 years, which is equivalent to 1.33 days. In this sense, its resolution is high enough to almost grasp the day-night cycles. In Fig. 4 we can observe the IMF 22. Comparing such image with the original time series (see Fig ?), it is clear that the 22 IMFs obtained through EMD reproduce qualitatively well the original time series.

5   Conclusions

In this work we presented the main frequency modes in the time series of temperature records from January 1st, 1986 to April 30th, 2019, with a sample interval of 1 h, at MER station close to Mexico City's Downtown. The detected periods were obtained through EMD after the series were interpolated through kriging method. The first frequency mode revealed a clear increasing tendency of temperature in the region under study, which surpassed the baseline period mean since August 29th, 1997. This temperature increment, most likely due to the direct impact of GW in the studied area, reached a value of 0.72 °C above such baseline at the end of the time series, i.e. April 30th, 2019. Furthermore, linear extrapolation of the tendency provides increments of 0.8491 °C, 1.0872 °C and 1.6826 °C on the key years 2030, 2050 and 2100, according to IPCC [92, 93].

On the other side, when removing the effect of GW on the time series, i.e. $D_1(t)$, the lower frequency components of the temperature time series are most likely driven by the solar activity. In order to better grasp this fact, in Table 5 we present a summary of the EMD obtained periods against with those reported in the literature. In such table, we also present the relative error between both values. It is noticeable that the greater periods ($D_2(t)$ and $D_3(t)$) have relative errors of $\approx 20\%$, so it remains to study which other factors may influence these IMFs. Nevertheless, that is out of the scope of this work.

Lower periods ($D_4(t)$ to $D_{10}(t)$) match to some reported periods in the solar activity with reasonable errors ($\approx 5\%$), so they are very likely to be driven by the sun. Finally, the lowest periods reported in Table 2 ($D_i(t)$ $\forall$ $i > 10$) are to be investigated by researchers in order identify if they are part of the several high frequencies present in solar activity, or if they are due to other physical factors.

6   Future Work

This work, still in progress, has three research directions to follow: (1) integrate other data into the analysis, such as population, pollution, industry, growth, etc., factors which could also affect the temperature increase in the metropolitan area; (2), extend this methodology to the temperature time series arisen from other strategically located along the MZVM so to build a more robust map of the effects of GW in a larger region; and (3) implement AI techniques to better extrapolate the increasing temperature tendency discovered in the first frequency mode (see Fig. 3a) to provide more realistic forecasts.

Acknowledgements. The authors want to acknowledge the Tecnológico Nacional de México/I.T. Mérida for the financial support provided through projects 6714.19-P and 6176.19-P, as well as partial economical support by projects 20195343 and 20190136, as well as EDI grant, provided by SIP/IPN. Some authors also thank the AAAI and the AAAI student chapter at Yucatán, Mexico, for the support provided to perform this work.

References

1. Nguvava, M., Abiodun, B., Otieno, F.: Projecting drought characteristics over East African basins at specific global warming levels. Atmos. Res. **228**, 41–54 (2019). Cited By 0
2. Yadollahie, M.: The flood in Iran: a consequence of the global warming? Int. J. Occup. Environ. Med. **10**(2), 54–56 (2019)
3. Suarez Gallareta, E., Hernández Gómez, J.J., Cetzal Balam, G., Orozco del Castillo, M., Moreno Sabido, M., Silva Aguilera, R.A.: Sistema Híbrido Basado en Redes Neuronales Artificiales y Descomposición Modal Empírica para la Evaluación de la Interrelación entre la Irradiancia Solar Total y el Calentamiento Global. Res. Comput. Sci. **147**(5), 319–332 (2018)
4. Interngubernamental Panel on Climate Change: IPCC: Working Group I Contribution to the IPCC Fifth Assessment Report, Climate Change 2013: The Physical Science Basis, IPCC, AR5. Interngubernamental Panel on Climate Change (2014)
5. Spratt, D., Dunlop, I.: Existential climate-related security risk: a scenario approach, Melbourne, Australia, May 2019
6. Xu, L., Chen, N., Zhang, X.: Global drought trends under 1.5 and 2 °C warming. Int. J. Climatol. **39**(4), 2375–2385 (2019). Cited By 0
7. Sen, Z.: Noah and Joseph effects: floods and droughts under global warming. Int. J. Glob. Warm. **16**(3), 347–364 (2018)
8. Ding, Y., Zhang, S., Zhao, L., Li, Z., Kang, S.: Global warming weakening the inherent stability of glaciers and permafrost. Sci. Bull. **64**(4), 245–253 (2019)
9. Kotlyakov, V.M., et al.: Glacier revival and advances in the period of global warming. Dokl. Earth Sci. **481**(2), 1113–1118 (2018)
10. Ying, J., Huang, P., Lian, T., Chen, D.: Intermodel uncertainty in the change of ENSO's amplitude under global warming: role of the response of atmospheric circulation to SST anomalies. J. Clim. **32**(2), 369–383 (2019)
11. Jiang, N., Zhu, C.: Asymmetric changes of ENSO diversity modulated by the cold tongue mode under recent global warming. Geophys. Res. Lett. **45**(22), 12506–12513 (2018)
12. González-Alemán, J., Pascale, S., Gutierrez-Fernandez, J., Murakami, H., Gaertner, M., Vecchi, G.: Potential increase in hazard from Mediterranean hurricane activity with global warming. Geophys. Res. Lett. **46**(3), 1754–1764 (2019)
13. Duan, H., Chen, D., Lie, J.: The impact of global warming on hurricane intensity. In: IOP Conference Series: Earth and Environmental Science, vol. 199, no. 2 (2018)
14. Khan, A.: Why would sea-level rise for global warming and polar ice-melt? Geosci. Front. **10**(2), 481–494 (2019)
15. Carvalho, K., Wang, S.: Characterizing the Indian Ocean sea level changes and potential coastal flooding impacts under global warming. J. Hydrol. **569**, 373–386 (2019)
16. Tang, L., Higa, M., Tanaka, N., Itsubo, N.: Assessment of global warming impact on biodiversity using the extinction risk index in LCIA: a case study of Japanese plant species. Int. J. Life Cycle Assess. **23**(2), 314–323 (2018)
17. Yamaura, K., Sakaue, S., Washida, T.: An assessment of global warming and biodiversity: CGE EMEDA analyses. Environ. Econ. Policy Stud. **19**(2), 405–426 (2017)
18. Nangombe, S.S., Zhou, T., Zhang, W., Zou, L., Li, D.: High-temperature extreme events over Africa under 1.5 and 2 °C of global warming. J. Geophys. Res.: Atmos. **124**(8), 4413–4428 (2019)

19. Verheyen, J., Delnat, V., Stoks, R.: Increased daily temperature fluctuations overrule the ability of gradual thermal evolution to offset the increased pesticide toxicity under global warming. Environ. Sci. Technol. **53**(8), 4600–4608 (2019)

20. Huo, D., et al.: Global-warming-caused changes of temperature and oxygen alter the proteomic profile of sea cucumber Apostichopus japonicus. J. Proteomics **193**, 27–43 (2019)

21. Yousefpour, R., Nabel, J., Pongratz, J.: Simulating growth-based harvest adaptive to future climate change. Biogeosciences **16**(2), 241–254 (2019)

22. Drappier, J., Thibon, C., Rabot, A., Geny-Denis, L.: Relationship between wine composition and temperature: impact on Bordeaux wine typicity in the context of global warming-review. Crit. Rev. Food Sci. Nutr. **59**(1), 14–30 (2019)

23. Di Lena, B., Silvestroni, O., Lanari, V., Palliotti, A.: Climate change effects on cv. Montepulciano in some wine-growing areas of the Abruzzi region (Italy). Theor. Appl. Climatol. **136**(3–4), 1145–1155 (2019)

24. Campbell, A., Becerra, T., Middendorf, G., Tomlinson, P.: Climate change beliefs, concerns, and attitudes of beef cattle producers in the Southern Great Plains. Clim. Change **152**(1), 35–46 (2019)

25. Duru, S., Baycan, S.: Change of daily milk yield during estrous period in Holstein cattle raised under Mediterranean climate. Trop. Anim. Health Prod. **51**, 1571–1577 (2019)

26. Geng, A., Ning, Z., Zhang, H., Yang, H.: Quantifying the climate change mitigation potential of China's furniture sector: wood substitution benefits on emission reduction. Ecol. Ind. **103**, 363–372 (2019)

27. Salman, A., Li, Y., Bastidas-Arteaga, E.: Impact of climate change on optimal wood pole asset management. In: Life-Cycle Analysis and Assessment in Civil Engineering: Towards an Integrated Vision - Proceedings of the 6th International Symposium on Life-Cycle Civil Engineering, IALCCE 2018, pp. 1727–1734 (2019)

28. Avelino, J., et al.: Survey tool for rapid assessment of socio-economic vulnerability of fishing communities in Vietnam to climate change. Geosciences (Switzerland) **8**(12), 452 (2018)

29. Sharifuzzaman, S., Hossain, M., Chowdhury, S., Sarker, S., Chowdhury, M., Chowdhury, M.: Elements of fishing community resilience to climate change in the coastal zone of Bangladesh. J. Coast. Conserv. **22**(6), 1167–1176 (2018)

30. Rowe, M.: Textile industry welcomes change prompted by Paris climate deal. Twist **1**(77), 14–15 (2016)

31. De L'Ecluse, S.: COP21: textile industry also acts against global warming [COP 21 le textile agit aussi contre le Réchauffement]. J. du Textile **52**(2275), 2–4 (2015)

32. Yang, D., Frangopol, D.: Societal risk assessment of transportation networks under uncertainties due to climate change and population growth. Struct. Saf. **78**, 33–47 (2019)

33. Markolf, S., Hoehne, C., Fraser, A., Chester, M., Underwood, B.: Transportation resilience to climate change and extreme weather events - beyond risk and robustness. Transp. Policy **74**, 174–186 (2019)

34. Meinel, U., Schüle, R.: The difficulty of climate change adaptation in manufacturing firms: developing an action-theoretical perspective on the causality of adaptive inaction. Sustainability (Switzerland) **10**(2), 569 (2018)

35. Carlsson Kanyama, A., Carlsson Kanyama, K., Wester, M., Snickare, L., Söderberg, I.L.: Climate change mitigation efforts among transportation and manufacturing companies: the current state of efforts in Sweden according to available documentation. J. Clean. Prod. **196**, 588–593 (2018)

36. Bastida, L., Cohen, J., Kollmann, A., Moya, A., Reichl, J.: Exploring the role of ICT on household behavioural energy efficiency to mitigate global warming. Renew. Sustain. Energy Rev. **103**, 455–462 (2019)
37. De Cian, E., Sue Wing, I.: Global energy consumption in a warming climate. Environ. Resour. Econ. **72**(2), 365–410 (2019)
38. United Nations: The world's cities in 2018: data booklet. Economics and Social Affairs series (2018)
39. World Bank: Urban population (% of total)—Data (2018). https://data.worldbank.org/indicator/sp.urb.totl.in.zs. United Nations Population Division. World Urbanization Prospects: 2018 Revision. Accessed 9 June 2019
40. United Nations Department of Economic and Social Affairs: 68% of the world population projected to live in urban areas by 2050, says UN—UN DESA, June 2018. https://www.un.org/development/desa/en/news/population/2018-revision-of-world-urbanization-prospects.html. Accessed 9 June 2019
41. Landis, J., Hsu, D., Guerra, E.: Intersecting residential and transportation CO_2 emissions: metropolitan climate change programs in the age of trump. J. Plan. Educ. Res. **39**(2), 206–226 (2019)
42. Trájer, A., Nagy, G., Domokos, E.: Exploration of the heterogeneous effect of climate change on ozone concentration in an urban environment. Int. J. Environ. Health Res. **29**(3), 276–289 (2019)
43. Baldermann, C., Lorenz, S.: UV radiation in Germany: influences of ozone depletion and climate change and measures to protect the population. Bundesgesundheitsblatt - Gesundheitsforschung - Gesundheitsschutz **62**(5), 639–645 (2019)
44. Orimoloye, I., Mazinyo, S., Kalumba, A., Ekundayo, O., Nel, W.: Implications of climate variability and change on urban and human health: a review. Cities **91**, 213–223 (2019)
45. Woodward, A., Baumgartner, J., Ebi, K., Gao, J., Kinney, P., Liu, Q.: Population health impacts of China's climate change policies. Environ. Res. **175**, 178–185 (2019)
46. Aminipouri, M., et al.: Urban tree planting to maintain outdoor thermal comfort under climate change: the case of Vancouver's local climate zones. Build. Environ. **158**, 226–236 (2019)
47. Sun, Y., Xie, S., Zhao, S.: Valuing urban green spaces in mitigating climate change: a city-wide estimate of aboveground carbon stored in urban green spaces of China's capital. Glob. Change Biol. **25**(5), 1717–1732 (2019)
48. Doan, V., Kusaka, H., Nguyen, T.: Roles of past, present, and future land use and anthropogenic heat release changes on urban heat island effects in Hanoi, Vietnam: numerical experiments with a regional climate model. Sustain. Cities Soc. **47**, 101479 (2019)
49. Chapman, S., Thatcher, M., Salazar, A., Watson, J., McAlpine, C.: The impact of climate change and urban growth on urban climate and heat stress in a subtropical city. Int. J. Climatol. **39**(6), 3013–3030 (2019)
50. Zhang, C., Li, S., Luo, F., Huang, Z.: The global warming hiatus has faded away: an analysis of 2014–2016 global surface air temperatures. Int. J. Climatol. **2019**, 1–16 (2019)
51. Shastri, H., Ghosh, S., Paul, S., Shafizadeh-Moghadam, H., Helbich, M., Karmakar, S.: Future urban rainfall projections considering the impacts of climate change and urbanization with statistical-dynamical integrated approach. Clim. Dyn. **52**(9–10), 6033–6051 (2019)
52. Dodman, D., Archer, D., Satterthwaite, D.: Editorial: responding to climate change in contexts of urban poverty and informality. Environ. Urban. **31**(1), 3–12 (2019)

53. Gran Castro, J., Ramos De Robles, S.: Climate change and flood risk: vulnerability assessment in an urban poor community in Mexico. Environ. Urban. **31**(1), 75–92 (2019)
54. Xiong, L., Yan, L., Du, T., Yan, P., Li, L., Xu, W.: Impacts of climate change on urban extreme rainfall and drainage infrastructure performance: a case study in Wuhan City, China. Irrig. Drain. **68**(2), 152–164 (2019)
55. De la Sota, C., Ruffato-Ferreira, V., Ruiz-García, L., Alvarez, S.: Urban green infrastructure as a strategy of climate change mitigation. A case study in Northern Spain. Urban For. Urban Green. **40**, 145–151 (2019)
56. Bellinson, R., Chu, E.: Learning pathways and the governance of innovations in urban climate change resilience and adaptation. J. Environ. Plan. Policy Manag. **21**(1), 76–89 (2019)
57. Martinez-Juarez, P., Chiabai, A., Suárez, C., Quiroga, S.: Insights on urban and periurban adaptation strategies based on stakeholders' perceptions on hard and soft responses to climate change. Sustainability (Switzerland) **11**(3), 647 (2019)
58. Lal, R.: Managing urban soils for food security and adaptation to climate change. In: Vasenev, V., Dovletyarova, E., Cheng, Z., Prokof'eva, T.V., Morel, J.L., Ananyeva, N.D. (eds.) SUITMA 2017. SG, pp. 302–319. Springer, Cham (2019). https://doi.org/10.1007/978-3-319-89602-1_35
59. Raimundo, I.: Food insecurity in the context of climate change in Maputo city, Mozambique: challenges and coping strategies. ROUTLEDGE in Association with GSE Research (2016)
60. Mahaut, V., Andrieu, H.: Relative influence of urban-development strategies and water management on mixed (separated and combined) sewer overflows in the context of climate change and population growth: a case study in Nantes. Sustain. Cities Soc. **44**, 171–182 (2019)
61. Januszkiewicz, K., Świtoń, M.: Climate change and population mobility - envisioning infrastructure to reduce disaster's impact on cities. In: International Multidisciplinary Scientific GeoConference Surveying Geology and Mining Ecology Management, SGEM, vol. 17, pp. 519–526 (2017)
62. Khavarian-Garmsir, A., Pourahmad, A., Hataminejad, H., Farhoodi, R.: Climate change and environmental degradation and the drivers of migration in the context of shrinking cities: a case study of Khuzestan province, Iran. Sustain. Cities Soc. **47**, 101480 (2019)
63. Trihamdani, A.R., Lee, H.S., Kubota, T., Iizuka, S., Phuong, T.T.T.: Urban climate challenges in Hanoi: urban heat Islands and global warming. In: Kubota, T., Rijal, H.B., Takaguchi, H. (eds.) Sustainable Houses and Living in the Hot-Humid Climates of Asia, pp. 529–539. Springer, Singapore (2018). https://doi.org/10.1007/978-981-10-8465-2_48
64. Li, G., Zhang, X., Mirzaei, P., Zhang, J., Zhao, Z.: Urban heat island effect of a typical valley city in China: responds to the global warming and rapid urbanization. Sustain. Cities Soc. **38**, 736–745 (2018)
65. Trejo-González, A., et al.: Quantifying health impacts and economic costs of $PM_{2.5}$ exposure in Mexican cities of the national urban system. Int. J. Public Health **64**(4), 561–572 (2019)
66. Konar, A.: Artificial Intelligence and Soft Computing: Behavioral and Cognitive Modeling of the Human Brain. CRC Press, Boca Raton (1999)
67. Woo, T.: Artificial intelligence-based modelling for global warming analysis incorporated with the nuclear energy productions. Int. J. Glob. Warm. **17**(4), 389–400 (2019)

68. Lu, Q., Joyce, J., Imen, S., Chang, N.B.: Linking socioeconomic development, sea level rise, and climate change impacts on urban growth in New York City with a fuzzy cellular automata-based Markov chain model. Environ. Plan. B: Urban Anal. City Sci. **46**(3), 551–572 (2019)
69. Woo, T.: Global warming analysis for greenhouse gases impacts comparable to carbon-free nuclear energy using neuro-fuzzy algorithm. Int. J. Glob. Warm. **17**(2), 219–233 (2019)
70. Gubareva, M., Gomes, O.: On the edge of climate change: in a search of an adequate agent-based methodology to model environmental dynamics. In: Sequeira, T., Reis, L. (eds.) Climate Change and Global Development. CE, pp. 37–57. Springer, Cham (2019). https://doi.org/10.1007/978-3-030-02662-2_3
71. Atuahene, S., Bao, Y., Yevenyo Ziggah, Y., Semwaah Gyan, P., Li, F.: Short-term electric power forecasting using dual-stage hierarchical wavelet-particle swarm optimization-adaptive neuro-fuzzy inference system PSO-ANFIS approach based on climate change. Energies **11**(10), 2822 (2018)
72. Mohammadi, B.: "Prediction of effective climate change indicators using statistical downscaling approach and impact assessment on pearl millet (Pennisetum glaucum L.) yield through genetic algorithm in Punjab, Pakistan" by Asmat Ullah, Nasrin Salehnia, Sohrab Kolsoumi, Ashfaq Ahmad, Tasneem Khaliq. Ecol. Indic. **101**, 973–974 (2019)
73. Yoon, E., et al.: Modeling spatial climate change landuse adaptation with multi-objective genetic algorithms to improve resilience for rice yield and species richness and to mitigate disaster risk. Environ. Res. Lett. **14**(2), 024001 (2019)
74. Vaghefi, S.A., Abbaspour, N., Kamali, B., Abbaspour, K.: A toolkit for climate change analysis and pattern recognition for extreme weather conditions - case study: California-Baja California Peninsula. Environ. Model Softw. **96**, 181–198 (2017)
75. Wu, C., Chen, Y., Peng, C., Li, Z., Hong, X.: Modeling and estimating aboveground biomass of Dacrydium pierrei in China using machine learning with climate change. J. Environ. Manag. **234**, 167–179 (2019)
76. Crane-Droesch, A.: Machine learning methods for crop yield prediction and climate change impact assessment in agriculture. Environ. Res. Lett. **13**(11), 114003 (2018)
77. Collados-Lara, A.J., Pardo-Igúzquiza, E., Pulido-Velazquez, D.: A distributed cellular automata model to simulate potential future impacts of climate change on snow cover area. Adv. Water Resour. **124**, 106–119 (2019)
78. Nile, B., Hassan, W., Alshama, G.: Analysis of the effect of climate change on rainfall intensity and expected flooding by using ANN and SWMM programs. ARPN J. Eng. Appl. Sci. **14**(5), 974–984 (2019)
79. Aslan, Z., Erdemir, G., Feoli, E., Giorgi, F., Okcu, D.: Effects of climate change on soil erosion risk assessed by clustering and artificial neural network. Pure Appl. Geophys. **176**(2), 937–949 (2019)
80. Quezada, R., Martinez Rossier, L., Hernandez Garduno, E., Catalan Vazquez, M., Quezada, E., Perez Neria, J.: Comparison of carbon monoxide levels in air expired from pedestrian in an urban area and a rural area. Rev. del Inst. Nac. de Enferm. Respiratorias **10**(1), 13–17 (1997)
81. Matheron, G.: Principles of geostatistics. Econ. Geol **58**(8), 1246–1266 (1963)
82. Krige, D.: A statistical approach to some basic mine valuation problems on the Witwatersrand. J. Chem. Metall. Min. Soc. S. Afr. **52**, 201–215 (1952)
83. Zhang, J., Li, X., Yang, R., Liu, Q., Zhao, L., Dou, B.: An extended Kriging method to interpolate near-surface soil moisture data measured by wireless sensor networks. Sensors **17**(6), 1390 (2017)

84. Liu, L., Cheng, Y., Wang, X.: Genetic algorithm optimized Taylor Kriging surrogate model for system reliability analysis of soil slopes. Landslides **14**(2), 535–546 (2017)
85. Huang, N.E., et al.: The empirical mode decomposition and the Hilbert spectrum for nonlinear and non-stationary time series analysis. Proc. R. Soc. Lond. A: Math. Phys. Eng. Sci. **454**, 903–995 (1998)
86. Kim, D., Oh, H.S.: EMD: a package for empirical mode decomposition and Hilbert spectrum. R J. **1**(1), 40–46 (2009)
87. Huang, N.E.: Review of empirical mode decomposition. In: Wavelet Applications VIII, vol. 4391, pp. 71–81. International Society for Optics and Photonics (2001)
88. Du, H.K., Cao, J.X., Xue, Y.J., Wang, X.J.: Seismic facies analysis based on self-organizing map and empirical mode decomposition. J. Appl. Geophys. **112**, 52–61 (2015)
89. Nunes, J.C., Bouaoune, Y., Delechelle, E., Niang, O., Bunel, P.: Image analysis by bidimensional empirical mode decomposition. Image Vis. Comput. **21**(12), 1019–1026 (2003)
90. Andrade, A.O., Nasuto, S., Kyberd, P., Sweeney-Reed, C.M., Van Kanijn, F.: EMG signal filtering based on empirical mode decomposition. Biomed. Signal Process. Control **1**(1), 44–55 (2006)
91. Drakakis, K.: Empirical mode decomposition of financial data. Int. Math. Forum **4**, 1191–1202 (2008)
92. Intergubernamental Panel on Climate Change: Homepage (2014). http://www.ipcc.ch/home_languages_main_spanish.shtml. Accessed 01 Apr 2019
93. Masson-Delmotte, V., et al.: Global Warming of 1.5C. An IPCC Special Report on the impacts of global warming of 1.5C above pre-industrial levels and related global greenhouse gas emission pathways, in the context of strengthening the global response to the threat of climate change, sustainable development, and efforts to eradicate poverty. Technical report 1, IPCC, Geneva, Switzerland (2018, in Press)
94. Orozco-Del-Castillo, M., Ortiz-Alemán, J., Couder-Castañeda, C., Hernández-Gómez, J., Solís-Santomé, A.: High solar activity predictions through an artificial neural network. Int. J. Mod. Phys. C **28**(06), 1750075 (2017)
95. Kane, R.: Short-term periodicities in solar indices. Sol. Phys. **227**(1), 155–175 (2005)

Moderate Resolution Imaging Spectroradiometer Products Classification Using Deep Learning

Javier Arellano-Verdejo[✉]

El Colegio de la Frontera Sur, Estación para la Recepción de Información Satelital
ERIS-Chetumal, Av. Centenario Km 5.5, 77014 Chetumal, Quintana Roo, Mexico
javier.arellano@mail.ecosur.mx

Abstract. During the last years, the algorithms based on Artificial Intelligence have increased their popularity thanks to their application in multiple areas of knowledge. Nowadays with the increase of storage capacities and computing power, as well as the incorporation of new technologies for massively parallel processing (GPUs and TPUs) and Cloud Computing, it is increasingly common to incorporate this kind of algorithms and technology in tasks with a deep social and technological impact. In the present work a new Convolutional Neural Network specialized in the automatic classification of Moderate Resolution Imaging Spectroradiometer satellite products is proposed. The proposed architecture has shown a high-generalization by classifying more than 250,000 images with 99.99% accuracy. The methodology designed also can be extended, with other types of images, to make detection of Sargassum, oil spills, red tide, etc.

Keywords: Deep learning · MODIS · Remote sensing · Data science · Machine learning

1 Introduction

The Artificial Intelligence (AI) concept, was proposed by John McCarthy in Dartmouth (United States) during the summer of 1956. The AI is the result of the synergy between multiple disciplines such as computer science, mathematics, and logic (to mention just a few), with the aim of getting a machine to imitate the human cognitive functions such as learning and solving problems in an independent way. As a result of AI, new areas of knowledge have emerged such as: case-based reasoning, expert systems, Bayesian networks, robotics, pattern recognition, neural networks and machine learning to mention just a few [1].

Remote sensing (RS) is based on the acquisition of information about an object or phenomenon without having physical contact with it. The RS is used by multiple areas of study including geography, hydrology, meteorology, oceanography, geology, humanitarian applications, etc. The main source of information

© Springer Nature Switzerland AG 2019
M. F. Mata-Rivera et al. (Eds.): WITCOM 2019, CCIS 1053, pp. 61–70, 2019.
https://doi.org/10.1007/978-3-030-33229-7_6

used by the satellital RS is provided by various sensors on board space missions such as Landsat, RADAR, Sentinel, and MODIS [2]. The Moderate-Resolution Imaging Spectroradiometer (i.e MODIS), is an instrument of Earth observation placed in orbit by NASA in 1999 aboard the space platform EOS AM-1 TERRA and in 2002 on board EOS PM-1 AQUA. MODIS has a spectral resolution of 36 bands between 0.4 to 14.4 μm, has a radiometric resolution of 12 bits and a spatial resolution of 250, 500 and 1000 m. The main use of the different bands of the MODIS sensor is related to the detection of clouds and aerosols (bands 1 to 7), ocean color, phytoplankton and biogeochemistry (bands 8 to 16) and water vapor (bands 16 to 19) however, the main application of the MODIS sensor is related to the generation of the "MODIS Products", which are used by scientists from all over the world to carry out studies related mainly to the global change of the planet. MODIS products can be classified into five major groups: level 1 products, atmospheric products, land products, cryosphere products, and sea products. Recently, the combination of MODIS satellite data with data science techniques and AI has given rise to many practical applications for Mexico such as the detection of Sargasso on the coast of Quintana Roo [3] and the study of the state of health of Banco Chinchorro [4]. Access to MODIS data is open and free through NASA websites, so developing tools to manipulate, classify and exploit them is essential for the development of algorithms and techniques related to the handling of this type of information and its application to remote sensing problems.

In the present work, a new AI algorithm based on a Convolutional Neural Network is proposed for the classification of MODIS satellite products. The proposed neural network has shown high performance and accuracy, classifying more than 250,000 images with 99.99% of accuracy.

2 MODIS Products Classification

2.1 Artificial Neural Networks

An Artificial Neural Network (ANN) is a computational model inspired by the interconnection and exchange of information between biological neurons of living beings. As can be seen in Fig. 1a, an ANN is formed by a set of artificial neurons organized in layers, in the classical model, these layers are organized into: input layer, output layer and one or more hidden layers. The artificial neurons (see Fig. 1b) are the minimum unit of computation of an ANN, its main function is to compute the weighted sum between the inputs X_i and the weights W_i. The result is processed by an activation function f which generates the final output S. Depending on the type of network architecture, the S output can be used as input for another neuron or simply be part of the network's output layer [9].

Within the field of Artificial Intelligence, RNAs are part of the Machine Learning (ML) discipline and belong to the set of supervised learning algorithms. Supervised learning is a technique that allows generating a mathematical model capable of correctly classifying information in different groups. It uses a set of pairs of tagged data and, through an iterative training process, approximates the

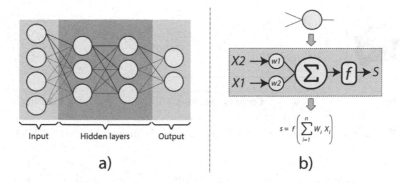

Fig. 1. BASIC architecture of a multilayer artificial neural network

model that best classifies the information. With this set of data and applying a learning algorithm called "retro-propagation" algorithm based on the descending gradient technique, the ANN generates a structure that has the ability to classify information that is not in the original data set correctly [10].

2.2   Convolutional Neural Network

The Convolutional Neural Networks or CNN, traditionally have been used almost specifically in the classification of images (Fig. 2). CNN has been used successfully in multiple areas such as computer science, medicine, economics, music, painting, and science, to mention just a few [5–8,11]. In CNN, neurons correspond to receptive fields in a manner similar to neurons in the primary visual cortex of the biological brain. The CNN is composed of a set of filters of one or more dimensions used to highlight specific features of the information you want to classify, at the end of each filter layer, a function that is responsible for performing a non-linear mapping is applied. Unlike the ANNs, during the CNN training process a set of specialized filters is obtained instead of w_i type weights. The main operation within CNN is called convolution. The convolution allows highlighting characteristics or specific aspects of the image and it is precisely this ability to extract features that have made the CNN widely used successfully in subjects related to computer vision and classification of images.

2.3   Construction of the Training Data Set

As with all supervised learning algorithms, an appropriately labeled data set is required to design, train an algorithm capable of classifying information appropriately. This data set is used during the training phase of the RN, additionally, it is necessary to have a set of data for the verification and validation of the same neuronal network. For the present work, a set of MODIS data products was generated consisting of 253,500 images of 28×28 pixels, which were extracted from more than 17 years of historical data from products. The study region where

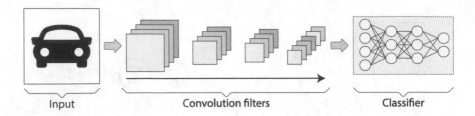

Fig. 2. General structure of a Convolutional Neuronal Network (CNN)

these images were extracted is located within the Caribbean Sea of Mexico and part of Central America. The images were obtained by applying a window with 25% overlap between images to preserve the spatial relationships between them (see Fig. 3). The data set is composed of four classes of MODIS products: chlorophyll, sea surface temperature, fluorescence and the photosynthetically available instantaneous radiation (IPAR).

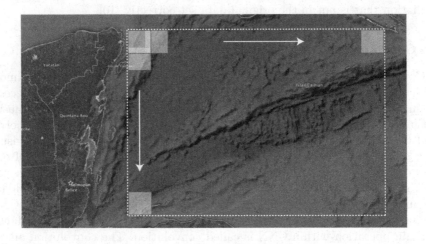

Fig. 3. Study region to create the data set

3   CNN for the Classification of MODIS Products

In Fig. 4, the convolutional neuronal network designed for the present is shown. The proposed CNN is composed of two parts; the block of convolutional layers and the block containing a classifier based on a multilayer perceptron. The block of convolutional layers is composed of two sets of filters, by one hand, the first of which consists of 32 filters of 3×3 pixels, on the other hand, the second block is composed of 64 filters of the same size. At the output of each set of filters, the rectified linear unit activation function (i.e. RELU) is used, finally, in order to extract the representative information of the last set of filters, in the last section of the convolutional block a two-dimensional "Max Pooling" operation, was used. The classifying block (multilayer perceptron) is composed of an input layer formed by 128 neurons with a RELU-like activation function and an output layer of 4 neurons with a softmax-type activation function.

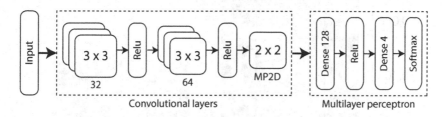

Fig. 4. Convolutional Neural Network for classification of MODIS products

For the implementation of the proposed neural network, the Python 3.7.0 programming language and the library Keras 2.2.4 with TensorFlow 1.10.0 as a backend were used. TensorFlow is an Open Source library developed by Google's Brain Team, it is used for the numerical calculation using "flow graphing programming". The nodes in the graph represent mathematical operations while the connections within the graph represent multidimensional data sets known as "Tensors". Tensor Flow contains a set of automatic learning algorithms as well as other tools that make it ideal for the development of new methods. Keras is a library that can be used by Python and provides an abstraction layer that facilitates access to TensorFlow to create deep learning models. The convolutional neural network was trained and tested using a Lenovo workstation with an 8-core Xeon EP processor with 64 GB of RAM and an Nvidia Quadro k5000 GPU with 1536 parallel processing CUDA cores using the Ubuntu 18.04 operating system.

4 Results

To carry out the training and testing of the proposed neural network, the k-fold procedure with $k = 5$ was used as a cross-validation method. The cross-validation process is used to estimate the ability of an CNN to classify information that has never been presented to the model (generalization), that is, a limited sample of information is used to estimate how the Model performs in general when used to make predictions about data that was not used during model training. K-fold is one of the most popular cross-validation methods because it results in a less biased or less optimistic estimate of the model's capacity than other methods, such as a simple trial-and-error division. During the training of the proposed network, 80% of data was used to design (training, and testing) the CNN while the rest 20% was used for the validation. As it can be seen in Fig. 5, both the data set and the validation data set are balanced, that is, the total number

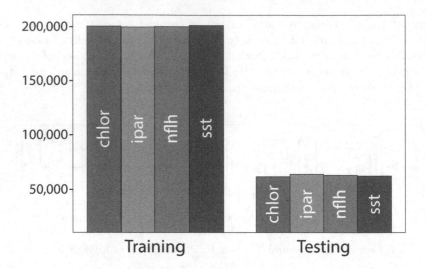

Fig. 5. Histogram of training and test data sets

of elements for the class used for each of the cases is similar. The purpose of avoiding biases when generating the model.

The training process was carried out for 20 epochs or iterations, in each iteration blocks (batch size) of 100 images were used. The optimization method used during the training phase was Adam's algorithm. The Adam optimization algorithm (Addictive moment estimation) was presented by Kingma Diederik in 2015 [12] and this is an extension of the stochastic gradient method, this algorithm has been adopted in the field of deep learning for its profound impact on the applications of computer vision and natural language processing.

Figure 6 shows the convergence graph during the training process, the black dotted line shows the behavior of the neural network during the training phase, it is evident, the network is able to obtain a good model of classification relatively fast. As you can see, at the epoch 10 of the training phase, it is clear that the neural network has learned to distinguish between different classes with an accuracy close to 100%. The continuous line of green color shows the validation of the neural network, that is to say, the capacity of the network to classify data that has never seen previously in other words, the generalization capability of the network. Thereby it is clear the overfitting is not present as it can be seen in the plot result. Finally derived from the behavior and trend of the data during the training process, it can be clearly distinguished that the network has not memorized the data, instead, it has generated a robust enough model for the successful classification of MODIS satellite products.

In Table 1, a summary with the results obtained is shown. As can be seen, the percentage of successful classification by the neural network was 99%. During the cross-validation phase, it was found that the architecture is able to classify up to 99.97% of the information correctly. Also in the same table, it can be seen

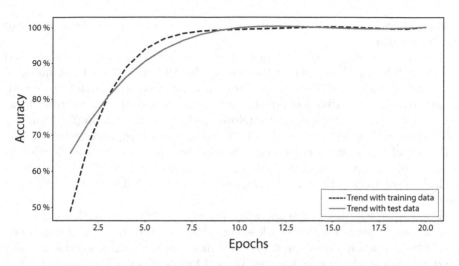

Fig. 6. Convergence plot during the training phase (Color figure online)

that the measures of central tendency and dispersion are similar between the training and test data sets, which implies that the results, at least from this classical point of view, they have the same tendency and statistical dispersion.

Table 1. Statistical data of the training process and data sets

Statistical measure	Value
Successful classification percentage	99.0
Best percentage of successful classification	99.973831
Training data set size	200,000
Size of the test data set	53,500
Average of the training data set	−0.09725764
Average of the test data set	−0.09741989
Standard deviation of the training data set	0.78812724
Standard deviation of the test data set	0.78970873

5   Discussion

The classification of images using neural networks and deep learning is not new, In general, the classification of images is done using three bands mainly (red, green and blue) however, depending on the complexity of the data set, neural networks, even convolutional networks, are not able to achieve optimal results. In many cases, for the correct classification of information, the development of new specialized architectures is required in such a way as to increase the accuracy of the classification.

The satellite images, depending on the sensor and platform, are composed of at least 8 bands (Landsat), in the case of the MODIS sensor, the number of bands increases to 36, which requires, for their classification, an architecture with optimal parameters. After a detailed study of the state of the art, no record was found showing the classification of satellite products such as chlorophyll, surface water temperature and fluorescence by using modern computation techniques, so the use of Deep Learning as a classification tool is in itself a contribution to the state of the art. A drawback of the lack of algorithms in the literature, is the lack of contenders in order to compare the results obtained with the state of the art.

The proper selection of the operating parameters of a convolutional network even of a multilayer neural network is not trivial, even today, it is still an open topic where in many occasions it becomes more an art than a science. Finally, the development of libraries such as TensorFlow or Keras allow researchers to concentrate on solving the problem rather than on the operational implementation of this, that is why (in addition to the increase in computing power and storage space) that in recent dates we have observed an exponential increase in the applications of Artificial Intelligence.

In this work, the appropriate parameters for a convolutional architecture capable of classifying satellite products derived from the 36 MODIS bands were developed and obtained. Achieving an accuracy of more than 98% the architecture shown is simple, however, the selection of the parameters has not been simple, these have been determined experimentally in order to find the best network performance.

Another important contribution of this work is the creation of an image bank, which was generated from the historical collection of more than 17 years of images obtained by the ERIS-Chetumal Satellite Information Reception Station, This image bank has information for the entire Mexican Caribbean and it has a total of 253,500 images, which can be used for other algorithms of classification, clustering and data processing.

6   Conclusions and Final Comments

The area of remote satellite detection has a great impact in the face of support in emerging problems and with a great social impact, such as the detection of sargassum, the study of soil change, the environmental impact in large-scale works, like the Mayan train among other.

The remote perception without a doubt, still has many challenges ahead such as for example the automatic classification of information. The use of algorithms based on artificial intelligence such as CNN presented in this work represent an alternative to be able to face this type of challenges. As shown in the results, with the use of convolutional neural networks, encouraging results are obtained for the automatic classification of MODIS satellite data.

In the present work, a convolutional neural network was presented for the automatic classification of MODIS satellite products. After the careful elaboration of a data bank with more than 250,000 images of MODIS products divided and correctly labeled in four classes for a wide region of the Caribbean Sea of Mexico, a CNN capable of automatically classifying these images was designed. As a result of using the k-fold cross-validation method, a CNN with a classification capacity of 99% accuracy was obtained. The application of measures of central tendency and dispersion showed that both the training data set and the validation data are statistically consistent, which, together with the results obtained, helps to conclude that the proposed network is capable of generalizing with a high degree of confidence.

7   Future Work

As part of the future work, the authors are currently working on the design of a new architecture of Neural Network for the automatic classification of more than 20 MODIS products. With a database of more than 1,019,200,000 data and more than 1,300,000 images for the Caribbean Sea, new storage, access and information manipulation challenges are being faced, which implies, among other things, the design of new algorithms as well as the use of from other disciplines such as data science, Big Data, parallel programming using graphical processing units clusters and specialized hardware units for the processing of tensors like Google TPU technology.

References

1. Russell, S.J., Norvig, P.: Artificial Intelligence: A Modern Approach. Pearson Education Limited, Kuala Lumpur (2016)
2. Jensen, J.R., Lulla, K.: Introductory Digital Image Processing: A Remote Sensing Perspective. Prentice Hall, Upper Saddle River (1987)
3. Arellano-Verdejo, J., Lazcano-Hernandez, H.E., Cabanillas-Terán, N.: ERISNet: deep neural network for Sargassum detection along the coastline of the Mexican Caribbean. PeerJ 7, e6842 (2019). https://doi.org/10.7717/peerj.6842
4. Lazcano-Hernandez, H.E., Arellano-Verdejo, J., Hernandez-Arana, H.A., Alvarado-Barrientos, M.S.: Spatio-temporal assessment of "Chlorophyll a" in Banco Chinchorro using remote sensing. Res. Comput. Sci. 147(12), 213–223 (2018)
5. Cheng, G., Yang, C., Yao, X., Guo, L., Han, J.: When deep learning meets metric learning: remote sensing image scene classification via learning discriminative CNNs. IEEE Trans. Geosci. Remote Sens. 56(5), 2811–2821 (2018)
6. Rajkomar, A., et al.: Scalable and accurate deep learning with electronic health records. NPJ Digit. Med. 1(1), 18 (2018)
7. Poplin, R., et al.: Prediction of cardiovascular risk factors from retinal fundus photographs via deep learning. Nat. Biomed. Eng. 2(3), 158 (2018)
8. Han, J., Zhang, D., Cheng, G., Liu, N., Xu, D.: Advanced deep-learning techniques for salient and category-specific object detection: a survey. IEEE Signal Process. Mag. 35(1), 84–100 (2018)

9. Haykin, S.S., Elektroingenieur, K., Haykin, S.S.: Neural Networks and Learning Machines, vol. 3. Pearson Education, Upper Saddle River (2009)
10. Michie, D., Spiegelhalter, D.J., Taylor, C.C.: Machine Learning. Neural and Statistical Classification, 13 (1994)
11. LeCun, Y., Kavukcuoglu, K., Farabet, C.: Convolutional networks and applications in vision. In: Proceedings of 2010 IEEE International Symposium on Circuits and Systems, pp. 253–256. IEEE (2010)
12. Kingma, D.P., Ba, J.: Adam: a method for stochastic optimization. arXiv preprint arXiv:1412.6980 (2014)

A Dynamic System Model Using Agile Method Techniques Applied to Geomatics

René Rodríguez Zamora[1]([⊠]), Álvaro Peraza Garzón[1],
and Iliana Amabely Silva Hernández[2]

[1] Universidad Autónoma de Sinaloa,
Av Ejercito Mexicano 1166, Fracc. Tellería, 82140 Mazatlán, Sinaloa, Mexico
rene.rodriguez@info.uas.edu.mx, aperaza@gmail.com
[2] Universidad Politécnica de Sinaloa, Carretera Municipal Libre Higueras KM 3,
Colonia Genaro Estrada, 82199 Mazatlán, Sinaloa, Mexico
isilva@upsin.edu.mx

Abstract. In this paper we propose the use of a model that represents a territory across a dynamic system. As part of the process in the definition of the model we used techniques adaptive software engineering, particularly construction tools associated with agile methods. The dynamic system modeling serves to simulate territorial scenarios and analyze their characteristics using geographical information systems. The approach is to design user stories as artifacts that can be used for example by decision makers, urban planners or researchers to more easily observe and read territorial scenarios that can be to present in the evolution of land-use changes in a geographical area of interest. This represents an important advantage because it reduces reading complexity and facilitates analysis because combining agile methods with a simulation model provide a macroscopic and simplified view of a scenario of nature complex.

Keywords: Dynamic systems · Geomatics · GIS · Agile methods

1 Introduction

The vertiginous advance of the digital technology has propitiated the whole transformation in the development of the activities that the persons realize daily. The evolution in the land use of the territory is a fundamental element in our society, since it manifests different variables that affect our daily life, for example, accessibility to different points of interest within the city, slopes of the land, etc. This evolution has gained interest mainly fueled by the different environmental problems especially those in urban areas [1–3].

Thanks to the advances in the computing field and the development of important analytical tools such as Geographic Information Systems (GIS) or simulation models, the study of the changes taking place in metropolitan areas has been promoted [4]. The analysis of the environmental alterations that result from these

© Springer Nature Switzerland AG 2019
M. F. Mata-Rivera et al. (Eds.): WITCOM 2019, CCIS 1053, pp. 71–82, 2019.
https://doi.org/10.1007/978-3-030-33229-7_7

changes and the development of new planning instruments, has caused that different disciplines, specifically the Artificial Intelligence (AI), approaches from a computer and mathematical point of view to give alternative solutions to this problem [5,6]. Numerous modeling tools have emerged in recent years. In the case of urban growth, the models based on cellular automata (CA) are the most widely used [7,8].

In this paper we present a discrete dynamic system represented by a cellular automaton that can be used to simulate a geographical area. We test the model by doing experiments from a digitalized map and generate a corresponding map from a simulation. Finally, as an additional element to the model definition we use user stories and scenario description as agile method techniques for communicating important aspects that characterize the model.

2 Dynamic Systems

The dynamic systems are systems which internal parameters (variables of the state) follow a series of temporary rules. There are called systems because they are described by a set of equations (system) and dynamic because its parameters change with regard some variable that generally is the time. The study of the dynamic systems can be divided into 3 subdisciplines:

- Applied dynamics: Modeling processes using state equations that relate past states to future states.
- Dynamics Mathematics: Focuses on the qualitative analysis of the dynamic model.
- Experimental Dynamics: Laboratory experiments, computer simulations of dynamic models.

The dynamic systems can split into two big classes: those in which the time changes continuously and in which the time passes discreetly. Dynamic continuous-time systems are expressed with differential equations; these can be ordinary differential equations, differential equations in derivative partial, and differential equations with delays. On the other hand if the time is discreet the systems are described by means of difference equations. In the following figures some examples of dynamic systems can be observed [9,10].

The cellular automata were conceived at the beginning of the 1950's by John Von Neumann, a mathematical brilliant interested in investigating about the required complexity so that a device could be auto-reproductive and the organization of this one to have a correct operation when repairing itself with part that could have and operation badly [11]. The results were not let hope, all a current of investigation has been developed with strong interrelation in fields like fractals and dynamic systems, as well as applications in: parallel cellular computing, simulation of dynamic systems and recognition of patterns, and simulation of socio-economical models, for instance (Figs. 1 and 2).

In general therms, we can say that a cellular automata is defined and operates based on the following elements [11]:

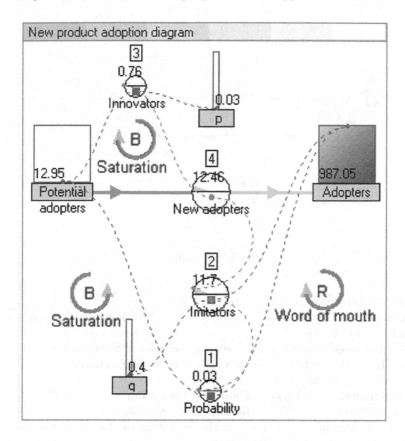

Fig. 1. New product adoption diagram.

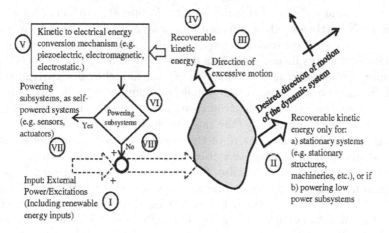

Fig. 2. Self-powered dynamic system.

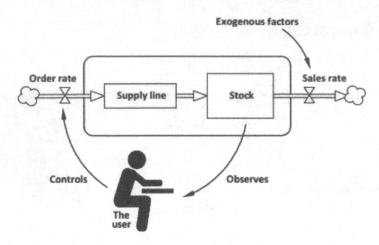

Fig. 3. Sales model.

– States, or attributes, e.g., "on" or "off", 0 or 1.
– Containers that store those attributes, e.g., a location in and array, a sector in a computer's memory.
– Behaviors associated with those states; formulated as conditional transition rules (IF, THEN, ELSE) that govern how and when automata react to information that is input to them.
– Neighborhoods from which the automata draw input, e.g., neighboring locations in an array, databases containing information.
– Temporal domain, through which the evolution of the automata proceeds, e.g., real-time, program cycles.

We can define cellular automata so that it operates in one, two or more dimensions. Nevertheless, the complexity to analyze them or to implement simulations of these in a computer is exponentially increased with the number of dimensions and states including in this definition Fig. 3.

Cellular automata are also extremely useful for modeling disease transmission [12]. By treating each cell as an individual and defining a few key constants we can model how much damage a given disease can be expected to do. The four key quantities are the infectivity (the rate at which the disease spreads), latency, (how long before it becomes active in the host), duration (how long it remains in the host and mortality (the percentage of people the disease kills).

Patterns show up often in nature, from the coloration of fur on a leopard to the shape a fern takes as it grows. The way in which these patterns for is poorly understood. However, Wolfram [13] has theorized that they are generated in a manner similar to cellular automata. In this model, each pigmentation cell behaves according to the state each of its immediate neighbors has taken on, much same way a cellular automata works. Another example of this is in the way mollusk shells are generated. Since the shell is extruded one cell layer at a time (much like your fingernails), the complex color patterns may be acting as a one-dimensional cellular automata. Examples of mollusk shells can be seen below. Below you can see an example of one such simulation [14] (Fig. 4).

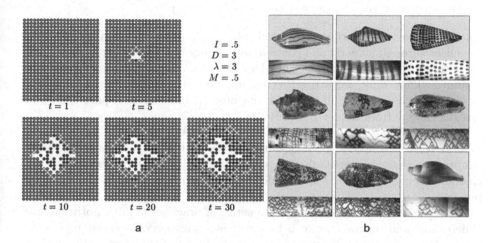

a   b

Fig. 4. Some cellular automata.

3   Agile Methods

There are methodologies based on classical paradigms within the scope of software development guided by models used at the time by software engineers like linear models represented in cascade, and the evolutionary, iterative and incremental represented in spiral and prototypes.

One of the most widely used standard methodologies is the Unified Process (UP) for different application areas and different classes of organizations [15]. There are three characteristics that distinguish the UP from the rest of the methodologies: is centered in the architecture, is iterative and incremental, and is oriented and directed by use case. Although these characteristics distinguish UP, do not leave aside the advantages offered by other methodologies, that is, they take advantage of their strengths in the development of stages and phases that are already well established in the field of software engineering, but increasing the flexibility and giving the first guidelines for which are known as agile methods [16].

The agile methods are part of a set of methodologies also known like light which use similar practices based on the results, the persons and its interaction. Exists a diversity of methodologies as the extreme programming (XP) Crystal Clear, Feature Driven Development (FDD), Adaptive Software Development (ASD) and Scrum. All these methodologies adopt the one that is known as an agile manifesto, which values:

- To individuals and their interaction, over processes and tools.
- The software that works over the exhaustive documentation.
- The collaboration with the client, above the contractual negotiation.
- The answer to the change over the follow-up of a plan.

These four postulates are implemented using agile principles such as: satisfying the client through an early and continuous delivery of the software, the fact that the requirements are changing, the elements of an organization are positively assumed. They must work together on a daily basis during the development of the project, it is established that the best architectures, requirements and designs emerge from teams that self-organize.

Agile methodologies seek at all times teamwork, multidisciplinary and collaborative, which allows to carry out projects with immediacy and flexibility, adapted to changes, demanding at any time modify the mentality, a cultural change based on respect, responsibility, values, competencies and skills of the person.

An agile methodology implements a series of practices (values, aptitudes and skills) short and repetable, that is to say, it is a question of iterating repeatedly to be adapting changeable requisites inside the frame of the scope of the project. It seeks to get ready entregables often, with preference to the period of time as short as possible, to refine and to converge to an acceptable solution.

In addition to the model incremental, some other differential aspects of agile methodologies are, without doubt, the following:

- Equipment self-governed, self-organized and multi-functional. It is not necessary to have a team leader, since the team itself is able to self-regulate.
- The team regularly reflects on how improving the efficiency, and fits to obtain it.
- The motivation of the team members is absolutely essential.
- Prioritizes face-to-face communications against the excessive documentation.
- Accepts without problems changing requirements that, in fact, are a fundamental part of its rationale.
- There are realized deliveries of the functional product with a frequency of between 1 to 4 weeks. It is the main progress measurement.
- Sustainable development with a constant rhythm.
- Search for technical excellence and the best possible design.
- One looks for the simplicity, to maximize the quantity of work that is not necessary to do, to do as well as possible the rest.

Within the set of agile methodologies is located SCRUM [17, 18], which provides a number of tools and roles for, iteratively, be able to see the progress and results of a project.

A way to use user stories [19, 20] to define in this case part of the dynamic system model is through the technique BDD (Behavior Driven Development) in which integrates the history a scenario description of behavior.

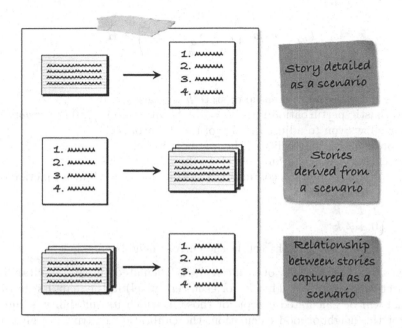

Fig. 5. Stories Scenarios Options.

4   Model Definition

The fundamental idea in CA Models is that the state of a cell at any given time depends on the state of the cells within its neighborhood in the previous time step, based on a set of transition rules [21]. The CA model used in this investigation is the one proposed by R. White (see Eq. 2), is a constrained cellular automata for high-resolution modelling of urban land-use dynamics [22,23]. The CA model is oriented towards the representation of the attributes of a given geographic region in a two-dimensional lattice, raster maps provides these data format to the CA.

A raster map can be represented formally by an array of real values. This matrix is represented as $A = a_{ij}$ of order mxn such that $0 \leq i \leq m, 0 \leq j \leq n$ where each element $A = [a_{ij}] \in \mathbb{R}$.

A neighborhood filter matrix 1 is required to analyze each element $A = a_{ij}$, this neighborhood is formally represented $B = b_{ii}$ of order nxn such that $0 \leq i \leq n$ where each element $B = [b_{ii}] \in \mathbb{Z}$.

$$B = \begin{bmatrix} b_{i-1j-1} & b_{i-1j} & b_{i-1j+1} \\ b_{ij-1} & b_{ij} & b_{ij+1} \\ b_{i+1j-1} & b_{i+1j} & b_{i+1j+1} \end{bmatrix} \qquad (1)$$

The neighborhood filter is used to calculate the transition potential from state h to j for each element $A = [a_{ij}]$. The calculation methodology is detailed below:

$$P_{hj} = v s_j a_j \left(1 + \sum_{k,i,d} m_{kd} I_{id}\right) + H_j \qquad (2)$$

where

P_{hj}: is the transition potential of state h to state j.

v: stochastic perturbation term. $v = 1 + [-ln(random)]^x$. $0 < random < 1$, and x allows you to adjust the size of the disturbance.

s_j represents the suitability of the state of the cell.

a_j: euclidean distance from the cell to the nearest road.

m_{kd}: calibration matrix, contains the weights of each cell as a function of its state k and distance d.

$$I_{id} = \begin{cases} 1, i = k \\ 0, i \neq k \end{cases}$$

where i is the index of the cell in the current neighborhood, k.

The transition potential P_{hj} of each cell A_{ij} is calculated only if the suitability of the objective state $s_j > 0$. That is, for each cell (pixel) in the map, its transition potential will be calculated except for those in which its suitability is equal to zero. For the neighborhood calculation, the calibration matrix m_{kd} gives each neighbor cell b_{ii} a weight based on its state and distance (subscript d in 2) concerning the analyzed cell a_{ij}. The nearby neighbor cells will generally have a higher weight, positive values are taken for an attractive effect and negative for repulsive effect, these values tend to decrease as the distance increases between the analyzed cell and its neighbor, this is called Distance Decay Effect. When analyzing the neighbor cells, the I_{id} component helps to filter (multiplying by 1) cells with the same state.

Visually, in Fig. 6(a) we have the urban land use map, in Fig. 6(b), the neighbor is set to 3×3 around the analyzed cell. Figure 6(c) calculates the transition potential of each cell from its current state to a desired state, the higher is selected. For this case we set as the higher to urban use. Figure 6(d) analyzed cell change its value to the higher urban use. Figure 6(e) shows observation window moves to the next cell. An epoch has been completed when the last cell of the map is calculated. A simulation may require one or more epochs. If we take into account that this calculation must be done for each pixel of the map, we find a problem of computational complexity $O(2^n)$, this means, larger size of the input maps would increase the execution time of the simulation exponentially. To handle this complexity we used the OpenMP library.

5   Results

From the model of dynamic system using a celular automata we take as parameters to define the states and the evolution space a map previously digitalized by means of a geographic information system (see Fig. 5). On the map are represented the land uses of an urban region of northwest Mexico. The Fig. 6 represents the result of the evolution of the celular automata model with the same

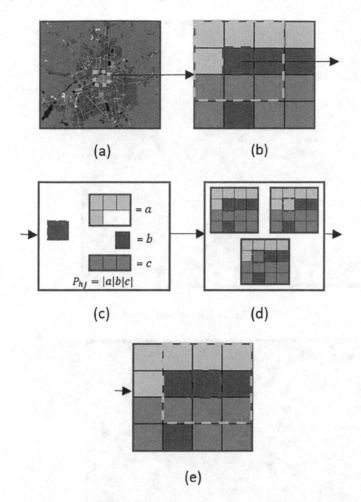

$$P_{hj} = |a|b|c|$$

Fig. 6. Transition potential process.

land uses for the same period. As can be seen in the evolution of the automaton there are 10 land uses. These land uses are expressed as user stories incorporating scenarios defined based on conditions that influence the permanence or change of state (land use) of the evaluated cell. With the above what we are looking for is that this can facilitate the characterization and communication with those who will read such a map, for example, an urban planner. Finally, with this model it is possible to carry out experiments later for other eras, which will allow to build territorial scenarios in the future to identify trends in the territorial space that are taken to obtain the parameters of the model (Figs. 7 and 8).

Fig. 7. Raster map 2004.

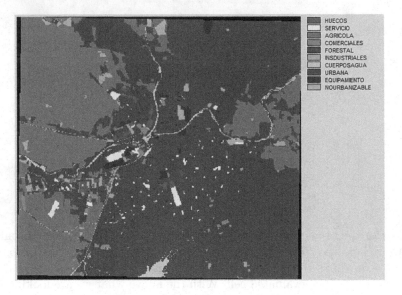

Fig. 8. Land-use map generated by CA.

6 Concluding Remark

Urban development and the territorial scenarios that derive from it are topics of increasing interest. Phenomena such as globalization and migration that produce among other things, changes in land uses. It is important to look for these changes in land uses to be sustainable to maintain balance in the various ecosystems that coexist. Thus, we present in this paper some maps obtained from a dynamic system model represented by a cellular automaton.

We use cellular automata due to its ability to represent complex behaviors from simple rules in its definition. Although reading and analyzing results is not a simple thing, mainly if they need to be transmitted to specialists from other areas. For instance urban planners or anyone who can use this information to support decision-making or in the development of a plan or project related to urban development. In this sense, we propose as an innovative additional contribution the integration of artifacts used in agile methods. Particularly we propose used user stories as part of a narrative that allows to describe and read in a simple way the scenarios possible in land-use changes. Seen in the latter as user stories that clearly illustrate trends for various territorial scenarios.

References

1. Plata-Rocha, W., Gomez-Delgado, M., Bosque-Sendra, J.: Simulating urban growth scenarios using GIS and multicriteria analysis techniques: a case study of the Madrid region, Spain. Environ. Plan. B Plan. Des. **38**, 1012–1031 (2011)
2. Li, S., Juhász-Horváth, L., Pedde, S., Pintér, L., Rounsevell, M.D., Harrison, P.A.: Integrated modelling of urban spatial development under uncertain climate futures: a case study in Hungary. Environ. Model Softw. **96**, 251–264 (2017)
3. Gounaridis, D., Chorianopoulos, I., Koukoulas, S.: Exploring prospective urban growth trends under different economic outlooks and land-use planning scenarios: the case of Athens. Appl. Geogr. **90**, 134–144 (2018)
4. Ralha, C.G., Abreu, C.G., Coelho, C.G.C., Zaghetto, A., Macchiavello, B., Machado, R.B.: A multi-agent model system for land-use change simulation. Environ. Model Softw. **42**, 30–46 (2013)
5. Yalew, S., et al.: Land-use change modelling in the Upper Blue Nile Basin. Environments **3**(3), 21 (2016)
6. Pontius, R.: Criteria to confirm models that simulate deforestation and carbon disturbance. Land **7**(3), 105 (2018)
7. Feng, Y., Qi, Y.: Modeling patterns of land use in Chinese cities using an integrated cellular automata model. ISPRS Int. J. Geo-Inf. **7**(10), 403 (2018)
8. Aguilera Benavente, F., Plata-Rocha, W., Bosque Sendra, J.: Diseño y simulación de escenarios de demanda de suelo urbano en ámbitos metropolitanos. Rev. Int. Sostenibilidad, Tecnol. y Humanismo 57–80 (2009)
9. Khoshnoud, F., Dell, D.J., Chen, Y.K., Calay, R.K., de Silva, C.W., Dwhadi, H.: The concept of self-powered dynamic systems. In: European Conference for Aerospace Sciences (EUCASS), Munich, Germany, 1–5 July 2013. EUCASS (2013)
10. Borshchev, A.: The big book of simulation modeling: multimethod modeling with AnyLogic. AnyLogic North America, Chicago (2013)
11. Zamora, R.R., Vergara, S.V.C.: Using de Bruijn diagrams to analyze 1d cellular automata traffic models. In: Sloot, P.M.A., Chopard, B., Hoekstra, A.G. (eds.) ACRI 2004. LNCS, vol. 3305, pp. 306–315. Springer, Heidelberg (2004). https://doi.org/10.1007/978-3-540-30479-1_32
12. Beauchemin, C., Samuel, J., Tuszynski, J.: A simple cellular automaton model for influenza A viral infections. J. Theor. Biol. **232**(2), 223–234 (2005)

13. Wolfram, S.: A New Kind of Science, vol. 5. Wolfram Media, Champaign (2002)
14. Brock, Z., Karst, N., Siripong, M.: Bio-inspired computing (2005). ca.olin.edu
15. Jacobson, I., Booch, G., Rumbaugh, J.: The Unified Software Development Process. Addison-Wesley, Boston (2000)
16. Priolo, S.: Métodos ágiles. USERSHOP (2009)
17. Abrahamsson, P., Salo, O., Ronkainen, J., Warsta, J.: Agile software development methods: review and analysis. arXiv preprint arXiv:1709.08439 (2017)
18. Cockburn, A.: Agile Software Development. Addison-Wesley Professional, Boston (2001)
19. Patton, J.: User Story Mapping: Discover the Whole Story, Build the Right Product. O'Reilly Media Inc., Cambridge (2014)
20. Trkman, M., Mendling, J., Krisper, M.: Using business process models to better understand the dependencies among user stories. Inf. Softw. Technol. **71**, 58–76 (2016)
21. Barredo, J.I., Gómez, D.J.: Towards a set of IPCC SRES urban land-use scenarios: modelling urban land-use in the Madrid region, pp. 1–16. European Commission - DG Joint Research Centre Institute for Environment and Sustainability, Department of Geography, University of Alcalá (2000)
22. White, R., Engelen, G.: High-resolution integrated modelling of the spatial dynamics of urban and regional systems. Comput. Environ. Urban Syst. **24**, 383–400 (2000)
23. White, R., Engelen, G., Uljee, I.: The use of constrained cellular automata for high-resolution modelling of urban land-use dynamics. Environ. Plan. B Plan. Des. **24**(3), 323–343 (1997)
24. Benavente, F.A., Montes, L.M.V., Lara, J.A.S., Delgado, M.G., Rocha, W.P.: Escenarios Y Modelos De Simulación Como Instrumento En La Planificación Territorial Y Metropolitana. Ser. Geográfica **17**, 11–28 (2011)
25. Montgomery, A.W.: Scrum framework effects on software team cohesion, collaboration, and motivation: a social identity approach perspective. Creighton University (2017)

Telematics and Electronics

Statistical Properties of Vehicle Residence Times for Fog Computing Applications

David Miguel Santiago[1](✉), Mario E. Rivero-Angeles[2],
Laura I. Garay-Jiménez[1], and Izlian Y. Orea-Flores[3]

[1] Instituto Politécnico Nacional SEPI UPIITA, Mexico City, Mexico
dmiguels1800@alumno.ipn.mx, lgaray@ipn.mx
[2] Network and Data Science Laboratory,
Instituto Politécnico Nacional (CIC-IPN), Mexico City, Mexico
mrivero@ipn.mx
[3] Telematics Department-UPIITA,
Instituto Politécnico Nacional, Mexico City, Mexico
iorea@ipn.mx

Abstract. Currently, new advances in the automotive industry are focused on implementing autonomous cars, since they are the future to avoid accidents and protect users. Even if safety is the main goal, many opportunities for technological developers are possible. Among them, Smart Cities is a major player in future communication networks. In a smart city context, hundreds or thousands of sensors will be deployed in many strategic parts of the city, including sensors in mobile devices, that can provide critical information for the city management and improve the resident's livelihood. However, this scenario entails extremely high volumes of information to be sent to different geographical locations. Because of this, the use of cellular base stations may be a highly expensive alternative.

In this work. We propose to take advantage of the use of autonomous cars as data mules for the efficient recollection of data in smart cities environments. Specifically, we consider interest points in Luxembourg City, where relevant data may be generated by sensors in mobile devices or fixed sensors in the city's infrastructure. Assuming that, autonomous vehicles know in advance the route that they are going to follow to reach their destination, sensors can profit the passage of these vehicles to transmit their data, making short-range, low-cost transmissions and reducing the implementation cost of these applications. Later, the vehicles can relay the data on the destination point. To this end, we evaluate the potential use of this system by obtaining the main statistics variables of the passage of the vehicles though these interest points in the city. We obtain the mean, variance and coefficient of variation of the resident times of vehicles to estimate the potential use of this communication system in Smart Cities.

Keywords: Fog Computing · Vehicle networks · Statistical characterization · Smart Cities

© Springer Nature Switzerland AG 2019
M. F. Mata-Rivera et al. (Eds.): WITCOM 2019, CCIS 1053, pp. 85–97, 2019.
https://doi.org/10.1007/978-3-030-33229-7_8

1 Introduction

Smart Cities are envisioned to be a major component of people's everyday lives in big cities for the near future [1]. This technology will connect a high number of sensors placed throughout the city to monitor highly sensitive processes in the city, such as, water supply, gas or toxic substances leakages, pollution levels, temperature, floods, urban wildlife (rats, dogs, cats, birds, etc.) monitoring [2], and even traffics jams [3] and criminal acts. Sensors can be integrated into the urban infrastructure but also, mobile devices which nowadays have many different types of sensors (gyroscopes, acceleration, sound, video, heart rate monitoring, light, etc.) [4], can be used to generate and convey relevant data for the city operation.

For instance, urban wildlife monitoring apps can send an alert for people in a specific point in the city, like a public park, to take sound samples searching for birds of interest. By recognizing the individual sound characteristics of birds in the environment. In this application, only users and sensors placed in a certain region are asked to send their data, while sensors and mobile devices outside this region are not involved in the data recollection process. This leads to the concept of Fog Computing [5], where devices in a certain region, inside the fog, communicate and process information that does not need to reach the cloud computing [6], i.e., this information is locally generated, stored and transmitted.

Also, relevant in the context of Smart Cities is the development of autonomous vehicles that will help us with our goal. For years, driver assistance, automation systems, and communications have been developed to guide us to the next generation of mobility [7]. The complexity of these developments tries to connect vehicles with other vehicles or with a controlled environment out of the car. Autonomous vehicles have the great advantage that the route can be known in advance. Indeed, before driving begins, the vehicle can calculate the adequate route based on the traffic conditions, driver's personal preferences, accidents in the routes, and weather conditions among many others.

Some works talk about how to make the roads safer and efficient the vehicular traffic through communications V2V (Vehicle-to-Vehicle) and V2I (Vehicle-to-Infrastructure) [8], in the last concept it is necessary to use the RSUs (Road-Side Units), i.e., devices that provide connectivity with vehicles in the range [9], this work has a similar concept in comparison with this paper but there are differences. We propose a fixed or mobile sensor to analyze in a determinate area, as Fog Computing, if a car can or cannot receive data to be used as a data mule without the necessity to have an RSU because the information can be received by a pedestrian or another mobile device.

On the other hand, there are advances as VANET's (Vehicular Ad hoc NETwork) [10] where a vehicle is considered as a communication unit and vehicles can trade information without a network or Fog Computing, this work is different than our propose. We make an emphasis on participation and collaboration between pedestrians and automobiles.

In this work, we make a study of the communication between vehicles and a sensor placed in specific parts of the city. Specifically, we consider a system where a sensor, fixed or mobile, generate information in strategic parts of the city and take advantage of the passage of autonomous cars. Since the routes of these vehicles are well defined, the sensor devices can determine if the passing vehicle can be used as a data mule to convey their data to another part of the city. Although, in this paper, the main goal is to analyze if the interaction between vehicles and a sensor, fixed or mobile, can be able viable or not.

To characterize these residence times, we use real vehicle trajectories from a well-known database on SUMO (Simulation of Urban MObility) [11] simulator about the traffic of vehicles in different parts of the city to analyze the behavior of vehicles in different traffic conditions.

SUMO [12] is a software that can provide a vehicular scenario of a real-world working with JOSM (Java OpenStreetMap) that provides the updated map of the city.

For this analysis, we work with an article published by the University of Luxembourg [13] called "Luxembourg sumo traffic (lust) scenario: 24 h of mobility for vehicular networking research." where it is possible to obtain a simulation scenario in a period of 24 h of traffic from Luxembourg. This work was compared with the Typical Traffic option in Google Maps and showed similar traffic with the real traffic in Luxembourg.

Then, we calculate the times that an automobile is in a street, waiting in a traffic light or moving with a specific speed. The position and the behavior of a vehicle are important parameters used to calculate the residence times of vehicles in a fog computing application. Luxembourg is a typical European city, and we assume that the results presented in this paper can be extended to other cities with similar conditions.

The realistic scenario was measured in a common day, during the morning the traffic is high density, in the afternoon is medium density and, in the night, the density is lower than other times of the day. In this scenario, there are vehicles, buses, and pedestrians that have different behaviors.

The rest of this paper is organized as follows: Sect. 2 presents the main assumptions and system set-up were the residence times where measured. Then, in Sect. 3 we explain how the characteristics of the residence times were obtained. Finally, Sect. 4 presents relevant results.

2   System Model

The vehicular analysis consists in considering 24 h of traffic observation in Luxembourg city. We focused on low density (during the night). In this real vehicle trajectories, 295,979 vehicles interacted in an area of 155.95 km². As such, it is computationally difficult to analyze all possible interactions between cars during all 24 h. Hence, we selected periods of ten minutes for each kind of traffic density and we identified five different places considered as tourists spots where a high vehicle concentration is expected. We selected these places based on recommendations of touristic attractions. In Fig. 1, we present the SUMO vehicle trajectories and we compare it to Google maps to identify both the touristic spots where many sensors (fixed and mobile) can gather relevant information and the traffic conditions to use vehicles as data mules.

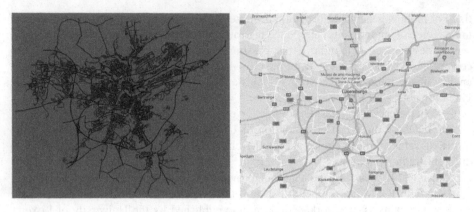

Fig. 1. Comparison between map in SUMO and Google maps.

We can observe that both images are similar, but some routes do not exist in the SUMO map. Then, based on both maps, we selected specific places to analyze vehicular concurrence. These points represent parts of a smart city scenario where information can be generated. Hence, all sensors (fixed and mobile devices) inside the range of interest will form the Fog Computing network, i.e., data is sensed, stored, processed and conveyed to passing vehicles to then transmit it to other parts of the city. Also, note that this information is not relevant to other parts of the city. As such, this information does not have to reach the cloud, effectively reducing the traffic and resource utilization in the cloud. For instance, a WiFi-based network has a range of about 100 m and Bluetooth about 10 m. Both these networks are typically enabled in any commercial smartphone and sensor nodes. We also considered ranges of 50 m and 100 m for completeness purposes, then we make a radius of 25 m and 50 m around the point to simulate a network. In Table 1, we showed the selected places.

Table 1. Places where residence vehicular were analyzed.

Place	Direction	Range
Schlassbréck bridge	*Montée de Clausen Av. & Rue Sisthéne Weis*	50 m, 100 m
Justice Palace of Luxembourg	*Franklin Delano Rooselvet Roundabout & René Konen Tunnel*	50 m, 100 m
Art Gallery Schorten	*Emile Reuter Av. & Royal Roundabout*	50 m, 100 m
Sofitel Luxembourg Le Grand Hotel	*Boulevard d'Avranches & Rue du Laboratoire*	50 m, 100 m
International School of Luxembourg	*Rue de Bouillon Roundabout*	50 m, 100 m

The first place is a bridge and is an intersection between Montée de Clausen street and under Rue Sosthéne Weis street, this location is near Casemates du Bock that is an antique architecture to defend the city called Schlassbréck bridge. As seen in Fig. 2, the radius is in red and, this circle simulates the network, i.e., all vehicles that enter on this circle is considered as potential data mule to convey data to other parts of the city.

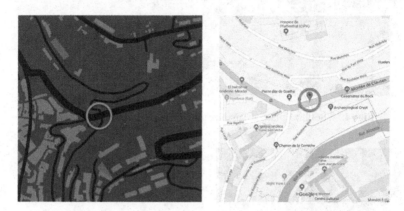

Fig. 2. The first place to analyze in SUMO map and Google map.

The second point of interest is shown in Fig. 3 and is located near Justice Palace, this place is between Franklin Delano Roosevelt boulevard and René Konen tunnel.

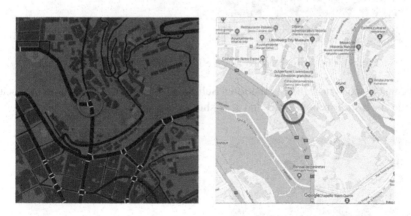

Fig. 3. The second place to analyze in SUMO map and Google map.

The third point of interest is depicted in Fig. 4 and is near the Art Gallery Schorten and is located between Emile Reuter avenue and Royal boulevard.

The fourth point of interest is shown in Fig. 5 is near a hotel called Sofitel Luxembourg Le Grand Hotel located in d'Avranches boulevard and Rue du Laboratoire street.

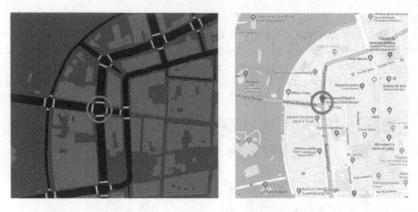

Fig. 4. The third place to analyze in SUMO map and Google map.

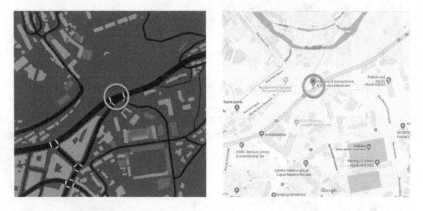

Fig. 5. The fourth place to analyze in SUMO map and Google map.

The last place is near the International School of Luxembourg Asbl and the location is in Rue de Bouillon boulevard and it is shown in Fig. 6.

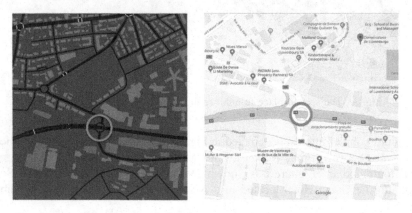

Fig. 6. The last place to analyze in SUMO map and Google map.

3 Distribution of Residence Times

Once the interest points are selected and the different communication ranges are placed around it, we now can calculate the residence times of all vehicles going through the circles described in the previous section. We analyze the information making a program in python because SUMO generates files with XML format. These files have several data characteristics about the vehicles but the information that we need is the position and time of each vehicle. The position is given as cartesian coordinates and, as mentioned before, we consider periods of 10 min because it was difficult to analyze the 24 h. The 10 min period is equal to 600 s; during this time, we analyze the position of each vehicle second inside the coverage data.

To find vehicles in a circumference we used the circumference equation given by:

$$x^2 + y^2 = r^2 \qquad (1)$$

Then, we added our coverage range to localize the vehicles inside the interest points as follows:

$$50 \geq \sqrt{(x - Origx)^2 + (y + Origiy)^2} \qquad (2)$$

or

$$100 \geq \sqrt{(x - Origx)^2 + (y + Origiy)^2} \qquad (3)$$

Where x and y are the coordinates of each vehicle and Origx and Origy are the interest points and all vehicles present in a radius equal or minor to 50 or 100 meters are considered in this analysis.

In this work, we are only interested in studying the statistical characteristics of this residence time. Then, we calculate the mean, variance and coefficient of variation of these residence times. The main data that we are going to use is the coefficient of variation because is a relation between the size of the mean and the standard deviation.

$$CV = \frac{\sigma}{\mu} \qquad (4)$$

These are some properties of CV.

1. It does not have units.
2. Based on these characteristics we can propose a distribution with similar behavior according to the following cases:
3. In the case that the CV = 1, the possible distribution that can describe the residence times is the exponential distribution. This distribution describes the time elapsed between two independent events.
4. In the case that the CV > 1, the possible distribution that can describe the residence times is the Hyper-exponential distribution.

5. In the case that the CV < 1, the possible distribution that can describe the residence times is the Erlang distribution. This distribution describes the wait time until an event occurs.

4 Numerical Results

We now present some relevant results of the residence times. In Figs. 7 and 8 we present the histograms of the residence times in the first point of interest considering low vehicle density with 50 and 100 m of coverage radio respectively.

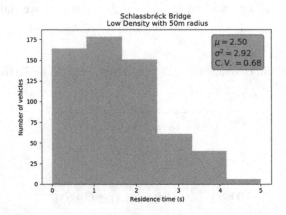

Fig. 7. Histogram in Schlassbréck bridge with 50 m radius.

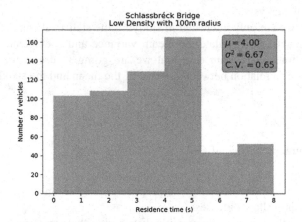

Fig. 8. Histogram in Schlassbréck bridge with 100 m radius.

For the second point of interest, we present the histograms in Figs. 9 and 10. For the third point of interest, we present the histograms in Figs. 11 and 12.

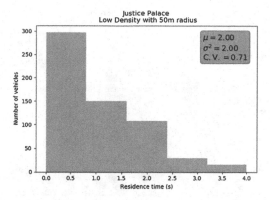

Fig. 9. Histogram in Justice Palace with 50 m radius.

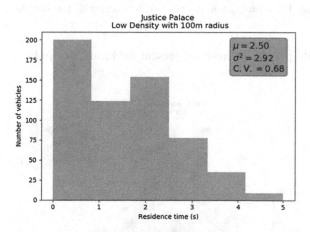

Fig. 10. Histogram in Justice Palace with 100 m radius.

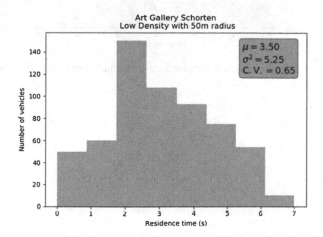

Fig. 11. Histogram in Art Gallery Schorten with 50 m radius.

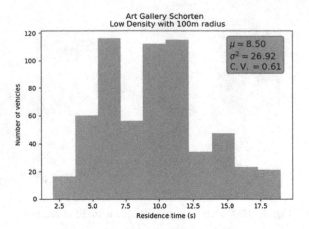

Fig. 12. Histogram in Art Gallery Schorten with 100 m radius.

For the fourth point of interest, we present the histograms in Figs. 13 and 14.

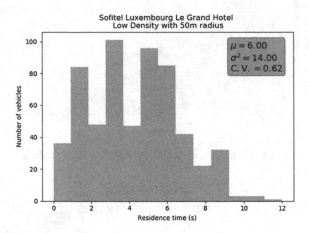

Fig. 13. Histogram in Sofitel Luxembourg Le Grand Hotel with 50 m radius.

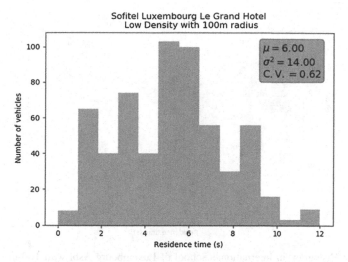

Fig. 14. Histogram in Sofitel Luxembourg Le Grand Hotel with 100 m radius.

Finally, for the fifth point of interest, we present the histograms in Figs. 15 and 16.

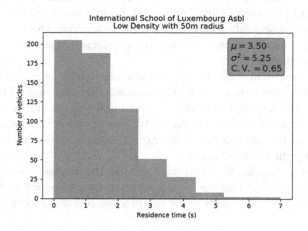

Fig. 15. Histogram in International School of Luxembourg Asbl with 50 m radius.

In each figure, we show the mean (μ), the variance (σ^2) and the coefficient of variation (CV). As we mentioned before, the CV is part of our interest since we can choose a hypothetical distribution that matches the statistical characteristics of the residence times. Building on this, we can see that the CV of all residence times measured in this work are lower than 1. Hence, the Erlang distribution can be used to model the times that the vehicles remain in the interest region.

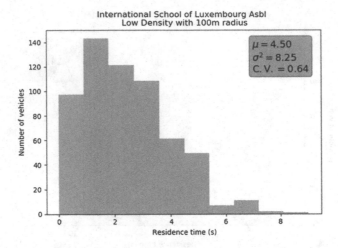

Fig. 16. Histogram in International School of Luxembourg Asbl with 100 m radius.

5 Conclusion and Future Work

In this work, we characterized the residence time of real traces of vehicles inside an interest region in Luxembourg City. To this end, we first locate touristic locations that are potential points where data can be gathered and disseminated for a future smart city scenario and autonomous vehicles, although if we could select several locations maybe we would expect similar results.

Another relevant result is that for the scenarios considered, an Erlang distribution is a good candidate distribution to model the residence times for future Fog Computing applications in smart city environments, we could link with the real results and test if these results are real and not a coincidence. We must prove mathematically.

If we could analyze all data, we would expect similar results, because we consider that vehicles have the same behavior.

These results can be used for future mathematical and simulation works to calculate the amount of information that can be conveyed to vehicles acting as data mules to transport information to other parts of the city in a low-cost scenario, it depends on the future works.

References

1. Albino, V., Berardi, U., Dangelico, R.M.: Smart cities: definitions, dimensions, performance, and initiatives. J. Urban Technol. **22**(1), 3–21 (2015)
2. Khan, Z., Anjum, A., Soomro, K., Tahir, M.A.: Towards cloud based big data analytics for smart future cities. J. Cloud Comput. **4**(1), 2 (2015)

3. Biswas, S.P., Roy, P., Patra, N., Mukherjee, A., Dey, N.: Intelligent traffic monitoring system. In: Satapathy, S.C., Raju, K.S., Mandal, J.K., Bhateja, V. (eds.) Proceedings of the Second International Conference on Computer and Communication Technologies. AISC, vol. 380, pp. 535–545. Springer, New Delhi (2016). https://doi.org/10.1007/978-81-322-2523-2_52

4. Ong, R., et al.: Traffic jams detection using flock mining. In: Gunopulos, D., Hofmann, T., Malerba, D., Vazirgiannis, M. (eds.) ECML PKDD 2011. LNCS (LNAI), vol. 6913, pp. 650–653. Springer, Heidelberg (2011). https://doi.org/10.1007/978-3-642-23808-6_49

5. Stojmenovic, I., Wen, S.: The fog computing paradigm: scenarios and security issues. In: 2014 Federated Conference on Computer Science and Information Systems, pp. 1–8. IEEE (2014)

6. Capponi, A., Fiandrino, C., Kliazovich, D., Bouvry, P., Giordano, S.: A cost-effective distributed framework for data collection in cloud-based mobile crowd sensing architectures. IEEE Trans. Sustain. Comput. 2(1), 3–16 (2017)

7. Sookhak, M., et al.: Remote data auditing in cloud computing environments: a survey, taxonomy, and open issues. ACM Comput. Surv. (CSUR) 47(4), 65 (2015)

8. Aissaoui, R., Menouar, H., Dhraief, A., Filali, F., Belghith, A., Abu-Dayya, A.: Advanced real-time traffic monitoring system based on V2X communications. In: 2014 IEEE International Conference on Communications (ICC), pp. 2713–2718. IEEE (2014)

9. Richter, A., Friedl, H., Scholz, M.: Beyond OSM–alternative data sources and approaches enhancing generation of road networks for traffic and driving simulations. In: SUMO2016–Traffic, Mobility, and Logistics, pp. 23–25 (2016)

10. Ge, X., Li, Z., Li, S.: 5G software defined vehicular networks. IEEE Commun. Mag. 55(7), 87–93 (2017)

11. Kastner, K.H., Pau, P.: Experiences with SUMO in a real-life traffic monitoring system. In: SUMO 2015–Intermodal Simulation for Intermodal Transport (2015)

12. Liu, W., Wang, X., Zhang, W., Yang, L., Peng, C.: Coordinative simulation with SUMO and NS3 for vehicular ad hoc networks. In: 2016 22nd Asia-Pacific Conference on Communications (APCC), pp. 337–341. IEEE (2016)

13. Codeca, L., Frank, R., Engel, T.: Luxembourg sumo traffic (LuST) scenario: 24 hours of mobility for vehicular networking research. In: 2015 IEEE Vehicular Networking Conference (VNC), pp. 1–8. IEEE (2015)

Text and Image Transmission and Reception Using Light from LEDs and a Light Sensor

Sergio Sandoval-Reyes[✉]

Centro de Investigación en Computación (CIC), Instituto Politecnico Nacional,
Av Juan de Dios Batiz s/n, Col. NI Vallejo, 07738 Mexico City, Mexico
sersand@cic.ipn.mx

Abstract. Visible Light Communication or VLC uses visible light from light emitting diodes (LEDs) to transmit information. Using a computing device and some hardware, the transmission of information is performed driving and modulating the light emitted by the LEDs. In the receiver side, the information carried by the modulated light is demodulated through a light sensor, connected to a similar computing device for the final recovering of the information. In this article we describe an application based on VLC using OOK (On-Off Keying) modulation, to transmit and receive a line of text and an image from a Raspberry Pi computer (using Python as the programming language), two yellow LEDs and a sensor light.

Keywords: Text and image · VLC · OOK · Raspberry Pi · Python

1 Introduction

Visible Light Communication [1, 2] can be used to transmit audio, voice and data using light from emitter diodes (LEDs), and light detectors at the transmitter and receiver ends respectively (Fig. 1). VLC works in the 380 nm to 780 nm optical band which is visible light [3–5].

To convey information this one has to be encoded, and then the light has to be modulated and demodulated at the transmitter and receiver sides. There are several methods to do this, some are briefly discussed in the following. Then, the received information has to be decoded and processed to recover it fully. The success of this recovery depends of several factors, among them: (1) The number, shape, and wavelength of the LEDs employed; (2) The number and type of light detectors (light-sensor, PIN-diode, reverse-biased LED, etc.) used; (3) The encoding method (RZ, NRZ, NRZP, etc.); (4) The modulation scheme (OOK, WPM, VWPM, PPM, OFDM, etc.), and (5) The synchronization and distance between the LEDs and the light detector. VLC is a technology that requires line-of-sight between both emitter and receiver [6].

In this work we describe an application based on VLC using OOK (On-Off Keying) modulation, to transmit a line of text and a color image using a Raspberry Pi 3 computer as the data source and sink (to simplify the synchronization problem between emitter-receiver), Python as the programming language, and several modules (LEDs and a sensor light) from littleBits, to easy the hardware implementation.

© Springer Nature Switzerland AG 2019
M. F. Mata-Rivera et al. (Eds.): WITCOM 2019, CCIS 1053, pp. 98–109, 2019.
https://doi.org/10.1007/978-3-030-33229-7_9

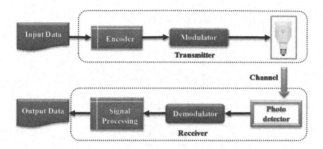

Fig. 1. A basic VLC link structure.

This paper is organized as follows: Part 2 presents a summary of works related to the transmission of text and images using VLC. Section 3 describes the design of our VLC application. Part 4 describe the experiments realized, the results obtained, and their analysis. The conclusions and future work are presented in Sect. 5.

2 Related Work

Several research works on VLC technologies to transmit text and images have been proposed. The most important are described in the following.

2.1 How Based VLC Text and Image Systems Work

Generally, VLC image systems are implemented modulating the intensity of light and a direct detection scheme with a line-of-sight (LOS) configuration [7]. In the transmitter, intensity modulation is implemented through the modulation of the transmitted signal into the instantaneous optical power of the LED by controlling the radiant intensity with the forward current through the LED (High modulation frequencies are used to avoid flicker). In the receiver, the transmitted signal is recovered using direct detection throughout a light sensor to convert the incident optical signal power into a proportional current. The following Fig. 2 shows a general flow chart for VLC text and image transmission [8].

2.2 VLC Text and Image Transmitter

A typical based VLC text and image transmitter contains a text and image generator (a PC with Matlab to convert the text and the image into bits), an interface (usually a USB cable) to send the bits to a microcontroller (for coding and modulation), and taken through one of its output ports to the LED driver and the LED optics. See Fig. 3 [9]. The modulated signals are used to switch on-an-off the LEDs at desired frequencies using LED drivers. These drivers rely on transconductance amplifiers to convert voltage signals into corresponding current signals to excite the LEDs array for communication purposes.

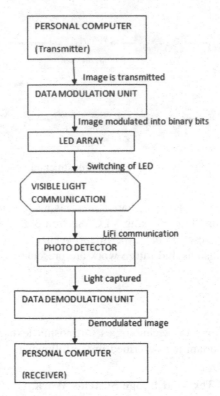

Fig. 2. A flow chart for VLC text and image transmission.

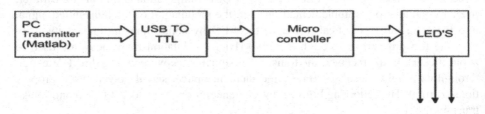

Fig. 3. VLC text and image transmission.

2.2.1   VLC Modulation

There exist different modulation schemes for VLC, the most common are: on-off keying (OOK), variable pulse-position modulation (VPPM), color shift keying (CSK) and orthogonal frequency division multiplexing (OFDM) [10]. However, OOK is the most commonly used modulation scheme in VLC due to its simple implementation. In this method essentially the LED intensity is changed between two distinguishable levels corresponding to the data bits (1 or 0). See Fig. 4. A modified OOK can also provide dimming. It is achieved by changing the data duty cycle through pulse-width modulation (PWM), with only 1 bit of information carried per symbol period.

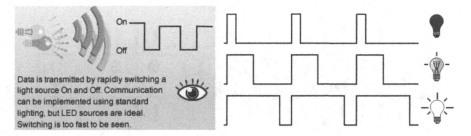

Fig. 4. On-Off Keying with PWM.

2.3   VLC Text and Image Receiver

A typical optical text and image receiver consists of a photo detector followed by an amplifier. The photo detector can be a photo transistor, a reverse-biased LED, or a Light Detect Resistor (LDR). The light captured by the photo transistor which acts as a sensor, passes the output to the comparator which compares the binary input, and similarly the original image is recovered using Matlab software in the PC. See Fig. 5 [8, 9].

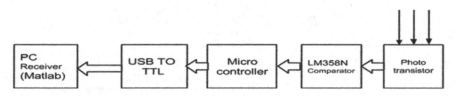

Fig. 5.   VLC text and image reception.

3   Text and Image Tx and Rx Application Using VLC

In this section we develop a VLC application to transmit and recover a line of text first, and then a color image using two LEDs in the transmitter, and a light sensor in the receiver.

We begin using in the transmitter as a data source, a Raspberry Pi 3 (RBPi) computer, and six littleBits bit-modules [12]: power, button, proto, split, and two bright LEDs. See Fig. 6. The RBPi using a software program written in Python will read a line of text or an image byte by byte, and will transmit each byte using the SPI MOSI (Serial Peripheral Interface, Master Output Slave Input) output port (Pin 19), toward the proto module, OOK signals to drive the two LEDs.

Similarly, in the receiver we will use three littleBits components: power, light sensor, and another proto bit. See Fig. 7. The light sensor captures the light emitted by the two LEDs and converts it into a digital signal which is fed to the proto module, which in turns outputs this signal and with a wire connector, feeds this signal toward the MISO (Master Input Slave Output) input port (Pin 21) of the RBPi.

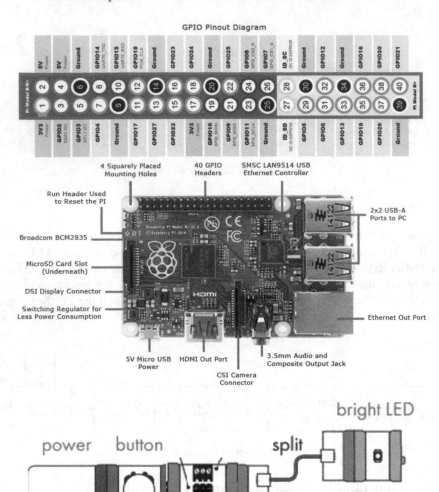

Fig. 6. Raspberry Pi 3, and six modules: power, button, proto, split and two LEDS

Fig. 7. Receiver components: light sensor and proto bits.

3.1   Transmitting a Line of Text and an Image via VLC

The program *hola_lifi.py* written in python transmits a line of text. See Fig. 8.

```
# hola_lifi.py
# Python code to transmit and recover the line of text "hola Li-Fi" using SPI and VLC
import spidev
spi = spidev.SpiDev()
spi.open(0,0)
spi.max_speed_hz = 4000000
buffer = bytearray()
tx_data = [ord(H"), ord("o"), ord("l"), ord("a"), ord(" "), ord("L"), ord("i"), ord("-"), ord("F"),
        ord("i")]
while True:
    # Transmit the text "Hola-Li-Fi", throught the Raspberry out pin 19 SPI-MOSI,
    # and receive it in the array rx_data, throught the Raspberry input pin 21 SPI-MISO
    rx_data = spi.xfer(tx_data)

    # Receive every byte in rx_data and store them in a  buffer to display them in the screen
    for byte in rx_data:
        buffer.append(chr(byte))
    print buffer
```

Fig. 8. Python code to transmit and recover a line of text via VLC.

Transmitting an image via VLC is very similar to transmit a line of text. Here the RBPi with a script written in Python, opens a picture file ("lenna.jpeg") and it reads it into a bytearray "b". Then with a "for" loop reads byte by byte of the picture and as before, it sends them to the SPI MOSI output port 19, using the spi.xfer () directive. This MOSI output is fed into the input of the proto module (lower middle connector in Fig. 7). As before, the proto module outputs and splits the OOK signals to drive the two LEDs; the LEDs light is picked up throughout the light sensor to recover the image. The Python program to execute the above mentioned is shown in Fig. 9.

In the code above, it is necessary to import the following libraries: "SPI", "PIL" (Python Image Library), and "Array". To drive the LEDs the power module was fed with a 9-V battery. This was necessary because the outputs of the RBPi are low-voltage (3.3 V) and low-current (Individual pins must not pull more than 16 mA and the entire GPIO must not source more than 50 mA), which are no good enough to drive two bright LEDS [13]. These LEDs are simple yellow LEDS with a wavelength of 550-to-600 nm, and consume around 16-to-20 mA each, with an aperture angle of about 120°. See Fig. 10.

3.2   Receiving Text and an Image via VLC

As it was mentioned, the line of text and the image was sent via VLC as LED light. This light is received through a light sensor module which then sends it back through out another proto module, to the MISO port 21 of the RBPi. This light sensor not only receives the OOK light signal but also has a transimpedance amplifier for high speed operation. The light sensor has two operational modes. In LIGHT mode (switch up in

```
# lena_spy.py: Python code to read, transmit, and recover a picture via Visible Light
import spidev
from PIL import Image, ImageFilter
import io
from array import array
spi = spidev.SpiDev()
spi.open(0,0)
spi.max_speed_hz = 4000000

b = bytearray()
buffer = bytearray()
try:
    # Load an image from Raspberry Pi
    with open ("lenna.jpeg", "rb") as img:
        f = img.read()
        b = bytearray(f)
    # Sending with SPI and converting the image, byte by byte into visible light
    for byte in b:
        rx = spi.xfer([byte])
        rx_data = rx[0]
        buffer.append(rx_data)
    # Recovering the bytes array and back into an image
    img_rec = Image.open(io.BytesIO(buffer))
    img_rec.save('lena_img_recovered.png')
    img_rec.show()
except:
    print "Unable to recover image"
```

Fig. 9. Python code to read, transmit and recover a picture via VLC.

Fig. 10. LittleBits bright LED.

Fig. 7), as the light shining on the sensor gets brighter, more signal passes through it. In DARK mode (switch down), the signal increases as it gets darker. Furthermore, the light sensor has a sensitivity dial or slide dimmer to adjust how much light it takes to recover the signal, and has a spectral sensitivity range from 500-to-600 nm similar to the LEDs wavelength. See Fig. 11.

The recovered text and image from the light sensor via the SPI MISO input (pin 21) is stored into a buffer, saved and displayed, as can be seen from the Python code lines of Figs. 8 and 9.

Fig. 11. Receiving text and an image via a light sensor.

4   Experiments and Results

For the experiments we use as was mentioned a RaspBerry Pi 3 computer with several LittleBits components. The whole setup is shown in Fig. 12.

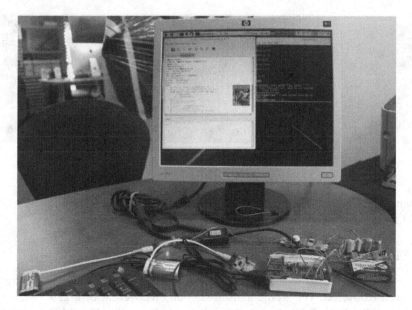

Fig. 12. Setup for the transmission and reception of text and an image using VLC.

Figure 12 shows the whole set up: the Raspberry Pi 3 computer, a HP display, keyboard and mouse, thus as the LEDs, the sensor light, and the proto modules, fed with 9 V batteries. Figure 13 shows the recovered text and picture after the execution of the line commands *"sudo python hola_lifi.py"* and *"sudo python lena_spi.py"*. Figure 13.

Figure 13 also shows that the recovered text and picture was no good enough. That was due to the presence of noise, mainly: Fluorescent light from ceiling lamps,

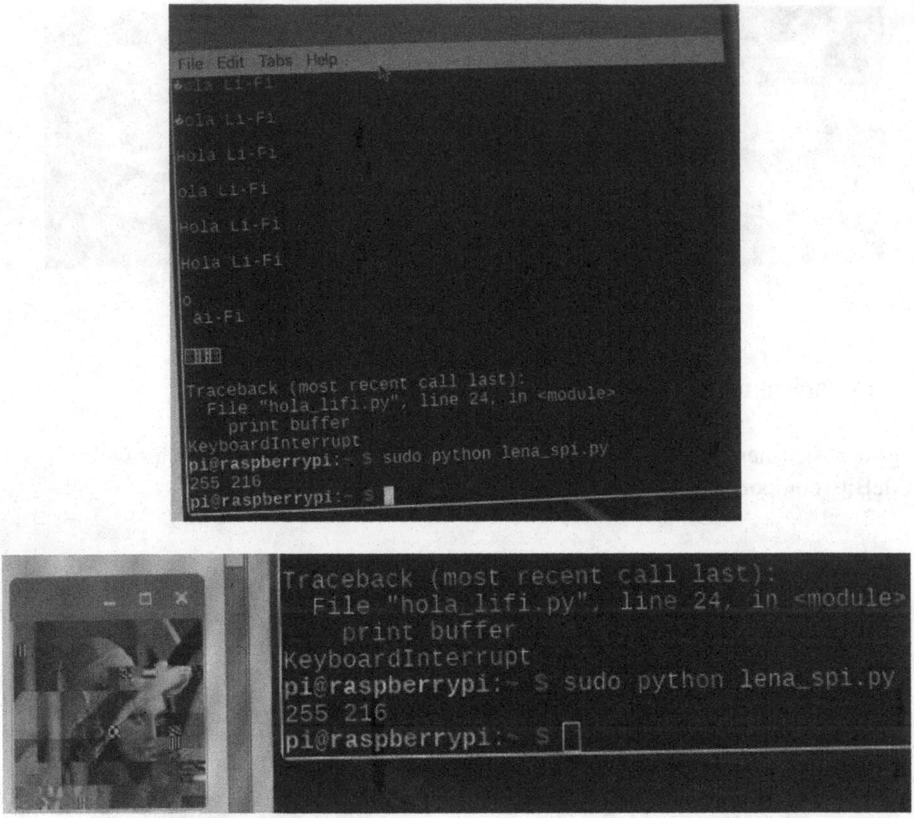

Fig. 13. Recovering of text and picture via VLC.

misalignment and distance between the LEDs and the light sensor, and low sensitivity to light from the light sensor.

4.1 Discussion of Results

After several adjustments to the setup and a few intents, the text and the picture was finally well recovered. The whole transmission and recovering of a 225×225 pixel color image weighting 8 Kbytes, took less than a second. See Fig. 14. Naturally, the noise cannot completely eliminated and increases when the misalignment and the distance between the LEDs and the light sensor is larger. Also the brightness of the LEDs influence the performance. That was the main reason for using two LEDs in parallel to increase the amount of light sent to the light sensor.

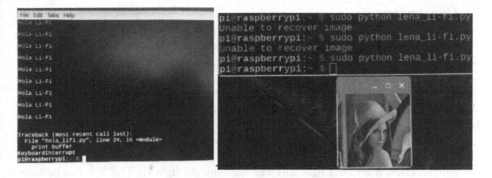

Fig. 14. Recovered picture via VLC after some adjustments.

4.2 Efficiency of the Recovered Text and Image via VLC

Due to the fact that the transmission (LEDs) and reception (light sensor) link is made using Raspberry SPI, two questions arise: (1) What percentage of the image and text was recovered correctly? and (2) How many times the image or the text was well recovered, versus the number of times the image or text could not be recovered?

(1) **Percentage of the image or text that was recovered correctly**: Initially without any kind of adjustments, the recovery of the image was around 50% as it can be seen from Fig. 13. Notice from this figure the pixelation of the image in certain areas. In contrast with the adjustments mentioned before, the image was 100% recovered as it is shown in Fig. 14. Similar results were obtained for the line of text.

(2) **Number of times the image or text was well recovered**: Although the adjustments made to the transmitter-receiver setup, the Tx-Rx link was somewhat shaky, requiring many tries to obtain a 100% image recovery. The number of times to get the image well recovered, was 3-out-of-10. In contrast, the recovery of the line of text required less tries.

4.3 Contributions

This work differs with respect to similar ones reported in [8–11], and [14–18], in the following. In some of them only a design model is proposed without any proof of implementation. In others a hardware setup is shown, but again, there is not any proof of sending and receiving any image. It also required to use two microcontrollers (one for transmission and one for reception). The main problem of using microcontrollers is that not all of them run good enough fast and have enough RAM memory to store a medium to large image sent by the PC. Furthermore, it requires software written in C or Matlab to reside at both PCs to connect with the microcontrollers and to process the picture transmission and reception. Some others, do not use visible light at all, but infrared light. Our work differs from the above in that we only use a Raspberry Pi computer, visible light from LEDs, littleBits modules, and simple code written in Python as the programming language.

5   Conclusions

A line of text and an image transmission and reception application using visible light was developed using a Raspberry Pi 3, two bright LEDs and a light sensor, thus as OOK modulation, and the Python Image Library. Both the line of text and the picture in color, were recovered acceptably well although with a small presence of noise. It should be noted that this noise is due to environment light, and the distance between the LEDs and the light sensor.

We concluded that the performance of the application depends on several factors: (1) The brightness of the LEDs: (2) The sensitivity of the light sensor with respect to the light received from the LEDs; (3) The surrounding light (in Fig. 7 it can be seen that the light sensor has a control for graduating the sensitivity in the presence of high or low light); and (4) The alignment between the LEDs and the light sensor influences the reception, and consequently the quality of the image and text recovery.

5.1   Future Improvements

A list of improvements to enlarge the efficiency of this application are the following: (1) Increasing the number and/or power of the LEDs to augment the reception distance; (2) Using different modulation schemes, and (3) Implement and include a continuous synchronization mechanism to improve the LED-to-light sensor VLC transmission-reception link.

Acknowledgments.   This work was supported by Instituto Politecnico Nacional Project SIP-IPN 20196133.

References

1. Haas, H.: Wireless data from every light bulb. TED: Ideas worth spreading (2011). http://www.ted.com/talks/harald_haas_wireless_data_from_every_light_bulb
2. Tsonev, D., Videv, S., Haas, H.: Light fidelity (Li-Fi): towards all-optical networking. In: Proceedings of SPIE (Broadband Access Communication Technologies VIII), vol. 9007, no. 2 (2013). https://doi.org/10.1117/12.2044649
3. Sherman, J.: How LED light bulbs could replace Wi-Fi. Digital Trends (2016). http://www.digitaltrends.com/mobile/light-bulb-li-fi-wireless-internet/
4. Haas, H.: High-speed wireless networking using visible light. SPIE Newsroom. https://doi.org/10.1117/2.1201304.004773, http://www.spie.org/newsroom/4773-high–speed-wireless-networking-using-visible-light. Accessed March 2016
5. Vincent, J.: Li-Fi revolution: internet connections using light bulbs are 250 times faster than broadband (2016). http://www.independent.co.uk/news/science/li-fi-revolution-internet-connections-using-light-bulbs-are-250-times-faster-than-broadband-8909320.html
6. Location Awareness Wikipedia (2018). https://en.wikipedia.org/wiki/Location_awareness
7. Jovicic, A., Junyi, L., Richardson, T.: Visible light communication: opportunities, challenges and the path to market (2013). https://doi.org/10.1109/mcom.2013.6685754, http://ieeexplore.ieee.org/document/6685754/

8. Mahendran, R.: Integrated LiFi (Light Fidelity) for smart communication through illumination. In: International Conference on Advanced Communication Control and Computing Technologies (ICACCCT), pp. 53–56. https://doi.org/10.1109/icaccct.2016.7831599, https://ieeexplore.ieee.org/document/7831599/?reload=true
9. Shah, V., et al.: 2D image transmission using light fidelity technology. Int. J. Innov. Adv. Comput. Sci. (IJIACS) **4**(4), 121–126 (2015). https://www.academicscience.co.in/admin/resources/project/paper/f201504241429887963.pdf, ISSN 2347-8616
10. Lee, K., Park, H.: Modulations for visible light communications with dimming control. IEEE Photonics Technol. Lett. **23**(16) (2011). https://doi.org/10.1109/lpt.2011.2157676, http://ieeexplore.ieee.org/document/5773477/
11. Perfecto, G.C., Godoy, R.S., Rios, A.A.: Transmision de imagenes de Matlab a Arduino via Puerto Serial. Boletín UPIITA-IPN, 644 CyT, No. 52 (2016). http://www.boletin.upiita.ipn.mx/index.php/ciencia/644-cyt-numero-52/1234-transmision-de-imagenes-de-matlab-a-arduino-via-puerto-serial
12. LittleBits. https://www.littlebits.cc/
13. Pi, R.: Raspberry Pi input and output pin voltage and current capability. Mosaic Documentation Web. http://www.mosaic-industries.com/embedded-systems/microcontroller-projects/raspberry-pi/gpio-pin-electrical-specifications
14. Vasuja, M., et al.: Image transmission using Li-Fi. In: IEEE Conference Publications (2018). https://ieeexplore.ieee.org/document/8473033
15. Raju, K.S., et al.: PC to PC transfer of text, images using visible light communication (VLC). Int. J. Adv. Eng. Manag. Sci. (IJAEMS) (2017). https://dx.doi.org/10.24001/ijaems.3.5.6
16. Hamand, A., Kuntawar, S.: An approach towards high speed communication using Li-Fi technology. IOSR J. Electron. Commun. Eng. (2018). http://www.iosrjournals.org/iosr-jece/papers/Vol.%2013%20Issue%204/Version-1/K1304017275.pdf
17. Chen, M., et al.: Real-time video transmission of visible light communication based on LED. Int. J. Commun. Netw. Syst. Sci. **10**(8B) (2017). https://doi.org/10.4236/ijcns.2017.108b007, https://www.scirp.org/journal/PaperInformation.aspx?PaperID=78373
18. Costa Mari, J.: Visible light communication for Internet of things. Trabajo final de grado, Universitat Politecnica de Catalunya (2018). https://upcommons.upc.edu/handle/2117/117811

12–18 GHz Microwave Frequency Band Microstrip Patch Antenna Design for the Radio Implant Medical Devices Application

Salvador Ricardo Meneses González[✉]
and Rita Trinidad Rodríguez Márquez

Instituto Politécnico Nacional, Escuela Superior de Ingeniería Mecánica y
Eléctrica, Unidad Zacatenco, 07738 Mexico City, Mexico
rmenesesg@ipn.mx

Abstract. The implantation of radio implant medical devices (IMD) into the
human body are becoming smaller, therefore and because to the high degree of
miniaturization and an efficient wireless link, antennas extremely small, which
satisfies gain, bandwidth, impedance, and low cost are demanded. This work
proposes a wide bandwidth ranging from 12 GHz to 18 GHz Microstrip Patch
Antenna, describing the design, simulation, implementation and measurement,
in order to be used on the IMD's.

Keywords: Microstrip antenna · Microwave band · Implant medical device

1 Introduction

Biomedical telemetry permits the measurement of physiological signals at a distance
through wireless communication technologies, that is, implantable medical devices
IMDs are implanted inside the patient's body and used for diagnostic, monitoring,
and/or therapeutic applications, but the human body is a lossy material for electromagnetic waves.

This means the body converts electric fields into heat, that is, the body absorbs
energy from electromagnetic waves and part of this energy is collected by the antenna,
an important element of the IMD, consequently, when an antenna is placed near the
body, the result is a large reduction of the antenna efficiency, this power loss is a
function of frequency which value is in accordance with the permittivity and con-
ductivity of the medium where the electromagnetic wave propagates, in this case,
human skin, fat, muscle, and due to its structure, these ones have different attenuation
factor, that is, human body tissue is a great attenuator [1], which increases with frequency. In this sense, these devices which use small antennas have become in a part of
body-centric wireless communications.

Several different antenna designs have been considered for medical implants, for
instance, [2] evaluates microstrip configurations, spiral and serpentine antennas were
simulated in order to compare their resonant frequencies, concluding that, serpentine
antenna is electrically shorter than the spiral antenna, [3–6] report challenges, limitations and benefits of different kind of antennas. Thus, it is known that the antenna size

© Springer Nature Switzerland AG 2019
M. F. Mata-Rivera et al. (Eds.): WITCOM 2019, CCIS 1053, pp. 110–120, 2019.
https://doi.org/10.1007/978-3-030-33229-7_10

with respect to the wavelength is the most important parameter influencing the antenna's radiation [3], and a relation between antenna size and its radiation characteristics is reported in [7] concluded that geometrically small but efficient antennas are required for high operating frequencies, and the antenna efficiency significantly decreases if lower operating frequencies are used. Likewise, implantable antennas operating at much higher frequencies (31.5 GHz) have also been reported in the literature [8].

On the other hand, inductive links formerly have been employed for the wireless telemetry of IMDs [9–11], but this kind of inductive low-frequency links shows low data rates, short communication range and unwanted emissions. Actually ITU-R Recommendation SA.1346 (ITU-R 1998) which outlined the use of the 402.0–405.0 MHz frequency band for medical implant communication services (MICS), in this sense, at 402 MHz–405 MHz, the wavelength of an electromagnetic wave is approximately 74 cm, as we know, the size of the microstrip antenna is directly proportional to the wavelength at the operating frequency, consequently an antenna with dimensions comparable to this wavelength cannot be used for an implant [12], so, different antenna structures that need to be addressed. In this sense, due to higher operation frequencies allow use of smaller-sized antennas and components, and without wanting to enter a conflict with ITU-R regulations, for this purpose the designed antenna in this work, is a just a proposal to be considered, due to wavelength corresponding to this frequency band (12–18 GHz), ranges between 25 mm to 16 mm.

Only for the sole purpose to observe the dimensions of the proposed microwave band patch antenna, this one was placed close to a RFID UHF Band meander antenna (915 MHz) [13], (see Fig. 1).

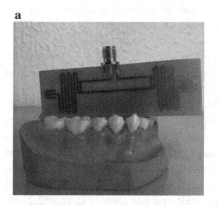 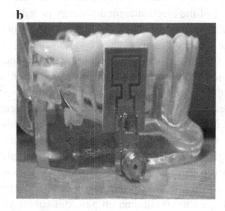

Fig. 1. (a) RFID UHF Band meander antenna (915 MHz) and (b) Proposed microwave band patch antenna (12–18 GHz).

Therefore, in view of the importance of their health role and because the body directly degrades the performance of the antenna, these kind of antennas should be safety, lightweight, extremely small, robust structure, it must be considered the interaction with the human body, in this sense, there are complex factors involved that have to be considered when dealing with this issue; [14] describes considerations related to the design and performance of implantable patch antennas. In this work, first part, it is limited to selection of the frequency band of operation, miniaturization of the antenna, the other issues relative to biocompatibility of the antenna, will be supported on a further work (part 2) in this area.

In this way, in this work, we propose a small slotted patch antenna operating in 12–18 GHz Microwave Band, in order to reduce the size antenna, increase the bandwidth, and improve the quality communication of the implantable antenna with exterior monitor/control equipment.

To determine the performance of design parameter, as impedance, resonance frequency, radiation pattern, wideband, etc., CST software (Computer Simulation Technology) has been used, in the same way, experimental tests have been applied.

The paper is organized as follows: Sect. 2 describes a brief tag antenna design basis, discusses simulation, Sect. 3 describes measurements results, and finalizing the present work with conclusions and references.

2   Antenna Design

2.1   Design Basis

The patch antenna is generally made of conducting material such as cooper and the substrate material should have dielectric constant, and it bases her behavior on the way in which the electromagnetic waves propagates through the antenna structure. Theses ones are reflected by the ground plane, traveling on the dielectric surface, guided by the conductive strip, when they reach the point between the face substrate an the free space, part of the electromagnetic energy is reflected, and part of it, it is radiated to free space; so, in order to increase the antenna efficiency, the radiated energy should be higher than the reflected energy.

In this work, we propose a small patch antenna which consists of a rectangular patch fed by a microstrip transmission line, operating at 12–18 GHz frequency band, in order to miniaturization of the antenna's occupied volume/size and achieve high efficiency and large bandwidth. Let us remember that thick substrates with low permittivity result in antenna designs with high efficiency and large bandwidths, thin substrates with high permittivity lead to small antennas but with a lower bandwidth and high radiation loss [15]; during the simulation stage, we have made a tradeoff between substrate thickness and permittivity for the purpose to define the kind of material, according to within our means in a cost-effective way, for that, we have used and built the prototype antenna on a duroid substrate, which electric permittivity is $\varepsilon r = 2.2$ and loss tangent $\delta = 0.0009$.

On the other hand, patch antennas, not all of them preserving the characteristics of the device in a frequency band broad enough and some of them are complicated in terms of design and have the disadvantage that bandwidth is limited, so, in order to enhance the antenna, some modifications on the structure are applied, based on slots to redistribute the current density. In fact, the antenna has been designed to be more simple, low cost, wide bandwidth, without the need of altering of substantial changes to the structure, maintain the small size.

Considering a design frequency equal to 15 GHz, this being the core of the proposed band, the wavelength is equal to λ = 20 mm. As we know, the size of the microstrip antenna is directly proportional to the wavelength at the operating frequency, in this sense, the following expressions [16] have been used, in such a way that, the substrate thickness h = 1.524 mm, strip width, W = 9 mm, which is approximately equal to λ/2.

Structure geometry and dimensions are shown in Figure.

Strip width:

$$W = \frac{1}{2f_r\sqrt{\epsilon_0\mu_0}}\sqrt{\frac{2}{\epsilon_r+1}} \tag{1}$$

Strip length:

$$L = \frac{1}{2f_r\sqrt{\epsilon_e}\sqrt{\epsilon_0\mu_0}} - 2\Delta L \tag{2}$$

Effective Permittivity:

$$\epsilon_e = \frac{\epsilon_r+1}{2} + \frac{\epsilon_r-1}{2}\left(\frac{1}{\sqrt{1+12\frac{h}{W}}}\right) \tag{3}$$

where:

f_r, resonance frequency
ε_r, relative permittivity
h, substrate thickness.

2.2   Antenna Simulation

Important parameters that define the antenna performance are the reflection coefficient or return loss, which is called Parameter, S_{11}, that, describes the performance antenna, for instance, if $S_{11} = -10$ dB, this implies 90% of power is delivered to the antenna, and 10% is the reflected power, when this value crosses the power magnitude line -10 dB value a certain frequency, this is the resonance frequency or bandwidth on a frequency range, if $S_{11} = 0$ dB, then all the power is reflected from the antenna and nothing is radiated. The other parameter is the radiation pattern (Fig. 2).

In order to achieve these parameters, the computer Simulation Technology Software [17] has been used to simulate the designed antenna (see Fig. 3), resulting the Magnitude vs. Frequency simulation graphic, parameter S_{11} (see Fig. 4).

It is possible to observe that from the magnitude vs. frequency simulation graphic, resonance frequency value is approximately equal to 15 GHz, bandwidth approximately equal to 1.5 GHz, from 13 GHz to 14.5 GHz and from the simulation trials

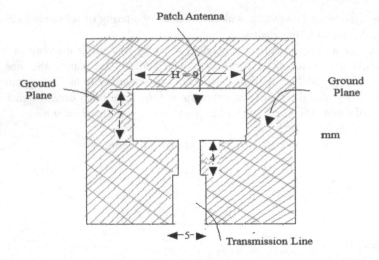

Fig. 2. Patch antenna dimensions.

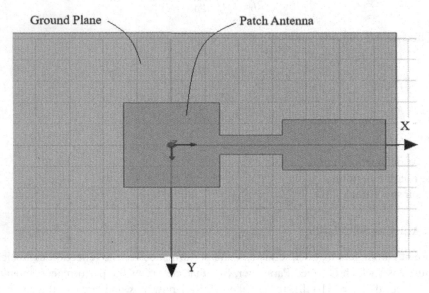

Fig. 3. Antenna structure simulation.

results gives the chance to identify the necessary dimension modifications, in order to adjust the resonance frequency value along the 12–18 GHz. Simulated radiation pattern (see Fig. 5) shows the vertical plane (E| vs. θ), called E-Plane and the 3D simulation pattern (See Fig. 6).

In the same way, it is possible to observe an omnidirectional performance, with no nulls, concentrated electromagnetic power on the −90°–90° plane, that is, the front side of the antenna, due to ground plane to its rear. This radiation pattern geometry is an

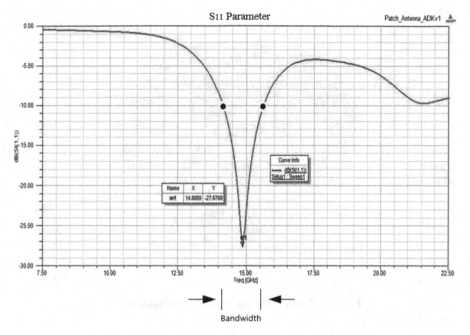

Fig. 4. Magnitude vs. Frequency (simulation).

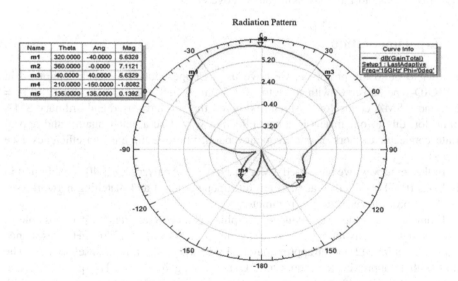

Fig. 5. Radiation pattern graphic, Plane-E (simulation).

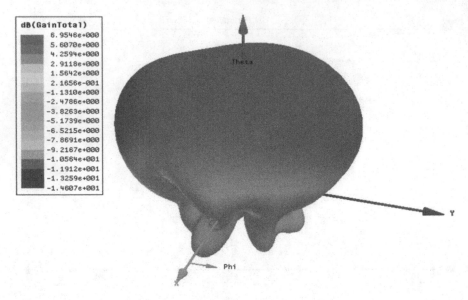

Fig. 6. 3D radiation pattern graphic (simulation).

advantage, because of point to point communication is required for this application and certain area close to the body skin can be covered.

3   Experimentation

In order to build the prototype, we have used Copper slotted by tracks engraved in DUROID-type substrate with a width of 1.5 mm, which electric permittivity is $\varepsilon r =$ 2.2, and a SMA connector. It should be noted that we have used and ordinary SMA connector, due to our means in a cost-effective way. Use a better-quality and appropriate connector to work at this frequency band, improve the antenna efficiency (see Fig. 7).

In the same way, we have used a Vector Network Analyzer ZVB 40 is calibrated in the band 10 GHz–20 GHz, at short circuit, opened circuit and matching network (see Fig. 8) in order to measure S_{11} parameter.

From the magnitude vs. frequency graphic achieved (see Fig. 9), it is possible to observe that the maximum antenna efficiency is achieved at 12.86 GHz, resonance frequency, point M2 and at approximately 13.2 GHz is the minimum efficiency. The bandwidth is approximately equal to 6 GHz, starting in 12.11 GHz (point M1) and ending in 18.5 GHz, that is, the designed antenna is a wideband antenna, bandwidth enough to support high data rate.

On the other hand, literature review present other architectures antennas, in the MICS (402.0–405.0 MHz) and ISM (433.1–434.8, 868.0–868.6 and 902.8–928.0 MHz) bands [18]. The proposed antenna is novel, useful, innovative antenna, in the microwave band (12–18 GHz), small dimensions and wide bandwidth.

Fig. 7. Prototype antenna.

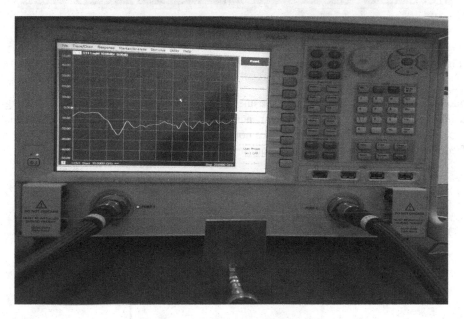

Fig. 8. Prototype antenna under test.

3.1   Limitation

The method used to measure and calculate the gain antenna and radiation pattern, consists of install the prototype antenna, into an anechoic chamber, acting as receiver antenna, and a known second antenna, a commercial antenna acting as a transmitter

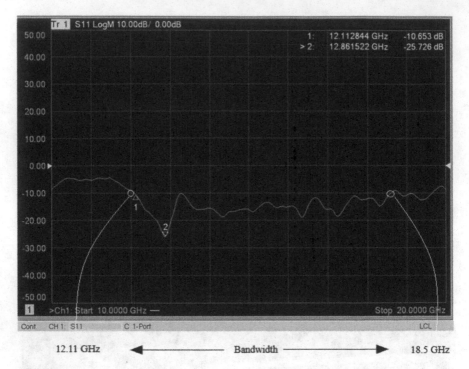

12.11 GHz   ◄──────────── Bandwidth ────────────►   18.5 GHz

Fig. 9. Magnitude vs. Frequency, S_{11} parameter (prototype antenna under experimental test).

antenna, both of them installed into the anechoic chamber, spaced 2.8 m apart, keeping a line of sight (see Fig. 10), however, actually, we are not be able to carry out this measurement due to our laboratory does not have capabilities to experiment at this band frequency (transmitter and receiver equipment).

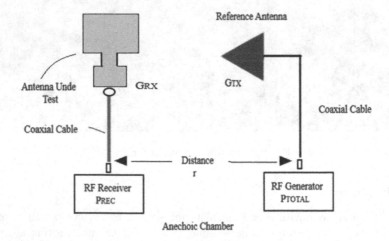

Fig. 10. Gain antenna measurement method.

4 Conclusion

A microstrip patch antenna array has been designed, meeting the resonance frequency, small size (millimetric), exhibiting a wide bandwidth (12–18 GHz), an appropriate geometry of the radiation pattern, low cost, and easily construction.

There are differences between simulation and measurement results on the S_{11}, respect to the maximum resonance frequency, 15 GHz and 12.86 GHz, respectively, due to certain construction defects, for instance, bad soldier, SMA connector, or adjust the exact dimensions, however, the experimental bandwidth result was far better than the simulated bandwidth result, due to the simulation bandwidth result is equal to 1.5 GHz and the experimental bandwidth result is approximately equal to 6 GHz.

The second part of this work consists of to continue the technical stage (gain measurement), as soon as we get the chance, as soon as the appropriate equipment at this band is in place, and, verify the antenna effectiveness (distance, penetration depth), testing the antenna performance on/under human or animal skin, it will be necessary the support biomedical research.

Finally, due the obtained results, the proposed antenna is a novel, useful and innovative antenna for IMD's application, in the microwave band, wide bandwidth, small dimensions, easily construction, meeting the resonance frequencies, input impedance requirements, an appropriate geometry of the radiation pattern, so that, we recommend this kind of small antenna as well as the proposed frequency band to be applied to Radio Implant Medical Devices corresponding to the health sector.

References

1. Xuyang, L.: Body Matched Antennas for Microwave Medical Applications. KIT Scientific Publishing, Karlsruhe (2014)
2. Soontornpipit, P., Furse, C.M., Chung, Y.C.: Design of implantable microstrip antenna for communication with medical implants. IEEE Trans. Microw. Theory Tech. 52(8), 1944–1951 (2004). Part 2
3. Kim, J., Rahmat-Samii, Y.: Implanted antennas inside a human body: simulations, designs, and characterizations. IEEE Trans. Microw. Theory Tech. 52(8), 1934–1943 (2004). Part 2
4. Norris, M., Richard, J.-D.: Subminiature antenna design for wireless implants. In: Proceedings of the IET Seminar on Antennas and Propagation for Body-Centric Wireless Communications, London, UK, April 2007, pp. 57–62 (2007)
5. Hall, P.S., Hao, Y.: Antennas and Propagation for Body-centric Wireless Communications. Artech House, Norwood (2006)
6. Skrivervik, A.K., Zürcher, J.F., Staub, O., Mosig, J.R.: PCS antenna design: the challenge of miniaturization. IEEE Antenna Propag. Mag. 43(4), 12–27 (2001)
7. Sánchez-Fernández, C.J., Quavado-Teruel, O., Requena-Carrión, J., Inclán-Sánchez, L., Rajo-Iglesias, E.: Dual-band microstrip patch antenna based on short 0 circuited ring and spiral resonators for implantable medical devices. IET Microw. Antennas Propag. 4, 1048–1055 (2010)
8. Ahmed, Y., Hao, Y., Parini, C.: A 31.5 GHz patch antenna design for medical implants. Int. J. Antennas Propag. 2008, 6, Article ID 167980 (2008). Hindawi Publishing Corporation

9. Freedonia: Implantable Medical Devices – Industry study with forecast for 2015 & 2020. The Freedonia Group, Study #2852 (2012)
10. Valdastri, P., Menciassi, A., Arena, A., Caccamo, C., Dario, P.: An implantable telemetry platform system for in vivo monitoring of physiological parameters. IEEE Trans. Inform. Technol. Biomed. **8**, 271 (2004)
11. Baghel, S., Yadav, N.K.: A review on micro electronic pill. Int. J. Res. Appl. Sci. Eng. Technol. (IJRASET), **3**(VI) (2015)
12. Kiourti, A., Nikita, K.S.: Implanted antennas in biomedical telemetry. In: Chen, Z.N., Liu, D., Nakano, H., Qing, X., Zwick, T. (eds.) Handbook of Antenna Technologies, pp. 2613–2652. Springer, Singapore (2016). https://doi.org/10.1007/978-981-4560-44-3_94
13. Meneses, R., Montes, L., Morales, M.: A small note about RFID technology applied to public safety. Part 1: RFID tag antenna design. In: Conference: Power, Electronics and Computing (ROPEC), 2013 IEEE International Autumn Meeting 2013, Ixtapa, Gro. México, November 2013
14. Li, X.: Body Matched Antennas for Microwave Medical Applications. Forschungsberichte aus dem Institut für Höchstfrequenztechnik und Elektronik (IHE) der Universität Karlsruhe (TH). KIT Scientific Publishing (2015). ISSN 0942-2935
15. Madhav, B.T.P., et al.: Multiband slot aperture stacked patch antenna for wireless communication applications. Int. J. Comput. Aided Eng. Technol. **8**(4), 413–423 (2016)
16. Wong, K.: Compact and Broadband Microstrip Antennas. Wiley, Hoboken (2002)
17. CST Homepage. https://www.cst.com/Academia/Student-Edition
18. Kiourti, A., Nikita, K.S.: Performance of miniature implantable antennas for medical telemetry at 402, 433, 868 and 915 MHz. In: Godara, B., Nikita, K.S. (eds.) MobiHealth 2012. LNICST, vol. 61, pp. 122–129. Springer, Heidelberg (2013). https://doi.org/10.1007/978-3-642-37893-5_14

Analytics for Basic Products in Mexico

Paul Millán[✉] and Félix Mata

Instituto Politécnico Nacional, Unidad Profesional Interdisciplinaria en
Ingeniería y Tecnologías Avanzadas, Avenida Instituto Politécnico Nacional
No. 2580, Col Barrio la Laguna Ticomán, Gustavo A. Madero,
07340 Mexico City, Mexico
luapmg@outlook.es, mmatar@ipn.mx

Abstract. In this research, it was designed a methodology to forecast prices of products In the Mexican Republic. The dataset is composed of basic basket products. The work consists of analyzing open and mixed data of this dataset. The approach is centered on studying how is the behavior in time and location domains for three products, tuna, detergent, and milk. The data ranges for five years. Neural networks were used to analyze data, and several experiments of price forecast were issued using different granularity levels. The regression models were validated using two traditional approaches of the machine learning area, coefficient of determination, and mean absolute error. The experiments showed that the price of basic products varies by zone and it is possible to give a forecast with a percentage of 80% of precision.

Keywords: Forecasting · Data analytics · Data science · Big Data · Machine learning

1 Introduction

Presently, the data of basket products have been studied from a wide range of perspectives mainly in financial and market aspects. Traditionally these approaches are dominated for statistical approaches. However, new opportunities of analyzing and studying these phenomenons from the perspective of data science, Big Data, and machine learning ara available today to discover or identify insights in such data.

For another hand, according to the National Survey of Household Income and Expenses (INEGI by its acronym in Spanish) [1]. The average household expenditure in Mexico is invested in products of a basic basket. In light of this knowledge, it is natural to be interested in analyzing the behavior of these products. The possible results of the data analysis of these products have a valuable and useful character. Future price forecasts can help commercial companies in the elaboration of control and financial planning processes. Governments can also benefit from this type of study for the creation of public policies.

© Springer Nature Switzerland AG 2019
M. F. Mata-Rivera et al. (Eds.): WITCOM 2019, CCIS 1053, pp. 121–129, 2019.
https://doi.org/10.1007/978-3-030-33229-7_11

2 Methodology

The data methodology proposed is composed of 4 phases: (1) ETL process, (2) Data Continuity, (3) Categorical Data transformation and (4) Feature Selection. Each of one are developed in the following sections.

2.1 ETL Process

The first phase of the methodology is based on the process of extraction, transformation, and loading (ETL).

The data used in this research are open and provided for a Mexican organism denominated PROFECO [2]. The data is available in CSV and JSON format. The data period includes from 2011 to 2016, in the Mexican Republic, with more than 62 million records. The nature of data is mixed, numerical, and categorical. The data was cleaned, eliminating records containing empty, null, or 'N/A' values. The data of the address (location) variable were homogenized since the oldest records only contained the street and the number, while the most current ones also contained the 'barrio'. An identity location procedure is running in order to match all the address. Two original variables, called latitude and longitude, were eliminated since it was not planned to work at this level of geographic granularity. Three new integer variables called day, month, and year were created, based on the original date variable. Finally, the Date-Time type variable is transformed into a continuous floating type value to work in the next process with them.

2.2 Data Continuity

It is necessary to guarantee certain continuity in the records so that there is homogenized information, which will help to create and evaluate better regression models as well as compare products taking into account the variability of their price over time. For the purpose of this research, a combination will be when a number of records have the same values taking into account a certain number of variables, except for this rule the date and price variables. In this way when there are two records that are the same except for the date and the price, it will be said that there are two records of this combination.

In the data of this research there was a serious problem of continuity over time, as an example, see the Fig. 1, where this problem can be seen for a combination of three variables of the milk powder product.

It required to create a new training dataset, where those combinations that met a certain condition of continuity were taken, in this case, it was proposed to keep those combinations that appeared at least 5 years and at least 8 months for each year. In the example in the previous Fig. 1, only the first combination would be selected, and the others would be omitted.

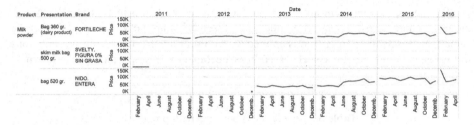

Fig. 1. Time continuity of milk powder records in the dimensions of product, presentation, brand.

2.3 Categorical Data Transformation

Currently, most data mining and machine learning techniques need numerical data. Therefore, categorical data such as those present in this investigation should be transformed into numerical values to which it is possible to apply these techniques. In this methodology it is recommended to use a binarization technique of type one against all, for example, One Hot Encoding, see Table 1. This technique is based on converting every possible value of a categorical attribute into a new column. The disadvantage is that this technique increases the number of columns in the dataset.

Table 1. Binarization sample: one versus all.

Brand	Price (MXN)	Brand			Price (MXN)
		Dolores	Herdez	Tuny	
Dolores	11.5	1	0	0	11.5
Herdez	11.9	0	1	0	11.9
Tuny	12	0	0	1	12

2.4 Feature Selection

One of the problems that were constantly presented during this investigation was the high computational cost, which translated into long periods to process the data, as well as for the stages of machine learning, mainly in the training stage. This was due in large part to the increase in dimensions that occurs when transforming categorical to numerical data through binarization. It was necessary to use feature selection algorithms to select the most important and discard those that provided little information when trying to predict the price. It was necessary to use feature selection algorithms to select the most important and discard those that provided little information when trying to predict the price. This was achieved by using cloud computing using the mutual information algorithm which can work with categorical data. Analyzing the characteristics using all the basic products we have as a result the Table 2 showing the most important variables.

Table 2. Feature selection for all basic products.

Presentation	Product	Brand	Category	Address	Tradename
1.5460	1.1770	1.0930	0.5070	0.0470	0.0390

The above is consistent since the products are being taken in a grouped manner, therefore characteristics such as product and presentation are very important. When the same feature selection algorithm is applied to certain products and certain presentations individually, other features such as address become more important. It is shown in Table 3.

Table 3. Feature selection for certain products.

	Product	Presentation	Brand	Address	Tradename	Year	Commercial Chain
Milk powder	0	1.0935	0.4702	0.2432	0.1401	0.1811	0.0748
Tuna	0	0.1216	0.0931	0.3733	0.2770	0.0965	0.2055
Detergent	0.292	1.1890	1.0550	0.152	0.1270	0.0090	0.09900

2.5   Parameter Selection and Model Generation

The regression algorithm used in this investigation is *MLPRegressor* [3–6]. To select parameters, the exhaustive search algorithm *GridsearchCV* was used, in addition to the latter, *TimeSeriesSplit* was used as a cross-validation technique with a number of divisions defined to 5. The previous algorithms belong to the library *Scikit-learn* [7] in python. The *MLPRegressor* class implements a multilayer perceptron (MLP) that trains using backward propagation [8, 9] with no activation function in the output layer, which can also be seen as the function of identity as a function of activation. Use the square error as the loss function, and the output is a set of continuous values. *MLPRegressor* uses the alpha parameter for the term regularization (L2 regularization) that helps avoid over-setting [10]. It makes use of a stochastic gradient-based optimizer called *adam* [11].

The *MinMaxScaler* algorithm is used to scale all values to a range between 0 and 1. The selection of the *alpha* parameter is very important since this parameter helps to control the over-adjustment, it is recommended to use a range of [1.e−01, 1.e−02, 1.e −03, 1.e−04, 1.e−05, 1.e−06] for the *MLPRegressor* algorithm [10]. As for the size of the neural network, it was tested with different sizes using *GridsearchCV*. The first size equal to the number of real entries, the second equal to the number of entries after binarizing the categorical data. The above was tested for each case from a single hidden layer to three.

2.6   Measure Performance with Grouped Products

The coefficient of determination with which model′s learning is being measured uses the variance of the set of samples to be defined, see formula 1. Now, the variance is the square of the standard deviation, therefore it is necessary to pay special attention to the cause of the latter.

$$R^2 = \frac{\sum_{i=1}^{m} (y_i - \hat{y}_i)^2}{\sum_{i=1}^{m} (y_i - \bar{y}_i)^2} \tag{1}$$

Looking at the previous formula it can be seen that the coefficient of determination is based on knowing how good the predictions generated by the model are, compared with simply having used the average of the samples as a prediction. If there is a larger standard deviation, there will be a larger error in the lower part of the equation, which will minimize the error produced by the model. Therefore, it is vitally important to know if this standard deviation is due to the variation of a product over time or if it is due to grouping, for example, different products and presentations. To clearly visualize this situation, a detergent model created from a dataset whit different presentations are used as an example. The presentations are as follows: bottle 1 L liquid, bottle 750 ml liquid, bag 500 g powder, bag 900 g powder, bag 1 kg powder, bag 5 kg powder. The presentation in bag 5 kg powder stands out in size from others, in the same way, its price is higher. In the test stage, the model demonstrated know to differentiate between this presentation and the others, clearly observing a distance between the forecasts, always because of the presentation of bag 5 kg powder that generated higher prices. The above can be seen in the Fig. 2.

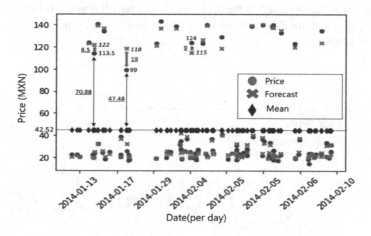

Fig. 2. Error comparison with the detergent product.

The predictions shown in Fig. 2 come from a model that obtained a coefficient of determination of 0.98.

2.7 Measuring the Model's Performance with Ungrouped Products

The models generated with datasets of ungrouped products will obtain a coefficient of determination that will reflect exclusively how good the predictions of a particular product and presentation are, taking into account their own variance over time.

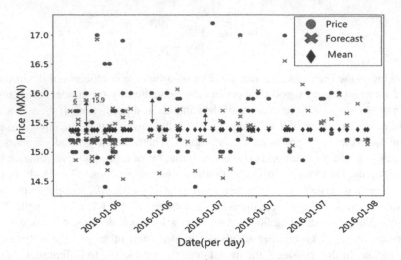

Fig. 3. Error comparison with the model of ultra-pasteurized milk, partially skimmed, box 1 L Lala light milk.

The model presented in Fig. 3 obtained a coefficient of determination of 0.7, this value is less than that obtained in the previous section which was 0.98. However, it can be seen in Fig. 4 that the forecasts are much closer to real prices, many of errors are in the order of cents.

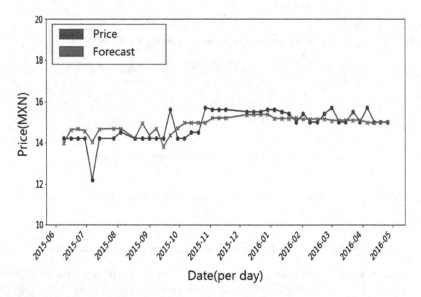

Fig. 4. Test for ultra-pasteurized milk, partially skimmed, box 1 L brand Lala Light in Chedraui, Toluca, Mexico, Alfredo del Mazo 705, col. Tlacopa CP 50010

3   Results

A model and predictions were created of ultra-pasteurized milk, partially skimmed, box 1 L brand Lala Light. A brief description of the dataset is presented in Table 4.

Table 4. Description ultra-pasteurized milk, partially skimmed, box 1 L brand Lala Light.

Number of records	39939
Mean	14.2270
Standard deviation	0.9732
Minimum	8.0000
25%	13.5000
50%	14.3000
75%	14.9000
Maximum	25.9000

The characteristics selected in this model are the following: *date, year, commercial name, address, municipality, state, commercial chain* and *month*. The result of the parameter selection can be seen in the Table 5.

Table 5. Results of the selection of parameters for ultra-pasteurized milk, partially skimmed, box 1 L brand Lala Light.

Alpha	Network size	Ranking
0.001	(527, 527, 527)	1
0.1	(8)	2
0.01	(527, 527)	3
0.000001	(527, 527, 527)	4

The training period was from January-2011 to June-2015. The yield obtained was 0.1722 of the coefficient of determination and an average absolute error of 0.5131, both in the test stage, which covered from June 2015 to April 2016.

Now, an example of the predictions generated during the test stage for an address, that is, an establishment, in this case of the Chedraui commercial chain in the state of Toluca. See Fig. 4.

Using this methodology, it was discovered that the prices of basic products in this database vary by address, prices are not kept by commercial chains. Even establishments of the same commercial chain in the same state and municipality, present their own prices, an example can be seen in Table 6. In this case, there is a price difference of more than 15%.

Table 6. The same detergent product offered at Walmart in two establishments at different prices on the same date.

Product	Presentation	Brand	Price	Date	Commercial chain	Address	State	Municipality
Dish detergent	Bag 900 g powder (green)	Salvo	16.91	2011-04-08	Walmart	Calzada de Guadalupe 431	Distrito Federal	Gustavo A. Madero
Dish detergent	Bag 900 g powder (green)	Salvo	19.50	2011-04-08	Walmart	Othon de Mendizabal Ote 343	Distrito Federal	Gustavo A. Madero

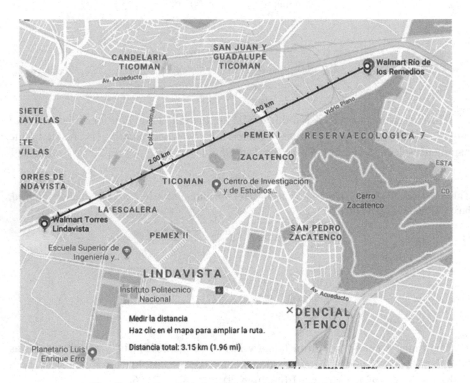

Fig. 5. Location and distance between two Walmart stores.

It is interesting how this variation occurs even in nearby locations, like in this case, two establishments belonging to the Walmart commercial chain at approximately 3 km away. It is depicted in Fig. 5.

4   Conclusions and Future Work

We conclude t is possible not only to know the behavior of the products but also to generate models of prediction of the prices of these products in a particular place and some period.

It is possible by combining the techniques of exploration and machine learning on time and location domains. It is applied to categorical attributes such as product, presentation, brand, and commercial chain, address, among others.

Nevertheless, It is necessary to work on other approaches that allow the transformation of qualitative or categorical data to numerical data. Considering the conditions: do not insert bias and not increase the number of columns.

The use of Feature selections algorithm allowed identifying datasets with better performance than the original ones to produce price predictions. However, it is proposed as future work to add new variables that can later be analyzed with other algorithms, to discover possible external variables to this dataset that influence the variation of prices products in Mexico.

References

1. INEGI Homepage. Encuesta Nacional de Ingresos y Gastos de los Hogares (ENIGH) (2014). https://www.inegi.org.mx/programas/enigh/tradicional/2014/default.html. Accessed May 2019
2. PROFECO Homepage. Quién es Quién en los precios. https://datos.gob.mx/busca/dataset/ quien-es-quien-en-los-precios. Accessed January 2018
3. Hinton, G.E.: Connectionist learning procedures. In: Artificial Intelligence, pp. 185–234 (1990)
4. Glorot, X., Bengio, Y.: Understanding the difficulty of training deep feedforward neural networks. In: Thirteenth International Conference on Artificial Intelligence and Statistics, Sardinia, Italy (2010)
5. He, K., Zhang, X., Ren, S., Sun, J.: Delving deep into rectifiers: surpassing human-level performance on ImageNet classification. In: Proceedings of the IEEE International Conference on Computer Vision, pp. 1026–1034 (2015)
6. Kingma, D.P., Ba, J.: Adam: a method for stochastic optimization (2014)
7. Pedregosa, F., Varoquaux, G., Gramfort, A., et al.: Scikit-learn: machine learning in Python. J. Mach. Learn. Res. **12**, 2825–2830 (2011)
8. Rumelhart, D.E., Hinton, G.E., Williams, R.J.: Learning representations by back-propagating errors. Cogn. Model. **5**(3), 1 (1988)
9. LeCun, Y.A., Bottou, L., Orr, G.B., Müller, K.-R.: Efficient BackProp. In: Montavon, G., Orr, G.B., Müller, K.-R. (eds.) Neural Networks: Tricks of the Trade. LNCS, vol. 7700, pp. 9–48. Springer, Heidelberg (2012). https://doi.org/10.1007/978-3-642-35289-8_3
10. Pedregosa, F.: «Scikit Learn» [En línea]. https://scikit-learn.org/stable/modules/neural_ networks_supervised.html\#regression. Accessed July 2019
11. Kingma, B.J.: Adam: a method for stochastic optimization. In: 3rd International Conference for Learning Representations, San Diego (2014)

Design and Development of Photovoltaic Power Meter

Jaime Vega Pérez[1]([⊠]), Blanca García[2], and Nayeli Vega García[3]

[1] Escuela Superior de Ingeniería Mecánica y Eléctrica,
Instituto Politécnico Nacional (IPN), San José Ticoman,
07340 Mexico City, Mexico
jvegape@ipn.mx
[2] Centro de Estudios Científicos y Tecnológicos No. 1 Gonzalo Vázquez Vela,
Instituto Politécnico Nacional (IPN), Pueblo de San Juan de Aragón,
07480 Mexico City, Mexico
blgarcia16@yahoo.com
[3] Escuela Superior de Cómputo, Instituto Politécnico Nacional (IPN),
Zacatenco, 07738 Mexico City, Mexico
nvegag0126@gmail.com

Abstract. The design, construction and test of an electronic system in order to measure of photovoltaic (PV) module power are reported. An interface electronic system was developed to couple the PV module toward an electronic control target with a personal computer. Samplings of the PV module current and voltage are captured analogically. The electronic system amplifies the electrical signal and converts to digital signal and also software was designed based in Matlab. After using this software the digital current and voltage signals are processed by the laptop to determinate the PV module power. The output short circuit current, open circuit voltage and maximum power of PV module were measured. In addition, the output current-voltage and power-voltage curves are achieved. This measurement system has advantages of simple, cost effective and applicable in the place where the modules are installed to measure the PV modules. Experimental results were done for different levels of incident solar power to measure capacity of PV modules installed in CINVESTAV-IPN, Mexico. The prototype developed has tolerance of 1.5% but it can be improved using precision electronic devices. We have obtained the I-V curve, P-V curve and maximum power point of the PV modules with the help of this prototype.

Keywords: Photovoltaic module · Photovoltaic power meter · Maximum power

1 Introduction

Till now, the greatest amount of electricity used by man is extracted from natural fossils fuels. The energy generation by fossils fuels has concerned due to its pollution on ecosystem and limited amount available. So that it is now necessary to look for alternating energy sources that can supply energy without producing harmful gases for long period. Among different alternative sources of energy, solar energy is sustainable and

M. F. Mata-Rivera et al. (Eds.): WITCOM 2019, CCIS 1053, pp. 130–141, 2019.
https://doi.org/10.1007/978-3-030-33229-7_12

renewable energy, which can be converted directly from sun energy to electrical energy by photovoltaic (PV) cells and modules [1]. The photovoltaic (PV) cell is an electronic device, which transforms the visible light into direct current electrical energy. The output power depends on area of cells, incident light level, efficiency but it is reduced for temperature increase. Due to the photovoltaic cell is a low voltage device (0.56 V) then photovoltaic modules are built that are integrated by several electrically connected cells in series to increase the voltage.

The basic module is designed to couple with an automotive type battery, its output voltage in the open circuit of the order of 17 to 19 V so that it can supply power to the battery. Its output power is variable from 20 W and depends of cell size.

The manufacturers are fabricating PV cells and modules of mono crystalline and polycrystalline silicon principally although many other semiconductor materials can be used [1]. The basic PV module is integrated by 36 PV cells connected in series connected to automotive battery of 12 V, but with least time PV modules with higher output power and voltages are being manufactured [2]. The PV cell or module is electronic device that converts the light energy from solar energy into the electrical energy or direct current (DC). The PV cell is a semiconductor diode the more common is done with silicon and phosphorus although there are many semiconductors materials to make PV cells [2]. The output current of photovoltaic module is represented by Eq. 1.

$$I_c = -I_0 \left[e^{\frac{q(V_c + I_c R_s)}{KT}} - 1 \right] + \frac{I_c R_s + V_c}{R_f} + I_g \tag{1}$$

The PV module output is represented mathematically by the equation of rectifier diode but guessing the serial resistance and shunt resistance as it is showed in Eq. 2.

$$P_o = V_o \left[I_g - I_0 \left(e^{\frac{q(V_o + I_o R_s)}{KT}} - 1 \right) - \frac{I_o R_s + V_o}{R_f} \right] \tag{2}$$

From Eq. 2, P_o is the output power, V_o is the output voltage, I_g is the generated current, q is the electron charge, I_o is the output current, K is the Boltzmann constant, T is the temperature, R_s is the series resistance [3]. When both are solved changing the voltage V_c from open circuit condition to short circuit condition, all the values of power and voltage are obtained, in order to get the current-voltage (I-V) and power-voltage (P-V) curves of the PV module (see Fig. 1).

The characteristic I-V and PV curves (see Fig. 1) of the photovoltaic module are very important because they have the information of their electrical variables. The maximum output power is used when a photovoltaic system is designed. But the power of the module is variable because it depends mainly on the environmental conditions of irradiance level, wind speed and module temperature. The modules are electrically characterized by the manufacturer in standard conditions (i.e. solar power of 1000 W/m^2, temperature of 25 °C) where in real working conditions the photovoltaic module is subjected to environmental changes all time, then it is necessary the PV module output maximum power must be measured on installation place.

According to the graph in Fig. 1, the I-V curve of solar module is nonlinear, and then it is not easy to locate the maximum power point (MPP). So, it is necessary to

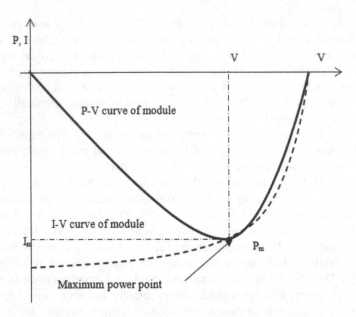

Fig. 1. Graphic representation of the Eqs. 1 and 2

develop techniques and prototypes to measure the maximum power. Several researchers have reported different methods to obtain the characteristic curves of the photovoltaic module to track the maximum power (MPPT).

Ashish et al. [4] developed an algorithm where proposed a variable step-size P&O method in which the perturbation step is obtained by a fixed ratio multiplies by the derivative of the power with respect to the voltage. This P&O method sampled the voltage and current, and the power can be obtained by multiplying the two values. When both, power variation and voltage variation, are greater than zero, the OP is on the left-hand side of the P-V curve and moves toward the MPP. If the power variation is greater than zero and voltage variation is smaller than zero, then the OP is on the right-hand side of the P-V curve and moves toward the MPP. Therefore, the direction of perturbation does not change under these two conditions. This method shortens the tracking time and reduces the steady-state oscillation as well.

Again, Khatib et al. [5] developed a new I-V curve prediction method using artificial neural networks, they include records of solar radiation, ambient temperature, current and voltage characteristics (open circuit voltage and short circuit current) for different photovoltaic modules by using MatLab software.

Danandeh et al. [6] also explain that there are still two important barriers in the path of PV cells, relatively expensive cost and low efficiency. Therefore it is completely necessary to extract maximum power of cells because of economic reasons and growing demand for energy. The solar cell output voltage and current increased with increasing the input solar radiation to the solar cell, but the PV cell temperature increases with increase of the solar radiation and temperature results in a decrease of both power and efficiency Solimana et al. [7]. Heat sink cooling system was used on the performance of solar cells because the temperature of the solar cell decreases the solar cell performance.

Through sampling and calculation, the maximum Power Point is tracked successfully by determining the step size according to the present and previous values of voltage and power variation to strike a balance between tracking time and tracking accuracy. Peng [8]. To solve the problem, variable-step size MPPT algorithms have been reported and they concluded the transient response of PI type P&O is the fastest among all. However, the complexity of this method is also the highest.

Santos et al. [9] proposed a traditional Perturbation and Observation to track the maximum power point (P&O) MPPT technique with trade-off between step-size, tracking-time and tracking-accuracy. The traditional P&O method sampled the voltage and current, and the power can be obtained by multiplying the two values. Farhat et al. [10]. Developed un algorithm based on the architecture Multi-layer Perceptron (MLP) to track real time, the maximum power point (MPPT). Maximum Power Point is a function of irradiance and temperature. In contrast, the PV systems must be designed to operate at their peak output power to extract and maintain the peak power of the PV panel even when climatic conditions are unfavorable. The obtained results show that the use of artificial neural networks present a precise estimate of the maximum power of PPV compared to the measured values.

Ramana et al. [11] described an MPPT algorithm to track the global peak out of many local peaks of PV module. The output of the PV array mainly depends on the irradiance and temperature where the non-uniform irradiance conditions occurs on PV module due to passing clouds, bird dropping, shadows etc. The MPPT algorithm tracks the global pick out of the many local peaks. The input to the PV array is irradiance and temperature of four modules and the output is the duty ratio. Pulse Width Modulator receives the duty ratio as input and generates pulses to the MOSFET of boost converter. Battery is used as load.

Wang et al. [12] defined an improved particle swarm optimization algorithm is proposed to track the maximum power point of the PV array when the PV array is partially shaded by object occlusion. The model of PV array is established, and simulation is carried out to verify the effectiveness of the algorithm. The method can avoid the local maximum and track the global maximum power point. Badis et al. [13] reported the conventional methods such as Perturb and Observe (P&O) and the Incremental Conductance and fails to extract the global MPP of the PV panel if the PV generator is partially shaded. They propose an Evolutionary Algorithms (AE), trough the Particle Swarm Optimization (PSO) and Genetic Algorithm (GA) is better. They developed an algorithm based in neural networks using MatLab software. Moreover, it is proven that PSO process mitigates more efficiently power losses caused by PS with lesser fluctuation and higher steady final output power.

2 Proposal

We propose an integrated prototype by an electronic circuit with two sensors for current and voltage (see Fig. 2). After they were used, two amplifier steps with integrated circuit LM308. The output signals of this amplifier are sent to analogical-digital converter. An electronic power circuit was designed [14] to drain up to 10 A which is coupled to the photovoltaic module, with the combination of analogic integrated circuits like TL081 and power transistor as MJ5529. A circuit generator was designed [15] to generate the random time to do the measurement. Tl081 integrated circuit, transistors as BC547, an electrolytic capacitor and several resistances were used. An electronic ramp voltage generator circuit was also designed [16] to activate the power circuit coupled to the PV module, using analogic integrated circuit MC308 combined with capacitors and resistance to get a time reference in which the electronic system can do the measurement This circuit was calibrated to get the range of 1 to 5 s so that the laptop can capture, the storage and processing of the electrical signals found during the measurement. Figure 3 showed the block diagram of this electronic circuit. Also the Arduino control target was used to link the electronics circuit with the laptop. For this, it is necessary to design the appropriate software based in Matlab.

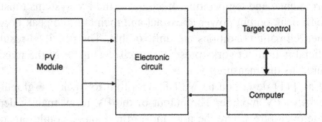

Fig. 2. Block diagram of proposed electronic system

3   Design of Electronic Circuit

The prototype proposed is integrated by electronic circuit, two sensors for current and voltage. After that, they were used as two amplifier steps with integrated circuit LM308 The output signals of this amplifier are sent to analogical-digital converter. An electronic power circuit was designed [14] to drain up to 10A which is coupled to the photovoltaic module, with the combination of analogic integrated circuits like TL081

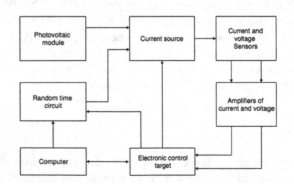

Fig. 3. Block diagram of the electronic circuit proposed

and power transistor as MJ5529. A circuit generator was designed [15] to generate the random time to do the measurement. Tl081 integrated circuit, transistors as BC547, an electrolytic capacitor and several resistances were used. An electronic ramp voltage generator circuit was also designed [16] to activate the power circuit coupled to the PV module, using analogic integrated circuit MC308 combined with capacitors and resistance to get a time reference in which the electronic system can do the measurement This circuit was calibrated to get the range of 1 to 5 s so that the laptop can capture, the storage and processing of the electrical signals found during the measurement. In Fig. 3 is showed the block diagram of this electronic circuit. Also, the Arduino control target was used to link the electronics circuit with the laptop. For this, it is necessary to design the appropriate software based in Matlab.

4 Software Design

For accessing the voltage and current signals, the Arduino electronic card was used between the developed electronic circuit and the PC and the software was designed guessing the following logical of the diagram on Fig. 4. The voltage signals were

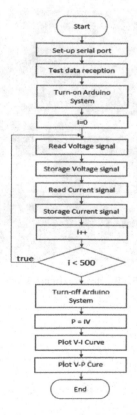

Fig. 4. Flowchart of proposed method to obtain the PV module maximum power

processed using Matlab software and an Arduino hardware was use in other to capture the electrical signal of current and voltage or PV module and transfer to laptop or computer where the electrical signals and determinate the characteristic curve or PV module.

5 Developing

All the analogies and integrated digital circuits, where signal transistors, resistances, and capacitors are installed, were assembled by a printed circuit board. The power transistor was installed on a heat sink because it works with 15 A of the current. The control target was used to link the electronic circuit designed with the computer. Both, electronics and control target are assembled into the cabinet. The electronic circuit developed is shown in Fig. 5. Also, a cabinet was used for the installation of the electric controls, as well as a digital display to show the values of current, voltage and power that are utilizing to measure efficiency in the photovoltaic module. Photovoltaic power meter prototype developed is shown in Fig. 6.

Fig. 5. Electronic circuit developed

Fig. 6. Photovoltaic power meter prototype developed.

6 Preliminaries Measurements

The maximum power, the I-V and P-V curves were measured with same level of incident solar power and room temperature. Several photovoltaic modules of different nominal powers were measured with the prototype developed. The measurements have done in a normal day and the incident solar power was changing around from 600 to 860 W/m^2. With the help of lux meter intensity (Solar power meter TES 1333R Datalogging), two PV modules of 20 W manufactured in CINVESTAV Mexico were used. The first measurement was done with one module and the second one was done with two modules connected in parallel. The short circuit current (*Isc*), open circuit voltage (*Voc*), maximum power (*Pm*), the maximum current (*Im*) and the Maximum voltage (*Vm*) of photovoltaic module were measured. The experimental results are shown in the Table 1.

Table 1. Shows the various parameters of PV module for the calculation of efficiency

PVm (W)	Light power (W/m^2)	I$_{scc}$ (A)	V$_{oc}$ (V)	I$_m$ (A)	V$_m$ (V)	Pm (W)
20	600	1.12	18.45	0.91	12.8	11.52
20	700	1.24	18.51	1.15	12.00	14.04
20	860	1.25	18.64	0.91	12.7	17.24
40	790	2.31	18.75	2.15	12.9	27.55
40	800	2.36	18.60	2.24	13.	30.52
40	820	2.4	18.82	2.35	13.6	31.42
40	850	2.42	19.25	2.3	14.20	32.30

Also, the I-V curve was measured. The previous results are showed in the Fig. 7.

Here, the power voltage curve of PV module was plotted with the same incident solar power was 700 W/m^2. The previous results are showed in the Fig. 8.

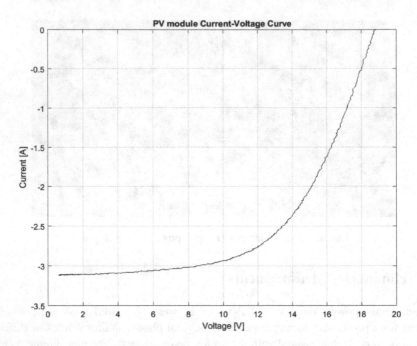

Fig. 7. I-V curve of PV module measured

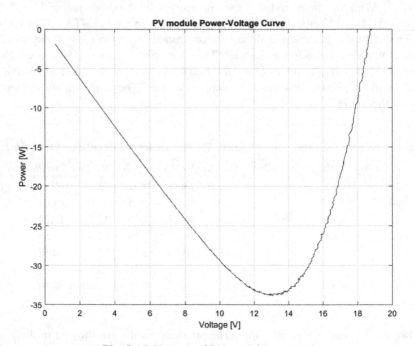

Fig. 8. P-V curve of PV module measured

7 Results and Discussion

Based on the experimental results of Table 1, it was found that the developed electronic prototype works correctly and can measure the maximum power of the photovoltaic module, and its current coordinates for varying levels of incident solar power. it is possible to see how voltage and power variables of the photovoltaic module were changed it was also confirmed by connecting two modules in parallel the current and power variables increased while the voltage was almost the same value as that of a only module.

In addition, it was observed that there was a greater change in current as a function of the incident light power, however, the voltage change was minimal, which corresponds to Eqs. 1 and 2 because the current changes exponentially while the voltage changes logarithmically. From the voltage-current curve reported in Fig. 2, it could be verified how the prototype developed can properly capture and process the current and voltage signals of the photovoltaic module, store the information and then measure the corresponding curve.

In the mentioned curve it was observed that the experimentally obtained curve starts from zero with the horizontal axis of voltage this is due to the fact that the measurement process of the photovoltaic module starts from the open circuit condition. On the other hand the curve does not touch the vertical axis of current that is because the electronic power circuit coupled to the photovoltaic module during the measurement has a minimum resistance of the order of 0.3 V, which causes a voltage drop of the order 0.6 V which prevents the curve from reaching the current axis. In relation to the voltage power curve of Fig. 3, it is verified that the computer program developed in Matlab which controls the measurement process works correctly because it is equal to the theoretical curve of Fig. 1, which verifies that the voltage current processing was right because it determines the power for all captured points.

However, it can be seen that the curve starts from the horizontal axis of voltage, which indicates that the measurement starts in the open circuit condition of the photovoltaic module but does not reach the crossing point or zero of the axes, therefore it reaches the short circuit condition, also due to the saturation of the power circuit of the prototype developed. The development of a method of measuring the maximum power of the photovoltaic module and its characteristic curves I-V and P-V propose is different of the proposed method. the purposed circuit is activated with a ramp voltage signal in contrast with the reported methods which use technics like oscillating voltage signal, pulse-width modulation, power signal derivation among others. Therefore, the measurement with the proposed prototype is more stable and the proposed computer program is simple. The proposed prototype can measure whatever photovoltaic module with any incident light power.

8 Conclusions

According with the experimental results, the electronic system developed works correctly and its experimental results are agreement with the theoretical method used in the design.

It is verified that the measurement technique of the photovoltaic module can be controlled with a ramp voltage signal, and it is not necessary to use sophisticated and complex methods such as those that have been reported. The electronic prototype has an error of around 2%, but it is possible to improve it by selects precision electronics devises and also by improving with the software. Although only 40 W power of modules was measured in our experiment, it can measure up to 100 W. The prototype was developed with electronics devices localized in Mexico; which is cheaper as well as very easy to manufacture.

Acknowledgments. The authors are thankful to National Polytechnic Institute from México, and also grateful to the project No. 20195869 SIP-IPN by their financial support.

References

1. Vega-Perez, J., Ponomaryov, V., Nino-de-Rivera, L.: Electronic system for power optimization of photovoltaic generator. Int. J. Electromagn. Waves Electron. Syst. **7–8**(8), 12–15 (2003)
2. Wanzeller, M., Cunha Alves, R., Fonseca Neto, J., dos Santos Fonseca, W.: Current control loop for tracking of maximum power point supplied for photovoltaic array. IEEE Trans. Instrum. Meas. **53**(4), 1304–1310 (2004)
3. Munji, M., Okullo, W., Van Dyk, E., Voster, F.: Local devise parameter extraction of a concentrator photovoltaic cell under solar spot illumination. Sol. Energy Mater. Sol. Cell **94**, 2129–2136 (2010)
4. Ashish, P., Nivedita, D., Ashok, K.: High-performance algorithms for drift avoidance and fast tracking in solar MPPT system. IEEE Trans. Energy Convers. **23**(2), 681–689 (2008)
5. Khatib, T., Ghareeb, A., Tamimi, M., Jaber, M., Jaradat, S.: A new offline method for extracting I-V characteristic curve for photovoltaic modules using artificial neural networks. Sol. Energy **173**, 462–469 (2018)
6. Danandeh, A., Mousavi, S.M.: Comparative and comprehensive review of maximum power point tracking methods for PV cells. Renew. Sustain. Energy Rev. **82**, 2743–2763 (2018)
7. Solimana, A., Hassana, H., Ookawara, S.: An experimental study of the performance of the solar cell with heat sink cooling system. Energy Proc. **162**, 127–135 (2019)
8. Peng, B., Chen, J., Liu, Y., Chiu, Y.: Comparison between three different types of variable step-size P&O MPPT technique. In: International Conference on Computer Information Systems and Industrial Applications (2015)
9. Santos, T., Galhardo, A., Perturbation, A.: Observation routine used to control a power converter. In: 2014 Sixth World Congress on Nature and Biologically Inspired Computing (NaBIC), pp. 78–83 (2014)
10. Farhat, S., Alaoui, R., Kahaji, A., Bouhouch, L.: Estimating the photovoltaic MPPT by artificial neural network. In: Proceedings of International Renewable and Sustainable Energy Conference (IRSEC), pp. 49–53 (2013)
11. Ramana, V., Jena, D.: Maximum power point tracking of PV array under nonuniform irradiance using artificial neural network. In: Proceedings of IEEE International Conference on Signal Processing, Informatics, Communication and Energy Systems (SPICES), pp. 1–5 (2015)

12. Wang, Y., Bian, N.: Research of MPPT control method based on PSO algorithm. In: Proceedings of the 4th International Conference on Computer Science and Network Technology (ICCSNT), pp. 698–701 (2015)
13. Badis, A., Mansouri, M., Sakly, A.: PSO and GA-based maximum power point tracking for partially shaded photovoltaic systems. In: Proceedings of 2016 7th International Renewable Energy Congress (IREC), pp. 1–6 (2016)
14. Rashid, M.: Power Electronics Handbook. Prentice Hall, Upper Saddle River (1999)
15. Malik, N.R.: Electronic Circuits: Analysis, Simulation, and Design. Prentice Hall, Upper Saddle River (1998)
16. Sedra, A.S., Smith, K.C.: Microelectronics Circuits. Oxford University Press, Oxford (1999)

Artificial Intelligence and Machine Learning

Clustering Methodology in Mixed Data Sets

Jacobo Gerardo González León[(⊠)] and Miguel Félix Mata Rivera[(⊠)]

Instituto Politécnico Nacional, Unidad Profesional Interdisciplinaria
en Ingeniería y Tecnologías Avanzadas, Avenida Instituto Politécnico Nacional
No. 2580, Col Barrio la Laguna Ticomán, Gustavo A. Madero,
07340 Mexico City, Mexico
jgonzalezll007@alumno.ipn.mx, mmatar@ipn.mx

Abstract. One of the most challenging tasks of data analysis is finding clusters in mixed data sets, as they have numerical and categorical variables, and lack a labeled variable to serve as a guide. These clusters could serve to summarize all the variables of a data set into one and be able to find information more easily than generating summarizations for each variable. In this research thesis, a methodology of clustering on mixed data sets is proposed, which yields better results than the methods applied in the state of the art.

Keywords: Clustering · Ensemble methods · Mixed data set

1 Introduction

At today the human activity generates data every time, the problem is what to do with them? How to find valuable information? As an interconnected technology society, we already have stable data structures, industrial algorithms, repositories of almost all topics, distributed computing to deal with large volumes but the problem remains, how to process them?

This paper begins with the assumption of the existence of a hidden phenomenon in these data sets that we will call a pattern [1]. The mathematic on which the data analysis is based is focused on finding this phenomenon. Due to the complexity of the high dimensions of the phenomena that describe our data sets, it is sometimes difficult with simple statistics to find this pattern. That is why science never stops working and keep looking for new ways to find information about the pattern hidden in our data because no method has the absolute truth.

Then a specific methodology is proposed to process, through unsupervised classification, mixed data sets through a series of steps, which lead us to satisfactory results as will be seen below, and which raises a new way of creating clusters beyond applying algorithms directly. The steps are quantified with stable metrics, and especially this methodology is intended to be usable in real problems.

The case study presented in this paper is the safe houses where the crime of kidnapping was committed, the complexity here was to integrate and process different mixed data sets from official surveys, to find valuable information that a specialist on issues of public safety you may be interested.

© Springer Nature Switzerland AG 2019
M. F. Mata-Rivera et al. (Eds.): WITCOM 2019, CCIS 1053, pp. 145–161, 2019.
https://doi.org/10.1007/978-3-030-33229-7_13

In order to propose a complete and novel methodology, an exploration of works related to "clustering for mixed data sets" in the formal scientific field in the 2013–2019 period corresponding to the 6 years prior to this proposal was made. The search term was the clustering ∩ mixed data, and 89 papers were found, of which only 14 are really related to the proposed work (10 algorithms, 2 methodologies and 2 implementations) because they meet the following criteria (see Table 1 where the works are summarized):

- Type of work: the contribution is explicitly mentioned.
- Algorithm or proposed model: the contribution is explained.
- Mixed data set: the data set used, and the source are mentioned.
- Comparison: the contribution is compared against other similar works.
- Evaluation: the results obtained are measured.

Table 1. Summary of related research papers found in the state-of-art.

Type of work	Algorithm or proposed model	Mixed data set	Evaluation
Modified algorithms	k-prototypes, FCM, Density Peaks	UCI MLR	Accuracy, F-measure, Rand Index
Methodologies	k-medoids, hierarchical clustering	Own case study	Dunn Index, Average Silhouette Width
Implementation	k-medoids	Own case study	Average Silhouette Width

2 Unsupervised Classification in Mixed Data Sets

2.1 Mixed Data Sets

A mixed data set is a collection of X data represented in a structured tabular way through an array of data of X rows, also called observations, instances, examples, objects, points, tuples, etc., by D columns, also called attributes, properties, variables, characteristics or dimensions and can be seen in Eq. 1 [2]:

$$X = \begin{pmatrix} & X_1 & X_2 & \ldots & X_D \\ x_1 & x_{11} & x_{12} & \ldots & x_{1D} \\ x_2 & x_{21} & x_{22} & \ldots & x_{2D} \\ \vdots & \vdots & \vdots & \ddots & \vdots \\ x_N & x_{N1} & x_{N2} & \ldots & x_{ND} \end{pmatrix} \tag{1}$$

In where $x_i = \{x_{1i}, x_{2i}, \ldots, x_{iD}\}$ are the observations, and $X_j = \{X_1, X_2, \ldots, X_D\}$ are the variables.

The main characteristic of mixed data sets is that the domain of their variables can take two types of values, numerical or categorical, also called quantitative and qualitative respectively; when a variable is numerical, its domain is of the real type, therefore, its values can be continuous or discrete, finite or infinite. Its elements can be part of any rational subset, integer, irrational or transcendent, then $\text{domain}(X_{\text{numerical}}) = \mathbb{R}$; when a variable is categorical, its domain has a set of finite symbols, its values can be numbers or characters that represent some category. These categorical can be of two types; nominal, when there is no order in the symbols, and ordinals, when, there is an order in the symbols, then $\text{domain}(X_{\text{categorical}}) = \{s_1, s_2, \ldots, s_n\}$.

2.2 Unsupervised Classification

The human being when trying to describe a phenomenon generates a series of rules or criteria, to understand the objects that describe its characteristics. Usually and given the properties of a specific object to the phenomenon, classifying the information provided by these objects, it may be useful to group these objects into categories to explain this phenomenon [3].

Classification systems based on machine learning can be supervised or unsupervised, it all depends on whether the characteristics of the object revolve around a specific characteristic or attribute, called labeled variable, or there is a lack of this variable, respectively. In the case of unsupervised classification, its objective is to separate a set of data into groups, based on the concept of similarity or dissimilarity, as the case may be, how similar or different are the objects?

This paper proposes the use of partition algorithms for unsupervised classification, this is based on the optimization of an objective function that will iteratively improve these partitions or clusters found. These algorithms have to be indicated the number of partitions or groups in which you want to group the data.

3 Proposed Methodology

The most common way to attack the problem of unsupervised classification in mixed data sets is through algorithms applied directly to the data, but in this research work, the hypothesis is through a specific methodology for this type of data set (see Fig. 1), could help in the search for clusters or groups in the data. Therefore, this thesis presents a methodology to find groupings of observations in mixed data sets through the pre-processing and application of an array arrangement of unsupervised partition classification algorithms.

Steps 1 and 2, *source* and *mixed data set*, are subjective since the data set can come from a specific experiment and the scientist who is analyzing the data, and they can have an accurate knowledge of the phenomenon that is wanted to find or may also be in exploration of the phenomenon.

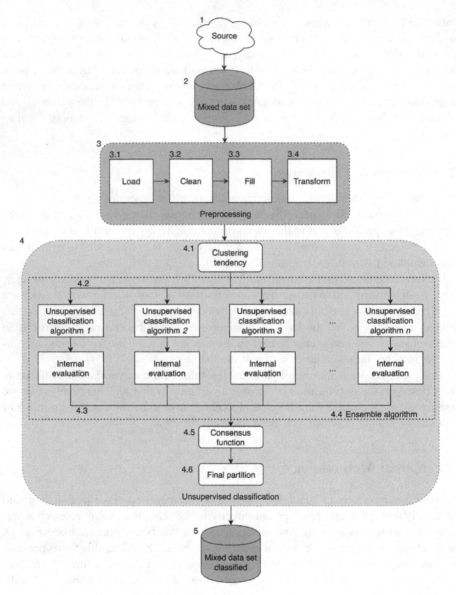

Fig. 1. General diagram of the proposed methodology.

3.1 Preprocessing

This step consists of 4 sub-phases, load, clean, fill and transform, which have the sequential sense to ensure the different actions: understanding the information, quality, integrity and homogeneity in the data.

The mixed data set must be loaded into the computer's memory to be able to analyze it, and regardless of the operating system. The cleaning of a data set is done so that the values correspond to the range of values that it should. One of the problems to which this step gives solution is to deal with erroneous, inconsistent, obsolete and/or redundant data. For this, it is proposed, with the help of metadata and/or prior knowledge of the subject, to search and count the unique values of each variable and compare the original domain with the current domain, in this way you can also easily detect outliers and extremes

Once the anomalies in the data have been cleared, and if it is the case that there are missing values, either spaces or any symbol that indicates a lack of data (NA, NaN, or NULL) this missing data can be filled. Although there are several conventional methods [4], among them, eliminating the rows that contain the missing values, or replacing the missing value with the average, you can also use predictive methods [5] based on supervised machine learning such as Linear Regression or Random Forest to complete this lack of values.

The last sub-phase of the preprocessing is a transformation of the data, this in order to normalize the domain in which the values of the variables are. As already mentioned before, a mixed data set has numerical and categorical variables, for each type there is a different transformation:

- Numerical: this transformation is made through the min-max normalization technique [6] with the minimum and maximum operations, respectively, which scales all values to a range between [0, 1], according to the following Eq. 2:

$$x_i := \frac{x_i - \min(X)}{\max(X) - \min(X)} \tag{2}$$

In where X is the vector of the numerical variable to transform, and x_i is the ith value of vector X.

- Categorical: this transformation replaces the symbolic values of the categories of a variable, the numerical values of its cumulative probability, and is based on the proposal of [7] through the following method:

  a. For each column of categorical data in the data set, the categories are sorted in descending order by frequency.
  b. Knowing the total observations, we find the probability p_{x_i} of each possible categorical value x_i through Eq. 3:

$$p_{x_i} = \frac{f_{x_i}}{N} \tag{3}$$

  In where x_i is the ith value of the variable x; f_{x_i} is the frequency of observations of the ith value of the variable x; and N is the total number of observations.

  c. The categorical value is replaced by the value of its cumulative probability a_{x_i} through Eq. 4:

$$a_{x_i} := \sum_i p_{x_i} \tag{4}$$

3.2   Unsupervised Classification

This step consists of 6 sub-phases, clustering tendency, unsupervised classification algorithms, internal evaluation, ensemble algorithm, consensus function, and final partition. The internal evaluation sub-phases, unsupervised classification algorithms, consensus function are found in an assembly structure, this structure combines different algorithms and with a consensus function chooses the best partition within those generated by the assembly.

Clustering Tendency

One of the first tasks when working with clustering data sets is to be able to measure if it has relevant groups, that is, if there are the "grouping" conditions in the data set to be analyzed. And although there is still no formal term, in [8] a "grouping function" is defined as one that can quantify the degree of "grouping structures", in other words, find out whether or not the data set has groups significant.

Unsupervised Classification Algorithms

Beginning from the theorem "No free lunch" [9], which says that there is no "better" machine learning algorithm that can solve a problem in a superior way because beyond the proposed optimization function, it is true that Each set of data is unique in dimensions, variables, and values. Then the grouping of the observations proposed in this thesis is through an assembly of unsupervised partition classification algorithms [10].

The unsupervised classification algorithms called "by partition" try to discover groups in the data sets by optimizing a specific function and iteratively improving the quality of these partitions [11] These algorithms require that they be previously indicated the number k of groups, to begin measuring, the distance between observations and these groups, is for this reason that this class of algorithms is also called "prototype" or "distance-based".

In two or three dimensions there is not much difficulty in proposing the initial value of the k clusters, because this parameter can be assigned visually, but in high dimensions, it is difficult to define this value. That is why internal evaluation is proposed, to find the best value objectively and measurably.

Internal Evaluation

Clustering is an unsupervised classification [12] that is, these algorithms attempt to find an intrinsic structure in the data sets, and although there are different types of algorithms of unsupervised classification, this structure commonly meets the similarity of the data. This type of unsupervised classification techniques is applied to data sets with no dependent variable, that is, they do not have a variable to predict.

In terms of accuracy and precision, and unlike the supervised classification, where this dependent variable is used to assess how much the model or algorithm approximated the generalization of the data [13], in clustering it cannot be measured in the same way, unless a priori the data set has the target variable and what you want, for example, is to find perhaps what are the "true groups" or "true classification" [14] by comparing the partition found against the classification original of the dependent variable.

The evaluation of the found partitions of a mixed data set without labeling variable, with unsupervised classification techniques, is called "internal evaluation" or "internal measure" and is used to evaluate the quality of the partitions that are generated. Testing different values of k [15] and measuring the quality of the partition, which found the unsupervised classification algorithm that was used, through the similarity within the groups and the separation between them, you can find this evaluation, commonly through an internal evaluation index that is expressed by reason (intra-group)/(inter-group) [16]. For example, in [17] 27 internal evaluation indices are proposed, whose value is the maximization or minimization of this ratio; the best partition generated will then be the one that can have the least compactness within its groups, and the highest among the separability among all.

Ensemble Algorithm

An ensemble of unsupervised classification algorithms and a heuristic that evaluate different values of k and different unsupervised classification algorithms are proposed in the following pseudocode:

```
Let k={1, 2, 3, ..., n} be the number of proposed groupings,
a={1, 2, 3,...,m} the different algorithms of unsupervised
partition classification, pₘ the current partition gener-
ated, i the index internal evaluation, eₘ the value of
the internal evaluation index, and vₘ=[∅, ∅, ∅,∅] a vali-
dation matrix:
For each value kₙ evaluate:
   For each aₘ algorithm evaluate:
```

$$p_m \leftarrow a_m(k_n)$$
$$e_m \leftarrow i(p_m)$$
$$v_m \leftarrow [k_n, a_m, p_m, e_m]$$

Consensus Function

Once you have the validation matrix $v_m[k_n, a_m, p_m, e_m]$, a decision function $f(v_m)$ will decide which is the best partition, by maximizing or minimizing the value of the internal evaluation index e_m for each proposed group k_n, in the following pseudocode is showed a consensus function that maximizes:

```
Let vm, a validation matrix, and which.max(·) be a deci-
sion function that returns the position of the maximum
value, posmax a variable position, k the best partition, a
the best algorithm, p the best partition, and e the best
value of the internal evaluation index:
```

$pos_{max} \leftarrow which.max(e_m)$

$k \leftarrow v_m[k_m][pos_{max}]$

$a \leftarrow v_m[a_m][pos_{max}]$

$p \leftarrow v_m[p_m][pos_{max}]$

$e \leftarrow v_m[e_m][pos_{max}]$

3.3 Case Study

The phenomenon that was proposed to investigate to find groups of observations with the proposed methodology for mixed data sets are: the safe houses where the crime of kidnapping was committed. The data of these security houses were found using the web scrapping extraction technique, searching for information in the following Mexican news sites: Proceso, La Prensa, Reforma, and El Universal; extracting the following information: site, link, year, colony, municipality, and state. The address of each safe house was found with the concatenation of the colony, municipality, and state variables.

Once the address of the safe houses was extracted, a geocoding function was applied to the address of each safe house to find its latitude and longitude. With 21 safety houses, a sample of 5 observations is presented in Table 2.

Table 2. Sample of 5 safe houses found.

Colony	Municipality	Latitude	Longitude
Desarrollo Urbano Quetzalcóatl	Iztapalapa	19.3263221	−99.050701
La Conchita Zapotitla	Tláhuac	19.3068385	−99.043425
Casas Alemán	Gustavo A. Madero	19.4783912	−99.089195
Manzanatitlán	Cuajimalpa	19.367977	−99.299582
Agrícola Oriental	Iztacalco	19.3956912	−99.088798

Figure 2 shows these security houses found on the map of Mexico City in the 2016–2017 period, in total 21 security houses were found distributed in 10 of the 16 municipalities.

The data found from the safe houses when being extracted from news do not come with some extra information, beyond the address, that would allow us to be able to identify the reason for the phenomenon, so it was devised to integrate different sets of data that had characteristics of the geography where these houses were found, in order to discover information.

Fig. 2. Map of the safe houses found in Mexico City.

According to the methodology developed in this thesis, these data must come from an official source. Therefore, it was chosen to take open data from regular household surveys of the Instituto Nacional de Estadística y Geografía (INEGI). Each of these surveys is a set of mixed data, as there are questions with binary, or categorical answers, as well as numerical data such as age, or amounts of money.

After completing the preprocessing phase proposed in the methodology, the mixed data sets from the resulting surveys are shown in Table 3. Once the preprocessed mixed data sets are done, in this case 5: HOGARES, SDEMT, TMOD, TPER_VIC1, VIVIENDA, the unsupervised classification can start.

Table 3. Description of the variables of the surveys found.

Survey	Mixed data set	Numerical	Categorical	Observations
ENIGH	Household information (HOGARES)	10	65	1,733
ENOE	Sociodemographic information (SDEMT)	5	63	76,397
ENVIPE	Victimization information (TMOD_VIC)	2	10	5,098
ENVIPE	Perception of security information (TPER_VIC1)	1	118	6,203
ENH	Housing information (VIVIENDA)	8	53	3,588

3.4   Implementation

To begin with the measurement of the clustering tendency of mixed data sets, Hopkins statistics were proposed [18] since this test that determines whether a data set has a random structure, that is, measures the probability that the data set comes from a uniform distribution of data. If the data sets do not come from a uniform distribution of data, it may contain well segmented groups.

In [19] they review the unsupervised classification algorithms used over 20 years, including partition algorithms, so it was proposed to use the k-means k-modes and k-medoids algorithms. These algorithms have the particularity that the main parameter is to indicate the k groups, so, according to this methodology, an internal evaluation index is needed to find this number k.

The proposed internal evaluation index is the Dunn index [20] since it measures the separation between groups, seeking the maximization of this inter-cluster distance, and cohesion within the groups, seeking the minimization of intra-cluster distance. The decision function will then be the maximization of this Dunn index [21] the larger the Dunn index, the better the partition found. The index implementation could be beneficial to find the optimal number of the k groups needed for the assembly algorithms since this number of k could vary between 1, the case where the whole mixed data set is a group, and N, where each observation is a different group.

4   Results

Earlier in the last chapter it was already mentioned, that the integration of information to the case study "safe houses" is explored to describe this phenomenon, with an unsupervised classification approach. It was also mentioned what is the source and mixed data sets chosen for analysis, 5 surveys with different topics.

After processing the mixed data sets, the result of the clustering trend measurement can be seen in Table 4.

Table 4. Result of the clustering tendency in mixed data sets from INEGI surveys.

Mixed data set	Clustering tendency: Hopkins statistics	
	Without methodology	With methodology
HOGARES	0.0461	0.3746
SDEMT	0.00814	0.2422
TMOD_VIC	0.0464	0.3759
TPERC_VIC1	0.1925	0.4908
VIVIENDA	0.1664	0.3552

Once it was measured how many significant groups, through the grouping trend, can be found in these data sets, the unsupervised classification was performed with the help of the algorithm assembly. Table 5 shows the result of the evaluation of the Dunn index of the assembly of unsupervised classification algorithms proposed in the methodology, against the algorithms that were found are used in the state-of-the-art k-medoids and k-prototypes.

Table 5. Result of internal evaluation in mixed data sets from INEGI surveys.

Mixed data set	Internal evaluation: Maximum Dunn Index				
	Without methodology		With methodology		
	k-medoids	k-prototypes	k-means	k-medoids	k-modes
HOGARES	0.1040	1.94e−05	0.3872	0.0598	0.2326
Clusters	10	9	4	2	2
SDEMT	0.1810	7.0460e−06	0.6779	0.0515	0.6779
Clusters	2	2	2	10	2
TMOD_VIC	0.0271	0.0238	0.0334	0.0162	0.0331
Clusters	3	3	6	2	3
TPERC_VIC1	0.0078	0.0083	0.2458	0.1959	0.2884
Clusters	4	4	2	10	9
VIVIENDA	0.0819	0.0064	0.1892	0.1091	0.1302
Clusters	2	3	3	3	2

The unsupervised classification, through the algorithm assembly, proposed in the methodology of this thesis, is designed to evaluate a set of mixed data at the same time. The result of the unsupervised classification can be visualized the different groups found with the help of the Principal Components Analysis (PCA) technique.

In Fig. 3 the different groups can be displayed, as well as the map of Mexico City, the delegations belonging to each group found from the HOGARES survey, and Table 6 shows a sample of 5 variables that characterize each group found.

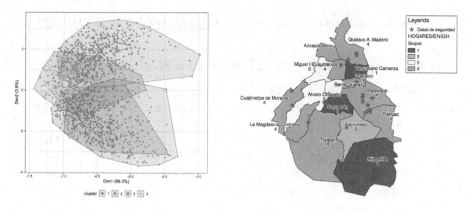

Fig. 3. Visualization of the groups found of the mixed data set HOGARES.

Table 6. Sample of 5 variables of the groups found in the mixed data set HOGARES.

Survey: HOGARES					
Variables	acc_alim1	acc_alim3	acc_alim6	alim17_2	alim17_4
Cluster	Meaning				
	Worry meal is over	Limited variety of food	Number of days they ate egg	Number of days they ate meat	Number of days they ate fruits
1	No	No	2	2	7
2	Yes	Yes	3	2	2
3	No	No	2	7	7
4	No	No	3	3	7

In Fig. 4 the different groups can be displayed, as well as the map of Mexico City, the delegations belonging to each group found from the SDEMT survey, and Table 7 shows a sample of 5 variables that characterize each group found.

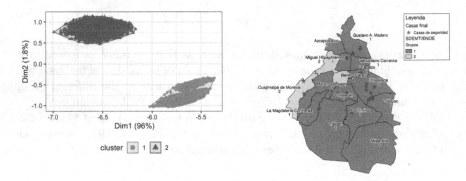

Fig. 4. Visualization of the groups found of the mixed data set SDEMT.

Table 7. Sample of 5 variables of the groups found in the mixed data set SDEMT.

Survey: SDEMT					
Variables	Sex	eda	cs_p13_1	cs_p17	e_con
Cluster	Meaning				
	Sex	Age	What degree did the school approve?	Do you currently attend school?	Marital status
1	Woman	21	Elementary	Yes	Single
2	Man	40	Undergraduate	No	Married

In Fig. 5 the different groups can be displayed, as well as the map of Mexico City, the delegations belonging to each group found from the TMOD_VIC survey, and Table 8 shows a sample of 3 variables that characterize each group found.

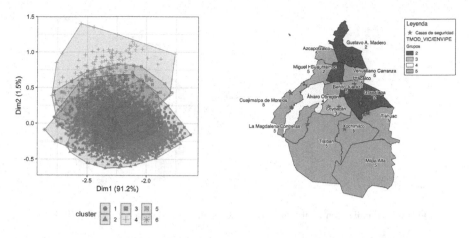

Fig. 5. Visualization of the groups found of the mixed data set TMOD_VIC.

Table 8. Sample of 3 variables of the groups found in the mixed data set TMOD_VIC.

Survey: TMOD_VIC			
Variables	BP1_1	BP1_5	BP1_3C
Cluster	Meaning		
	What month did the crime happen?	Where place did the crime happen?	In which municipality did the crime occur?
1	May	On the street	Álvaro Obregón
2	February	On the street	Iztapalapa
3	December	On the street	Iztapalapa
4	December	In his house	Álvaro Obregón
5	August	On the street	Benito Juárez
6	December	In his house	Cuauhtémoc

In Fig. 6 the different groups can be displayed, as well as the map of Mexico City, the delegations belonging to each group found from the TPER_VIC1 survey, and Table 9 shows a sample of 3 variables that characterize each group found.

In Fig. 7 the different groups can be displayed, as well as the map of Mexico City, the delegations belonging to each group found from the VIVIENDAS survey, and Table 10 shows a sample of 5 variables that characterize each group found.

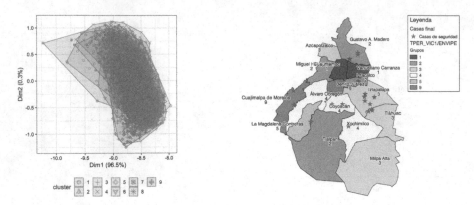

Fig. 6. Visualization of the groups found of the mixed data set TPER_VIC1.

Table 9. Sample of 3 variables of the groups found in the mixed data set TPER_VIC1.

Survey: TPER_VIC1			
Variables	AP4_10_01	AP4_10_04	AP4_10_06
Cluster	Meaning		
	For fear of being a victim of a crime, did you stop going out at night?	For fear of being a victim of a crime, did you stop taking a taxi?	For fear of being a victim of a crime, did you stop carrying cash?
1	Yes	No	Yes
2	No	No	No
3	Yes	No	Yes
4	No	No	No
5	No	No	Yes
6	No	No	No
7	No	No	Yes
8	No	No	No
9	Yes	Yes	Yes

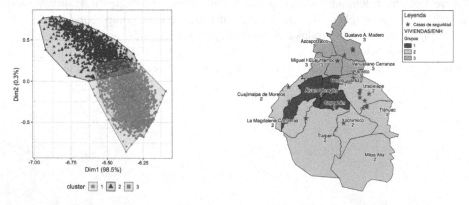

Fig. 7. Visualization of the groups found of the mixed data set VIVIENDAS.

Table 10. Sample of 5 variables of the groups found in the mixed data set VIVIENDAS.

Survey: VIVIENDAS					
Variables	antiguedad	tipo_viv	num_cuarto	cuart_dorm	auto_pick
Cluster	Meaning				
	Housing age	Type of housing	Number of rooms	Bedroom	Own car availability
1	27	Independent house	5	2	Yes
2	25	Independent house	3	1	No
3	32	Department	4	2	Yes

5 Discussion

With only the information from the mixed data sets from the INEGI surveys in Table 3, we could begin to generate hypotheses about how many groups these data sets could have. For example, from the SDEMT table that contains more observations, we might think that there are many more groups than the others, or that the HOGARES table that contains fewer observations, there are few groups. So, when we apply the methodology, we realize that only two groups were found in the SDEMT survey, while four groups were found in the HOGARES survey. There is not yet a rule that, depending on the number of observations or variables, so many groups will be obtained, which is why the unsupervised classification exists and makes sense, to propose this number of partitions in the data that at first glance cannot be defined. Also, with the basic information of the groups for each mixed data set, summaries could be made with their variables. but summary tables should be made for each variable that contains the mixed data set, this can take a long time and many tables, so it might not be useful.

One advantage of finding clusters in the data is to simplify this task to only one table, as for example, in the case of Table 6 of the first HOGARES survey analyzed. It is the case similar to wanting to see on a map the characteristics of each delegation, the same number of maps would have to be made to be able to visualize all the variables, as is the case of Fig. 3 of the HOGARES survey, where the map is seen with the delegations belonging to each group found, it is easier to read and interpret the variables of a mixed data set, based on the groups found with this methodology.

Then the interpretation for each of the data sets, based on the question: which delegations do not have safe houses? You can respond by summarizing the groups found. Even with the methodology supported by the different measurements that are made, questions remain that perhaps only an expert on the subject could answer. Questions like if the groups found have any interest value? Or in what range of k clusters should the heuristics of the algorithm assembly be run?

5.1   Conclusion and Future Work

This work is aimed to improve the search for groups in mixed data sets based on a review of the state of the art, to see how the unsupervised classification of their observations was being done. A methodology was then proposed with a series of steps that show a better generation of groups, than simply applying an algorithm to these data sets. The results obtained from the implementation of this methodology, in the case of study and the extension, are satisfactory and show that they improve the creation of groups.

To find the best partition, or the best groups, Hopkins's statistics were proposed so that before processing, one could know what the distribution of the data set is like, because if it has a uniform nature, few groups could be found, and if it has a non-uniform nature, significant groups could be found. This can be seen in the case of the SDEMT survey, which was the least valuable data set, almost 0 and only 2 groups were found; contrary to the TPERC_VIC1 survey, which was the most valuable data set, almost 0.5 and 9 groups were found. This number of clusters was found with the maximization of the Dunn index, which, the larger, is interpreted as which better groups have been created.

As future work, more internal validation rates, other measures to evaluate the clustering tendency, could be integrated, as well as other real mixed data sets to continue measuring the effectiveness of this methodology.

References

1. Ströing, P.: Scientific Phenomena and Patterns in Data. Ludwig-Maximilians-Universität, München (2018)
2. Zaki, M.J., Meira, W.: Data Mining and Analysis. Cambridge University Press, Cambridge (2014)
3. Bramer, M.: Principles of Data Mining. Springer, London (2016). https://doi.org/10.1007/978-1-4471-7307-6
4. Soley-Bori, M.: Dealing with missing data: key assumptions and methods for applied analysis, vol. 23. Boston University (2013)
5. Yadav, M., Roychoudhury, B.: Handling missing values: a study of popular imputation packages in R. Knowl.-Based Syst. **160**, 104–118 (2018)
6. Larose, D., Larose, C.: Discovering Knowledge in Data: An Introduction to Data Mining, 2nd edn. Wiley, Hoboken (2014)
7. Patki, N., Wedge, R., Veeramachaneni, K.: The synthetic data vault. In: IEEE International Conference on Data Science and Advanced Analytics (DSAA), pp. 399–410. IEEE (2016)
8. Adolfsson, A., Ackerman, M., Brownstein, N.: To cluster, or not to cluster: an analysis of clusterability methods. Pattern Recogn. **88**, 13–26 (2019)
9. McCue, C.: Public-safety-specific evaluation. In: Data Mining and Predictive Analysis: Intelligence Gathering and Crime Analysis, pp. 157–183. Butterworth-Heinemann (2015)
10. Wu, X., Ma, T., Cao, J., Tian, Y., Alabdulkarim, A.: A comparative study of clustering ensemble algorithms. Comput. Electr. Eng. **68**, 603–615 (2018)
11. Jukes, E.: Encyclopedia of machine learning and data mining (2nd edition). Ref. Rev. **32**, 3–4 (2018)

12. Loshin, D.: Knowledge discovery and data mining for predictive analytics. In: Business Intelligence. The Savvy Manager's Guide MK Series on Business Intelligence, 2nd edn., pp. 271–286 (2013)
13. Tharwat, A.: Classification assessment methods. Appl. Comput. Inform. (2018)
14. Hennig, C.: What are the true clusters? Pattern Recogn. Lett. **64**, 53–62 (2015)
15. Gurrutxaga, I., Muguerza, J., Arbelaitz, O., Pérez, J., Martín, J.: Towards a standard methodology to evaluate internal cluster validity indices. Pattern Recogn. Lett. **32**, 505–515 (2011)
16. Jauhiainen, J., Kärkkäinen, S.: Comparison of internal clustering validation indices for prototype-based clustering. Algorithms **10**, 105 (2017)
17. Desgraupes, B.: Clustering Indices. University of Paris Ouest-Lab Modal'X, vol. 1, pp. 34 (2013)
18. Han, J., Kamber, M., Pei, J.: Cluster analysis: basic concepts and methods. In: Data Mining, pp. 443–495 (2012)
19. Benabdellah, A., Benghabrit, A., Bouhaddou, I.: A survey of clustering algorithms for an industrial context. Proc. Comput. Sci. **148**, 291–302 (2019)
20. Rodriguez, M., Comin, C., Casanova, D., Bruno, O., Amancio, D., Costa, L., Rodrigues, F.: Clustering algorithms: a comparative approach. PLoS One **14**, e0210236 (2019)
21. Yang, Y.: Temporal Data Mining via Unsupervised Ensemble Learning. Elsevier Science, Amsterdam (2016)

American Sign Language
Electromiographic Alphabet
Sign Translator

Edgar-Armando Catalan-Salgado[✉], Cristhian Lopez-Ramirez,
and Roberto Zagal-Flores

Instituto Politecnico Nacional (IPN), Escuela Superior de Cómputo (ESCOM),
Av. Juan de Dios Batiz s/n, GAM, Mexico City, Mexico
{ecatalans,rzagalf}@ipn.mx, cristhlopram@gmail.com

Abstract. Communication between people is complicated, thus is due
to correct idea and thought expression. But for the deaf or mute people
this is even worse due to that our main communication channel is sound.
They can use their own language using sign and ideograms made with
hands, called American Sign Language. But as every language it is needed
to learn and the population that dominate this language is small. In this
work we propose an American Sign Language translator for 24 alphabet
signs, using a wearable that give us eight electromiographic signals and
KNN classifier for signs processing with 80% of accuracy.

Keywords: American Sign Language · KNN · Pattern recognition ·
Artificial intelligence and health

1 Introduction

Communication is in some way complicated between different beings. Correct
ideas, thoughts and desires transmission is not ever correctly or fully realized.
But this is even harder for impaired people, particularly deaf or mute people,
this is due to the fact that spoken language is our main communication language.

Disability is a result between people with impairments and the barriers that
arises due to attitudes and environment that restrain them for the fully participation in society [7,8]. In Mexico, this definition is specified for people with
some physical, mental, intellectual or sensorial deficiency [5].

Already exists a variety of languages that only uses hands signs and move-
ment to establish communication, one of them is called American Sign Language
(ASL) [1], is mainly used by deaf or mute people and his family or near friends.
But find other people that dominates this language can be a challenge.

In this paper we establish a novel method to translate the signs corresponding to the ASL alphabet to text, in order to give the opportunity to establish
communication for impaired people.

© Springer Nature Switzerland AG 2019
M. F. Mata-Rivera et al. (Eds.): WITCOM 2019, CCIS 1053, pp. 162–170, 2019.
https://doi.org/10.1007/978-3-030-33229-7_14

Automatic sign recognition is a well established problem and exist different approaches in literature. First of all, it is necessary to consider the gesture components such as hand shape, location and movement [2].

Many artificial vision systems have been developed in [2, 9–11], nevertheless they are based on a camera using and lighting dependency. In other words, their performance is affected on situation where there is high or a low illumination. For example, when a leap motion controller (LMC) is used that uses a combination of 2 cameras to make a three-dimensional reproduction of hands and their space movement [3], using this sensor and considering 26 alphabet letter, *Chang et al.* produces 80.30% of accuracy using a Support Vector Machine (SVN), but using a deep neural network (DNN) a 93.81% of performance is developed.

An alternative to vision artificial systems is the use of forearms wearables and uses electromiographic and motion sensors. An example of this is the Myo Arm band, which one deliver Inertial and Electromiographic (EMG) data. This kind of wearable approach have already been used in previous research, particulary Fatmi et al. [4] used two myo arm band devices, one for each forearm, and considering the IMU and EMG data as time series tested Artificial Neural Networks (ANN), Support Vector Machines (SVM) and Hidden Markov Models (HMM) with a mean accuracy of 93.79, 85.56, and 85.9 respectively.

We used as input eight electromiographic signals, given for EMG sensors of a Myo Arm Band in the right forearm person. Each one signal was preprocessed getting a *muscle activation parameter*. Using the eight activation parameter as feature vector for each sign a KNN classifier was used. Experimentation using 24 signs of ASL alphabet deliver a 80% accuracy.

2   American Sign Language

A sign language uses visual-manual modality to convey meaning [14]. It is expressed through manual articulations and full fledged natural languages with its own grammar and lexicon [12]. Wherever a deaf people exist a version of sign language arises. The 2013 edition of Ethnologue list 137 sign languages [6].

American Sign Language (ASL) is an the predominant sign language used mainly by deaf and mute community in United Sates and canada [13], with a user number range between 250,000 and 500,000 persons. It consist in signs and ideograms, made with hands and specific movements that transfer a specific letter or idea. ASL possesses 26 signs know as the American Manual Alphabet that are shown in Fig. 1. Fingerspelling or dactilology is the representation of the letters of a writing system and numcral systems using only the hands. In ASL, fingerspelling is used for proper nouns, abbreviations and for technical terms with no native ASL equivalent.

3   Electromiographic Sensors

Electromyography (EMG) and nerve conduction study (NCS), are tests that use electrodes to detect, translate, and record the electrical signals in muscles

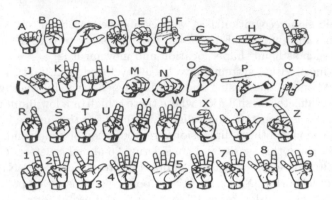

Fig. 1. American Sign Language Alphabet

and nerve cells, generally used by specialist in order to determine the causes of diseases that affect muscles and nerves, but lately have been used to make automatic ASL translation.

Between the commercial grade devices, the Myo Arm band excels over others, it have a EMG sensors and Inertial Movement Unit (IMU), at a relative low price, the wearable is shown in Fig. 2.

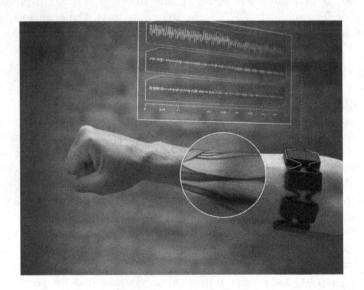

Fig. 2. Myo arm band

Data collected is transmitted to a compatible device using bluetooth, IMU data at 50 Hz and EMG data at 200 Hz. In synthesis, IMU data collect information from a three axis giroscope, three axis magnetometer and three axis accelerometer; EMG collect information of eight EMG sensors, delivered as a byte array of eight elements whose values are between -128 and 127 and unitless. So trough a time the signals would be as shown in Fig. 3.

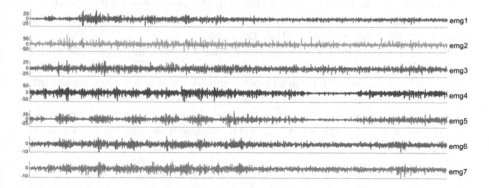

Fig. 3. Sensors values in time

4   Method

When we made a sign, the position of our fingers, hand and wrist changes. Thus undoubtedly changes the tension of our forearm muscles, changing also the *emg* signals. So theoretically the combination of the eight signal values in time t can represent a sign, but can't be directly used due to their oscillating nature, so a processing is needed in order to be useful as a muscle activation measure.

As a muscle activation measure for a given time t, a standard deviation σ of each sensor s is calculated for the period $[t-n,\ t]$, where n is a period size. This is calculated as follows:

$$\bar{x}_t^s = \sum_{i=t-n}^{t} \tag{1}$$

$$\sigma_t^s = \sqrt{\frac{\sum_{i=t-n}^{t}(x_i^s - \bar{x}_t^s)^2}{n-1}} \tag{2}$$

With this we can get the following row vector in a given time t:

$$X_t = \left[\sigma_t^1, \sigma_t^2, \sigma_t^3, \sigma_t^4, \sigma_t^5, \sigma_t^6, \sigma_t^7, \sigma_t^8\right] \tag{3}$$

For sign recognition purposes the time is not needed, so we can take it out from vector showed in *3*, and let it as follows:

$$X = \left[\sigma^1, \sigma^2, \sigma^3, \sigma^4, \sigma^5, \sigma^6, \sigma^7, \sigma^8\right] \tag{4}$$

This vector can be interpreted as a measure of the forearm muscles activation detected by each sensor s. Graphically this abstraction can be observed in Fig. 4. Some things worthy to remark are:

First, the mean value is almost zero for every sensor.

Second, the range values is not the same in this case for some is $[-10, 10]$, for others $[-25, 25]$ and for others $[-50, 50]$, but according to technic specifications could be any possible between $[-127, 127]$.

Third, exist a correlation between value range of each sensor, and the muscles used to make a sign.

Finally, by definition, high variations in considered window time would bring high values in standard deviations values.

From previous points our theory is that we can use standard deviation values as a measure of muscle activation in a given window time, and used it to classify hand signs.

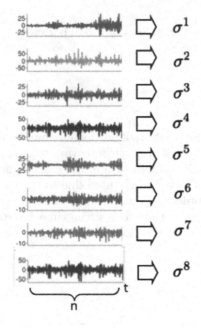

Fig. 4. Standard deviation in a range $[t-n, t]$

4.1   Classifier

For simplicity a KNN classifier was used for testing, due to is a easy algorithm and doesn't have parameters that can alter or bias to the final classification, allowing a general behaviour. In this case, we used the value 1 for K parameter.

4.2   Learning Phase

The number of signs taking in account is 24. Then, an index $g \exists [1, 24]$ is defined and each sign can be addressed by g. The KNN clustering algorithm is used for one sample per sign, in order to create a matrix of 24 rows and 8 columns. This strategy allows to simplify the learning phase.

The learning algorithm is defined as follows:

1. Get X vector for each sign g.

$$X_g = [\sigma_g^1, \sigma_g^2, \sigma_g^3, \sigma_g^4, \sigma_g^5, \sigma_g^6, \sigma_g^7, \sigma_g^8] \tag{5}$$

2. Introducing Xg in KNN matrix:

$$m_{g,i} = x_g^i \tag{6}$$

In this way the matrix M becomes in:

$$M = \begin{bmatrix} \sigma_1^1, & \sigma_1^2, & \sigma_1^3, & \sigma_1^4, & \sigma_1^5, & \sigma_1^6, & \sigma_1^7, & \sigma_1^8 \\ & & & \cdots & & & \\ \sigma_g^1, & \sigma_g^2, & \sigma_g^3, & \sigma_g^4, & \sigma_g^5, & \sigma_g^6, & \sigma_g^7, & \sigma_g^8 \\ & & & \cdots & & & \\ \sigma_{24}^1, & \sigma_{24}^2, & \sigma_{24}^3, & \sigma_{24}^4, & \sigma_{24}^5, & \sigma_{24}^6, & \sigma_{24}^7, & \sigma_{24}^8 \end{bmatrix} \tag{7}$$

4.3   Recall Phase

A euclidean distance d is used to recall, due to the fact that for each sign g only exists one input in the KNN matrix M, then a 1-NN classifier was chosen.

The recall algorithm is:

1. Get the X vector for the unknown sign

$$X = [\sigma^1, \sigma^2, \sigma^3, \sigma^4, \sigma^5, \sigma^6, \sigma^7, \sigma^8] \tag{8}$$

2. Get the euclidean distance to each one of the learned patterns.

$$d(x, m_g) = \sqrt{\sum_{i=1}^{8} (x^i - m_g^i)^2} \tag{9}$$

3. Assign as output class those whose $d(x, m_g)$ is the minimum.

5   Experiments and Results

The signs corresponding to the letters j and z was excluded due that they need some hand movement. Also the numbers was excluded and would be considered in future work. So the remaining 24 signs in the ASL alphabet are the letters that the classifier can recognize as the possible output classes.

First of all a time window n = 20 is considered in order to get the standard deviations.

For training phase the X vector of standard deviation was obtained for each one of the 24 sign considered and learned with the KNN.

For recall phase ten different instances of each sign from the same user is considered. For each one the X vector of standard deviations is obtained and tested with with the KNN.

As validating method a confusion matrix is used, this is due to additional information about the algorithm behaviour that can be achieved by this matrix. Due to the matrix confusion size this was divided in three parts of seven signs each one, showed in Tables 1, 2 and 3.

Table 1. Confusion Matrix part 1, a–h

X	a	b	c	d	e	f	g	h	i	k	l	m	n	o	p	q	r	s	t	u	v	w	x	y	%
a	10	0	0	0	0	0	0	0	0	0	0	0	0	0	0	0	0	0	0	0	0	0	0	0	100
b	0	4	0	0	0	5	0	0	0	0	0	0	0	0	0	0	0	0	0	0	0	0	1	0	40
c	0	0	2	0	0	0	0	0	0	0	0	0	0	0	0	0	0	8	0	0	0	0	0	0	20
d	0	0	0	5	0	0	0	0	5	0	0	0	0	0	0	0	0	0	0	0	0	0	0	0	50
e	0	0	0	0	9	0	0	0	1	0	0	0	0	0	0	0	0	0	0	0	0	0	0	0	90
f	0	6	0	0	0	4	0	0	0	0	0	0	0	0	0	0	0	0	0	0	0	0	0	0	40
g	0	0	0	0	0	0	10	0	0	0	0	0	0	0	0	0	0	0	0	0	0	0	0	0	100
h	0	0	0	0	0	0	0	10	0	0	0	0	0	0	0	0	0	0	0	0	0	0	0	0	100

Table 2. Confusion Matrix part 2, i–q

X	a	b	c	d	e	f	g	h	i	k	l	m	n	o	p	q	r	s	t	u	v	w	x	y	%
i	0	0	0	0	0	0	0	0	10	0	0	0	0	0	0	0	0	0	0	0	0	0	0	0	100
k	0	0	0	0	2	0	0	0	0	0	0	0	0	2	0	0	6	0	0	0	0	0	0	0	0
l	0	0	0	0	0	0	0	0	0	0	10	0	0	0	0	0	0	0	0	0	0	0	0	0	100
m	0	0	0	0	0	0	0	0	0	0	0	8	0	0	0	0	0	2	0	0	0	0	0	0	80
n	0	0	0	0	0	0	0	0	0	0	0	0	10	0	0	0	0	0	0	0	0	0	0	0	100
o	0	0	0	0	0	0	0	0	0	0	0	0	0	10	0	0	0	0	0	0	0	0	0	0	100
p	0	0	0	0	0	0	1	0	0	0	1	0	0	0	6	2	0	0	0	0	0	0	0	0	60
q	0	0	0	0	0	0	0	0	0	0	0	0	0	0	1	9	0	0	0	0	0	0	0	0	90

This gave us a global performance of 80%, that is a high percentage considering the number of classes.

Table 3. Confusion Matrix part 3, r–y

X	a	b	c	d	e	f	g	h	i	k	l	m	n	o	p	q	r	s	t	u	v	w	x	y	%
r	0	0	0	0	0	0	0	0	0	0	0	0	0	0	0	0	10	0	0	0	0	0	0	0	100
s	0	0	0	0	0	0	0	0	0	0	0	0	0	0	0	0	0	7	3	0	0	0	0	0	70
t	0	0	0	0	1	0	0	0	0	0	0	0	0	0	0	0	0	0	9	0	0	0	0	0	90
u	0	0	0	0	0	0	0	0	0	0	0	0	0	0	0	0	0	0	0	10	0	0	0	0	100
v	0	0	0	0	0	0	0	0	0	0	0	0	0	0	0	0	0	0	0	0	10	0	0	0	100
w	0	1	0	0	0	0	0	0	0	0	0	0	0	0	0	0	0	0	0	0	0	9	0	0	90
x	0	0	0	0	0	0	0	0	0	0	0	0	0	0	0	0	0	0	0	0	0	0	10	0	100
y	0	0	0	0	0	0	0	0	0	0	0	0	0	0	0	0	0	0	0	0	0	0	0	10	100

6 Conclusions and Future Work

According to the result the measure of muscle activation is a good discriminant for hand sign recognition, using a KNN classifier with 80% of efficiency is achieved. As a result, it becomes an excellent feature, because our approach uses low computational and spacial cost, this advantage is very important when the recognition algorithm it is necessary to be implemented in a limited hardware capabilities such as mobile devices, wearables or other small devices, allowing the use of low-computational and low-space cost algorithm like Nearest neighbour algorithm (1NN). In contrast, more complex algorithms like ANN or support vector machines would take advantage of this measure and achieve even better results.

Although comparison with other algorithms is desired, there isn't a basic data set, an alternative option is to choose ideograms randomly but any comparison isn't fairly. In this paper the 24 static alphabet sign was considered as a data set, while others authors such Fatmi et al. [4] used only 13 signs obtaining 82.91% of accuracy as minimum, but the ideograms considered both hands and movement, it could be a disadvantage.

The most similar dataset in literature is the used by Chong et al. [3], they used the 26 alphabet sign letters, achieving a 80.30% accuracy using a Support Vector Machine and 93.81% using a Deep Neural Networks (DNN). In the case of SVM is almost the same accuracy, but using DNN they won by at least 14%, however both algorithms have high computational cost.

Making a deeper analysis of confusing b with f, and k with r, because hands signs are very similar and only change orientation. Others would need more analysis in a different levels like the worst result that is confusing c and v and doesn't seem to be a logical reason and the proposed measure fails.

As future work, the reduction of this confusion and improvement of the classification is desired, in order to use additional features or another classifier that brings weight to features, maybe an Artificial Neural Network. Another important task is to consider the hand movement analysis for not only to include the j and z letters based on ideograms recognition, also the analysis the Inertial

Movement Unit of the Myo Arm Band. Another way to improve this research is the use of two arm band, one for each forearm, in order to be able to recognize ideograms made with two hands. In fact, the research of low cost features would benefit all the sign recognition disciplines.

Acknowledgments. The authors are grateful to *Instituto Politecnico Nacional* for the economic support given to the research project number *20196065* given through the *Secretaria de investigacion y posgrado*.

References

1. ASL: Ethnologue Definition, American Sign Language (ASL) (2019). https://www.ethnologue.com/language/ase
2. Banerjee, A.E.A.: Generation of movement explanations for testing gesture based co-operative learning applications. In: Proceedings - 2019 IEEE International Conference on Artificial Intelligence Testing (2019)
3. Chong, T.W., Lee, B.G.: American sign language recognition using leap motion controller with machine learning approach. Sensors (Switzerland) **18**, 3554 (2018)
4. Fatmi, R., Rashad, S., Integlia, R.: Comparing ANN, SVM, and HMM based machine learning methods for American sign language recognition using wearable motion sensors. In: 2019 IEEE 9th Annual Computing and Communication Workshop and Conference (2019)
5. INEGI: Disability in Mexico. INEGI (2014)
6. Lewis, M.P., Simons, G.F., Fennig, C.D.: Ethnologue: Languages of the World, 17th edn. SIL International, Dallas (2013)
7. OMS: World report on disability. OMS (2014)
8. ONU: impaired people rights conference. ONU (2017)
9. Pansare J.R., Ingle, M.: Vision-based approach for American sign language recognition using edge orientation histogram. In: 2016 International Conference on Image, Vision and Computing, ICIVC 2016 (2016)
10. Torung V.N.T., Yang, C.K., Tran, Q.: A translator for American sign language to text and speech. In: 2016 IEEE 5th Global Conference on Consumer Electronics, GCCE 2016 (2016)
11. Vanco, M., Minarik, I., Rozinaj, G.: Evaluation of static hand gesture algorithms. In: International Conference on Systems, Signals, and Image Processing (2014)
12. Sandler, W., Lillo-Martin, D.: Sign Language and Linguistic Universals. Cambridge University Press, Cambridge (2006)
13. Wikipedia: American Sign Language. https://en.wikipedia.org/wiki/American_Sign_Language
14. Wikipedia: Sign Language. https://en.wikipedia.org/wiki/Sign_language

Artificial Intelligence as a Competitive Advantage in the Manufacturing Area

Juvenal Mendoza Valencia[✉], Juan José Hurtado Moreno,
and Felipe de Jesús Nieto Sánchez

Instituto Politécnico Nacional, UPIITA, G.A. Madero, 07340 Mexico City, Mexico
juvenalmv69@gmail.com, hurtadoupiicsa@yahoo.com, felnieto73@gmail.com

Abstract. Since the beginning of the industrial revolution, manufacturing has gone through different stages: the 1st technological islands, 2nd the mass production, 3rd the lean manufacturing and the 4th IIoT (for the year 2025); we must keep in mind the leadership in the production of goods today what the Eastern countries have (and are using stage 3), so that the current guidelines have the necessary meaning, which establishes a new way of producing more as the potential of technologies that are in the process of maturation such as: Artificial Intelligence, Big Data, 3D Printing and Robotics; find original solutions to the problems of productivity, customization, just in time and services.

Artificial Intelligence is taking a leading role in solving manufacturing problems, with the purpose of eliminating all those areas that are blindly worked, and that therefore it is not possible to improve by suffering from data to: analyze them, obtain information, establish controls and improve. The above is achieved by establishing disruptive technologies that take control in real time.

Keywords: Industry 4.0 · Artificial Intelligence · Big data · 3D Printing and Robotics

1 Introduction

The Oriental companies that apply the Lean concept (3rd stage), have two fundamental guidelines and without them it cannot operate properly [11]. **The First one**, a hierarchical structure is horizontal (democratic), which implies that all the members of the company have administrative and operational functions, so that decision-making is the result of a consensus.

The Second one, its based on first sell and then produce, that means, what the company is looking for is not to work blindly, the programming of the orders is the result of real orders; for this purpose it is necessary to bring transparency to the entire production process, making visible the stoppages in real time; achieving this comply with the agreed with customers.

Western companies [11]. **Been preferred** to maintain a vertical structure (Authoritarian), so the work environment is very stressful and they seek to produce and then sell; but when the first premise is not fulfilled, it is generated that

© Springer Nature Switzerland AG 2019
M. F. Mata-Rivera et al. (Eds.): WITCOM 2019, CCIS 1053, pp. 171–180, 2019.
https://doi.org/10.1007/978-3-030-33229-7_15

the established work program is not achieved, generating delays, poor quality products and penalties; the above is the result of the low participation of workers in making decisions, as well as excessive rotation of them at different levels.

In the different research works in manufacturing companies in Mexico, it has been found that their managers are more focused on achieving short-term results, such as compliance with the volume of production, leaving aside quality, variety and time of delivery.

The problem is that managers do not understand the philosophy of lean manufacturing, so by not complying with the premises indicated above, their companies do not have the possibility of joining a global production chain, which requires them to comply with the times of delivery, international prices and quality of its products.

As companies of Japanese origin have arrived, they have worked with their suppliers in the teaching and understanding of their work methods, which has allowed a greater number of CEO, managers and workers to understand these forms of production.

25 years have passed since the signing of the free trade agreement between the United States, Canada and Mexico, it is expected that in this second stage governments will require their companies as a requirement to operate the implementation of Lean Manufacturing, which will put their companies of manufacturing at the same level as the Oriental companies.

With the above [10], the foundations are laid for equitable competition between the different countries, which means that they are able to move to industry 4.0. They have 5 years for the installation of 5G communication technology, which will allow the development of the IIoT industry (Internet of industrial things).

1.1   4.0 Industry Considerations

Lean Manufacturing was born from the idea of controlling production through the computer [3], for this purpose the Kan-Ban was created, this is nothing more than a set of cards that were taken to the computerized processing center in periods of 2 h and In this way it was possible to know if the volume of goods corresponded to what was programmed; from this restriction the requirement arises that all the flow of internal and external materials had to be done in lots that will not exceed that time; By involving all areas of the company, there was a need to develop a set of methodologies to solve the different manufacturing problems.

The use of the computer in the 60s represented a great innovation in the production processes and this did not stop there, also followed developments such as the use of robots, networks and communication equipment, CNC machines, PLCs, ERP Software (planning of the business requirement), etc. All these new technologies were introduced harmoniously in the industry and helped each other to increase its productivity, quality and flexibility.

Each new technological development that was introduced in the industry generated changes in the way of producing, resulting in the elimination of jobs, which were rewarded by a considerable increase in productivity, as well as the profits of the company, the above made that it grows and demands workers in areas such as: technical, administrative, logistics, marketing, etc., resulting in a benefit of the economy as a whole.

We have many disruptive technologies in the 4.0 industry [2], each one solving a specific problem, we would have to ask, which of these has a strategic importance in the production of goods?; The answer is Artificial Intelligence, it allows machines to do their jobs better and improve in time, never in the history of mankind have we transferred intelligence to them, since the beginning of the industrial revolution equipments have been built, which they follow a set of steps in a mechanical, electrical or electronic way, which has allowed the human being to be released from monotonous and dangerous work.

With the creation of the smartphones in 2007 [10], companies have developed a set of smart devices and softwares, as a way to differentiate themselves from their competitors, in many cases it has represented a competitive advantage, which forces those who do not to imitate these, as a way to remain in the market.

We must consider Artificial Intelligence [2], as a new element of integration of the different areas of the company, being part of the ERP system, whose main function is to take control of production in real time with the advantage of knowing all the productive incidents at throughout the entire production chain; quantifying therefore all the delays that occur in the same, presenting in a graphic way the state that the different orders keep "e.g." (red delay of more than 2 h, Yellow of 1 h and green without delays).

We must consider Artificial Intelligence as a new element of integration of the different areas of the company, being part of the ERP system, whose main function is to take control of production in real time with the advantage of knowing all the productive incidents at throughout the entire production chain; quantifying therefore all the delays that occur in the same, presenting in a graphic way the state that the different orders keep "e.g" (red delay of more than 2 h, Yellow of 1 h and green without delays). To this day it is how control of the manufacturing plants is carried out; but in reality the use of the different applications that make up this platform is between 50 to 80%, this is due to the problem of transferring information from different because of geographical issues and productive conditions, thus leaving many areas that work blindly.

2   Methodology

If we consider that Western companies have a Vertical Organization, it does not generate an effective participation of workers, they are only limited to following orders, without analyzing whether these are adequate to the needs of the particular production of the company, seeing the results of these decisions at the end of the fiscal year.

It is evident that all this generates a poor work culture and a lack of interest of workers to solve everyday problems, because they are excluded as an element that can bring creative ideas to the company, If this is taken into account, it will substantially change the way it operates, being part of the solution of the production process.

2.1   Inefficiency of Equipment and Staff Turnover

We must have defined where our strengths and weaknesses are, they will make us aware of the importance of technology to the achievement of the development of a new competitive strategy, as well as the elimination of our inefficient areas, One of the most frequent problems that manufacturing companies have is the separation of the master production program and the actual execution of the same, due to the fact that they have countless number of machine tools, these occur when operating endless of failures, which have to be repaired at the time of production, which generates a cumulative amount of time that consumes more than scheduled.

For the measurement of the problem of failures, the most appropriate solution so far, is to apply the measure called: General Equipment Efficiency (OEE), which establishes that for world-class companies you must have an efficiency of 85% [9], therefore there is a 15% for the correction of machine failures, if it will work optimally we would only charge an over 15% cost and delivery times would be those involved when considering this percentage of inefficiency at the time of scheduling production; But for this to be true, we must have low staff turnover and that it perform decision-making functions, which does not occur in most of Western companies.

To reduce staff turnover, it is an essential requirement to have a minimum level of technological baccalaureate studies, which allows workers to understand the potential of new technologies and therefore make contributions to the improvement of processes in an innovative way, achieving development and job satisfaction, creating a healthy work culture.

If this is fulfilled in terms of complying with the specifications of the equipment failures, minimum academic training and job satisfaction, we will be able to use disruptive technologies to build a competitive advantage.

2.2   Artificial Intelligence and Disruptive Technologies that Support Production

If we apply [7] Artificial Intelligence, intelligent machines, robots, products with embedded systems with Radio Frequency Identification (RFID) and digital twins companies, would be able to receive production orders in real time, analyze the financial part, define time of delivery, track orders, analyze delivery logistics, see how the products work with the customer, update the product software offline, make fault diagnostics and define a solution.

It is important to explain how these technologies would interrelate, [15] in the first place, the function of Artificial Intelligence (AI), is to give intelligence to things, for this purpose it is necessary that they have an embedded system, which monitors the actuators and motors For this purpose, sensors must be included: temperature, position, speed, geolocation, touch, visualization, listening and speaking, with which it is possible to communicate directly between the manufacturer and the user, to indicate the required maintenance to indicate the changes of the parts, the time of life and define the date of replacement of the device; It would increase the productivity of the company with the use of this new technology (AI), being able to analyze data and make decisions before the problem of equipment failures occurs, thus achieving a general efficiency of the 100% equipment (OEE), and therefore eliminating the 15% cost overrun, which had to be considered before, when they worked without an effective communication.

What we seek with the technologies of Industry 4.0 is to move from static to dynamic systems [13] (that is, they can be changed over time), the reason is that markets are unpredictable (customers request goods at any time), from There the importance of disruptive technologies, each fulfills a specific purpose. Artificial Intelligence is in the center of all of them, being the one that allows the company to adapt to the change, by analyzing all the information produced in the production chain and take the most appropriate decisions when knowing the general operation of the company, And when this determination is reached, it is necessary that this must be transformed into real actions, for this it is essential to define the communication network, so nodes have to receive the information, which machines will execute the action and what effects occur; for which it is necessary to retransmit the executions of the machines to the general body control, so that it makes the pertinent corrective actions. The previous process will be carried out all the time, with the different systems that make up the company.

Once the Artificial Intelligence analyzes, transmits the orders and receives feedback, it is able to perform this action with all the devices that are in the company in real time, which will allow managing the overall operation of the system, when determining in advance the series of processes that must be executed, At the time of any problem of any kind in the system, the solution will be sought, in case of a direct human intervention: to make a mechanical change of a device, reprogramming a robot, register a drone, electrical failure, earthquakes, etc. reprogramming of the master production program could be done to define new delivery dates, thereby reducing losses.

In the production lines we currently have areas with industrial robots [5]: 90% Welding, 50% Painting, 80% Die-cutting, 20% Assembly; but new robots such as collaboratives robots are appearing, which can cover the percentage that is missing, if this happens, the productivity of these areas must necessarily be increased. In the case of humanoid robots, they could be applied in areas of customer service at the window, in bureaucratic offices, sales agencies, etc., so that the procedures can be done faster, not having the need to move to find information, for being connected wirelessly to the general database.

In the case of 3D printing you have many of opportunities in the printing of: car bodies, cabinets, casings, metal parts, etc., you must be aware that at this time the construction time is very long; but it has the advantage that once the design order is given immediately, the execution order is given, which makes them ideal for new products, metal parts with hollow interiors, parts that are out of the market, construction of spare parts in advance, in general manufacturing of any pieces with irregular shapes that the only way is that this type of device, which, once they leave the printer can begin with the assembly of the other parts.

A problem in the manufacturing lines is that to make a product it is necessary to have a car body that contains all the parts that it will carry, for which manufacturers use different techniques to build these, such as injection processes for the car of electronic products, car body building stamping, die-cutting with oxyacetylene for metal structures, etc., which consume a lot of time for its design, construction and installation, which makes any mistake or design change very expensive.

On the other hand, if we use 3D printing, it would allow us to build the entire car body of the product, make the necessary adjustments, change the design, in an economical and fast way; if 3D printing goes hand in hand with artificial intelligence [4], we would obtain additional potential, having the ability to see what the market demands in real time, changes in production volume, changes in design, order and cancellations, resulting in a decrease in costs, which will give the company a competitive advantage.

A very revolutionary application is represented by the digital twins companies [7], that which consists of a physical part (the product) and the virtual part (Artificial Intelligence), within the virtual part there is a set of designs that correspond to the different models that it has The company, at the time the customer makes the order for any of them, the system gives a code which is associated with the following data: customer, model and place of delivery; This production order is transferred to the corresponding plant to define the delivery time, in turn the plant assigns the start-finish time and the manufacturing line; When the scheduled date arrives, the body or cabinet is manufactured in a 3D print, a motherboard with the code corresponding to the personalization of the product is placed.

This motherboard is part of the embedded system that will be the one that will control the different production phases, the most important sensors in manufacturing are RFID [8] (which defines the work cells) and GPS geolocation (for external logistics), To fulfill this purpose, the communication must be wireless, the ERP control system with Artificial Intelligence, would track the product in real time, thus eliminating that of working blindly.

When the product leaves the production line [6], the system will define the route and the means of transport required; The GPS geolocation sensor will keep you informed of the time and distance traveled, in this way you can check the total time consumed, as well as those unforeseen for future improvements in the same process, so that in external logistics blind work is eliminated.

Once the product reaches the customer's hands, Artificial Intelligence will be able to monitor [14] the behavior of the product, the habits of use, the energy consumption, the general performance of the product, for this it will use the different sensors that have the same such as: temperature, vision, listening, speaking, vibration, GPS, RFID, etc., so that with this information the buyer can be indicated about the required maintenance, software updates, available applications and product life time (which is depending on mechanical use), so that suitable precautions may be taken. As the manufacturer can sell thousands, hundreds or millions of products, Artificial Intelligence along with Big Data, Analytics and the cloud, can make a comparison of the use of all its products, the failures, the communication problems presented, the spare parts used, satisfaction surveys, comments on social networks of the product, sales areas, characteristics of the population, religion professed, culture and comments on the company, This way you can make a very approximate profile of the thinking of customers, to know what you like or dislike, improvements and possible models for different ages of the population.

All of the above can not be possible today because of many countries, as well as companies suffer from 5G communication (24 to 100 GHz transmission range), which can work with massive information and transmit it in milliseconds; The most extreme case is the ability to receive information from 100 devices in a square meter, which is inferred from having a hyperconnected world.

3   Results

Companies are constantly changing due to the emergence of soft and hard technologies, which cause them competitive disadvantages, these have to be eliminated in order to remain in the market, for this purpose they should not be lost in the multiple technological alternatives that are they present, for which it is important to identify their strengths and weaknesses, to have the right human talent and the most efficient technological option to create the competitive advantage.

It is important to keep in mind that artificial intelligence, intelligent machines, robotics, digital twins and 3D Printing are in the phase of growth in the curve of the technological life cycle, so it has to start to be implemented in the productive processes, with the purpose of knowing their capacities and deficiencies, as well as defining the technological profile of the collaborators, the training programs, the life plan, as well as the most appropriate organizational design for the fulfillment of the objectives and goals of the company.

We must also keep in mind that we have other technologies such as, cloud computing, big data, mobile internet, augmented reality and virtual reality, that allow us to increase automation and efficiency in production processes, which are complementary to the previous ones and which together will allow us to solve complex problems of the everyday world, as would be the case with smart cities. Which generate a large number of solutions to problems in the fields of: health, safety, transport, housing, energy, water and food, among others.

The purpose of the 4.0 revolution is to change the current paradigms, of how we understand technology and its future implications, to have a more inclusive world, where ethics plays an important role in defining its regulation to maintain a harmony between humans and machines.

Data analytics and the use of the cloud will be part of a complex and intelligent process that allows for reliable and well-processed data that helps genetic algorithms work with quality information, generating reliable solutions for the current requirements of the company.

For the production of a set of different and personalized goods, a real-time transmission of information is necessary, as well as the control of the process, in order to comply in a timely manner with what the market demands, and also consider that the consumer does not follow any rules at the time of establishing their requirements, this causes that you constantly have to be planning, to adapt the production to these needs.

It is very important that companies determine the time that consumes the different custom goods, so that in their computer platforms customers obtain the delivery time and the price, in a few seconds, which will imply a communication with the entire value chain (suppliers, manufacturing and distribution), in this way comply with the agreement.

By having a more informed client, it becomes more demanding, for the reason that in a few minutes you can visit different Web pages of each of the companies that interest you, making it necessary to have your own vision that distinguishes it from the rest of the competition, otherwise the chances of remembering it will be minimal.

4   Discussion

We are getting to the point that if we want to be competitive it is important to use smart manufacturing, cloud-based manufacturing, cognitive manufacturing, etc. Which have a very close relationship with artificial intelligence, we are allowed to design and develop intelligent systems that contribute to the creation of machines, which have the ability to collect and analyze data, and communicate with other systems that have the characteristic of solving complex problems.

We are in a social transformation at this time, which is reflected in a constant change in the way of doing and seeing the world, the new generations of young people are more qualified for work in smart factories, they are accustomed to change, so they are more familiar with these new technological innovations, as well as their use, application and new solutions, so they will continue being a factor of change.

Many of the ways in which the company works will tend to disappear and will be replaced by intelligent methods, which will be constantly changing, for which they must have a life of their own, to deal with unexpected changes in the production processes, models business and agile project management because it will demand capacity and speed of response to the demand for new solutions.

With respect to manufacturing companies they have to be workplaces that allow workers to have a good work culture, which will be reflected in the development of their potential, with organizational structures that have as their purpose innovation, caring for the planet and respect for the different ways of thinking, all this within the framework of tolerance and respect for others.

We have 5 years to define how manufacturing companies 4.0 will be, in what they have to do with their organizational structure, this is very important, since it defines the rights and obligations of all those involved in the manufacture of products, as well as with the plant distribution, which until now is online, which implies the sequencing of activities. With new technologies such as: artificial intelligence, robotics, 3D printing, Big Data, the cloud and intelligent machines, we must think of other ways of organizing production, technological possibilities allow.

5   Conclusions

Although much of the current literature indicates that the future of humanity will be of abundance and mass unemployment, where machines will have control of all daily activities, it should be remembered that at the time a technological development is used in general, the people learn to see its advantages and disadvantages, if this happens we can say that there is a real understanding of it, so it will take another technological revolution to solve the new needs of the population.

We must also bear in mind that at present people only use 10% of our brain mass, and that as we use it more, it will necessarily have to increase the percentage that is not used, so we can be in a future beings that can travel in the galaxy and see how it is and the machines will continue to be the tools that allow us to achieve this purpose and generating the right conditions, so that human beings can inhabit, eat and live on these planets.

The use of disruptive technologies, such as the Artificial Intelligence, is only paving the ground for the aforementioned to happen and for human beings to abandon the phase of scarcity of resources, hunger, injustices, etc. for a new one where the search for happiness, finding our true selves and facing any unknown challenges ahead will be the ideals of this new era.

Acknowledgments. To the Academic Community of the Master's Degree in Industrial Engineering of the Postgraduate Studies and Research Section at Professional Interdisciplinary Unit of Engineering and Social and Administrative Sciences from the National Polytechnic Institute.

References

1. Aggour, K., Gupta, V., Ruscitto, D.: Artificial intelligence/machine learning in manufacturing and inspection: a GE perpective. MRS Bull. **44**, 545–558 (2019). Materials research society. www.mrs.org
2. Bartodziej, C.: The Concept Industry 4.0, 1st English edn. Springer, Wiesbaden (2017). https://doi.org/10.1007/978-3-658-16502-4
3. Brau, S.: Lean 4.0 Manufacturing, 1st English edn. (2016)
4. Bukkapatnam, S., Afrin, K., Dave, D., Kumara, S.: Machine learning and AI for long-term fault prognosis in complex manufacturing systems. CIRP Ann. - Manuf. Technol. **68**, 459–462 (2019)

5. Ford, M.: Rise of the Robots, 1st English edn. Basic Books, New York (2015)
6. Hu, L., Miau, Y., Wu, G.: iRobot-Factory: an intelligent robot factory based on cognitive. Future Gener. Comput. Syst. **90**, 569–577 (2019)
7. Joyanes, l.: Industria 4.0, 1a edición en español. Alfaomega, México (2018)
8. Knapciková, L., Balog, M.: Industry 4.0: Trends in Management of Intelligent Manufacturing System, 1st English edn. Springer, Cham (2019). https://doi.org/10.1007/978-3-030-14011-3
9. Leflar, J.: Practical TPM, 1st English edn. Productivity, Portland
10. López, J.: La gran transición, 1a edición en español. Fondo de cultura económica, México (2018)
11. Monden, Y.: Toyota Production System. 4th English edn. CRC Press, Boca Raton (2012)
12. Moreira, L., Li, W., Fitzpatrick, M.: Supervision controller for real-time surface quality assurance in CNC machining using artificial intelligence. Comput. Ind. Eng. **127**, 158–168 (2019)
13. Ostrosi, E., Fougeres, A.: Intelligent virtual manufacturing cell formation in cloud-based design and manufacturing. Eng. Appl. Artif. Intell. **76**, 80–95 (2018)
14. Qin, J., Chian, L.: Advances and opportunities in machine learning for process data analytics. Comput. Chem. Eng. **126**, 465–473 (2019)
15. Ustundag, A., Cevikcan, E.: Industry 4.0: Managing the Digital Transformation, 1st English edn. Springer, Cham (2018). https://doi.org/10.1007/978-3-319-57870-5

Software Engineering and Education

Mobile Application for the Support in the Learning of the Alphabet, Verbs and Pronouns of the Mexican Sign Language Based on Augmented Reality

A. Gordillo-Ramírez[1], O. Alonso-Cuevas[1], D. Ortega-Pacheco[2(✉)],
and U. Vélez-Saldaña[1]

[1] National Polytechnic Institute, ESCOM,
Av. Juan de Dios Bátiz s/n esq. Av. Miguel Othón de Mendizabal, Col. Lindavista,
Gustavo A. Madero. C. P., 07738 Mexico City, Mexico
almagoram@gmail.com, osvaldo.alocue@gmail.com, ulises.velez@gmail.com
[2] National Polytechnic Institute, UPIICSA,
Av. Té #950 esquina Resina, Col. Granjas, Iztacalco, C.P.,
08400 Mexico City, Mexico
jdortegap@ipn.mx

Abstract. In this paper we present a mobile application for android operating system focused for children's, for the support in the learning of the alphabet, verbs and pronouns in the Mexican Sign Language context. The parents or teacher will be able to download the markers for each Lesson or Game. Once the markers are available, the child will be able to carry out his activity with the support of the augmented reality.

Keywords: Augmented reality · Mexican Sign Language · Mobile learning · Mobile application

1 Introduction

An alternative to address the child learning process for Mexican Sign Language is through the technology we currently have, since the fast advancements of technological developments allows to find wide possibilities in the learning environment, such as the use of mobile devices and augmented reality. There are benefits of using mobile devices in the learning process, such as: improves student's autonomy, facilitates feedback and helps to understand topics with multimedia elements (by augmented reality, for example).

This learning way is good for topics like: Problems solving, to acquire skills, languages, continuous learning, exploratory and transversal competences, games, science and model representation. This learning method is called Mobile Learning and it is a new strategy for education. In this learning method, the materials are important: videos, conceptual maps, images, models, conferences, simulations, test, etc. The contents should be optimal and suitable for mobile devices.

© Springer Nature Switzerland AG 2019
M. F. Mata-Rivera et al. (Eds.): WITCOM 2019, CCIS 1053, pp. 183–191, 2019.
https://doi.org/10.1007/978-3-030-33229-7_16

In M-Learning the automated organization of content (topics) is promoted more in a similar manner when the teachers work with learning objectives, and this strategy recommends sectioning the topics in little units, it forms complete information, learning activities and contextualization elements [1].

In the educational context, there are previous works that have endeavored to support learning as in [2], which describes how augmented reality can be used to teach concepts in the field of health, using a mobile device; in [3] shows how augmented reality is used to support children with learning disabilities. In the specific context of sign language learning, there is, for example, in [4], where augmented reality is used on a PDA for the teaching of Brazilian Sign Language, focusing only on the alphabet; in [5] the elements of augmented reality are used through a personal computer or a tablet, using an exercise book to support learning, which contains the markers that trigger augmented reality to visualize learning objects, in this case the alphabet, and in [6] the elements for the augmented reality are words and letters of the Arabic Alphabet in an mobile environment. With the above we can realize that in terms of learning, in regard to Sign Language, the works focus on the alphabet and not on more language elements such as verbs, pronouns, articles or phrases, which are important for learning that language, independently of the country.

The present work described below, pretend to be a mobile application tool, that intends to integrate basic elements for child learning of Mexican Sign Language such as: Alphabet, Pronouns and Verbs, based on augmented reality and its use in mobile devices with Android operating system.

2   Learning Environment

The learning environment is based on the use of a mobile application, whose development focuses on the concepts of Mobile Learning, Gamification and Augmented Reality, as described in Fig. 1. The application is designed for children in first year of primary school, and pretend to be a supporting tool for the learning of the alphabet, verbs and pronouns, that are the base for more complex structures in the Mexican Sign Language context.

Each child must have access to a mobile device with android operating system, which according to the statistics obtained from [7], for May 2019 has 82.28 % of use in mobile devices in Mexico.

Each learning element (alphabet, verbs or pronouns) has a lesson, which is carried out by the child and supervised by the teacher in the classroom or by one of his parents in other place. Each lesson is based on the use of augmented reality technology through printed markers. Once the child completes a lesson, the parent or teacher can record the evaluation corresponding to the child's performance. There is also a game for the alphabet, which is not intended to make an evaluation, the aim is to motivate the child to practice the elements of the corresponding lesson of alphabet. The approach for the mobile application development, are described as follow.

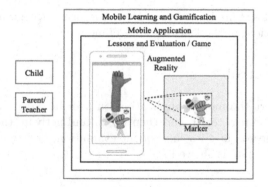

Fig. 1. Learning environment

3 Mobile Application Development

We have use the agile development approach: Mobile-D (more detail in [9]), witch consists in five stages: Explore, Initialize, Productionize, Stabilize and System test and fix. We developed the mobile application as follows:

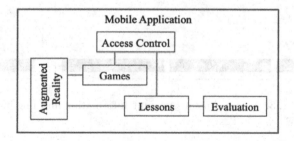

Fig. 2. Mobile application architecture

- **Explore**. In this stage, we define the software scope (requirements), user environment and the architectural design (See Fig. 2).
- **Initialize**. In this stage we prepare and verify all critical development issues for requirements implementation and carried out the concept proofs for augmented reality, 3D models and android application development.
- **Productionize**. In this stage we implement the functionality associated in each module for the architecture design, applying an iterative and incremental development cycle.
- **Stabilize**. In this stage we ensure the quality of each implementation, and if it was required, we carried out the necessaries adjustment.
- **System test and fix**. In this stage, we obtained the team feedback for the application functionality and fix the found defects for the stabilization

between modules. Finally we carried out the users acceptance tests for the mobile application, in the learning environment.

4 Access Control

Before a child start the mobile application on a device, one of the parents or the teacher must be registered, and then log in and activate the corresponding activity, either a lesson and its subsequent evaluation, or a game. The account Information and Log in, is showed in Fig. 3.

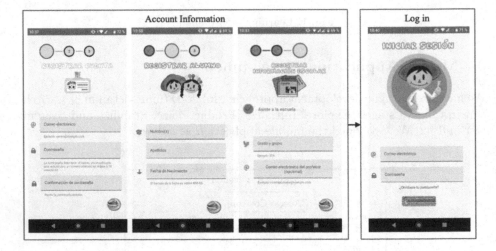

Fig. 3. Access control: Account Information and Log in

5 Augmented Reality

The augmented reality in the mobile application is based on the use of the ARToolKit API, in his 5.3.3 version, for more detail see [8]. The general operation of this module is showed in Fig. 4.

Each element is described as follow:

– **Marker.** Has the design showed in Fig. 5, that contains the dimensions and sections for each marker, and represents the relationship between signified and signifier, in the Mexican Sign Language context. In the example, the bee image (Abeja in Spanish) is the signified, and the image with the letter A and the corresponding Mexican Sign Language representation, are the signifier. This concepts presents in the marker, are crucial for language acquisition process.

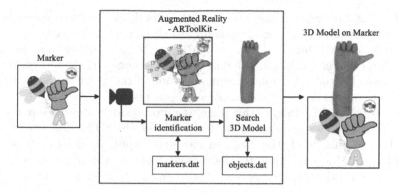

Fig. 4. Augmented reality operation

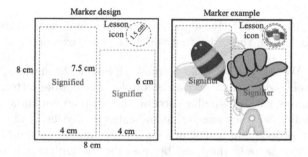

Fig. 5. Marker design and example for letter A

Fig. 6. Feature map image: edge points in green crosses and textured areas in red squares (Color figure online)

- **Marker identification.** The camera in the mobile device, is the responsible for processing the marker. For each image frame, the object tracking method (part of the Natural Feature Tracking), is used to for process natural interest points of an image such as: texture-patches, edges, color blobs, etcetera. This method generate a image with a feature map with this interest points (see Fig. 6). The input marker identification, is performed by the comparison between his feature map image processed in each image frame by the camera, with all feature map images stored in the mobile application, referenced by the markers.dat file, and corresponding to all recognizable markers.

- **Search 3D Model.** If the input marker is identified, the module should search the corresponding 3D Model, that is referenced by the objects.dat file. This model is the 3D graphical representation of the Mexican Sign Language signifier corresponding in the identified input marker.
- **3D Model on Marker.** In this stage, the module identifies the input marker ubication, and show on the mobile device screen, the 3D Model over the input marker. At this point, the user can move the input marker to left or right, and the 3D Model reacts to this movements showing the corresponding view. To accelerate the augmented reality processing, OpenSceneGraph (OSG).

6   Lessons

The lessons corresponding to the alphabet, pronouns and verbs in the application are described below, in the order that which they are executed:

1. **Alphabet.** We use the Mexican Spanish alphabet: 28 markers, and we considered vowels, consonants and an example of a double letter, however we show the vowels without spelling accent and without umlauts. Each marker has the signified with an image that indicates an object, it also has the first letter of the object that kids can view in the image. In the 3D models for this lesson, we use only the hand because for the alphabet is not necessary to show the complete body, so the model must have a hand with five fingers and the corresponding arm that allows the movement of the Sign. The child performance is evaluated in the mobile application by the parent or teacher. An example is showed in Fig. 7.

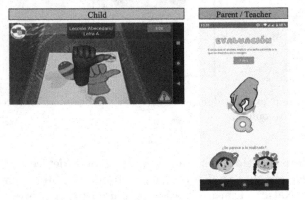

Fig. 7. Example of alphabet lesson and evaluation

2. **Pronouns.** The second lesson is personal pronouns in Mexican Spanish Language, and we have 9 pronouns (if we think about feminine and masculine pronouns) therefore in LSM the signs for female and male are different each other. We decided to have only 5 signs to put on view, and each marker has signified so in this lesson we did 3 people to represent the pronouns and has signifier represented by the word and sign. In the special case of the pronoun "Nosotros", there are three ways to do the same sign "Nosotros", but the sign that we show is the most actual and it is used by young people. The child performance is evaluated in the mobile application by the parent or teacher. An example is showed in Fig. 8.

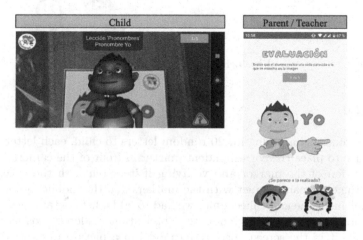

Fig. 8. Example of pronouns lesson and evaluation

3. **Verbs.** The last lesson is verbs, we have knowledge of Spanish Language has a lot of verbs, but first we were taking into account that in Spanish, the LSM verbs do not indicate mode or time, also in LSM, the verb "Ser o estar" (To be) is very rarely used, for these reasons we selected some verbs related to the school and then we carefully chosen some of them that have easier movements. When we selected the five verbs, we designed the markers only with signifier represented by the word and sign because the marker is too small to include much information. In this time, we have be careful with the position and structure of the hands because some verbs can be confused with other sign. The child performance is evaluated in the mobile application by the parent or teacher. An example is showed in Fig. 9.

Fig. 9. Example of verbs lesson

7 Game

This game consists on asking for 20 random letters to child, each letter at time, so they have to place the correspondent marker in front of the camera, allowing the recognition of the marker and verifying if it match with the asked letter, therefore the child can interact with the markers and the mobile application.

To implement the game mechanics we had to add a list containing the letters and it's corresponding marker index, the application randomly extracts a letter and asks for it in the screen, also, a 3D model of a picture frame is displayed to provide feedback, so the user knows the application is detecting a marker, besides, we added a GIF image of the letter's sign as assistance to recognize the correspondent marker. We implemented a reward system based on trophies represented by candies, if the child place the 20 letters correctly in a time less or equal to two minutes, three candies will be provided, if the letters are placed in a time higher than 2 min and less or equal to 3 min, the child will be rewarded with two candies, and finally, if the child place the letters in a time higher than 3 min, the reward will be one candy. An example is showed in Fig. 10.

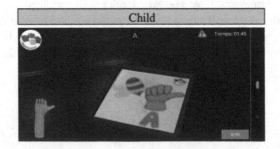

Fig. 10. Alphabet game

8 Discussion and Future Work

With this application, it is shown how augmented reality can support more actively on the learning of elements of Mexican Sign Language, integrating elements that are the basis of it: Alphabet, Pronouns and Verbs; this leaves the basis for later reaching a mobile application that helps to represent more complex phrases, where the execution of a sign has a dependence on the position of the body where it is performed. An additional element will be to be able to use pattern recognition techniques to be able to automatically evaluate the performance of a child in the use of the mobile application.

Acknowledgements. The authors would like to thank to the National Polytechnic Institute (IPN) of Mexico, for the support in the development for this project.

References

1. Ramírez Montoya, M.: Dispositivos de mobile learning para ambientes virtuales: implicaciones en el diseño y la enseñanza. Educación de la Universidad Virtual del Tecnológico de Monterrey. Monterrey, México (2008)
2. Aurélio Galvão, M., Roberto Zorzal, E.: Augmented Reality Applied to Health Education. In: 2013 XV Symposium on Virtual and Augmented Reality. IEEE (2013). https://doi.org/10.1109/SVR.2013.54
3. Vinumol, K.P., Chowdhury, A., Kambam, R., Muralidharan, V.: Augmented reality based interactive text book: an assistive technology for students with learning disability. In: 2013 XV Symposium on Virtual and Augmented Reality. IEEE (2013). https://doi.org/10.1109/SVR.2013.26
4. Rabelo Nazareth, D., Dos Santos Alencar, M., José Francisco de Magalhães Netto: ELRA - teaching brazilian sign language using augmented reality. In: 2014 XVI Symposium on Virtual and Augmented Reality. IEEE (2014). https://doi.org/10.1109/SVR.2014.37
5. Cadeñanes Garnica, J.J., Arrieta, M.A.G.: Augmented reality sign language teaching model for deaf children. In: Omatu, S., Bersini, H., Corchado, J.M., Rodríguez, S., Pawlewski, P., Bucciarelli, E. (eds.) Distributed Computing and Artificial Intelligence, 11th International Conference. AISC, vol. 290, pp. 351–358. Springer, Cham (2014). https://doi.org/10.1007/978-3-319-07593-8_41
6. Al-Megren, S., Almutairi, A.: Assessing the effectiveness of an augmented reality application for the literacy development of arabic children with hearing impairments. In: Rau, P.-L.P. (ed.) CCD 2018. LNCS, vol. 10912, pp. 3–18. Springer, Cham (2018). https://doi.org/10.1007/978-3-319-92252-2_1
7. Mobile Operating System Market Share in Mexico - May 2019 Homepage. StatCounter. http://gs.statcounter.com/os-market-share/mobile/mexico. May 2019
8. ArToolkit Homepage. http://www.hitl.washington.edu/artoolkit/. May 2019
9. Mobile D. Electronics Agile Homepage. http://virtual.vtt.fi/virtual/agile/mobiled.html (2019)
10. Neumann, U., You, S.. Natural feature tracking for augmented reality. In: IEEE Transactions on Multimedia, vol. 1, No. 1, March 1999. https://doi.org/10.1109/6046.748171

Augmented Reality with Swift in ARkit and Their Applications to Teach Geometry

Eduardo Eloy Loza Pacheco[1](✉) ⓘ, Mayra Lorena Díaz Sosa[1](✉) ⓘ,
and Miguel Jesús Torres Ruiz[2] ⓘ

[1] Universidad Nacional Autónoma de México, Acatlán Edomex,
08544 Mexico City, Mexico
{eduardo.loza,mlds}@apolo.acatlan.unam.mx
[2] Instituto Politecnico Nacional, CDMX, Mexico City, Mexico
mtorres@ipn.mx

Abstract. Augmented Reality technologies are now entering in a maturing process. We can see major computer technologies companies developing it. For example Google with ARCore born in 2018 or Apple with ARKit born in 2017. These options allow us to develop a very friendly augmented reality environment with a few steps and a very friendly computer-human interaction. An iOS App needs to be developed using Swift a young language born in 2014. This work shows the application of ARkit to ease the learning of Geometry in R3 space.

Keywords: Augmented reality · Teaching geometry · Swift and ARkit

1 Introduction

In the past two decades, we can see several technologies of virtual reality and augmented reality such as OpenGL, VRML [1], X3D that is web technology [2]. These technologies have a limited impact on educations because of the availability of computer equipment. Twenty years ago the reduction cost of computer technologies permits the democratization of access to the Internet. The reality now is different mobile devices are part of the fourth revolution [3]. Two technological firms Apple and Google are developing two different and independent implementations called ArKit and ArCore respectively to exploit the augmented reality market, which is becoming standards [4]. Education is one of the greatest beneficiaries thanks several students have access to mobile devices. It is possible to teach several mathematics topics with the help of augmented reality. Specifically, geometry that is one of the main topics in engineering at Universities because develops our abilities of spatial reasoning. Examples of applications we can find in GI Science where we need to teach Cartesians to polar transformations, robotic planning the student will need concepts such as vector, planes in order to describe the states of an agent, etc. Swift is a programming language born in 2014 and open to the Open Source community in 2015. The ArKit API was released in 2017 [5] and multidevice integration in the fall of 2018 [6]. On WWDC 2019 Apple introduced new advances on Augmented Reality, ARKIT 3 and Reality

© Springer Nature Switzerland AG 2019
M. F. Mata-Rivera et al. (Eds.): WITCOM 2019, CCIS 1053, pp. 192–202, 2019.
https://doi.org/10.1007/978-3-030-33229-7_17

Composer. The present very interesting novelties such as: People Occlusion, Motion Capture Multi-Face Tracking, Simultaneous front and Back camera, Collaborative Sessions, y and improvement on image recognition. People Occlusion allows to insert animation in front of people or hide some part of their bodies. Motion Captures scan the body of a person to track their movement and generate a 3D model. Front a Back camera are now available to captures images in order developers can program more interactive applications. Face tracking allows to sense the face of a person so we can develop more interesting applications, these features is presents in all devices with iOS 13 or higher [7]. Reality composer is a full framework designed to integrate all applications not just. For iOS but for MACOS, integrates Animations and audios, can record and play [8] (Fig. 1).

Fig. 1. Arkit 3, motion capture taken from: [9]

2 Didactic Strategy

Virtual reality and augmented reality allow us to visualize elements and environments as never seen before. Although education has been enriched by these tools, there are few documented cases of its use to promote the learning of abstract concepts of mathematics and exact sciences. But these environments can be useful to create learning objects for analytic geometry under a playful approach. In Fig. 2 we can see a Virtual environment develop in Java 3D, that we have developed in class.

Fig. 2. Virtual reality Tic-Tac Toe develop in Java 3D

In contrast a we can see, the same game in Augmented reality using Arkit in Swift in Fig. 3. The environment can be combined with elements in reality that teacher can be used to add additional information, with the help of another element such as blackboard or projector.

Fig. 3. Augmented reality Tic-Tac Toe developed ARKit

3   ArKit Implementation

Arkit implementation is simple and reduces the complexity that can be found in many programming languages such as Java using the API Java 3D [10], or VRML [1]. For example in Java, the programmer has to write large sums of code, in VRML the code has no expressivity. Instead Swift keeps important concepts such as the definition of a root object and all objects heritage of it. As the majorities of all Graphics programming languages, As we can see in Fig. 2 shows the design of the virtual world is the same as in VRML. Where the "transform" node has the regular transformation actions such: translation, rotation and scale and geometric attributes. Similar to VRML in Java 3D we can see the same structure (see Fig. 4).

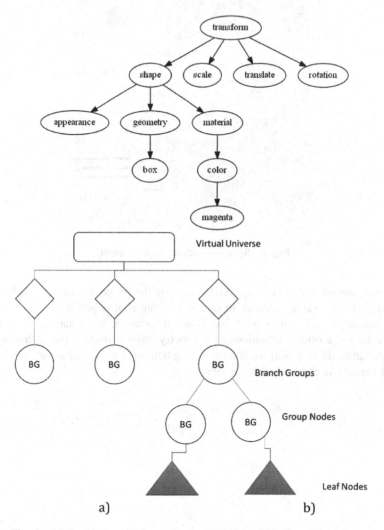

a)   b)

Fig. 4. (a) Semantic net of a scene for VRML and (b) Java 3D structure.

However Swift can create scenes from programmatically as we can see in the previous images. Or Visually by adding objects in art.scrassets View. Here we can modify objects such: color, transparency, transformation (translation, scale, rotation). As we can see in Fig. 5.

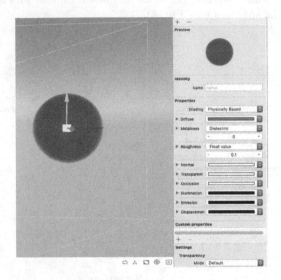

Fig. 5. Sphere transformation in Swift

The programmatical we can see ARKit divides the properties of the graphic object in material, shape, and appearance in one leaf of the root object of the scene and the transformation properties in another like scale, translation, and rotation. Also, we can be found the same object definitions of geometry objects such, textures, transparency and illumination. In Fig. 6(a) we can see a fragment of the code of a part of a scene in Java 3D versus the Swift implementation.

```
31   public TransformGroup DibujarFigurasCili(float radio,float alto,
32          float traslacion_x,float traslacion_y,float traslacion_z,
33          double rotacion_x,double rotacion_y,double rotacion_z,
34          float red,float green, float blue){
35
36
37   Transform3D translateCilindro1=new Transform3D();
38
39   Transform3D RotTmp2=new Transform3D();
40   Transform3D RotTmp2_1=new Transform3D();
41   Transform3D RotTmpZ=new Transform3D();
42
43
44     translateCilindro1.set(new Vector3f(traslacion_x,traslacion_y,
45          traslacion_z));
46
47
48     RotTmp2.rotX(rotacion_x);
49     RotTmp2_1.rotY(rotacion_y);
50     RotTmpZ.rotZ(rotacion_z);
51     RotTmp2.mul(RotTmp2_1);
52     RotTmp2.mul(RotTmpZ);
```

a)

```
var colorBola = UIColor.cyan

let bola = SCNNode(geometry: SCNSphere(radius: 4))
bola.geometry?.firstMaterial?.diffuse.contents =
    colorBola

let plano = SCNPlane(width:
    imagenDeReferencia.physicalSize.width, height:
    imagenDeReferencia.physicalSize.height)

plano.firstMaterial?.diffuse.contents = UIColor.blue

let nodoDelPlano = SCNNode(geometry: plano)

nodoDelPlano.opacity = 0.25

node.addChildNode(nodoDelPlano)

node.addChildNode(bola)
```

b)

Fig. 6. (a) Java code in Java 3D and (b) Swift code in Swift ARKit.

Using ArKit in Geometry. The API allows us to create an AR scene and combine them with real-world images. Additionally, as is common in AR implementations, AR Kit has an implementation that permits image recognition. For this purpose, we create a project in XCode (New iOS Project/Augmented Reality App). So we can see a environment like this un Fig. 7. Then we add a new AR resource Group, so we can add the set of images we would like to recognize (New AR Resource Group), the result is shown in Fig. 8. The images are the place in the real world where Swift will place the AR scene [11, 12].

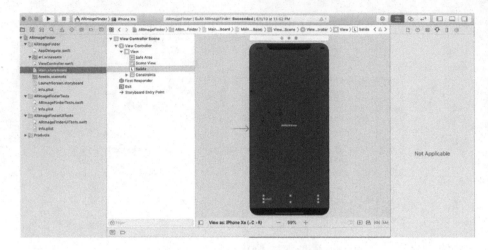

Fig. 7. Xcode environment using ARkit

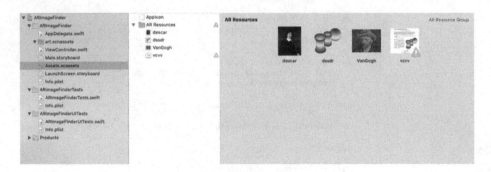

Fig. 8. AR Resource groups.

After that we need to enable the application the possibility to recognize images, as is seen in line 43 of Fig. 9 in the function *viewwillAppear(...)*, we will need to create the object that can discover the images. Also, we need to specify the Folder name where the images are stored (The image should have good resolution). Then we just need to add different images and program a different behavior for everyone.

```
35    override func viewWillAppear(_ animated: Bool) {
36        super.viewWillAppear(animated)
37
38
39        let imagenesDeReferencia =
              ARReferenceImage.referenceImages(inGroupNamed:
              "AR Resources", bundle: nil)!
40        // Create a session configuration
41        let configuration = ARWorldTrackingConfiguration()
42
43        configuration.detectionImages = imagenesDeReferencia
44        // Run the view's session
45        sceneView.session.run(configuration)
46    }
47
```

Fig. 9. Enabling tracking configuration object in line 43.

Having built the Environment, we need to select the size of our screen in order to develop for that size. In Fig. 10(a), we can see the different size XCode allow us to use. In Fig. 10(b) We can select the compatible technology we would use.

Finally, with these few lines of code, it is possible to develop an application that works with hybrid objects. Where part of the implementation is in virtual scenes of AR and others in a physic document. This gave us the opportunity to integrate mobile devices and conventional educational resources. For example, whether we need to explain planes and surfaces of Geometry. Part of the learning process can have a theoretical background, and the practice can be the human-machine interaction with the virtual world. In Fig. 11 we can see a small learning object applied to this matter.

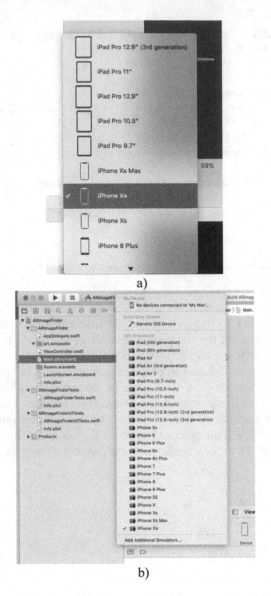

Fig. 10. (a) Different iOS devices (b) Different version of devices.

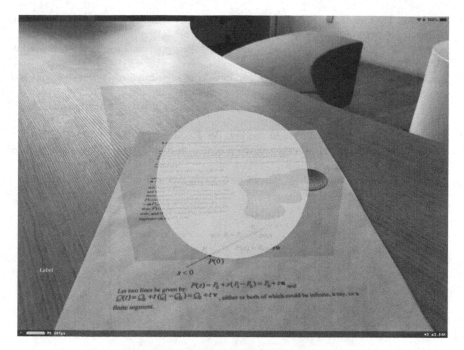

Fig. 11. AR scene with a physic document.

4 Conclusion

Modern technologies of AR are becoming very popular despite the fact there are new. In the case of ARKit of Apple, has been eased the form we develop AR Applications. Also, with the decreasing cost of mobile technologies. Today we have a great opportunity to integrate AR to a variety of applications in areas where the society can be benefited. The areas of applications are wide such as education, GIS, robotic planning, engineering, spatial reasoning, etc.

Acknowledgements. The authors would like to thank to CONACyT and DGAPA-UNAM (PAPIME PE 304717) for the funds to support this work.

References

1. Carey, R., Bell, G.: The Annotated VRML 2.0 Reference Manual, vol. 15. Addison-Wesley, Reading (1997)
2. Web3d.org Homepage. What is X3D?| Web3D Consortium. http://www.web3d.org/x3d/. Accessed June 2018
3. Toffler, A., Alvin, T.: The Third Wave, vol. 484 (1980)
4. Stallings, W.: Network and Internetwork Security: Principles and Practice, vol. 1. Prentice Hall, New Jersey (1995)
5. Apple Inc. Homepage, ARKit. https://developer.apple.com/arkit/. Accessed June 2019

6. Apple Inc. Homepage, ARKit. https://developer.apple.com/documentation/arkit/creating_a_multiuser_ar_experience. Accessed June 2019
7. Apple Inc Homepage., ARKit. https://developer.apple.com/augmented-reality/arkit/. Accessed 2 July 2019
8. Apple Inc., ARKit. https://developer.apple.com/augmented-reality/reality-composer/. Accessed July 2019
9. Andy O`Sullivan video page. https://www.youtube.com/watch?v=VKSFVLO_qaI. Accessed June 2019
10. Pratdepadua, J.: Programación en 3d con java 3d, Ra-Ma (2003)
11. Apple Inc. Homepage, Intro to App development with Swift, Apple Education. Accessed 2018
12. Apple Inc. Homepage, App development with Swift, Apple Education. Accessed 2018

Computer Tool Prototype for the Selections of Views to Materialize in Data Cubes and Frequent Pattern

Elizabeth Moreno Galván[(✉)] and Enrique Alfonso Carmona García

UPIITA-IPN, Av. Instituto Politécnico Nacional 258,
Gustavo A. Madero, 07340 Mexico City, Mexico
elizabeth.moreno.galvan.05@gmail.com,
eacarmona860920@gmail.com

Abstract. The widespread availability of new computational methods and tools for data analysis represents a great challenge for new students who need to now the basics. It is difficult the selection of the most appropriate strategy and the collection of methods in data mining it's a good example. Some of these methods require guidelines that may help practitioners in the appropriate selection of data mining tools. In the present paper it is showed the proposal of a tool which shows visually the implementation of an algorithm for the selection of the optimal set of views to materialize from a multidimensional cube, being the main parameter the materialization cost of those views. The tool allows defining operations with cubes on different dimensions from a list of business questions that can be performance on them, all this in order to ease students the learning and understanding of data cube generation in data mining discipline.

Keywords: Data mining · Data cube · Educational data mining · Big data

1 Introduction

Over the last years, the term data mining has been increasingly used in scientific literature and implies the use of different methods and tools to analyze large amount of data. Also, data mining term refers to data sets that are so massive or complex in nature so that traditional data processing methods and methodologies are inadequate to effectively analyze them [1, 2]. Data mining and big data has been successfully applied to different fields of human endeavor, including environmental and pollutant studies [3–6], disease detection and m-health [7–10], IoT and smart cities [11–13], but it does not only apply to these fields; these are just some of the recent fields of application of these techniques, they also apply to economic studies such as price prediction, marketing, or banking operations to name a few.

The data warehouse were created in response to the need to gather all the information of an organization in a single database, for analysts and administrators in order to find valuable data or verify situations that are related to different types of decisions where it is also necessary to reduce the time to obtain it [14–16]. The generation of a warehouse requires applying processes of extraction, integration, transformation and

© Springer Nature Switzerland AG 2019
M. F. Mata-Rivera et al. (Eds.): WITCOM 2019, CCIS 1053, pp. 203–212, 2019.
https://doi.org/10.1007/978-3-030-33229-7_18

cleaning data. The design and construction of a data warehouse is a complex and delicate task [16–18], since it must be outlined the multidimensional model to be used, as well as defining the optimal set of views to materialize. Finally, the last process consists of determining the necessary tools for data visualization.

This paper focuses on the data organization process from a warehouse using a software tool that automatically designs a multidimensional model and carries out the materialization of the hypercube to subsequently apply the algorithm of selecting the optimal set of views to materialize (Harinarayan method) [19]. The tool is also able to determine the frequent patterns present in the data taking into account a certain support and confidence, calculating also the association rules. The results of execution of the software tool developed are analyzed and finally the conclusions are presented.

2 Literature Review

The use of data mining in educational fields is knowing as Educational Data Mining, which emerges as a paradigm oriented to design models, methods and algorithms for exploring data from educational settings [20]. In this section are analyzed some frequently used educational data mining tools and techniques.

In [21] a review of works was presented; identifying statistics-visualization and web mining as a couple of techniques to classify. Related to visualization, four works are referenced and web mining is split into three tasks:

1. Clustering, classification and outlier detection
2. Association rules and sequential pattern
3. Text mining

Some features that are commonly present in friendly educational data mining tools for non-technical users, are the standardization of data mining methods and data, the integration of data mining functionalities and the design of techniques devoted to educational data mining.

In [20] an interpretation of educational data mining review is present, it shows a detailed analysis about:

1. Disciplines involved in data mining such as probability, machine learning, statistics, soft computing, artificial intelligence and natural language, where probability, machine learning and statistic are the principal approach used.
2. Data mining models, where two models are analyzed: descriptive models (unsupervised learning functions to produce patterns) and predictive models (supervised learning functions to estimate unknown or future values).
3. Data mining tasks such as clustering, association rules, correlation analysis, produce descriptive models, classification, regression and categorization generate predictive models. The most typical tasks are classification and clustering.
4. Data mining methods and techniques such as Bayes theorem, decision tree, instance-based learning and hidden Markov model are the most popular methods. Logistic, linear regression, frequencies and hierarchical clustering are the most popular techniques.

5. Algorithms, equations and frames used for data mining are implemented to mine the source data. The most popular are K-means, expectation maximization and Naïve-Bayes are the most used algorithms. Statistical equations are the most used equations. Several version of Bayesian networks are the most popular frames.

In [22] some of the tools for research and practice in educational data mining are analyzed, discussing where relevant tools are used in data science communities, but tools for creating structural equations model and multilevel models are not covered. The tools analyzed are resumed as follows:

6. Two tools for manipulation, cleaning and formatting the data are discuss (Microsoft Excel and EDM Workbench).
7. Six tools for determining the test can be conducted, what models can be constructed, what relationships can be mapped and explorer and how ca be validating the findings are analyzed (RapidMiner, Weka, KEEL, KNIME, Orange and SPSS).
8. Tree visualizations tools was analyzed (Tableau, d3js and InfoVis).

In all previous work nothing is mentioned about a tool which shows visually the implementation of an algorithm for the selection of the optimal set of views to materialize from a multidimensional cube, neither it is not taken in account the views materialization cost. Our proposal is a tool that allows defining operations with cubes on different dimensions from a list of business questions that can be performed on them.

3   Materials and Methods

The algorithm was implemented with the use of programming structures known as a linked list, which is filled from a data source file and emptied into various views within a database, forming what is known as the data cube. In a complementary way and to be able to adequately construct the structure of the data cube a modified B tree is implemented since each node has several children, it is necessary to take account that a node, in turn, can also have several parents. In the application interface named the file selection screen from which the user has to introduce the source file name in CSV format. If the user does not know the path or source file name, it can be selected from a file chooser, and once the source file is selected, the application can read the data source chosen in CSV format.

The data cube is used to represent the facts; in this case, the learning and understanding of data cube generation in data mining discipline. A data cube generally is a multi-dimensional concept; it can be from one to n dimensions. In this study, each dimension represents a separate measure, whereas the cells in the cube represent the facts of interest (how to generate the cube). Sometimes cubes hold a few values with the rest being *empty*, e.g., undefined, sometimes most or all cube coordinates hold a cell value of this type.

The tool was developed using Java programming language and was designed to read any text file sequentially and interpret it appropriately if it contains the data in a format where the column headings are in the first row separated by commas, as well as each data within tuple. The program is responsible for calculating the views on the MySQL database and manage a cached memory file in the form of a simple linked list and a modified B tree, where each node of the tree constitutes a cuboid or view, generating both a logical and a visual cube of data, where the calculation of data is carried out the cardinality of each dimension and its using an algorithm [19, 23] to determine the views to materialize. The first tests of the execution were made on a data cube created in a synthetic way; that is, the data was created by a computer program and the measurements were generated with random values.

4   Analysis and Design of the Multidimensional Model

Once the necessary data have been loaded, we work on the obtained database, so the schema of a cube is composed of Dimensions (D1, D2, ... , DN) that corresponds to the attributes of the database, obtained from the column headings reading of the file that contains the data store. The cube generated (Grill L = D1 × D2 × ... × DN) contains as nodes the cartesian product of dimensions D1, D2, ... , DN, where each node is called cuboid and represents potentially useful aggregations [19, 23].

Once the structure is generated, in order to answer any business questions, we must take advantage of the order in the structure of lattice that store the disk views in its nodes, besides it may a good option to materialize or pre-calculate all the cuboids, however the limitation of the size on disc it important to know. On the other hand, it is recommended to materialize the total base (maximum detail or apex) since with it can be answer any question and then move to the views with less cost, resulting into less time in obtaining the answer.

The formulation of business questions can be carried out through expressions of the structure query language (SQL), based on data obtained from the reading of the data file. The results of answering expressions or queries are known as view. In addition, operators can be created in order to work with views or data cubes. So, in a query as follows:

SELECT field, Op (field) **FROM** table **GROUP BY** field

Where:

- Field: is a subset of attributes within the database called dimensions of the form $D = \{d_1, d_2, ... , d_n\}$
- Op(field): is an operation in a numeric type dimension, such as **COUNT, SUM, MAX, MIN**.

The views are all those business questions that make use of the **GROUP BY** clause of at least one field and can be executed using the apex view. The cost of a view $C(v)$ is the cost of using that view to evaluated the average question and is proportional to the size of the view v. So, the construction of the lattice is done as follows:

$$A \rightarrow B \, si \, A \supset B$$

- Goes an arc from A to B, if B is a proper subset of A
- If mean that a question to B (if B does not exist) can be answered by looking only at A

If $A \cap B \neq 0$ but $A \not\subseteq B$ and also $B \not\subseteq A$, then there is no a arc from A to B

It has been implemented the Greedy algorithm [19] in order to get an efficient views generation, the algorithm works as it follows: Let $C(v)$ be the cost of a view v, which is the cost of using that view to evaluate a business question. Due to the disk size, there is a limit of k views (plus the total or top) to use. After selecting some set S of views, it has to be defined the benefit of the view v relative to S, denoted by $B(v, S)$. The only views that benefit from having v materialized are those that can be calculated from v, including v itself, we call each of them w. So the total benefit is the sum of all the benefits of the w views. Figure 1 shows the resulting pseudocode.

```
S = {top view};
for i=1 to k do begin
       select that view v not in S such that B(v,S) is maximized;
       S = S union {v};
end;
resulting S is the greedy selection;
```

Fig. 1. The greedy algorithm [19].

Figure 2 shows the Compute cube implementation with average by top-k H-tree-based implemented for the efficient views generation.

```
procedure htree_cubing(m, H, c);
{
(1)  for i = m downto 1 do {
(2)      for each a_i ∈ A_i if avg'^k(M) ≥ v, then {
(3)          let c[i] = a_i, if avg(M) ≥ v, output c;
(4)          if i > 1 then {
(5)              create a new header table H_{a_i}, only rows for attribute values in A_1,...,A_{i-1} are needed;
(6)              traverse side links started from row a_i in header table H once, do
                     (i) collect quant-info for header table H_{a_i};
                     (ii) copy quant-info in child node to parent node; and
                     (iii) link parent nodes with the same label using side-links;
(7)              call htree_cubing(i - 1, H_{a_i}, c);
(8)          }
(9)      }
(10)     if i > 1 then traverse side-links started from row a_i ∈ A_i in H once, do // roll up quant-info
                 (i) merge quant-info from children nodes to parent nodes; and
                 (ii) link parent nodes with the same label using side-links;
(11)     c[i] = *; // re-initialization for the new, current dimension,
(12)}
}
```

Fig. 2. Compute cube with average by top-k H-tree-based [23].

Where:

- Let C(v) be the cost of sight v
- Due the size of the disc, there is a limit of k views to use
- After selecting some set S of views (which of course includes the apex), the benefit of the view v relative to S is defined, denoted by B(v, S)
- Calculate B(v, S), the benefit of materializing the view v when the views of the set S have already materialized
- The only views that benefit from having v materialized are those that can be calculated from v, including v itself. Its denotated by w
- For each $w \leq v$, define B_w
- The view w can be calculated from v
- The lowest cost view is selected and denoted as u
- The benefit of B_w is C(v) < C(u), B_w = C(u) − C(v); otherwise B_w = 0
- If v has lowest cost than u, the benefit is the difference
- $B(v, S) = \sum_{w \leq v} B_w$.

In plain terms, the benefit of materializing v is calculated by looking at how the cost of evaluating other views, including itself, can be improved.

5   Results

The results obtained in the tool developed when loading the generated synthetic data are presented below. In Fig. 3 the result of loading the data in the application is observed.

Fig. 3. Data warehouse reading. Source: Self-made.

Subsequently, the views that can be generated from data cube in which the names of the dimensions are replaced by an alias is represented in Fig. 4.

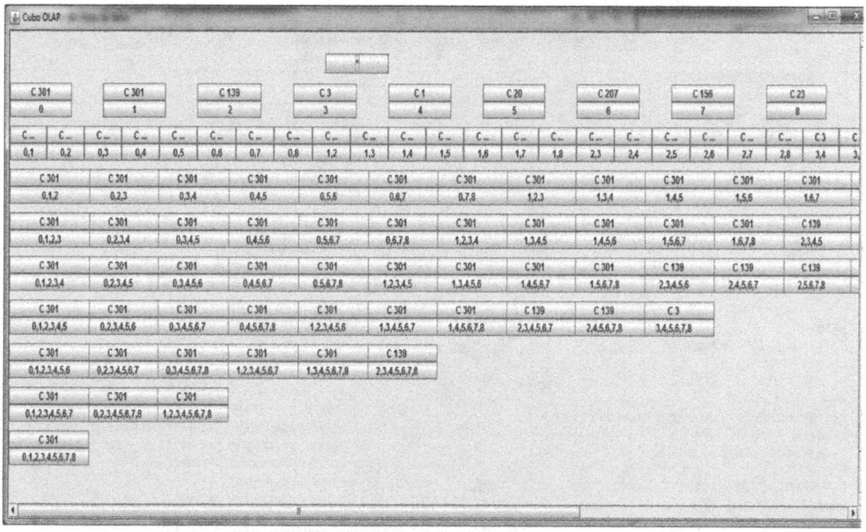

Fig. 4. Generation of data cube and its possible views. Source: Self-made.

Having all possible views to generate, we proceed to make the analysis of those that are suitable to materialize through the use of the proposed algorithms. Each view represents a set of fixed dimensional data in relation to a variable dimensional data. The frequent patterns are highlighted in the interface and determined by stablishing the required values of minimum support as Fig. 5 shows.

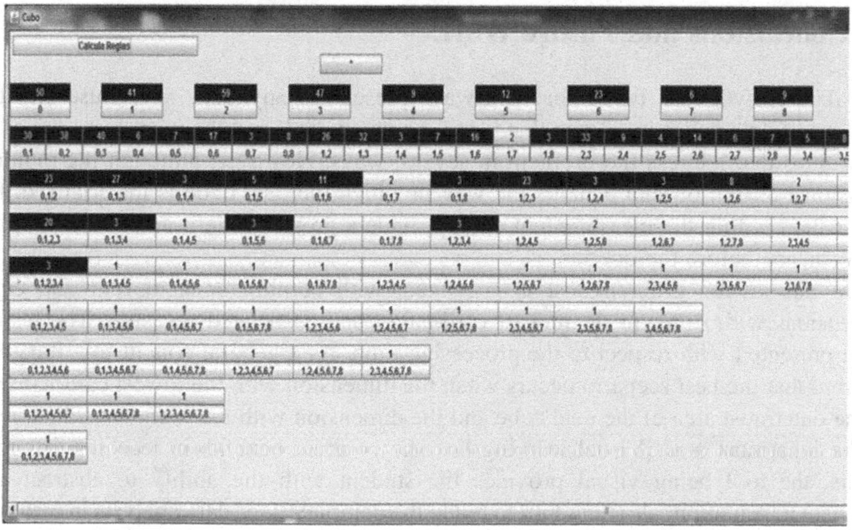

Fig. 5. Frequents patrons finding. Source: Self-made.

Finally, the existing association rules are determined by stablishing the required values of minimum confidence as Fig. 6 shows.

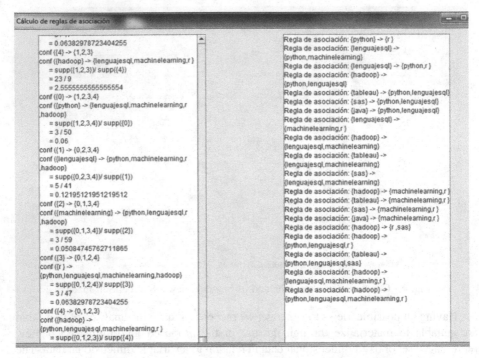

Fig. 6. Associations rules finding with min support = 3 and min conf = 80%. Source: Self-made.

6   Conclusions and Future Work

The data growth is a factor that is always present in any data warehouse and the analysis of data cubes is an area that is still being studied, and there are many types of algorithms that address the problem in several ways. However, although the multidimensional design of data benefits the way in which the data cube is materialized, the null values within the measurement data, provide a greater benefit and a much higher performance before the queries.

In this article, different test is presented, with combinations of four and eight dimensions with different degrees of cardinality and associated measure. The results were presented with respect to the processing time. As a general conclusion, it can be inferred that the best scenario occurs when the dimension with the lowest cardinality is in the outermost area of the data cube and the dimension with the highest cardinality is in the innermost area. Visual learning has shown great benefits in teaching environments, the tool being visual provides the student with the ability to abstract and organize information, allowing him to relate the complexity of data analysis in a natural way and faster that conceptually as has been done traditionally.

Some works that are considered interesting are:

- Accelerate the load of the base to the structure by means of chunks if there is limited memory.
- Improve the capture interface and the result interface.
- The capture of the expression that defines the business questions is not simple for a business analyst and the answer is delivered in text format, that makes difficult the interpretation.
- To include some other analysis algorithms implementations in order to show their performance and the comparison between them.

References

1. Bellazzi, R., Zupan, B.: Predictive data mining in clinical medicine: current issues and guidelines. Int. J. Med. Inform. **77**(2), 81–97 (2008). https://doi.org/10.1007/978-3-540-30576-7183
2. Wong, Z.S.Y., Zhou, J., Zhang, Q.: Artificial intelligence for infectious disease big data analytics. Infect. Dis. Heal. **24**(1), 44–48 (2019). https://doi.org/10.1016/j.idh.2018.10.002
3. Wang, J., Boesch, R., Li, Q.X.: A case study of air quality - pesticides and odorous phytochemicals on Kauai, Hawaii, USA. Chemosphere **189**, 143–152 (2017). https://doi.org/10.1016/j.chemosphere.2017.09.045
4. Wang, Q., Wang, J., He, M.Z., Kinney, P.L., Li, T.: A county-level estimate of PM2.5 related chronic mortality risk in China based on multi-model exposure data. Environ. Int. **110**, 105–112 (2018). https://doi.org/10.1016/j.envint.2017.10.015
5. Uni, D., Katra, I.: Airborne dust absorption by semi-arid forests reduces PM pollution in nearby urban environments. Sci. Total Environ. **598**, 984–992 (2017). https://doi.org/10.1016/j.scitotenv.2017.04.162
6. Bari, M.A., Kindzierski, W.B.: Ambient fine particulate matter (PM2.5) in Canadian oil sands communities: levels, sources and potential human health risk. Sci. Total Environ. **595**, 828–838 (2017). https://doi.org/10.1016/j.scitotenv.2017.04.023
7. Vijayakumar, P., Ganesh, S.M., Deborah, L.J., Rawal, B.S.: A new SmartSMS protocol for secure SMS communication in m-health environment. Comput. Electr. Eng. **65**, 265–281 (2018). https://doi.org/10.1016/j.compeleceng.2016.11.016
8. Kazemi, Y., Mirroshandel, S.A.: A novel method for predicting kidney stone type using ensemble learning. Artif. Intell. Med. **84**, 117–126 (2018). https://doi.org/10.1155/2018/6798042
9. Echeverría, M., Jimenez-Molina, A., Ríos, S.A.: A semantic framework for continuous u-health services provisioning. Proc. Comput. Sci. **60**(1), 603–612 (2015). https://doi.org/10.1016/j.procs.2015.08.187
10. Acharya, U.R., et al.: Data mining framework for breast lesion classification in shear wave ultrasound: a hybrid feature paradigm. Biomed. Sig. Process. Control **33**, 400–410 (2017). https://doi.org/10.1016/j.bspc.2016.11.004
11. Malik, K.R., Sam, Y., Hussain, M., Abuarqoub, A.: A methodology for real-time data sustainability in smart city: towards inferencing and analytics for big-data. Sustain. Cities Soc. **39**(April), 548–556 (2018). https://doi.org/10.1016/j.scs.2017.11.031

12. Ye, Y., Zhao, Y., Shang, J., Zhang, L.: A hybrid IT framework for identifying high-quality physicians using big data analytics. Int. J. Inf. Manag. **47**(January), 65–75 (2019). https://doi.org/10.1016/j.ijinfomgt.2019.01.005

13. Allam, Z., Dhunny, Z.A.: On big data, artificial intelligence and smart cities. Cities **89** (January), 80–91 (2019). https://doi.org/10.1016/j.cities.2019.01.032

14. Zhang, L., Wen, J.: A systematic feature selection procedure for short-term data-driven building energy forecasting model development. Energy Build. **183**, 428–442 (2019). https://doi.org/10.1016/j.enbuild.2018.11.010

15. Wang, F., Liang, J.: An efficient feature selection algorithm for hybrid data. Neurocomputing **193**, 33–41 (2016). https://doi.org/10.1016/j.neucom.2016.01.056

16. Lin, Y., Wang, H., Zhang, S., Li, J., Gao, H.: Efficient quality-driven source selection from massive data sources. J. Syst. Softw. **118**, 221–233 (2016). https://doi.org/10.1016/j.jss.2016.05.026

17. Manbari, Z., AkhlaghianTab, F., Salavati, C.: Hybrid fast unsupervised feature selection for high-dimensional data. Expert Syst. Appl. **124**, 97–118 (2019). https://doi.org/10.1016/j.eswa.2019.01.016

18. Mahdiyah, U., Irawan, M.I., Imah, E.M.: Integrating data selection and extreme learning machine for imbalanced data. Proc. Comput. Sci. **59**(ICCSCI), 221–229 (2015). https://doi.org/10.1016/j.procs.2015.07.561

19. Harinarayan, V., Rajaraman, A., Ullman, J.D.: Implementing data cubes efficiently. SIGMOD (1996). https://doi.org/10.1145/235968.233333

20. Peña-Ayala, A.: Educational data mining: a survey and a data mining-based analysis of recent works. Expert Syst. Appl. **41**(4 PART 1), 1432–1462 (2014). https://doi.org/10.1016/j.eswa.2013.08.042

21. Romero, C., Ventura, S.: Educational data mining: a survey from 1995 to 2005. Expert Syst. Appl. **33**(1), 135–146 (2007). https://doi.org/10.1016/j.eswa.2006.04.005

22. Slater, S., Joksimovic, S., Kovanovic, V., Baker, R., Gasevic, D.: Tools for educational data mining: a review. J. Educ. Behav. Stat. **42**(1), 85–106 (2017). https://doi.org/10.3102/1076998616666808

23. Han, J., Pei, J., Dong, G., Wang, K.: Efficient computation of Iceberg cubes with complex measures, In: Proceedings of the ACM SIGMOD International Conference on Management of Data, vol. 30, no. 2, pp. 1–12 (2005). http://www.scopus.com/inward/citedby.url?scp=0034825777&partnerID=8YFLogxK

Intelligent Learning Ecosystem in M-Learning Systems

Diana Carolina Burbano Gonzalez[1],
Clara Lucia Burbano Gonzalez[2(✉)], and Cristian Barria Huidobro[3]

[1] Universidad San Buenaventura, Cali-Valle, Colombia
caritoburg@yahoo.com
[2] Corporación Universitaria Unicomfacauca, Popayán-Cauca, Colombia
cburbano@unicomfacauca.edu.co
[3] Universidad Mayor, Santiago, Chile
cristian.barrio@mayor.cl

Abstract. This article refers to the background of Education and educational technology; To understand, they are theoretical-explanatory links in the teaching-learning process in today's networked society. The configuration of the learning environment and the development of experiences that generate learning by integrating the monitoring of real-time experiences into ecosystems that guide the learning outcomes common to all and desirable. The epistemological approach is an "alternative" proposed by [1], it facilitates the construction of new knowledge and the method is a research action of analysis the exchange of mixed studies mediated by mHealth in the thematic of the pathological oral anatomy. Data were obtained through focus groups to students; The data analysis was performed in MaxQd v 2018 from the analysis categories. The results are organized according to the analysis categories for students, a saber: dialogue; interaction with teachers, interaction with peers, perceived learning; Mediation with applications.

Keywords: Digital learning ecosystem · Intelligent learning · Learning interaction and m-learning

1 Introduction

The current information society poses an environment in which ICTs play a strong role in all areas, including education [2]. This demands the establishment of pedagogical models aimed at both the design of educational materials in digital format and their mode of application [3] In this sense, higher education institutions have been forced to adopt strategies to respond to new trends in information and communication by competing with a greater advantage among their peers; by offering alternatives to access knowledge different from traditional forms, which require the convergence of teacher and student time-space. The use of information and communication technologies (ICT) offers a wide variety of tools in the educational process, consequently, by themselves, they do not guarantee appropriate learning, which is why the importance of pedagogical strategies that support the learning of learning is evident. Collaborative way

M. F. Mata-Rivera et al. (Eds.): WITCOM 2019, CCIS 1053, pp. 213–229, 2019.
https://doi.org/10.1007/978-3-030-33229-7_19

Identifying student learning at any time is important, on the one hand, because of prior learning conditions the construction of new learning and, on the other hand, because of monitoring, both by the same apprentice and by whoever oriental is a fundamental condition for its control and direction. This dimension of research requires the application of measurement methods and statistical procedures [4].

The use of intelligent learning systems with analytical methods in online education focuses on the collection, analysis, and reporting of data on student online actions [5]. The learning analysis has aroused the interest of academic institutions and teachers by displaying information that was not available before, allowing them to better understand how students learn and, therefore, to take actions with information to support the process [6]. Advances in technology in recent years have changed student learning behaviors and teaching methods with new environments and ubiquitous resources methodologies. Consequently, our goal is to provide a theoretical and analytical understanding of the pedagogical model and its implications in teaching and learning. The analysis of the pedagogical model and didactic sequence (thematic of basic sciences in oral pathology anatomy) is implemented by generating interactions with students in the new m-learning environments, which integrate students into learning outcomes common to all and desirable. The m-learning education allows both teachers and students to connect through their mobile devices generating communicative interaction.

This article reveals how technological mediation is generated in learning, from a trans and interdisciplinary perspective, by establishing relationships between knowledge. This is possible because the authors root their discourse in an epistemic framework and an objective that makes all knowledge common, through reflexive and dialogical analysis.

2   State of the Matter

The technology has offered a line of advancement to the attention in intelligent learning and the creation and efficient use of intelligent learning environments mediated with ubiquitous technology.

2.1   Ubiquitous Learning and Intelligent Learning

The rapid advance of the networks of communication wifi, 4 g, 5G .., and the use of the Smartphone have allowed the students to access digital resources and interact with computer systems without being limited by location and time. This has been investigated in this perspective by [7], and with criteria based on learning by [8]; The authors call this learning approach that uses mobile and wireless communication technologies, "mobile learning" [9] or "ubiquitous learning" [8]. The other pillar is the detection technologies: GPS (global positioning systems), RFID (radio frequency identification), QR (rapid response); they have allowed the learning systems to detect the real-world locations and contexts of the students [10] and the recommendation systems [11, 12].

Various studies have evidenced these approaches and have emphasized the relevance that students learn from the real world with access to digital resources they use in their activities and are assisted by their teachers in technology-mediated learning and web-based learning, towards mobile learning and especially "ubiquitous context-aware learning" [13].

2.2 Reference Framework of the McLuhan Tetrad

McLuhan Media Laws are based on the idea that all artifacts have an effect on people and the society that adopts them. From this perspective, each new tool that is introduced becomes an extension. The word "extension" refers to the idea that, by building new things, humans increase their bodies and these changes are, in the long term, transforming the social and physical environment. We need an answer to a fact, the transit of the intelligent university (intelligent learning systems); through analysis based on experiences and interaction in learning ecosystems (m-Learning).

The data sources used in the learning analysis tools can come from a variety of academic systems, such as student information, library services, learning management systems, student admissions and grades [5]. Among those sources, research on learning analysis has tended to focus on the possibilities of using data in LMS learning management systems. According to Vernet, the potential uses of learning analysis are related to the following areas: (1) prediction of student performance and student modeling, (2) suggestion of relevant learning resources, (3) increased reflection and awareness, (4) improvement of social learning environments, (5) detection of undesirable learning behaviors and (6) identification of student emotions.

The research field of learning analytics is interdisciplinary, consequently, it combines aspects of educational data mining, social network analysis, artificial intelligence, psychology - theory and educational practice. In educational research, it is important to define two related areas: learning practice and organizational development. Both use educational data, although with different interests. While, in the practice of learning, the analyzes focus on improving student success, in organizational development the pressure has been on productivity and business solutions. In the domain of the organization, the analysis combines student information with institutional data to improve administrative efficiency [14].

The literature on learning analysis tools also suggests that it can be used to address data from a variety of perspectives. Some of the most prominent are social networks, discourse analysis [15, 16], content analysis [17, 18], disposition analysis [19] and student-centered analysis [20], among others. In all of them, learning analysis tools are expected to improve teaching and support student success.

2.3 Cognitive Sciences

From the cognitive sciences, including neurosciences and their relationship with psychology, anthropology and information sciences, innumerable contributions are made to the understanding of m-learning teaching and learning. How people learn using digital media, how information processing is carried out, how perceptual, associative and integrative processes carried out in the brain are involved, what are the best ways to teach from the functioning of the nervous system, or As meanings are built and skills are acquired, they are some of the questions to which cognitive sciences can contribute to answer.

2.4   Learning Analysis Tools

There are multiple definitions of the concept of "learning," and these depend on the epidemiological position on which it is based. For this article, the conceptualized one of [21] has been selected, who sees learning as A persistent change in human performance or its potential for performance, which must be the result of the subject's experience and interaction with the world

Based on the McLuhan axiom, all media are extensions of people, we analyze how the tools of learning analysis broaden our senses as human beings. Learning analysis tools reveal "hidden" information, it connects with the idea of a sixth sense, in this case to perceive learning behaviors that are not visible. By displaying this data, the learning analysis allows another view of what happens when students participate in online learning. The expectations of the learning analysis go beyond having a different view on teaching and learning. In this sense, education professionals and academics have expressed their hopes in the learning analysis by predicting learning performance and identifying learning models. Customize learning, control the activity of teachers, as well as the performance of the institution, understand social interaction and participation and engage students in their learning processes.

The prediction of student success or failure in learning, particularly in e-learning, has received considerable attention. Research in this area has led to the definition of profiles to model different types of learners, as well as the identification of different learning styles. Personalization is the core of many approaches to learning analysis; The data collected on students' online behaviors inform decisions about what type of learning resources or activities are most significant, given the student's current skills and knowledge on a given topic. Taking into account individual aspects, the tools of learning analysis improve a broader vision of learning that recognizes the importance of building prior knowledge and skills of students.

Learning analysis tools seek personalization, are based on the idea of how students learn, therefore, to ensure that students acquire the desired skills, teaching practice must adapt to the diversity of needs and challenges faced by students.

In many learning analysis tools, in addition to individual performance, data on group activity is also available. This feature intensifies the comparison between the individual and the group and indirectly pushes students to work harder when their activity falls below the group average. Educational institutions have used learning analysis to recruit students [22] and sometimes speculate on the possibility of human resources in the analysis of future learning. This scenario forces people to compete to guarantee access to the university or the labor market.

Nowadays societies need collaboration and cooperation instead of competition, the idea that educational institutions need to prepare students to work in a competitive society has been described as myth [23]. One of the main effects of Competition is homogenization: people need to share the same objectives and rules to compete [23]. In learning, standardization implies that everyone must learn the same in the same period. Continuous monitoring and pressure to meet academic expectations can create anxiety and distrust among those interested in education. [24] has studied these phenomena in learning in the workplace, and has concluded; in the monitoring of the online learning activity negatively affects the collaboration of workers, communication and knowledge sharing. Although formal education differs from learning in the workplace, the stress on students caused by fulfilling their curriculum on time while staying at the same level as the group does not support creativity and innovation [24]. Therefore, to the extent that the tools of learning analysis do not recognize the value of experimentation and risk-taking, they intensify a vision of learning based on the efficiency in which failure is penalized.

Digital data has become a key element in management techniques that are "evidence-based." Educational institutions are subject to a logic similar to that of contemporary organizations, which are based on the use of data and information. A good example of this trend can be found in the university and the school, in which the emphasis on the indicators has been questioned, therefore hiding good practices in teaching and learning. From this perspective, the most critical voices They affirm "the analysis of learning, especially the academic analysis, intensifies the management culture in education" [25], some sectors of the academic community affirm that the analyzes can improve the understanding and performance of the students [26] For teachers, the possibility of accessing the data generated by the students allows them to reflect on the ins design and management of the courses they teach. In this case, the learning analysis is presented as a tool that promotes the knowledge and reflection of educators about some aspects of their professional practice.

Learning analysis is part of a trend based on decision-making informed by data. From this perspective, automatic collection and analysis of student behavior data are assumed to be relevant and reliable, or at least more reliable than subjective percep-tions. The trust dedicated to computer algorithms is not exclusive to learning analysis, and similar attitudes towards data in business, medical care, social services, sports, etc. can be found. Although stakeholders in education recognize that learning analysis enriches teaching and learning, we could question the extent to which learning analysis is affecting the credibility we give to personal impressions. In a data-driven society, can we rely on subjective and qualitative data collected through individual experiences?

The learning analysis modifies certain aspects of the role of teachers, especially in online education. Here, we could say that the confidence in the data of the learning analysis is closely related to the emergence of educational programs online. As Mazza and [27] point out, in e-learning courses, students face related challenges such as loneliness, technical problems or loss of motivation [28]. In these cases, the lack of visual guidelines from teachers that help them recognize when students are poorly motivated, anxious or overwhelmed is compensated through learning analysis. In mixed learning scenarios, the learning analysis affects the teacher's ability to perceive group feedback, as there is a growing tendency to rely on the information collected through the back channels during large conferences. The ultimate goal of these efforts is to improve adaptation and improve teaching. But as McLuhan and McLuhan [29] pointed out, the simultaneous effect is the disappearance of certain practices. In this case, the praxis that is being relegated is the ability of certain teachers to detect individual and group behaviors.

2.5   Interactions

The pedagogical design currently proposed by the traditional education system requires the adequacy of the design of competent and individualistic producing minds that accommodate an industrialized social context. This learning structure based on the mass production paradigm seeks to retake the "feed-feed" model within the educational processes; a model that uses different pedagogical practices of collaborative interaction that involve technological and virtual communication scenarios [30].

This type of learning scenarios generally considered communication devices are centralized in the development of participatory cognitive structures within the social and educational environment, with the support of convergent interactive technologies to articulated languages for different purposes [31]. This technological accompaniment from the constant interactivity of individuals within a currently techno-mediated environment [32], arises amid the need to create new collaborative relationships of dissimilar transmissions.

The manifestation of these transmissions based on interaction relationships forms a connective knowledge based on autonomy, diversity, openness and connectivity/interactivity [31]. For Badillo, these interactions arise from the dialogue and argumentation of individuals, which allows the reciprocal exchange of different opinions, perspectives, and reconstruction of meanings, where new technologies are fundamental in collective interaction, differentiators in the reorganization of mental functions; they assign the meaningful concept of learning and enable the basic principle of knowledge transfer to real situations [31].

2.6   Mobile Learning

The new century is going through an era where information and knowledge are accessible from anywhere and at any time. It can be said that this is a society saturated with information influenced by technology and science available to the world. A society that is characterized by the variety of autonomous contexts differentiated by resources, willing to take on technological innovation challenges to improve their development, it can be said that this society is going through the phenomenon of ubiquitous training [33]. The current society adapts to the new mediated techno ecosystem [32], must emerge from its traditional roots to establish an educational system that integrates new models of quality, knowledge, and resources [34].

This is a challenge that the current educational model must take with care and responsibility, which goes through an outdated stage that refers to the beginning of its development before the emergence of information and communication technologies [34]. The current model, based on the face-to-face design of traditionalist practices [31], is aimed at educating a certain segment of the population. Therefore, it is important that training begins to be restored from the educational model of teachers; adapt them to the modern education system that includes technology among its practices.

We must not forget the work that these devices play in formal education since they are considered excellent administrators of academic material. They provide valuable and interactive multimedia learning content for educational purposes [35]. Also, learning strategies appropriate to this context can help educators facilitate the mobile learning process and reach their educational goals. Likewise, when these materials are properly adapted to their educational formats, the student can take full advantage of spaces that until now were not part of the learning time [36].

It is necessary to analyze the options for adapting training content (which are generally considered robust) to mobility scenarios, that is, transferring learning methods to a mobile context-based on flexible and interactive styles that are not difficult to grasp [37]. The use of technology alone does not directly include improvements in training. Cañizares points out through the author [38], artificial intelligence theorist and learning expert, the skepticism about a large part of the courses offered online; It considers that there is no sample of changes in the educational models and they are conditioned to offer the same materials as always. Schank is committed to learning based on experience. As a student of the human mind, he states that mental processes evolve greatly from experience, given that he faces real situations. Contrary to what happens with conventional learning, based on questions and answers outside the real context and far from the individual's praxis [36].

Education should examine how educational resources are designed and delivered and take into account the needs and characteristics of the new student generation. For example, in the delivery of improved technology to the student, what is the purpose of the tool at the educational level? Does it fit the current training needs? The current generation of students uses this technology in continuous transformation, such as mobile devices, which require the support of teachers as well as information and timely feedback. It must be taken into account that these changes occur according to the training needs supported by current technologies that arise in a society with high information demand [39]. The educational system must rescue informal learning practices adapted to the new connective and flexible world in the use of mobile technology, which is aimed at the autonomous and collaborative learning of students. Without a doubt, this is a knowledge society that must be willing to take on the challenges associated with communicative and informational technologies [40].

3 Research Design

Information and communication technologies (ICT) represent each, new challenges and possibilities in the educational field. The term educational technology acquires a new meaning that refers to the incorporation of ICT in teaching and learning processes. This emerging field called technological mediations in education supposes its epistemological status, supported by positioned epistemic tendencies, which reveal cognitive configurations that focus its interest in categories such as learning and collaboration, privileging interactivity, under the assumption that it gives meaning to experience and applicability of the contents learned to real-life situations.

Following the reflections of [41], it is possible to overcome the false dichotomy between quantitative research and qualitative research in the social and human sciences, for which he postulates an integrative vision called "alternative research". "The two types of techniques need each other most of the time ... every existence or phenomenon has quantitative and qualitative attributes … Consequently, some authors propose overcoming this false dichotomy."

4 Research Method

The Research-Action (I-A) Lewin's work in the period immediately after World War II. Lewin identified four phases in I - A (planning, acting, observing and reflecting) and imagined it based on the principles that could lead "gradually towards independence, equality, and cooperation" [42]. Throughout these years, the I-A method has been configured based on numerous contributions from different geographical and ideological contexts. The great diversity of conceptions that currently exist around I-A, both from a theoretical and experiential perspective, makes it less than impossible to arrive at a unique conceptualization. However, there are many common features in which most authors are coincidental. In the first place, it is worth highlighting the preponderant nature of the action, as defining this research method. This dimension is specified in the active role assumed by the subjects who participate in the research, which takes as a start the problems arising from educational practice, reflecting on them, breaking in this way with the separatist dichotomy theory/practice. "Action research is a form of research carried out by practitioners on their practices" [43].

5 Hypothesis

There is a significant transformation of the preconceptions that, on oral pathology, periodontics students bring, under the use of the mHealth application.

6 Techniques and Instruments for Information Gathering

In the present investigation, the following instruments will be used for the collection of the information: script of questions for focus group (qualitative analysis) and the questionnaire (pre-test) in the mobile application (quantitative analysis).

7 Population and Sample

The target population is heterogeneous and is made up of the academic program of Specialization in Periodontics and Osseointegration existing in the Cooperative University of Colombia, Bogotá headquarters; attached to the Faculty of Dentistry, which has informed consent or voluntary acceptance of participation in the project. The number of residents 15, enrolled according to Helmsman in the second and fourth semester in the second half of 2018.

8 Consent to Participate in the Study

In line with internationally accepted standards to ensure the ethical treatment of people involved in scientific research, an informed consent form was developed. The document will explain to the research participants in the focus groups the nature of the study, its objectives, as well as the right not to participate or to suspend their participation at any time and the confidentiality of the information provided to the participants.

9 Data Analysis Plan

The proposed methodology is complementary (quantitative and qualitative), the analysis of the data obtained according to their nature will be performed. For the processing and analysis of quantitative data, the statistical software SPSS (statistical package for the social science), version 20 for Windows, was used. As recommended by various authors such as [44], first the descriptive statistics will be kept, including frequencies, calculation of measures of central tendency (mean, median and mode) and dissension (variance and standard deviation). The analysis is performed between differences of groups (T students test for independent samples and analysis of variance of a factor) and the degree of association or relationship between the variables (Pearson's correlation coefficient and chi-square tests).

The qualitative information collected will be analyzed with the MaxQda software, version 2018. The interviews are made recorded in audio format and subsequently transcribed and incorporated into the software for the organization and classification of data, summarize and tabulate them (data reduction). It will be done following the inductive method, based on the information obtained, the analysis categories will arise. Therefore, following the suggested methodology, qualitative data will pass to an analytical description to extract relevant information, from coding to the interpretation of its meaning and importance [45].

The preparation of qualitative data includes: The transcription of interview recordings, observation and field notes (computer programs for optical recognition of OCR characters and voice recognition).

Thematic coding and categorization: coding is a way of indexing or categorizing the text to establish a framework of thematic ideas.

Narratives: storytelling or storytelling is one of the fundamental ways people organize the understanding of the world. In the stories, people make sense of their experience and share their experience with others. Therefore, careful analysis of the themes, content, style, context, and narrative reveals people's understanding of the meaning of events in cultural contexts.

Comparative analysis: the coding provides the shorthand synthesis between different people, objects, scenes or events (situations, actions, stories or experiences of the members), data of the same people, scenes, objects or types of events, some matches with others.

Typology: a typology is a way of classifying things that can be multidimensional or multifactorial, can be based on two (or more) different categories of things.

Quality of analysis and ethics

10 Data Analysis of Focus Groups with Qualitative Analysis Techniques

In the present study the classic content analysis will be used, it implies the creation of small pieces of data (Chunks) and the subsequent assignment of a code to each one of them. However, instead of creating a theme from the codes, these are placed in similar groups and then accounted for. Using the three-element coding framework there are only three ways to use classical content analysis with focus group data: a. the analysis can establish if each participant uses a given code; b. the analyst can determine if each group used a given code; c. the analyst can identify all instances in which a certain code appears [46]. Researchers should not only provide information on the frequency of each code (that is, quantitative information) but also complement it with a description of each code (qualitative information); which will create a mixed modality of content analysis [47].

11 Analysis of Quantitative Data

11.1 Interpretation of Pre Test Results

Regarding the content of m-learning educational applications by students, the results show a 30% difference between women and men. 40% of women contain educational applications on their mobile devices, unlike 70% of men. However, the data show the lack of good use of the mobile device in educational contexts by men, because women predominate communicative and interactive participation in different learning environments.

Although the methodology used by the teacher has shown good results, it is important to clarify that from the technological - pedagogical perspective, there is a need to include information and communication technologies (ICT) in their training processes. The study shows low rates about the use of the mobile device in the educational field, as well as the management of mobile educational applications. Therefore, the support of ICT, specifically mobile devices (m-learning) for the teaching-learning process, is undoubtedly the opportunity to transform formal education into a mobile and ubiquitous context applied to the reinforcement of knowledge in the subject of pathological oral anatomy.

11.2 Post-test Analysis

Once the pedagogical - technological and communication model has been implemented, the interaction - gender variable continues to stand out the intervention of women in terms of conditions of a teacher-student relationship, synchronous and asynchronous technological interaction), active participation in the subject, and the Access to resources on the platform.

The analysis of the comparative statistical results of the pre-test and post-test shows in the study of interactions in collaborative learning environments, mediated by m-learning, a significant difference is reported in the present comparative study. Figure 1 shows a before and after the m-learning test between the two samples.

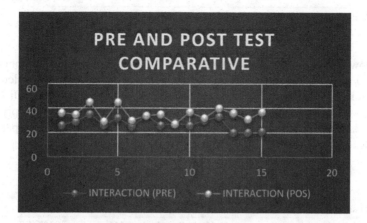

Fig. 1. Pre test and post test behavior. *Source own elaboration*

The behavior of the graph demonstrates the changes obtained once technological mediation has been applied in periodontics residents, due to the fact that a high frequency of technological and social interaction is evident. The average score that marked the difference between pre and post was 7.86.

Technique: T-Student Test for Related Simples
The t-student test was applied, to calculate and know the values of the mean, standard deviation and the standard mean error of the sample, as shown in Table 1.

Table 1 Paired samples 1. *Source own elaboration*

Paired sample statistics

		Half	N	Standard deviation	Mean standard error
Pair 1	INTERACTION (PRE)	27,40	15	4,837	1,249
	INTERACTION (POS)	35,27	15	5,244	1,354

The results show a difference of the average between the pre and post-test at a 7.867 higher in the result of the evaluation of the interactions that the post-test throws. For the standard deviation, the dispersion of the data is more significant in the post-test with a score of 5,244 compared to 4,837 that produced the pre-test; This is due to atypical data presented within the post-test results.

Regarding Pearson's linear correlation (Table 1), in this case, it is 0.100. As this value of significance is greater than the value of alpha (0.05), it can be statistically deduced that the scores in both registration conditions do not correlate, that is, there are differences in their results.

Table 2 Paired samples 2. *Source own elaboration*

Matched sample correlations

		N	Correlation	Sig.
Pair 1	INTERACTION (PRE) & INTERACTION (POS)	15	,440	,100

To know if there is a significant statistical difference in the results obtained, the difference between the P-value (0.000) and the value of alpha (0.05) was calculated. In this case, since P-value is less than alpha, it can be deduced that the statistical difference between the tests is significant (Table 2). Another condition for complying with this theory is shown in the relationship between the lower limit and the upper limit of the confidence interval is not 0 (Table 3).

Table 3 Paired samples 3. *Source own elaboration*

Test paired samples

		Half	Standard deviation	Mean error are-given	95% difference confidence interval
Pair 1	INTERACTION (PRE) - INTERACTION (POS)	−7,867	5,343	1,380	−10,826

		95% difference confidence interval			
		Higher	t	gl	Sig(bilateral)
Pair 1	INTERACTION (PRE) - INTERACTION (POS)	−4,908	−5,702	14	,000

It can be concluded that there is a significant difference in the means of the interaction variable before and after the technological mediation because P-value (level of significance) is less than 0.05 (alpha), so the test m -learning has significant effects on student interaction.

11.3   Qualitative Analysis

In qualitative research, the categories of analysis are dynamic and are built throughout the process, therefore general categories are established, derived from the research question. The initial proposal of analysis categories was based on theoretical revision and conceptual construction for the study.

11.4   Data Analysis

Concerning the interpretation and discussion of the data, it was done by contrasting the experiences of students and teachers with m-learning, dialogue, interaction, and learning. The information collected was analyzed based on categories with the help of the MaxQA 2018 software program. The method includes data reduction, coding, theoretical sampling. The principle of qualitative information analysis was that of "saturation", thus the cyclical analysis of the information comparing data to form categories, relating them to each other and resorting to new data and informants to confirm, modify or reject them, special attention was given to even a saturation point, that is, the new cases will not provide new information, which indicated that at that time the analytical process should conclude.

11.5 Interpretation of Qualitative Results

Analysis Category: The function of the dialogue with classmates and teachers

The dialogue functions are congruent with the predominant use of discussion forums. in m-learning, when conducting debates, exchanging perspectives among students and raising doubts with teachers. The possibility of contrasting opinions and interacting with other people with different experiences is positively valued by students, as it contributes to the development of professional skills.

The characteristics of the dialogue with codes were: communication is very important, respect and trust in the interaction, dialogue with peers are enriching, large and heterogeneous groups generate communication, communication with peers is fluid, communication with the teacher is fluid and generates feedback.

In general, the dialogue is perceived as relevant, respectful and enriching; Highlights the recognition by students of the importance of communication, as well as the elements of respect and trust, which are part of the very concept of dialogue. On these aspects, in a dialogical relationship, the student affirmed:

"Dialogue in apss-mediated learning, with respect and confidence in the fulfillment of acquired commitments."

Interaction with Teachers: What is the degree of interactivity between students and teachers? What is the quality of the interaction? And How does it take place?

The analysis of this category, derived from the focus groups, was broken down into four sets of codes: tools used to interact with teachers; functions of interaction with teachers, frequency of interaction with teachers, quality of interaction with teachers. About how interaction with teachers takes place, the most frequently used media were the asynchronous discussion forums, as well as email.

Interaction with Students: How is dialogue between students encouraged? and what role does it play in the student's learning process?

The analysis of the information provided by students in the focus groups resulted in code groups: tools used when interacting with peers, frequency of interaction, functions of interaction with peers, quality of interaction with peers. Then a representative appointment of the forms of communication used: "We communicate through telephone messages and emails. Communication through electronic messages and emails is given to share opinions about the course and organize better group work, interact constantly, even more than in the classroom.

12 Discussion of Results from the Conceptual Framework

Dialogue. In terms of dialogue, the virtual courses analyzed, from the perspective of the students, have an appropriate level of dialogue, understood as a bidirectional, horizontal, respectful and learning-centered relationship, between students and teachers and between the students themselves. The intensity of the dialogue is variable, although none of the courses presented a major difficulty that prevented the learning process. The availability of technological tools allows an acceptable level of dialogue.

Structure. Students perceive that the courses have an appropriate level of structure: course program, reading material, support material, links and activities scheduled according to a schedule. However, sometimes the lack of structure is a factor that negatively affects students' perception of teacher performance and the degree of perceived learning.

Direct instruction is exercised by teachers asynchronously, through a "mediated dialogue", as previously seen; They use written materials available on the platform, as well as announcements and messages to intervene in the presentation of content. However, students must assume their understanding of the material by reading and evacuating doubts at the time required, mainly with the use of the question forums and email.

13 Conclusions

A current trend in the "teaching-learning system", as opposed to the pedagogical practice of the teacher; Currently, teaching is less interesting than learning, and less interesting what the teacher presents and more what the student learns (training focused on learning).

It was found that students generally demonstrated an adequate level of satisfaction in m-learning, by separating the analysis between the best-rated courses was the discussion forum, the exchange of opinions and experiences with classmates were assessed as teaching-learning strategies.

Learning in collaborative or cooperative environments allows greater reception in educational settings. The student these learning options is in the ability to make decisions about their process and identify their own needs, specifically in the subject of networks which presents a high degree of student dropout.

Collaborative learning allows each student to develop their creative thinking, self-learning, commitment and responsibility of their peers, and their participatory spirit, achieving group growth.

The present investigation demonstrated the effectiveness of peer interaction generates skills in the subject of networks and stimulates cognitive improvement; At the time of exchange, we establish a relationship between the interacting subjects, motivations, and interests.

Interaction with peers has the function of coordinating tasks in group work or projects, as well as exchanging opinions and learning from the experiences of others. The degree of interaction is adequate but depends largely on the design of the activities. The teacher's role remains important as a promoter of the interaction in the group.

The main contribution of this research is the approach of three elements directly related to the positive perception of pedagogical presence by students, namely: feedback, academy, and socialization. In general, both students and teachers consider the contribution that peer interaction makes learning as important.

References

1. Paramo, P.: La investigacion en ciencias sociales: estrategias de investigacion. Universidad piloto de Colombia, Bogota, p. 332 (2003)
2. Galvis, E., Sánchez, J.: A critical review of knowledge management in software process reference models. J. Inf. Syst. Technol. Manag. 10 (2013). https://doi.org/10.4301/S1807-17752013000200008
3. Rosanigo, Z., Bramati, P.: Objetos de aprendizaje. XIII Workshop de Investigadores en Ciencias de la Computación, pp. 574–869 (2011). http://sedici.unlp.edu.ar/bitstream/handle/10915/19934/Documento_completo.pdf?sequence=1. Accessed 7 Sept 2013
4. Maldonado, L.: Virtualidad y autonomía pedagogía para la equidad. ICONK Editorial, Colombia (2012)
5. Lockyer, L., Heathcote, E., Dawson, S.: Informing pedagogical action: aligning learning analytics with learning design. Am. Behav. Sci. 57(10), 1439–1459 (2013)
6. Dawson, S., Gašević, D., Siemens, G., Joksimovic, S.: Current state and future trends: a citation network analysis of the learning analytics field. In: Proceedings of the Fourth International Conference on Learning Analytics and Knowledge, March 2014, pp. 231–240. ACM (2014)
7. Hwang, G., Chang, H.: A formative assessment-based mobile learning approach to improving the learning attitudes and achievements of students. Comput. Edu. 56, 1023–1031 (2011)
8. Zapata-Ros, M.: Teorías y modelos sobre el aprendizaje en entornos conectados y ubicuos. Bases para un nuevo modelo teórico a partir de una visión crítica del "conectivismo". Teoría de la Educación. Educación y Cultura en la Sociedad de la Información, vol. 16 (2015)
9. Sharples, M., Arnedillo-Sánchez, I., Milrad, M., Vavoula, G.: Mobile learning. In: Balacheff, N., Ludvigsen, S., de Jong, T., Lazonder, A., Barnes, S. (eds.) Technology-Enhanced Learning, pp. 233–249. Springer, Dordrecht (2009). https://doi.org/10.1007/978-1-4020-9827-7_14
10. Hwang, G., Furuchi, T., Naganuma, A.: The ubiquitin-conjugating enzymes, Ubc4 and Cdc34, mediate cadmium resistance in budding yeast through different mechanisms. Life Sci. 82(1182–5), 23–24 (2008)
11. Pazzani, M., Billsus, D.: Content-based recommendation systems. In: Brusilovsky, P., Kobsa, A., Nejdl, W. (eds.) The Adaptive Web. LNCS, vol. 4321, pp. 325–341. Springer, Berlin (2007). https://doi.org/10.1007/978-3-540-72079-9_10
12. Chen, Y., Cheng, L., Chuang, C.: A group recommendation system with consideration of interactions among group members. Expert Syst. Appl. 34(3), 2082–2090 (2008)
13. Liu, G., Hwang, G.: A key step to understanding paradigm shifts in e-learning: towards context-aware ubiquitous learning. Br. J. Edu. Technol. 41, E1–E9 (2010)
14. Siemens, G., Long, P.: Penetrating the fog: analytics in learning and education. Educause Rev. 46(5), 30 (2011)
15. De Liddo, A., Shum, S., Quinto, I., Bachler, M., Cannavacciuolo, L.: Discourse-centric learning analytics. In: Proceedings of the 1st International Conference on Learning Analytics and Knowledge, pp. 23–33 (2011). ACM

16. Ferguson, R., Shum, S.: Learning analytics to identify exploratory dialogue within synchronous text chat. In: Proceedings of the 1st International Conference on Learning Analytics and Knowledge, pp. 99–103. ACM (2011)
17. Drachsler, H., Bogers, T., Vuorikari, R., Verbert, K., Duval, E., Manouselis, N.: Issues and considerations regarding sharable data sets for recommender systems in technology enhanced learning. Procedia Comput. Sci. 1(2), 2849–2858 (2010)
18. Verbert, K., Drachsler, H., Manouselis, N., Wolpers, M., Vuorikari, R., Duval, E.: Dataset-driven research for improving recommender systems for learning. In: Proceedings of the 1st International Conference on Learning Analytics and Knowledge, pp. 44–53. ACM (2014)
19. Crick, R., Broadfoot, P., Claxton, G.: Developing an effective lifelong learning inventory: the ELLI project. Assess. Edu.: Principles Policy Pract. 11(3), 247–272 (2004)
20. Kruse, A., Pongsajapan, R.: Student-centered learning analytics. CNDLS Thought Papers, 1–9 (2012)
21. Driscoll, M.: Psychology of Learning for Instruction. Allyn & Bacon, Needham Heights (2000)
22. Van Harmelen, M., Workman, D.: Analytics for learning and teaching. CETIS Analytics Ser. 1(3), 1–40 (2012)
23. Combs, A.: Myths in Education: Beliefs that Hinder Progress and their Alternatives. Allyn and Bacon, Boston (1979)
24. Wesley, D.: A critical analysis on the evolution of e-learning. Int. J. E-learn. 1(4), 41–48 (2002)
25. Selwyn, N.: Data entry: Towards the critical study of digital data and education. Learn. Media Technol. 40, 64–82 (2014)
26. Graf, S., Ives, C., Rahman, N., Ferri, A.: A tool for accessing and analysing students' behaviour data in learning systems. In: Proceedings of the 1st International Conference on Learning Analytics and Knowledge, pp. 174–179. ACM (2011)
27. Mazza, R., Dimitrova, V.: Visualising student tracking data to support instructors in web-based distance education. In: Proceedings of the 13th International World Wide Web conference on Alternate track papers & posters, pp. 154–161. ACM (2004)
28. McLuhan, M.: Understanding Media. The Extensions of $man. Sphere Books, London (1964)
29. McLuhan, M., McLuhan, E.: Laws of Media: The New Science, vol. 1. University of Toronto Press, Toronto (1988)
30. Aparici, R., Silva, M.: Pedagogía de la interactividad. Comunicar: Revista Científica Iberoamericana 19(38), 51–58 (2012). https://doi.org/10.3916/C38-2011-02-05
31. Badillo, E.: Tensiones Comunicativas Emergentes En Estrategias Colaborativo. Red de Revistas Científicas de América Latina, El Caribe, España Y Portugal, vol. 9, pp. 188–201. http://www.redalyc.org/articulo.oa?id=265428385012
32. Ortiz, R., Ramirez, A.: Ellos vienen con el chip incorporado. Editorial, Bogotá
33. Gros, B., Maina, M.: The Future of Ubiquitous Learning. https://doi.org/10.1007/978-3-662-47724-3. Barcelona
34. Ramírez, M.: Modelos y estrategias de enseñanza para ambientes innovadores. In: Modelos y Estrategias de Enseñanza para ambientes innovadores, pp. 1–55 (2013). https://www.editorialdigitaltec.com/materialadicional/ID254_RamirezMontoya_Modelosyestrategiasdeensenanza.cap1.pdf
35. Jeng, Y., Wu, T., Huang, Y., Tan, Q., Yang, S.: The add-on impact of mobile applications in learning strategies: a review study. Edu. Technol. Soc. 13(3), 3–11 (2010)
36. Del Campo Cañizares, E.: M-Learning y aprendizaje informal en la educación superior mediante dispositivos móviles. Ilu, vol. 18, pp. 231–242. https://doi.org/10.5209/rev_HICS.2013.v18.44239

37. Nielsen, J.: Usability 101: Introduction to Usability. Nielsen Norman Group. https://doi.org/10.1145/1268577.1268585. Articles
38. Schank, R.C., Fano, A., Bell, B., Jona, M.: The design of goal-based scenarios. J. Learn. Sci. 3(4), 305–345 (1994). https://doi.org/10.1207/s15327809jls0304_2
39. Vidal, M., Gavilondo, X., Rodríguez, A., Cuéllar, A.: Aprendizaje móvil. Revista Cubana de Educacion Medica Superior 29(3), 669–679 (2015). https://doi.org/10.7238/rusc.v12i1.1944
40. Ally, M., Prieto, J.: What is the future of mobile learning in education? RUSC. Revista de Universidad Y Sociedad Del Conocimiento 11(1), 142 (2014). https://doi.org/10.7238/rusc.v11i1.2033
41. Paramo, P.: La investigacion en ciencias sociales: estrategias de investigacion, p. 332. Universidad piloto de Colombia, Bogota (2013)
42. Lewin, K.: La investigación-acción y los problemas de las minorías. In: Salazar, M.C. (1992)
43. Carr, W., Kemmis, S.: Teoría crítica de la enseñanza. La investigación-acción en la formación del profesorado. Martínez Roca, Barcelona (1988)
44. Lopez, L., Hernandez, J.: Estadística descriptiva, test y ejercicios, 2ª ed. Ediciones Académicas. (EDIASA) edn, pp. 1–33. Madrid, España (2016)
45. Cofffey, A., Atkinson, P.: Encontrar el sentido a los datos cualitativos. Universidad de Alicante, Alicante (2003)
46. Morgan, D.: Focus Groups as Qualitative Research. SAGE, Thousand Oaks (1997). https://doi.org/10.4135/9781412984287
47. Onwuegbuzie, A., Teddlie, C.: A framework for analyzing data in mixed methods research. In: Tashakkori, A., Teddlie, C. (eds.) Handbook of mixed methods in social and behavioral research, pp. 351–383. SAGE, Thousand Oaks (2003)

Application of Cyberphysical Systems Through Logistics as a Mediating Component in Learning Processes

Andrés Felipe Córdoba U.$^{(\boxtimes)}$, Clara Lucia Burbano Gonzalez$^{(\boxtimes)}$, Julio E. Mejía M.$^{(\boxtimes)}$, and Jessica María Montilla M.$^{(\boxtimes)}$

Corporación Universitaria Unicomfacauca, Popayán-Cauca, Colombia
{andrescordoba, cburbano, jmejia,
jessicamontilla}@unicomfacauca.edu.co

Abstract. Technological advances make it possible to improve the industrial sector, particularly in the management of production, one of the cases happens in companies that use robots with decision-making capacity. This paper presents the development of a serious game that integrates 3 logistic processes: organization, production, and transport, in addition to an evaluation process applied to students of two academic programs of the Comfacauca University (Mechatronic and Industrial Engineering), where 30 students are taken into groups of 15 for each program. The data were subjected to the normality test using the Shapiro-Wilk criterion and with the obtained results the T-Student parametric test was applied which allowed establishing statistical differences between the groups. To establish statistically significant differences P-Value less than 0,05 for production and transport skills, while for the case of the organization no significant differences were found.

Keywords: Education · Industrial revolution · Logistics · Shapiro-Wilk · T-Student

1 Introduction

Logistics has been applied since the first era of human beings, being conceived as a component in development, necessary for survival processes, a time when tribes were in charge of storing, transporting and distributing raw materials or food. Later, in the Middle Ages, the first technological advances were made: wheelbarrows, boats and horse-drawn carriages, using them in processes applied to distribution, in order to supply points of commerce in each community.

Then, the era of the industrial revolution arose, which integrated manual and mechanical processes, leading to the manufacture of steam engines [1]. The industry sought to improve the quality of life of human beings with the intention of optimizing production processes. In the 1950s, the term "integral logistics" came into being, defined by [2] as "the control of the flow of materials from the source of supply to place the product at the point of sale, in accordance with customer requirements and with two basic conditioning factors: a. Maximum speed in the flow of the product and b.

M. F. Mata-Rivera et al. (Eds.): WITCOM 2019, CCIS 1053, pp. 230–244, 2019.
https://doi.org/10.1007/978-3-030-33229-7_20

minimum operational costs", expecting companies to generate subcontracts with other suppliers, thus dividing production processes at a lower cost, with high quality standards, satisfying the customer's [3], the "Just in Time" method was originated, inherently associated with technology, with the intention that industries improve strategies linked to clients in logistics processes, obtaining as a result the elaboration of a product in an exact time and quantity [4]. Since the year 2000, production processes tend to be optimized on a large scale with complementary collaborative robotics in the industry; it seeks to automate manufacturing lines using logistics as a main tool, development plans aligned to manufacturing methods.

The companies reach the point of automating each process, fulfilling standards in industry 4.0 [5]; in this way it is projected to industrialize the robotic stages for production processes, defining a logistics plan in production stages: 1. Distribution of goods in the company 2. Return of goods. 3. Product development 4. Waste management and 5. Selection of raw material; the processes have the possibility of being executed by a robotic device in order to work collaboratively, grouping characteristics of artificial intelligence, in business development, the case of manufacturing robots with efficient tasks, capable of multiplying and overcoming human capabilities, among them is articulated: a. Manage resources b. Distribute materials c. Transport merchandise and d. Loading heavy elements [6]. Suffering an expansion: 1. Professional 2. Work 3. Business and 4. Academic. The above refers to the importance of permeating contents intervened in university careers in the Corporación Universitaria Comfacauca, where students of Industrial Engineering and Mechatronic Engineering, from the sixth semester incursion in the area of manufacturing processes, logistics and supply chain, while students of Industrial Engineering continue their training in this field deepen in topics such as distribution logistics and international trade. The above is intended to infer how relevant it should be to integrate this type of process to train professionals with technological skillsn [7], integrating current topics that can innovate the way they do their work, in effect, "to know the innovations that lead to logistics 4.0, to develop fluently in the digital environment, to master the new channels of management and sales, such as eCommerce, and to be able to make decisions based on data are also essential skills for the logistics professional of tomorrow" [8] and [9].

2 Methodology

The development of this research used a holistic approach, based on the methodology proposed by Jacqueline Hurtado de Barrera, the project line is implemented, with seven necessary phases. As it can be seen in Fig. 1, entitled "Research methodology".

For each phase presented in the methodology a description was made: Phase 1: Exploration based on antecedents, Phase 2: Description framed in technical and general concepts; Phase 3: Describe the process, characteristics and aspects in Logistics; Phase 4: Diagnosis, recognize how the business sector is innovating; Phase 5: Description of the technological resource; Phase 6. Reflection on the relationship of technology in society and Phase 7: Conclusions.

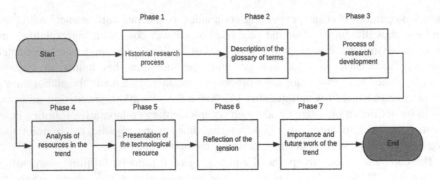

Fig. 1. Research methodology.

Additionally, a serious game evaluation was carried out in order to establish differences between the results obtained from the two analysis groups; the first one of the Mechatronic Engineering program (GEVIM) and the second one of Industrial Engineering (GEVII), each one of the groups with 15 students who belong to the semester of VI (Manufacturing Processes) and VIII (Logistics and Distribution) of the programs. Each student was evaluated at each of the three levels through the score obtained and the results were compared in order to establish the characteristics in relation to the topics of 1. Organization Process 2. Production Process 3. Transportation process.

3 Conceptual Framework

One of the biggest challenges that faces the logistics industry today is the availability of labor. It is not easy for companies around the world to find enough high-quality employees to move products from customers to customers. Two conflicting factors make this especially difficult: the first is the growing need for more logistics workers and this is being driven by the e-commerce revolution and its need for more package shipments; the second is a decrease in the size of the available workforce due to declining population levels in the western world.

Robotics applied to logistics and collaborative work - robots - human or robots - robots - performs work in predetermined spaces [6], fulfilling market strategies: 1. Movement of resources 2. Support to staff 3. Inventories of materials and 4. Distribution of goods [10].

The movement of resources implies increasing the effectiveness in relation to time, this indicates that the robots that transport goods must have capacity to detect the obstacles that represent a decision at the time of carrying out their work, these devices have the capacity to geo-locate themselves by means of sensors and incorporated cameras, to distribute goods or control the storage system, an example that currently bet on this type of technologies are Amazon, Google, Vodafone, Fedex and Alibaba, seeking to reduce their management of processes in less time.

In terms of storage of products in inventory, it is taken into account counting and location within the store, each package has an identifier code in the registration system, so the robot finds a package in the plant with efficiency of 20%, unlike a person; in other words, a device lasts about 15 min, while an operator takes 90 min.

This evidences the contrast that exists between the optimization of processes by the robot, the inventory systems currently use intelligent cameras that help to read bar codes or QR with artificial vision, where they specify type of product and location in the store, the robots have the ability to register each package in the software that manages the company's storage.

Platforms such as Kiva or Betty bot [11], have the ability to move heavy items to operators in storage areas by facilitating freight forwarding processes. The distribution of packages uses robots such as Wiki bot, FedEx, Sorthing Robot and livraison, generating impact on society due to the autonomy of going to a point outside the company delivering products: a. Fast foods b. Pharmaceutical drugs and c. Messaging packages; this type of technology generates reliability when providing the service, so it is necessary to use security codes or facial recognition of people.

3.1 Relationship Between Trend and Education

Education plays a fundamental role in carrying out research into the design and construction of intelligent mechanisms applied in logistics processes, for which educational institutions update their programs focused on topics such as artificial intelligence, artificial vision, neural networks, algorithm development and robotics.

The Corporación Universitaria Comfacauca offers programs oriented to a practical learning in relation to Information Technologies mediated by laboratories with mbot prototypes, necessary events for the logic of the collaborative work [12].

In addition to this, it can be used in logistics processes: 1. Implement robots to organize and distribute elements in plants 2. Make use of robots in a collaborative way, favoring group work 3. Promote Learning spaces in the field of Mobile Robotics (SR) [13].

In the sense of understanding how learning is produced in the classroom [14], it was necessary to appropriate different types of Logistics in the Training of Mechatronic and Industrial Engineering professionals, generating a classification for the Logistics processes, oriented to Functionality and Evolution.

By functionality of a company reflected in the organization in logistics, distributed in 4 types as it can be illustrated in Table 1 entitled "Classification of logistics by function".

Table 1. Classification of logistics according to its function.

Types of logistics	Description
Procurement logistics	It is a set of tasks whose mission is to distribute and receive the proportional amount of raw material or goods requested
Distribution logistics	This type of logistics is aimed at the customer, which aims to transport the goods requested from it
Production logistics	For the development of the manufacture of the product, this logistics is presented, which is in charge of the elaboration and packing processes
Reverse logistics	The process of this logistics is very important, as it can occur in the case where the customer is dissatisfied with the purchase and wants to make a return of the goods

By evolution in technology, evidencing an advance through time as shown in Table 2 entitled "Classification of logistics according to its evolution".

Table 2. Classification of logistics according to their evolution.

Logistics versions	Description of technologies
Logistics 1.0	In 1950, during the industrial revolution, the first steam engines were introduced
Logistics 2.0	Then in the year 1970 the machines with greater distribution and management of the products are illustrated with ports, shelves, and platforms that work in an electrical way
Logistics 3.0	In the year 2000, industries began to use digital systems that were responsible for managing the management of the plant, in addition to designing a network that communicates the entire company
Logistics 4.0	For the present time the companies propose to make a global connection in such a way that it is worked by subcontracting or as Smart Factory, mixing the technology with the manpower for a better efficiency in the processes

The development of Logistics introduces us to understand the fundamentals in regulations applied to the development of Logistics processes, as it is explained below:

3.2   Technical Standard in Robotic Safety

Collaborative robots work together with humans, performing repetitive work tasks, most often on assembly lines or in CNC manufacturing functions. Unlike fixed robots, which are programmed to operate independently of immediate human guidance, collaborative robots can work with human assistance because people can be in direct contact with these types of robots, whether with guidance or monitoring, there are stricter safety standards that apply to their operation. In this document, we will look at the various types of operations and the standards that guide them.

In a company's manufacturing processes, operators can cause an accident, in relation to: 1. malfunction of the plant 2. damage to the mechanical or electrical part 3. overloading of the robotic structure. Inadequate handling of equipment due to lack of proper instruments, as indicated in the standard "ISO EN10218 Safety requirements for industrial robots". This standard is responsible for handling safety requirements in the manufacture and integration of a robot into industry.

4 Technological Resource

In the development of the application it was decided to develop a serious game, in order to appropriate knowledge, executing possible tasks that are carried out in a company. For this purpose, the program Construct 2 was used as a development tool; creating HTML5 applications that allow the implementation of 2D games, contributing to the integration of learning processes for people who are not experts in the field of Logistics. The game development process is shown in Fig. 2 named "Construct 2 Work Interface".

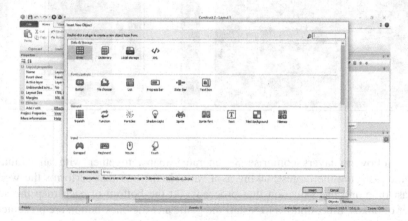

Fig. 2. Construct 2 Work Interface.

The development of the game was focused in strategy mode with the tilemap method, by means of different layers, where type layers is specified. The first layer shows the main menu composed by the title of the game and three options, the second option sets credits, and in addition to that you can select the exit button from the men. The second layer constitutes the beginning of the game, demonstrating the main objective aligned to interact within it, then press the accept button to continue with the manipulation of the game. The game provides help information, explaining its intention to execute a process at the shortest time, where each map corresponds to a logistics process: 1. Organization Process 2. Production Process 3. Process of Transportation; the fourth layer belongs to a menu of maps, evidencing three options that indicate each logistic process, finally the option to return with the button return is offered. As it can be seen in Table 3 named " LogiBot Layers".

Table 3. LogiBot Layers

The following layers comprise 3 generated maps, together with an evaluation system, classifying the largest, taking as a variable the one that performs the work in the least time and the valuation that proceeds. At the bottom of each map the score, number of boxes, time, options to restart the game and the back button are presented: 1. The first map conforms the organization process, which aims to group by type of elements in 4 specific areas called A1, A2, A3 and A4, the main component lies in the manipulation of the avatar conceived as a robot, changing its size depending on the load it has. The other moving robots act as obstacles for the avatar, the second map is production, the objective is to collect each of the elements: 1. Bottles 2. Tapes and 3. Boxes, to then take them to the blue colored area, then the avatar enters the yellow zone to activate a production mode, generating a box with the final product, taking it to the store in the shortest time possible; the last map consists of a transport mechanism, the idea is to collect a box of each color with the avatar: 1. Red 2. Green 3. White and 4. Blue to go to the house that has the same color, it is there where the person receives it and then moves to another box to meet the objective. This is presented in Table 4 named "LogiBot Maps".

Table 4. LogiBot Maps

Map 1: Organization	Map 2: Production
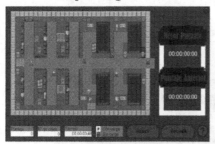	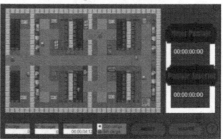

Map 3: Transportation

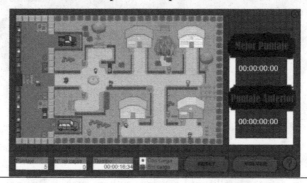

5 Discussion

The transformation in the industrial sector reflects changes from the way of managing processes to the innovation of technological equipment used in production lines, including cyberphysical systems; countries such as Japan attributed by its technological scope, plans to develop robots on a large scale, wanting to fulfill tasks in any sector: 1. Commercial 2. Industrial 3. Business and 4. Sports. One of the most important advantages is the reduction of expenses at the moment of avoiding hiring employees; in spite of advances obtained in technological field, allowing an efficiency and improvement for the control of times, emphasizing that the robots have favorable attributes, even better in performance, efficiency or force, making use of tools as the artificial intelligence or autonomous robots in different contexts. The benefits lie in the hyper-connectivity and automation of processes, properties highlighted under the rise of the industrial revolution 4.0 that allows a better effectiveness at a productive level, also it is evidenced by the transition from Digital User to Digital Citizen. In this context a transformation takes place, this expands new forms of interaction, enabling intelligent robotic systems, components such as: 1. Artificial Intelligence 2. Autonomous Vehicles 3. Internet of Things 4. Networked Systems 5. Big Data 6. Smart Cities 7. Drone System and ultimately 8. Intelligent learning. The above is entitled cyberphysical systems [14]. For the reader's further illustration, a graph was used, showing the contrast captured over time in the industrial revolutions from 1.0 to the current 4.0. This is presented in Fig. 3 named "Evolution of the Industrial Revolutions".

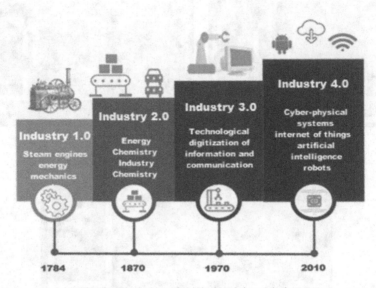

Fig. 3. Evolution of the industrial revolutions

In Education, refer to Intelligent Learning, authors such as Ros points out a type of adaptive and contextualized learning with mechanisms of detection, response and recommendation, supported by learning environments with technology, according to the individual needs of students, where they practice analysis of learning behaviors, performance trajectories, and online and real-world contexts. The possibility of integrating artificial intelligence, making use of intelligent learning or Smart Learning in robots applied to logistics, provides aid to learning, in relation to the fields of technology and robotics. Finally, it is concluded that social processes in relation to technology are associated with the training of Engineers in Fields of Mechatronics and Industrial Engineering.

5.1 Relationship with Emerging Technologies

Since the 1800s the idea of recreating the first versions of robots with artificial intelligence was generated, thanks to science fiction, which illustrates intelligent mechanisms that make their own decisions, today this idea has not changed much to present robots with neural networks that have the ability to perform high-risk work, by teaching certain intervals of data to help it determine the right decisions. Currently the universities that develop programs in artificial intelligence identify 5 types which are derived: 1. Voice 2. Vision 3. Robotics 4. Natural Learning Processing and 5. Machine learning; however, the most appropriate way to apply an appropriate learning is sought, supervised, not supervised or reinforced in such a way that towards a future it has the capacity to think as if it were a human being when determining a decision with

Table 5. Trend Applications

1. Drones Spray Sequence	2. Drones in logistics for goods delivery

Taken from:https://www.linkedin.com/in/jean-pierre-grimaud-77629696	Taken From: https://www.mediagroup.es/amazon-drones-marketing-sevilla/
3. Truck loading and unloading system	**4. Use of drones for terrain simulation**

Taken from: http://www.abconveyors.com.mx/Soluciones-Roboticas/	Taken from: https://www.xdrones.es/levantamientos-topograficos-con-drones-fotogrametria-aerea/

5. Logistics in 3D printing

Taken from:
https://ultimaker.com/en/blog/52750-6-overlooked-benefits-of-3d-printing-for-your-supply-chain

cognitive learning. On the other hand, this trend is related to knowledge of Big Data to contribute to Data Learning that seeks to establish decisions with stored data to find the right method. At present, educational projects are presented that take the characteristics of students such as grades, stratum, income, class schedules, and that generate platforms in academic processes.

5.2 Robotics Applied to Logistics

A variety of applications are presented: 1. Sprinkling sequence with drones: considered as a high category project for business development, centralized in the irrigation of agricultural crops, where its functionality allows to identify the type of plant selected, ideal to generate a route within a geographical plane [15]. 2. Use of drones in logistics for goods delivery. 3. Truck loading and unloading system: Companies such as Wynright intend to implement intelligent robotic systems that contribute to optimizing logistical processes for loading and unloading trucks [16], 4. Use of drones for land simulation: This allows its application in the art of mining, providing a topographical recognition of land with the support of an integrated vision system [17], 5. Logistics in 3D printing: According to the contribution that [18]: the logistics applied in distribution of material for several printers [19] and [20], in view of selecting type of material and exact quantity, in order to perform specific tasks. This is shown in Table 5 named "Trend Applications".

6 Results and Analysis

The students of each of the programs interacted with the game, having only one opportunity in each of the levels and the results obtained by them were recorded. It is important to highlight that the score obtained by each of the participants takes into

Table 6. Results by maps - game use

User	GEVIM			GEVII		
	Map 1	Map 2	Map 3	Map 1	Map 2	Map 3
1	1235	1850	2050	1135	1420	1956
2	1482	1760	2350	1282	1610	2010
3	1356	1568	2200	1453	1386	1910
4	1236	1750	1968	1316	1530	1689
5	1357	1820	2010	1136	1220	2102
6	1206	1796	2120	1109	1264	2010
7	1420	1783	2169	1230	1573	2067
8	1230	1860	1965	1125	1402	1735
9	1502	1745	2200	1001	1552	2009
10	1750	1576	2189	1150	1368	1990
11	1330	1642	1985	1420	1523	1852
12	1386	1750	2010	1296	1602	1901
13	1278	1726	2120	1487	1662	1902
14	1310	1805	2150	1525	1452	1950
15	1420	1598	2210	1580	1184	1930

account the fulfillment of the objectives and the time spent in the development of each map. In Table 6 named "results by maps - game use" you can see each of the ratings obtained by the students.

The data were analyzed descriptively in order to understand the behavior of the data obtained for each of the analysis groups, then in Table 7 named "descriptive statistical results for collected data".

Table 7. Descriptive statistical results for collected data

Group	Mean	Standard deviation
GEVIM Map 1	1,366.53	140.44
GEVIM Map 2	1,734.66	96.87
GEVIM Map 3	2,113.07	111.99
GEVII Map 1	1,283.00	176.49
GEVII Map 2	1,449.87	147,16
GEVII Map 3	1,934.20	112.13

As it can be seen from the Table, the mean values for map 1 do not differ substantially. The opposite occurs in relation to maps 2 and 3 of each of the groups where the calculated mean values have differences of 284.79 and 178.87 correspondingly in favor of the results obtained by the Industrial Engineering analysis group. In relation to the deviation of the data a very similar behavior is presented showing uniformity in the groups of evaluation that can be seen in the Fig. 4 denominated "Radial graph for abilities of the groups of analysis".

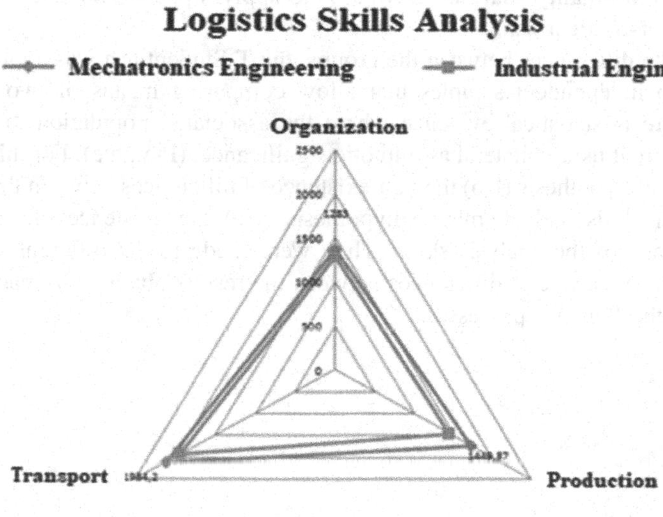

Fig. 4. Radial graph for abilities of the groups of analysis

Table 8. Shapiro-Wilk test for normality analysis of the knowledge test performed. *Source own elaboration*

Group	Statistics	gl *	P-Value
GEVIM1	0.944	15	0.438
GEVIM2	0.948	15	0.494
GEVIM3	0.932	5	0.293
GEIIM1	0.881	5	0,051
GEIIM1	0.893	15	0.073
GEIIM1	0.928	15	0.253

As can be seen in Fig. 4, the results obtained present a greater difference for the concepts of production, this is mainly because the students of Mechatronics Engineering do not adopt this concept within their academic curriculum. The data collected were subjected to normality tests to subsequently perform inferential analysis of the data in Table 8 called "Shapiro-Wilk test for normality analysis of the knowledge test performed." You can see the values obtained for the test statistic, for this case we proceeded to perform the "Shapiro-Wilk test" [21] highlighted by its frequent use in case studies and with better validity at the statistical level, it is applied in groups with samples less than 50 individuals. The normality test raises a null hypothesis (Ho) related to the origin of the data from a normal distribution and an alternative hypothesis (Ha) that states, as the data deviates significantly from a normal distribution; To validate the hypothesis, the bilateral asymptotic significance of the test (p-Value) is taken into account.

As can be seen in the values obtained for each group analyzed, the P-Value obtained is greater than 0.05 ($P > 0.05$) which allows to accept the null hypothesis (Ho) and affirm that the data collected comes from a Normal distribution, these results obtained from the normality analysis allowed us to apply a parametric analysis of the data through the T-Student test.

To analyze the differences between the groups, the T-Student test was applied. The t-test directed to independent samples that allow comparing means of two groups, indicating if there is statistical evidence where the associated population means are significantly different using bilateral asymptotic significance. (P-Value). For this case it was defined as null hypothesis (Ho) the non-existence of differences between the means of the analytical skills and alternative hypothesis (Ha) the existence of difference between the means of the analysis skills, They were made to the different skills, in order to verify the existence of differences between the results obtained for each of the maps related to the logistics processes.

Table 9. T-Student test for analysis of difference of means. *Source own elaboration*

T-test for equality of means					
Ability	t	gl	Sig. (bilateral)	Mean difference	Typ. error of the difference
Organization	1,434	28	0.163	83.53	58.23
Production	6,261	28	0,000	284.8	45.49
Transport	4,371	28	0,000	178.8	40.91

As it can be seen in the Table 9, the value of bilateral asymptotic significance is less than 0.05 ($P < 0.05$) for the Production and Transport cases, which leads to rejecting the null hypothesis Ho and accepting the alternative hypothesis Ha, allowing to establish that the scores obtained by the different groups generate differences depending on the academic program. In the case of organizational ability, it can be observed that the bilateral asymptotic significance is greater than 0.05 ($P > 0.05$), which allows accepting the null hypothesis Ho, establishing that this competition in the organizational field does not present a difference between the two groups.

7 Conclusions

The adaptation of technological tools when applying a serious game allows to establish didactic methodologies to evaluate the technical and technological competencies related to logistics processes, the results obtained from the application of the t-Student test allowed to establish statistically significant differences obtaining a P-value less than 0,05 ($P < 0,05$), allowing to conclude that the Mechatronics and Industrial Engineering groups presented significant differences related to Logistics and transportation skills, in relation to the organizational skill, did not appear statistical.

The use of a serious game related to robotics applied to logistics processes significantly improved the Learning processes within the subject of manufacturing and logistics processes in the Mechatronics and Industrial Engineering program of the Comfacauca University on the other hand. The combination of technological and communication tools Smart Factory intends to maintain an appropriate solution for efficiency, punctuality, productivity and quality in the services of the company, allowing to favor meaningful and collaborative learning in professionals that enhanced their logistics.

The use of Robotics, in industrial environments, in Revolution 4.0, integrates human capabilities with potentials of robots such as repetitiveness, speed, strength, security, allowing to improve logistics processes, about to efficiency and science. efficiency increasing up to 20% in pre-established work in the activities developed by the operators.

References

1. Barros, T.: La Industria 4.0: Aplicaciones e Implicaciones, Universidad de Sevilla, pp. 1–52 (2017). http://bibing.us.es/proyectos/abreproy/91146/fichero/La+Industria+4.0+Aplicaciones +e+Implicaciones.pdf

2. Anaya, J.: Logística integral: La gestión operativa de la empresa, pp. 25–27. Libros profesionales. ESIC Editorial, Madrid (2015)
3. Sarria, I., Lozano, B., Tenorio, W.: MÉTODO JAT JUSTO A TIEMPO, pp. 1–96. Universidad Libre Seccional, Cali (2015)
4. Tipping, A., Prümm, D., Kauschke, P., Smith, J.: Shifting patterns. PWC **11** (2016). http://www.ncbi.nlm.nih.gov/pubmed/8974216
5. Azmi, I., Hamid, N.A., Nasarudin, M., Hussin, M., Ibtishamiah, N.: Logistics and supply chain management: the importance of integration for business processes. J. Emerging Econ. Islamic Res. **5**(4), 73–80 (2017). http://www.jeeir.com
6. Sanz, J.: Robots industriales colaborativos: Una nueva forma de trabajo. Segurdad y salud en el trabajo **95**, 6–10 (2018)
7. Bensusán, G.: Los mecanismos de fijación de los salarios mínimos en México en una perspectiva comparativa: el marco institucional y los actores sociales. In: Mancera, M.A. (Coordinador), Del salario mínimo al salario digno, pp. 205–253. Consejo Económico y Social de la Ciudad de México, México (2015)
8. Roig, M.V.: Logística y cadena de suministro en la nueva era digital. Revista de economía, empresa y sociedad (2018)
9. Chaparro-Peláez, J., Agudo-Peregrin, A.F., Pascual-Miguel, F.J.: Conjoint analysis of drivers and inhibitors of E-commerce adoption. J. Bus. Res. **69**(4), 1277–1282 (2016)
10. Rayo, J.: La logística en el sector industrial. Logistics Assistant en Técnicas Reunidas **12**, 64–69 (2016)
11. Wu, Y., Ge, D.: Key technologies of warehousing robot for intelligent logistics. In: The First International Symposium on Management and Social Sciences (ISMSS 2019). Atlantis Press (2019)
12. Patiño, J.G., et al.: La cuarta revolución industrial. Ingenierías USBMed **10**(1), 1 (2019)
13. Báez Sánchez, X.E.: Efectividad del "Robot Milo" en el desarrollo de habilidades sociales y comunicación en niños de 5 a 7 años con trastorno del espectro del autismo de grado 1. Bachelor's thesis, Quito (2018)
14. Barrera, P.: Diseño de un en el área de la logística organizacional sistémico proyecto educativo mediante las tic. Universidad Militar Nueva Granada **7**(2), 1–21 (2017)
15. Amortegui, D., Betancurt, J., Soler, A.: Diseño de un sistema autonomo para fumigacion aerea (2014)
16. Mendez, J.: Logística colaborativa como herramienta para mejorar el nivel de servicio y disminuir los costos de distribución. Universidad militar nueva Granada, pp. 1–20 (2018). https://repository.unimilitar.edu.co/bitstream/handle/10654/17745/MendezBohorquezJulioAlexander2018.pdf?sequence=1&isAllowed=y
17. García, M.S.: Uso y aplicaciones de drones en minería (2017). http://bio-digestores.blogspot.com.co/2012/06/uso-y-aplicaciones.html
18. Lopez, J.: Fabricación aditiva y transformación logística: la impresión 3D. Oikonomics **9**, 58–69 (2018). http://oikonomics.uoc.edu
19. Telefónica, F.: Sociedad Digital en España 2018. Fundación Telefónica (2019)
20. del Val Román, J.L.: La Transformación Digital de la Industria Española. In: Conferencia de Directores y Decanos de Ingeniería Informática Ind, p. 10 (2016). https://doi.org/10.1080/14015430802688385
21. Dean, A., Morris, M., Stufken, J., Bingham, D.: Handbook of Design and Analysis of Experiments, 1st edn, pp. 140–148. Chapman and Hall/CRC, Boco Raton (2015)

Internet of Things

IoT Botnets

Pamela Beltrán-García, Eleazar Aguirre-Anaya[⊠],
Ponciano Jorge Escamilla-Ambrosio, and Raúl Acosta-Bermejo

Laboratory of Cybersecurity, Centro de Investigación en Computación,
Instituto Politécnico Nacional, Mexico City, Mexico
pam.belt.g@gmail.com,
{eaguirre,pescamilla}@cic.ipn.mx, racostab@ipn.mx,
http://www.cic.ipn.mx

Abstract. This paper presents a comprehensive state-of-art review that discusses the IoT botnet behaviour, including topology and communication between botmaster and bots, thus is possible to make a comparison of IoT botnets, based on their topology, type of attack, target, kind of propagation and operation. In several investigations, it is explained that a significant problem is an increase in the development of IoT botnets, such as attacks like DDoS. To this aim, understanding the behaviour of the IoT botnets could be helpful to prevent them.

Keywords: IoT · Botnet · Bot

1 Introduction

The concept of Internet of Things was initially expressed as "computers everywhere," formulated by Ken Sakamura at the University of Tokyo in 1984. In 1999, Kevin Ashton was the first to devise the term "Internet of Things" [1]. The phrase "Internet of Things," which is also shortly well-known as IoT composed of two words: first is "Internet" and second is "Things."

The Internet is a global system of interconnected networks that use the standard Internet protocol suite (TCP/IP) to serve billions of users worldwide [3]. Devices with few resources in computation and energy capacity characterize the term "Things" in IoT; these can have sensors, actuators, and processing unit; which have an IP address assigned for Internet connectivity, either wired or wireless networks [2, 4]. Due to the few IoT devices resources, complicates the task of installing security controls and causes them to be vulnerable to be infected and execute DDoS attacks by flooding a service with legitimate requests [27].

With the increase in the development of IoT devices, security has become an essential factor due to attacks that are multiplying; one way is the use of botnets. Silva et al. [24] discuss that approximately 16–25% computers connected to the Internet are members of botnets. Other studies report that at the beginning of the year 2008, e-mail spam was generated only by six botnets [25]. Also, Symantec Internet Security Threat Report indicates that 5.06 million distinct botnet computers; 61,940 active computers per day, and 4,091 bot command servers have been observed [26].

M. F. Mata-Rivera et al. (Eds.): WITCOM 2019, CCIS 1053, pp. 247–257, 2019.
https://doi.org/10.1007/978-3-030-33229-7_21

Actually, according to Spamhaus Malware Labs, 10,263 botnets hosted on 1,121 different networks in 2018 were identified and blocked. That is an 8% increase from the number of botnet C&C in 2017 [32].

2   Botnets Background

The botnet term is a combination of two main words, Bot as a Robot abbreviation and Net for Network; so, it can be defined as a "network of infected hosts called bots, which are controlled by a human operator, better known as the Botmaster."

Botnets recruit vulnerable hosts by using a type of malware that exploits vulnerabilities; an infrastructure is created between the now infected hosts and the Botmaster who takes the control of these hosts remotely using a Command and Control server (C&C), through the sending of commands to perform malicious activities, such as DDoS, spam, or information theft.

In the context of IoT, botnet is a network of compromised IoT devices, such as cameras, modems, DVR, sensors and other devices that use the IP protocol with the characteristic to transmit data over the Internet, infected with malware. Such networks allow an attacker to control the devices performing malicious tasks, as well as propagate their malware [5].

2.1   Botnet Stages

Botnets perform their actions in three main stages [7, 8]:

- Infection: The malware used for recruit new bots can be propagated by exploiting vulnerabilities, downloading by web/mail, installing software from unreliable sources, then executed, and the host became part of the botnet.
- Command and Control: Once infected, the bot communicates with the host that controls the botnet to receive commands.
- Malicious Activities: Execution of attacks such as DDoS, spam, etc.

2.2   Botnet Topologies

According to Vormayr et al. [9] and Dhinnesh et al. [10], the topology of the botnets is defined by the command and control process they execute:

- Centralized: The Botmaster controls and monitors all bots from a single central point, which makes the latency low, that is, all bots receive commands and reports to the center point (C&C server). Likewise, there are two centralized topologies: Star and hierarchical, in which the Protocols Internet Relay Chat (IRC) and Hyper Text Transfer Protocol (HTTP) are mostly used; like in the Chuck Norris or Aidra IoT botnet (Fig. 1(a)).
- Decentralized: Also known as Peer-to-Peer (P2P), in which the bot acts as a server and client, each one is connected to another bot at least. The commands can reach each bot only if all the bots are connected (Fig. 1(b)).

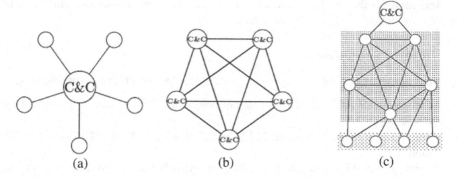

Fig. 1. (a) Centralized [9], (b) Decentralized [9] and Hybrid [9]

- Hybrid: It's a combination of centralized and decentralized topologies since there are two types of bots, some of them have the functionality as servers and clients others just as clients, makes the message latency high (Fig. 1(c)).

Authors in [9, 11, 12, 28], described the communication between the C&C server and bots, as shown in Table 1.

Table 1. Communication C&C server and bots

	Advantages	Disadvantages	IoT Botnet application
IRC	Channel protected by authentication mechanisms	Use of a centralized topology, this means a single failure point for the botnet	Close ports that were used to gain access to IoT device, i.e., like in the IoT Linux/Hydra botnet
HTTP		Use of a centralized or P2P topology, in which case has to prevent loops or replicated messages	Such as the Mirai botnet gained remote access to the device over Telnet, SSH, or HTTP
SMB		Often blocked by a gateway, so is mainly used for local networks	Bashlite IoT Botnet makes use of this channel by downloading two scripts to gain remote access, then inject malicious code into files, generating keep-alive messages exchanged every 60 s between the botnet C&C and the bot

As mentioned in Sect. 2.1, for an IoT botnet the main botnet stages are the communication between the botmaster and the bots due to the botmaster does not have direct communication with the bots, it makes use of the C&C server.

According to the topology and communication channel, botnet detection can be attached by building a C&C server detector.

2.3 Botnet Communication

Therefore, an exchange of messages sequence is needed to achieve a specific task:

- Coordination: If the particular task is not automatic, it is necessary to instruct the bot what to do.
- Scan: Network scan, can be an ICMP echo request, UDP or TCP scan for vulnerable services.
- Data: It can be a binary bot, arbitrary files, or network data that communicates to the botnet or other bots.
- Register: Message required for a record.
- Execute: Tasks executed by bots.

As well, it can be separated as presented in Table 2.

Table 2. Botnet stages

Infection	Operation
• It is used to recruit new bots • It can be active (when the botnet tries to infect additional hosts) or passive (when the binary bot is distributed by other means)	• The C&C sends commands to the active bots • The stage in which botnet performs the task

According to Vormayr et al. [9] botnets continuously recruit new bots by infecting hosts for launching a specific attack, this infection stage occurs in two different ways as exposed in Table 3.

Table 3. Infection stage

Active infection	Passive infection
• Makes use of existing vulnerabilities • Through commands or automatically 1. Coordination: Scan and parameters configuration to be exploited 2. Scanning: Host detection achievable with an ICMP echo request or directly in the vulnerabilities of the UDP and TCP ports 3. Infection: Vulnerabilities exploitation 4. Download additional data 5. Registration: Monitoring the botnet status, as well as the size and location of the bots	• Via email, web pages, or storage media • Users infect their host by a click or an action • The binary bot is executed on the infected host • Downloading additional data 1. Register: Monitor the botnet status, as well as the size and location of the bots

These two infection ways are applied to IoT devices due to, i.e., infected cameras by exploiting existing vulnerabilities such as default credentials; or like tablets where the user infects their device by a click allowing the binary bot download, these being helpful to understand botnet communication and therefore install detection mechanisms.

2.4 Communication Hiding and Obfuscation

To increase the probability of survival, botnets tries to evade detection using hiding and obfuscation techniques in the operation stage [9, 12]:

- Covert channels: They are used to hide the existence of communication.
- Encryption: Used to hide transmitted commands as well as the protocol used. If a botnet uses a predefined key and fixed commands, the botnet can be disabled.
- Compression: A compression algorithm can hide the data.
- Steganography: Hiding information in non-communicating containers, similar to covert channels with the difference of being used as carriers.

Knowing botnet communication and obfuscation techniques, network-based signature detection can be applied. According to Vormayr et al. [9], the operation stage can be categorized, as shown in Table 4.

Table 4. Operation stage

Operation stage	Actions
Data Upload: Data collected from bots	• C&C sends commands to bots with specific instructions • Instructions are executed • Report results to C & C
Data Download: storing data onto bots, i.e., botnet binary update	• C&C indicates the bot which file to download and where to find it • Download file in the bot • Store or install the download
Forward Proxy: Uses the botnet to hide the actual origin of the communication	• Unidirectional: It consists of data sent from the bot to a target, used to overload a single service with requests • Bidirectional: It consists of requests and responses that transmit through the bot, used if the Botmaster or a third entity needs the results of a request
Reverse proxy: Reverse for retransmission to a specific source host	• C&C indicates the bot which port to open and which internal address should connect so that other hosts or bots can connect to the source
Instruction: Execute tasks on behalf of the Botmaster	• The botmaster indicates the bots what tasks must be executed and provides the necessary parameters • The current command executes

During the operation stage, the sequence of exchanging messages depends on the botnet specific task, IoT botnets examples are in Sect. 3.

Studying the exchanging messages could be possible to collect information packets and determine the type of botnet used so that detection mechanisms can be used.

3   IoT Botnet Attacks

The use of a botnet is for several purposes such as malicious activities, better known as attacks. In a DDoS attack, the network bandwidth is consumed by the compromised IoT devices injecting malicious packets into the network targeting a particular server; this means it floods the traffic with service request and processed by a server [29, 30].

Specifically, the most executed IoT botnets flooding attacks are:

- **TCP SYN Flood:** exploits a known weakness in the TCP connection sequence, the requester sends multiple SYN requests, but either does not respond to the host's SYN-ACK response or sends the SYN requests from a spoofed IP address. Either way, the host system continues to wait for acknowledgment for each of the requests, making binding resources until no new connections, and ultimately resulting in a denial of service.
- **UDP Flood:** a large number of User Datagram Protocol (UDP) packets are sent to a targeted server to overwhelm that device's ability to process and respond.
- **HTTP Flood:** the attacker exploits seemingly-legitimate HTTP GET or POST requests to attack a web server or application.
- **ICMP Flood:** overwhelms the target resource with ICMP Echo Request (ping) packets, generally sending packets as fast as possible without waiting for replies.
- **ACK/ACK PUSH Flood:** receives no legitimate ACK packets that do not belong to any of the sessions on the server's list of transmissions. The server under attack then wastes all its system resources (RAM, processor, etc.) trying to define where the packets belong. The results in productivity loss and partial server unavailability.
- **TCP XMAS Flood:** Send a very explicitly crafted TCP packet to a device on the network with FIN, URG and PUSH flags set.
- **DNS Flood:** Attackers send validly but spoofed DNS request packets at a very high packet rate and from a large group of source IP addresses. The DNS server can be overwhelmed by the number of requests.

A single IoT device as bot is not a threat, but the recruitment of several bots can attached flooding attacks, due to these devices can send connections requests affecting the availability of services. By determining the type of a botnet attack, it is possible to apply a network-anomaly detection technique.

4   Related Work

As briefly mentioned in Sect. 3, IoT botnets are performing many attacks. In this section, an IoT botnet comparison is done at Table 5 based on model architecture, attacks, target, operation, and propagation [6, 13–23, 28].

Table 5. IoT botnets

Botnet	Archit. model	Attacks	Target	Infection	Operation
Linux/Hydra (2008)	IRC	SYN & UDP Flood	Routing devices based on MIPS architecture	Active: Dictionary attack, known specific authentication vulnerability	Download data: the attacker had to edit one of the source files to provide the URL address of the C&C IRC server as well as the link to download the malicious binary
Psyb0t (2009)	IRC	SYN, UDP & ICMP Flood	Routers & DSL modems	Active: Access to Telnet and SSH using brute force with 6000 predefined user names and 13000 passwords	Download Data: Once a shell of the vulnerable device is acquired, Psyb0t downloads itself from a remote server
Chuck Norris (2010)	IRC	SYN, ICMP & ACK Flood	D-Link routers & DSL modems	Active: Brute force, as well as the authentication override vulnerability	Download Data: Download SSH
Tsunami (2010)	IRC	SYN Flood, UDP Flood & ACK Also, HTTP Flood & TCP XMAS	Linux Mint Official ISO	Passive: Modifies the DNS server setting in the configuration of the infected devices such that the traffic redirects from the IoT device to malicious servers	Download Data: Download file (s) from remote servers
LightAidra/Aidra (2012)	IRC	SYN Flood & ACK Flood	Architectures such as MIPS, ARM, and PPC	Active: Search open Telnet port using default credentials Propagates over TCP on port 23, for install a backdoor.	Download Data: Download a shell script from buonapesca. altervista.org The script downloads and executes

(*continued*)

Table 5. (*continued*)

Botnet	Archit. model	Attacks	Target	Infection	Operation
					additional malicious files, also receive a command from the IRC server to perform the attack
The Moon (2014)	P2P	Bring down websites and servers by overwhelming them with requests; obfuscate information online	Linksys, ASUS, MikroTik, and D-Link routers	Active: Exploiting a command vulnerability in the POST request parameter	Reverse proxy: download an additional proxy module that opens a SOCKS5 proxy on infected devices, who knows the web page and the parameters to which the redirection of the uplink node must be accessed, and the port no longer opens directly on the infected node
Bashlite (2014)	IRC	SYN, UDP, HTTP & ACK Flood	Linux-based IoT devices such as cameras and DVRs	Active: Brute force with default credential of devices with open Telnet ports	Upload Data: In the malware's binary has the IP address of the C&C server. It also has the IP addresses hard-coded into it
Mirai (2016)	Centralized	Generates floods of GRE IP, GRE ETH, SYN, ACK, STOMP, DNS, UDP, & HTTP	Closed-circuit television, cameras, routers, and DVR	Active: 10 predefined attack vectors Dictionary attack based on 62 entries	Upload Data: loading the malware to the vulnerable IoT devices detected, scan the network for new victims while waiting for instructions from the C&C. Scan traffic uses random

(*continued*)

Table 5. (*continued*)

Botnet	Archit. model	Attacks	Target	Infection	Operation
					parameters to avoid identification and fingerprinting
Linux/IRCTelnet/New Aidra (2016)	IRC	SYN, ACK-PUSH, & UDP Flood	Routers, DVR, and IP cameras	Active: Brute force and code injection, list of Mirai credentials	Upload Data: In the malware's binary has the IP address of the C&C server. It also has the IP addresses hard-coded into it

Table 5 lists the botnets analyzed in this work along with their topology, targets, types of attacks and the infection/operation stages studied in Sect. 2; each column gives information about how the IoT botnet operates, making possible the use of detection mechanisms. Some mechanisms such as signatures-bases detection are referring to the analysis of known or abnormal patterns or characteristics of threats from intruders into a system, or by honeypots, which are used as traps to collect bot's information and activities, making possible to analyze them to detect botnets. These detections are performed when the attack is executed [31].

5   Discussion

Botnets grow in size and complexity as potential nodes in the Internet of Things time to time, making difficult to identify malicious from benign traffic even monitoring the common ports used, like 23,2323 and 22 to gain access to the IoT device.

From a diverse set of IoT attacks described in Sect. 3 and the botnet communication in Sect. 2, different botnets were chosen in the state-of-art to identify the type of infection and operation used. These botnets have been analysed according to their topology, target, and type of attack, for determining the way it infects new hosts and how it operates.

It was observed similar characteristics in most IoT botnets, such as centralized topology due to the IoT devices resources cannot function as a server the main cons of this topology is the single failure point by detecting the C&C server, although the pros are management and monitoring of the botnet by the botmaster that communicates directly with each bot, and the low latency.

As compare to decentralized and hybrid topology, there are more than one C&C server, and because of the IoT devices resources, these can not function as a server, these are cons. Although, the pros lies in the detection complexity of a failure point because if one C&C server is taking down, the other servers can manage and monitor the botnet.

The application of a centralized topology still exists, by creating new botnets following the evolution of applications on the Internet. According to the previous research, it is provided a comprehensive state-of-art review of botnets that are evolving time to time making important and understandable point their application to a new target, IoT devices, highlighting how evolution and behaviour can be expanded to perform different attacks in the IoT context.

6 Conclusion

This paper presented a comprehensive review and analysis that discusses the IoT botnet development with distinct variation targets, attacks, and type of propagation and operation. Being helpful to have a better knowledge of the communication between different IoT botnets that use similar techniques or a combination of them, so that botnet prevention can be created or even disable the botnet, i.e., the use machine learning to extract message exchanges from network traffic for identifying possible botnet communication.

Acknowledgment. The authors would like to thank the Instituto Politécnico Nacional (IPN), the Centro de Investigación en Computación (CIC) and the Consejo Nacional de Ciencia y Tecnología (CONACYT) for the support in this research.

References

1. Escamilla-Ambrosio, P.J., Rodríguez-Mota, A., Aguirre-Anaya, E., Acosta-Bermejo, R., Salinas-Rosales, M.: Distributing computing in the internet of things: cloud, fog and edge computing overview. Stud. Comput. Intell. **731**, 87–115 (2018)
2. Madakam, S., Ramaswamy, R., Tripathi, S.: Internet of Things (IoT): a literature review. J. Comput. Commun. **03**(05), 164–173 (2015)
3. Nunberg, G.: The Advent of the Internet: 12th April, Courses (2012)
4. Stavrou, A., Voas, J., Fellow, I.: DDoS in the IoT Mirai and Other Botnets-2017-Computer (2017)
5. Botnet de IoT Homepage (botnet de internet de las cosas). https://searchdatacenter.techtarget.com/es/definicion/IoT-botnet-botnet-de-internet-de-las-cosas
6. Angrishi, K.: Turning Internet of Things (IoT) into Internet of Vulnerabilities (IoV): IoT Botnets, pp. 1–17 (2017)
7. Tyagi, A., Aghila, G.: A wide scale survey on botnet. Int. J. Comput. Appl. **34**(9), 9–22 (2011)
8. Zhaosheng, Z., Zhi, J.F., Guohan, L., Phil, R., Yan, C., Keesook, H.: Botnet research survey. In: Proceedings of the International Computer Software and Applications Conference, pp. 967–972 (2008)
9. Vormayr, G., Zseby, T., Fabini, J.: Botnet communication patterns. IEEE Commun. Surv. Tutorials **19**(4), 2768–2796 (2017)
10. Sundareswaran, N.: Botnet life cycle and topologies. Int. J. Pure Appl. Math. **119**(17), 421–429 (2018)

11. Dwivedi, S.K., Bist, A.S., Chaturvedi, P.K.: Recent trends in botnet research. Int. J. Eng. Sci. Res. Technol. **6**(7), 280–295 (2017)

12. Khattak, S., Ramay, N.R., Khan, K.R., Syed, A.A., Khayam, S.A.: A taxonomy of botnet behavior, detection, and defense. IEEE Commun. Surv. Tutorials **16**(2), 898–924 (2014)

13. De Donno, M., Dragoni, N., Giaretta, A., Spognardi, A.: DDoS-capable IoT malwares: comparative analysis and mirai investigation. Secur. Commun. Netw. **2018**, 1–30 (2018)

14. Spognardi, A., De Donno, M., Dragoni, N., Giaretta, A.: Analysis of DDoS-capable IoT malwares. In: Proceedings of the 2017 Federated Conference on Computer Science and Information Systems, vol. 11, pp. 807–816, September 2017

15. Meidan, Y., et al.: N-BaIoT-network-based detection of IoT botnet attacks using deep autoencoders. IEEE Pervasive Comput. **17**(3), 12–22 (2018)

16. Durfina, L., Kroustek, J., Zemek, P.: PsybOt malware: a step-by-step decompilation case study. In: Proceedings of the Working Conference on Reverse Engineering WCRE, pp. 449–456 (2013)

17. Hallman, R., Bryan, J., Palavicini, G., Divita, J., Romero-Mariona, J.: IoDDoS – the internet of distributed denial of service attacks. In: IoTBDS (2017)

18. Janus, M.: Heads of the Hydra. Malware for Network Devices, 16 August 2011. https://securelist.com/heads-of-the-hydra-malware-for-network-devices/36396/

19. Barnett, R.: New Tsunami/Kaiten Variant: Propagation Status, 11 September 2018. https://blogs.akamai.com/sitr/2018/09/new-tsunamikaiten-variant-propagation-status.html

20. Symantec "Linux.Aidra" Writeup By: Kaoru Hayashi. https://www.symantec.com/security-center/writeup/2013-121118-5758-99

21. Cyware "The Moon IoT botnet is proxying traffic for Youtube ad fraud scheme", 1 February 2019. https://cyware.com/news/themoon-iot-botnet-is-proxying-traffic-for-youtube-ad-fraud-scheme-e17d6945

22. Netlab website. https://blog.netlab.360.com/themoon-botnet-a-review-and-new-features/

23. NJ Cybersecurity and Communications Integration Cell "Linux/IRCTelnet", 3 November 2016. https://www.cyber.nj.gov/threat-profiles/botnet-variants/linux-irctelnet

24. Silva, S.S.C., Silva, R.M.P., Pinto, R.C.G., Salles, R.M.: Botnets: a survey. Comput. Netw. **57**(2), 378–403 (2013)

25. AsSadhan, B., Moura, J.M.F., Lapsley, D., Jones, C., Strayer, W.T.: Detecting botnets using command and control traffic. In: Proceedings of the 2009 8th IEEE International Symposium on Network Computing and Applications NCA 2009, no. 4, pp. 156–162 (2009)

26. Symantec Internet Security Threat Report: Trends for July–December 2007 (Executive Summary), vol. XIII, April 2008

27. Makhdoom, I., Abolhasan, M., Lipman, J., Liu, R.P., Ni, W.: Anatomy of threats to the internet of things. IEEE Commun. Surv. Tutorials **21**(2), 1636–1675 (2019)

28. Ceron, J.M., Steding-Jessen, K., Hoepers, C., Granville, L.Z., Margi, C.B.: Improving IoT botnet investigation using an adaptive network layer. Sensors **19**(3), 1–16 (2019)

29. Ahmed, M.E., Kim, H.: DDoS attack mitigation in internet of things using software-defined networking. In: Proceedings of the 3rd IEEE International Conference on Big Data Computing Service and Applications, BigDataService 2017, pp. 271–276 (2017)

30. Gupta, B.B., Badve, O.P.: Taxonomy of DoS and DDoS attacks and desirable defense mechanism in a cloud computing environment. Neural Comput. Appl. **28**(12), 3655–3682 (2017)

31. Lange, T., Kettani, H.: On security threats of botnets to cyber systems. In: 6th International Conference on Signal Processing and Integrated Networks, SPIN 2019, pp. 176–183 (2019)

32. Spamhaus Malware Labs: Spamhaus Botnet Threat Report 2019, pp. 1–15 (2018)

Traffic Light Control Through Intelligent Agents, Sensors and Arduino

René Alberto Ojeda-Cepeda, Larissa Jeanette Peniche-Ruiz[(⊠)],
Iván Antonio Castro-Ynurreta, and Edwin Moises Pool-Couoh

Tecnológico Nacional de México, Instituto Tecnológico de Mérida,
Mérida, Yucatán, Mexico
rene_ojeda_96@hotmail.com, larissa.peniche@itmerida.mx,
castroynurreta@gmail.com, edwinpoolcouoh@gmail.com

Abstract. Car traffic control is an everyday problem in a city large enough to hold more than a million population. This paper presents an intelligent traffic light control system based on intelligent agents, Arduino and sensors, which produced data is used as entry to a scale model of a busy street intersection. The project succeeds at managing car flow on the model street crossing allowing to set variables such as time of the day, emergency vehicles and number of cars on each street to display solutions to traffic jam situations.

Keywords: Intelligent agents · Traffic control · Sensors

1 Introduction

Traffic congestion in the cities of the world is a problem which directly impacts both in the journey time and in the number of car accidents. This kind of incidents increase during rush hour with well-known consequences like delays, drivers and passengers annoyance, material damages and even casualties. Traffic jam consequences often end up in car accidents mostly because drivers lose control when they are forced to wait for a long time in a saturated street, which in turn stresses drivers to the point of speeding up when the street is clear. The excess of traffic may evolve into violent episodes, disturbing other drivers and increasing time loss and traffic congestion. In the same way other collateral damages may be produced, like excessive gas consumption while cars wait in line for a long time in the same place, thus environmental pollution with CO_2 rises considerably [1–3].

The most common system in the cities to control car flow is the traffic lights, which basically work with green, yellow and red lights to signal go, go with caution and stop, respectively. Their aim is to regulate and speed up car flow in the streets. However, traffic lights nowadays do not have the ability to intelligently manage traffic congestion on a public street at any given time; traffic lights work with timing devices which allow cars flowing on streets according to synchronized allotted time slots. There are a few traffic lights which consider the general state of the surrounding driveways to adjust their performance intelligently, as to give way or stop the car flow out of their programmed schedule. This is one challenge still to be solved for IoT and smart cities development [3].

© Springer Nature Switzerland AG 2019
M. F. Mata-Rivera et al. (Eds.): WITCOM 2019, CCIS 1053, pp. 258–267, 2019.
https://doi.org/10.1007/978-3-030-33229-7_22

Cars in México are the main source of pollution which contributes to the formation of tropospheric ozone, with serious consequences on cardiopulmonary illnesses, so the government must not keep delaying the update of regulations for emissions at national scale, as declared by officers of the Centro Mexicano de Derecho Ambiental AC (CEMDA, Mexican Center for Environmental Rights), the CTS Embarq México, and International Council of Clean Transportation (ICCT); these institutions remark that México currently has very mild standards to control emissions of ozone precursors pollutants [2].

Particularly, the city of Mérida, capital of the state of Yucatán, has become a city where the automobiles are reducing spaces for the more than 2 million citizens and they are flooding the streets of the historical downtown. According to the IMPlan, the Municipal Institute for Mérida's Planning, six hundred thousand private motor vehicles are estimated in the city, that is to say there is one car for every two inhabitants in average [4]. Since Mérida is a colonial capital city, with narrow streets, it is important to find alternatives that help clear traffic congestions which are inevitably often produced in the main streets and surrounding areas downtown Mérida [5].

This paper describes a traffic control system based on intelligent agents, sensors and Arduino to control traffic lights to improve every day traffic and emergency vehicles. A scale model of a two streets intersection with traffic lights and sensors is built to perform tests.

2   Reference Framework

This project involves intelligent agents, such as deliberative, reactive and information agents; there are also four type of sensors which are key to show the conditions on the streets and the system's behavior during testing.

2.1   Intelligent Agents

An intelligent agent may be defined as a software entity which, based on its own knowledge performs a set of operations aimed to satisfy the needs of a user or another program, either by its own initiative or because of a user's request [6].

All intelligent agents are programs but not all searching programs are intelligent agents. An agent can be considered as an individual entity, sort of a part of a program with control over its own functions; they are continuously performing processes that tell them what to do and how to do it, they also communicate with other agents to solve their given tasks adequately [7].

When a highly complex problem needs to be solve it is recommended to design a multiagent system which is a system made of multiple intelligent agents able to fulfill goals individually to solve a global goal [8].

According to [6], intelligent agents can be classified as deliberative, reactive, information and hybrid agents. Deliberative agents are based on an internal symbolic reasoning model which allows them to manage and coordinate tasks with other agents according to action plans. This kind of agent uses a decision taking scheme based on condition - cognition – action, to identify the environment conditions so that it can plan the next step. There are also reactive or static agents whose functions are specific and they are unable to perform any task out of those previously assigned; this does not imply that they are not able to interact with other agents to achieve specific joint objectives. They do not save previous information therefore they are fast an efficient in decision making but they do not adapt to change. Information agents are those that have access to one or more sources of information and they are capable of filtrating or manipulating data obtained from those sources in order to respond to user petitions or to other information agents in cooperative environments. Information sources can be of different nature from databases up to other agents. It is necessary to mention that a particular implementation of an intelligent agent may show more than one behavior at the same time, in which case it is classified as a hybrid agent. This allows to maximize the strengths of some agents and minimize deficiencies of others, thus taking the best of each type such as decision taking precision from the deliberative agents and speedy response time from the reactive agents.

2.2 Related Work Review

Controlling traffic in the cities is an escalating problem with repercussions beyond the trivial complication of waiting time and driver's annoyance, and in a worldwide scope there are pollution and smart cities development issues to consider. This is palpable with the large selection of published related work from which we have only mentioned those closer to the main subject of the present work. To improve waiting time autonomous traffic control systems have been used with real time data reception to control traffic lights and even to impose fines to reckless drivers [9], Q-learning algorithm has been applied in [10] and in combination with particle swarm optimization algorithm as in [11]. There are also proposals based on microcontroller hardware devices which control infrared sensors and they adjust traffic light timing as in [12] and [13], where the traffic light configuration is controlled via Bluetooth. Other developments are focused on emergency vehicles to control traffic in an emergency route by means hardware as in [14], and, in contrast there are proposals which privilege pedestrians crossing of highways as in [15]. There are more elaborated systems that incorporate fuzzy logic [16] and study cases involving air quality measurement [17] with very interesting results in software simulations.

Some of the developments mentioned above share transit flow and traffic lights sequences configuration with the present project; they take into account similar variables with variations in their definitions although mostly within the same range. Some include other aspects such as fuzzy logic control and pedestrian crossing which are not included in the present proposal. The scale model is the differentiator, which is a great asset in a classroom environment and is quite useful to visualize testing results.

3 Design and Implementation

The system displays a multiagent architecture combining software and hardware. It is built on a 0.80 cm by 0.80 cm wooden base with the programmed Arduido and sensors mounted on a scale model of the street crossing with the traffic lights. Model size cars can be moved about to see how the system reacts on each situation the user wishes to test.

3.1   Architecture Design

The environment is perceived with a number of sensors connected to a programmed Arduino with the three intelligent agent controlling the output, in this case three traffic lights (actuators) on the streets. On the side of the software, the system consists of three agents (see Fig. 1): a reactive agent which collects data from the sensors, a hybrid agent (information and reactive agent) which gets, selects and sends information, and a deliberative agent which takes decisions to control the traffic lights.

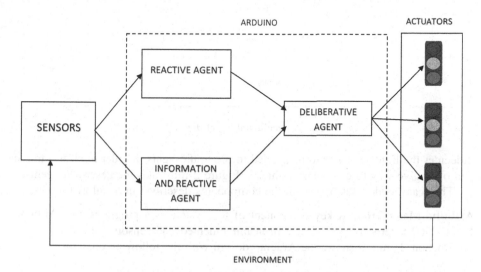

Fig. 1. Multiagent architecture (Color figure online)

The emergency agent is essentially a reactive one and it receives readings form the color and sound sensors to determine the presence of emergency vehicles; it disregards information related to traffic and time of the day, and it is sensible only to red or blue lights. Once light is detected the emergency agent compares the sound levels on each street to select the one with the highest noise so that such a street is identified as the one with an emergency vehicle, (police patrol, ambulance or fire truck). Once an emergency is detected and the street is tagged as that of preferential way, the emergency agent sends data to the control agent which adds an information component to the former agent and it is possible to classify the emergency agent as a hybrid one. The traffic sensor agent receives readings from the distance and motion sensors which means it is an information agent. All three distance sensors are identified individually and they indicate if the line of cars waiting on each street has reached a certain point (where the sensor is placed). In other words, these sensors alert when there is a traffic jam on each street. Also, the motion sensors placed under each of the traffic lights count the passing vehicles and this data is saved on a file for statistical purposes. Also, there is the intelligent control agent which collects data from the emergency and traffic agents and

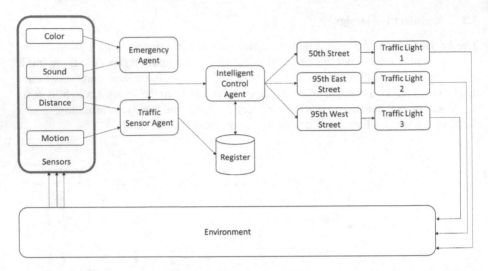

Fig. 2. Intelligent agent diagram

it decides the light sequence to be applied to the traffic lights in order to clear a traffic jam or to give way to emergency vehicles. Figure 2 illustrates the described agents.

The scale model was built with the components described in detail as follows.

Arduino Mega 2560. A key component of the system is a programmable Arduino Mega 2560 where the agents have been implemented and sensors are set to receive information. Figure 3 shows the Arduino design with the following components.

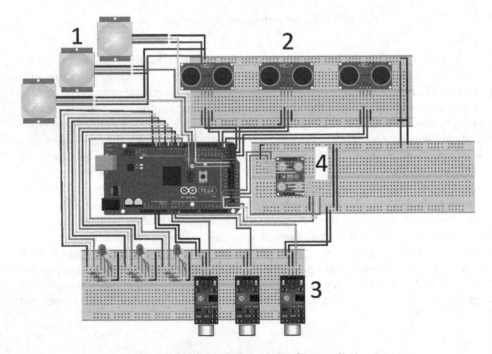

Fig. 3. Arduino design (Color figure online)

Motion Sensor PIR HC-SR501. It detects when an object crosses directly in front of the sensor and so it is programmed on the Arduino as a counting device. There are three motion sensors to count vehicles passing on each street; this information shows how many vehicles cross under the traffic lights after a light change. See number 1 on Fig. 3.

Ultrasonic Distance Sensor HC-SR04. This sensor continuously detects the distance between its position and an object directly in front of it from 3 to 300 cm (see number 2 on Fig. 3). In this case, when consecutive readings remain constant and under 7 cm for an allotted period of time it means that a car has remain in front of the sensor without moving, hence it is interpreted as a jam on the street.

Sound Sensor KY038. It analogically detects the amount of generated noise in the environment; the values range from 0 to 1023 (see number 3 on Fig. 3). The highest value identifies the street where an emergency vehicle may be coming.

Color Sensor TCS230. This sensor is able to detect red, blue and green light around it. To sense emergency vehicles it was programmed to react only to red and blue light, because they are commonly used on such vehicles. The color sensor activates the sound sensors on each street. See number 4 on Fig. 3.

3.2 Implementation

In Mérida, Yucatán, one of the busiest streets is the 50th st. which runs North to South; at one point it is intersected by 95th street, which is a two-way road (see Fig. 4). This intersection is represented on the scale model; it has 3 traffic lights, one is on 50th and two more are on 95th. There are sound, distance, motion and light sensors installed on this scenario. There are 3 ultrasonic sensors placed approximately at a distance of 3 to 5 average cars from the intersection. Traffic lights have a motion sensor installed underneath each one. One light sensor on this scale model has been installed next to the

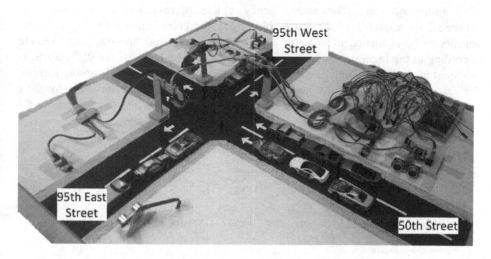

Fig. 4. Scale model of the streets intersection (Color figure online)

programmed Arduino as to have easy access to the sensor during testing. Sound sensors are placed approximately at the same distance as the ultrasonic sensors on each street. As it is still a prototype the whole system is sensible to malfunction of the sensors, in which case the results will not be as expected.

4 Results

A number of tests were designed to verify the behavior of the agents on each set of conditions (states) designed purposely to evaluate the results. Five typical states were selected and they are explained in detail in the following paragraphs, according to the corresponding 50th St, 95th East St and 95th West St. with a 10 s allocated time for each traffic light on a regular basis.

1. Normal state. This state shows a normal sequence for the three traffic lights. It starts with Traffic Light 1(TL1) allowing 8 cars to go for 10 s, followed by Traffic Light 2 (TL2) allowing 5 cars for 10 s and finally Traffic Light 3 (TL3) allowing 3 cars for 10 s, as detailed in Table 1. The count of cars is performed by each street's motion sensor. Since none of the distance, sound or color sensors are activated, the normal sequence is followed.

Table 1. Normal state.

50th street				95th East street				95th West street				
TL 1	D	M	S	TL 2	D	M	S	TL 3	D	M	S	C
Stop				Go (10 s)		5 cars		Stop				
Stop				Stop				Go (10 s)		3 cars		
Go (10 s)		8 cars		Stop				Stop				

2. Emergency state. When an emergency vehicle approaches on one road, the color sensor (C) is activated by the red or blue light; the color sensors allows the sound sensors to be evaluated in order to decide which street has an emergency vehicle according to the highest sound sensor reading. Table 2 shows how the 95th East St is cut short after allowing only 3 cars in 6 s on TL2 and then the sound sensors identify 50th street needing clearance for ambulance or patrol car; TL1 stays on for 20 s allowing 6 cars to pass including the emergency vehicle. When that vehicle is far

Table 2. Emergency state.

50th street				95th East street				95th West street				
TL 1	D	M	S	TL 2	D	M	S	TL 3	D	M	S	C
Stop				✓	Go (6 s)		3 cars		Stop				✓
Go (20 s)		6 cars		Stop				Stop				
Stop				Stop				Go (10 s)		4 cars		

enough and the sound is no longer perceived, the traffic lights go back to a normal schedule, as shown in TL3 with 10 s for 4 cars to pass on 95th West St.

3. Traffic jam state. In this context, a traffic jam is identified on a street with a long line of unmoving cars according to the ultrasonic distance sensor value which will be constant and less than 7 cm. after an allotted time. When such a situation arises, that sensor requests a preference on the way to clear the blocked street, in other words, the sensor requests a green light to be activated for as long as needed and when the blockage is no longer sensed the system will go back to normal state. Table 3 illustrates this situation, where TL2 allows 3 cars on a normal 10 s time slot; then it is TL3 turn but two distance sensors on streets 50th and 95th East are activated, thus cutting down to 8 s the time of TL3 to allow the system to decide which of the two jammed streets should be served first: it gives way to the 50th street allowing 12 cars to circulate for 15 s while 95th East street needs to wait. After 50th street is cleared, 95th street is granted a green light and a longer time slot of 12 s of green light was needed to allow 9 cars to go. Since both jammed streets are now cleared, the traffic light schedule goes back to the normal state with 10 s on TL 3 with only 2 cars passing through.

Table 3. Traffic jam state.

50th street				95th East street				95th West street				
TL 1	D	M	S	TL 2	D	M	S	TL 3	D	M	S	C
Stop				Go (10 s)		3 cars		Stop				
Stop	✓			Stop			✓	Go (8 s)		0 cars		
Go (15 s)		12 cars		Stop			✓	Stop				
Stop				Go (12 s)		9 cars		Stop				
Stop				Stop				Go (10 s)		2 cars		

4. Night state. From 00:01 h to 04:00 h, the night schedule is activated; this means that the 50th street will have only flashing yellow light to yield or slow down and cross the road carefully; on the other hand, the drivers on both ways of the 95th street will have flashing red lights as to indicate drivers to be aware and cross after a full stop. The night state disregards the distance sensor since no traffic congestions are expected during late night. See Table 4.

Table 4. Night state.

50th street				95th East street				95th West street				
TL 1	D	M	S	TL 2	D	M	S	TL 3	D	M	S	C
Stop				Yield				Yield				

5. Night state with emergency. During the night, TL1 stays on flashing yellow mode and streets 95th East and West stay on red lights. As Table 5 shows, when an emergency vehicle is identified on 95th East street, a green light is granted for as long as needed (in this example it was 10 s) before going back to the preventive flashing lights.

Table 5. Night state with emergency.

50th street				95th East street				95th West street				
TL 1	D	M	S	TL 2	D	M	S	TL 3	D	M	S	C
Yield				Stop				Stop				
Yield				Stop			✓	Stop				✓
Stop				Go (10 s)				Stop				
Yield				Stop				Stop				

5 Final Remarks and Conclusions

The intelligent agent system devised for traffic light control on a scale model has been successful to identify a set of conditions and it has reacted adequately according to each situation. The control agent implemented on the Arduino allows sensors to perceive the environmental variables to test the response of the multi agent system performance in each situation, showing good decisions to regulate traffic flow on both streets. The results show the system is able to change the environment favorably as traffic flow concerns. The agent system implemented on the scale model is able to identify a traffic jam and offers a way to free the blocked roads, as showed on state 3 Table 3, which portrays an everyday situation in that particular street crossing in Mérida. Emergency situations are recognized and handled adequately by the control agent thanks to the sensors reading the environment in conjunction with the programmed Arduino.

The prototype was built using the Arduino which is easy to program using a variant of C Language. This also allows the user to modify some parameters and test the results on the scale model.

There is also the advantage of having extra ports in which case the system can be scaled to model more sensors o traffic lights.

There is a lot to be done as future work on this incipient project: one line of study is for this model to be a generator of patterns which can be the input for a more complex traffic control learning system.

The authors would like to thank the Tecnológico Nacional de México, campus Mérida, for the support and resources devoted to this work.

References

1. New York Times. https://www.nytimes.com/2019/01/21/upshot/stuck-and-stressed-the-health-costs-of-traffic.html?ref=nyt-es&mcid=nyt-es&subid=article. Accessed 01 Aug 2019
2. Milenio. https://www.milenio.com/estados/autos-primera-fuente-de-contaminacion-en-el-país. Accessed 01 Aug 2019
3. INEGI. http://www3.inegi.org.mx/contenidos/app/saladeprensa/aproposito/2015/trafico31.pdf. Accessed 01 Aug 2019
4. Diario de Yucatán. http://yucatan.com.mx/merida/urbanismo/pobre-educacion-vial. Accessed 16 Apr 2019

5. Diario de Yucatán. https://www.yucatan.com.mx/merida/uso-mas-eficiente-de-vehiculos. Accessed 01 Aug 2019
6. Wooldridge, M., Jennings, N.: Intelligent agents: theory and practice. Knowl. Eng. Rev. **10** (2), 115–152 (1995). https://doi.org/10.1017/S0269888900008122
7. Inteligencia Artificial Agentes. https://sitiointeligenciaa.wordpress.com/agentes/. Accessed 01 Aug 2019
8. Universidad Nacional del Centro de la Provincia de Buenos Aires. http://www.exa.unicen. edu.ar/catedras/optia/public_html/2018%20Agentes%20inteligentes.pdf. Accessed 01 Aug 2019
9. Universidad Nacional Abierta y a Distancia. https://stadium.unad.edu.co/preview/UNAD. php?url=/bitstream/10596/17725/1/7702768.pdf. Accessed 01 Aug 2019
10. Rosyadi, A., Wirayuda, T., Al-Faraby, S.: Intelligent traffic light control using collaborative Q-Learning algorithms. In: 2016 4th International Conference on Information and Communication Technology (ICoICT), pp. 1–6. IEEE (2016)
11. El Hatri, Ch., Boumhidi, J.: Q-learning based intelligent multi-objective particle swarm optimization of light control for traffic urban congestion management. In: 2016 4th IEEE International Colloquium on Information Science and Technology (CiSt), pp. 794–799. IEEE (2016)
12. Ghazal, B., et al.: Smart traffic light control system. In: 2016 Third International Conference on Electrical, Electronics, Computer Engineering and Their Applications (EECEA), pp. 140–145. IEEE (2016)
13. Universidad Autónoma del Estado de México. http://hdl.handle.net/20.500.11799/99060. Accessed 01 Aug 2019
14. Kuzminvkh, I.: Development of traffic light control algorithm in smart municipal network. In: 2016 13th International Conference on Modern Problems of Radio Engineering, Telecommunications and Computer Science (TCSET), pp. 896–898. IEEE (2016)
15. Universidad Politécnica de Madrid. http://oa.upm.es/48212/1/TFG_SILVIA_MONINO_ ESTEBAN.pdf. Accessed 01 Aug 2019
16. Orozco, H., Lazcano, S., Landassuri, V.: Simulación basada en agentes para el control inteligente de semáforos mediante lógica difusa. In: Pistas Educativas No. 128 (SENIE 2017), México, pp. 1206–1223 (2018)
17. Scientific Electronic Library. http://www.scielo.org.mx/pdf/poli/n50/n50a10.pdf. Accessed 01 Aug 2019

A Clustering-Based Approach
to Base Station Assignment
in IoT Cellular Systems

Edgar Adrian Esquivel-Mendiola[1]([✉]), Hiram Galeana-Zapién[1],
and Edwin Aldana-Bobadilla[2]

[1] Centro de Investigación y de Estudios Avanzados del I.P.N., Unidad Tamaulipas,
Ciudad Victoria, Mexico
{eesquivel,hgaleana}@tamps.cinvestav.mx
[2] Conacyt-Centro de Investigación y de Estudios Avanzados del I.P.N.,
Unidad Tamaulipas, Ciudad Victoria, Mexico
ealdana@tamps.cinvestav.mx
http://www.tamps.cinvestav.mx

Abstract. We address the optimal base station assignment for each
device in IoT networks. In this regard, we extend the well known k-
means clustering algorithm wherein each device is represented as a n-
tuple which encompasses the channel conditions for a set of candidates
base stations to be assigned. Our solution firstly computes the number of
clusters in the scenario, and then determines the objects (devices) belonging to each cluster (group). Simulations results show that our approach
achieves competitive results in terms of the average sum throughput and
load balancing between the cluster heads.

Keywords: Base station assignment · Clustering · Internet of Things

1 Introduction

Cellular communication systems will play a key role in the provision of services
in the Internet of Things (IoT) systems. This is particularly critical in scenarios
where mobile sensing objects are expected to be deployed over large areas (e.g.,
logistics, fleet management, etc.), requiring the support of cellular networks to
seamlessly transmit/receive information to/from Internet. However, the support
of IoT imposes several challenges relative to the cellular communication systems,
such as: (a) the expected number of connected devices per access point or base
station (BS), leading to a significant traffic increase per service area [1]; (b) het-
erogeneity of devices and quality of service (QoS) requirements; and (c) resource
constraints either in the device (e.g., energy, computation) or network side (e.g.,
resource availability) [2]. In order to efficiently support IoT in cellular networks,
resource management strategies are required which in turn must guarantee QoS
requirements of connected devices, as well as limiting interference and tackling
new resource bottlenecks like the backhaul [3–5].

© Springer Nature Switzerland AG 2019
M. F. Mata-Rivera et al. (Eds.): WITCOM 2019, CCIS 1053, pp. 268–283, 2019.
https://doi.org/10.1007/978-3-030-33229-7_23

In this context, one of the most challenging problem is to find that assignment of BS that optimizes radio transmission to/from mobile devices. This poses an optimization problem where the objective function is defined typically in terms of utility and cost functions associated to a potential assignment. Such an optimization problem can be subject to a set of constraints (i.e., device and system capacity constraints) which in turn can induces non-convex solution spaces, in which case several authors resort to heuristic approaches [CITE]. For instance, given the heterogeneous characteristics of IoT devices, some scenarios poses constraints in terms of computation, sensing, and communication capabilities.

Implicitly the assignment of BS induces a partition with subsets that include devices with "similar" features wherein the similarity can be defined in terms of a metric (e.g. relative to channel conditions). This assumption allows us to treat such a problem as a clustering problem. This approach has been explored in [6], where the similarity metric is based exclusively on a proximity measure between devices (Euclidean distance). This implies that the approach in groups nearby devices without taking into account channel conditions (i.e., slow and fast fading), and thus the resulting BS assignment might not be the most appropriate from the air interface performance point of view.

In order to define a clustering-based BS assignment, we define a device representation which is a scalar value that denotes the overall channel conditions of each device with respect to the potential candidate set of BSs. Such representation is needed to be used as criterion to group devices according to channel conditions instead of Euclidean distance. Furthermore, we focus on IoT cellular systems, in which devices are expected to be connected to the Internet either via a macro-cell BS or by means of a cluster heads acting as the serving BS or Sink. In this work we concentrate in this latter case to determine the BS assignment solution (i.e., the associations between IoT devices and cluster heads), where a given mobile and the cluster head is supported via device-to-device (D2D) communications.

1.1   Contributions

This work provides the following significant contributions:

- Algorithms from data mining cannot be applied directly to group devices in cellular systems, given that the attributes of devices are mainly related to the spatial position in the cell. Thus, we provide a device representation that accounts for the channel conditions (i.e., path-loss, shadowing) of devices to group them using the well-known k-means algorithm.
- The proposed clustering-based BS assignment approach allows to control the load among cluster heads, so that when a cluster head exceeds a given load threshold our approach triggers a process to select a device to become a cluster head to have a new group of users.

- In conventional k-means implementations, an input requirement to the algorithm is the number of cluster heads (i.e., k, the number of groups). In this sense, our approach allow us to compute the appropriate number of cluster heads that improve the system capacity and provide balance conditions among cluster heads.
- The proposed approach can operate in a distributed way as each cluster head decide separately which devices are accepted according to load conditions.

The remainder of this paper is organized as follows. In Sect. 2 the related work is presented. The Sect. 3 introduces a reference BS assignment framework, system model and the formalization of the BS assignment problem. Then, in Sect. 4, we detail the proposed clustering-based BS assignment algorithm for which a suitable devices' representation of devices is described. The simulation experiments along with numerical results are discussed in Sect. 5. Finally, the conclusions remarks are summarized in Sect. 6.

2   Related Work

The BS assignment problem has been extensively studied in the literature, where greedy to heuristic-based algorithms have been proposed so far. On the one hand, in greedy solutions, the devices are associated with the BS that offers the highest signal to noise ratio (SNR). On the other hand, for heuristic approaches the problem is formulated as an optimization problem, imposing different resource constraints [7–10]. In [7], the authors formulated the BS assignment problem as the Multiple-Choice Multidimensional Knapsack Problem and proposed a heuristic approach to solve the problem. In [11] the authors studied the joint BS assignment and resource allocation problem, and proposed solution based on dynamical programming. Similarly, in [9] the authors modeled the problem as a supply and demand scheme. Game theoretic-based solutions have also been applied in [10] leading to a distributed-based assignment decision.

Recently, there is a trend to study the design of clustering-based solutions for the BS assignment problem in cellular networks [12–14]. This is mainly boosted by the supporting of device-to-device communications, where devices are modeled to communicate directly with the minimum coordination of the BS [15–17]. Most of the approaches proposed so far are based on the extensively work presented for wireless sensor networks, where clustering solutions have been proposed to perform the grouping of devices and the selection of the sink nodes [18,19]. In particular, the attributes of devices are determined by their spatial position inside the cell, and a clustering algorithm determines the membership of a device to one group. The criterion to decide the clusters of devices is mainly based on the Euclidean distance. In [20], the authors studied the support of machine-to-machine communications under cellular networks scenarios and proposed a method for grouping the devices and cluster head selection. In [13] a clustering approach is studied for the joint BS assignment and load balancing problem. Authors in [6] proposed a cluster head selection and a clustering scheme based on k-means. Similarly, in [21], the authors proposed a cluster head selection method based on resource availability at devices. In [22], the authors proposed a clustering solution based on physical position and social interaction metrics between devices. The work in [23] proposed a method to group devices that are configured to operate in D2D mode. Similarly, an energy-constrained scenario is studied in [24], where the selection of cluster heads is determined by the energy budget of devices.

It is worth noting that in most of the analyzed works the attributes of devices are characterized by their position in the cell. However, this representation does not account for the channel conditions observed between devices and their potential cluster head candidates. Moreover, devices are associated with nearest cluster head according to the similarity function based on the Euclidean distance, which may lead to a poor system performance since devices may not be associated with an adequate cluster head that satisfies their minimum requirements.

3   Reference Framework

In order to evaluate the BS assignment problem, herein we define a generic single-cell cellular system. Yet simple, the presented reference framework allow us to design and to validate a clustering-based algorithm to solve the BS assignment problem. Specifically, we assume that there are M total devices camped in the service area of a single-cell coverage. Each device $i \in M$ could be considered as a cluster head mode with $C \subset M$ or an IoT device with $D \subset M$, but not both modes at the same time. As depicted in Fig. 1, we assume that there exist the following type of devices:

- **IoT devices.** These devices are assumed to be resource-limited nodes that require to be connected to a cluster head for downlink and uplink data transfer. Each IoT device can only be connected to one cluster head (i.e., no partial associations are considered), which is defined as a device-to-cluster (D2C) association. Moreover, each IoT device requires to meet a minimum data rate requirement in the downlink, denoted as R_i^{min}.
- **Cluster heads.** Devices acting as cluster heads are directly connected to the macro-cell BS (C2N). As cluster heads provide connectivity to a given number of IoT devices, they are assumed to be constrained with an amount of radio resources.

At this regard, in this paper we concentrate on the problem of allocating IoT devices to a given cluster head. For the sake of simplicity, we refer to this problem as BS assignment problem.

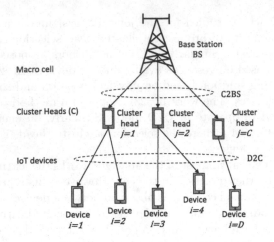

Fig. 1. Generic hierarchical single-cell scenario. Cluster heads are assumed to be connected to the macro-BS, whereas the association of IoT devices to a cluster head is determined using a clustering-based approach.

3.1 System Model

All devices can be selected as cluster heads. The suitability of a given device i to become a cluster head is determined in terms of the signal to noise ratio (SNR). Thus, we compute the SNR between each device with respect to each of the rest of devices. Hence, the computation of the SNR achieved by device i being served by cluster head j (with $i \neq j$) is computed as:

$$SNR_{ij} = \frac{G_{ij} P_{ij}}{\eta} \tag{1}$$

where G_{ij} accounts for the radio channel gain between device i and device j (including path-loss, shadowing and noise figures), P_{ij} is the transmit power of device j being in cluster head mode to device i, η denotes the thermal noise. Taking this into account, the achievable transmission rate of device i assigned to cluster head j (i.e.. downlink direction), denoted by r_{ij}, is determined by:

$$r_{ij} = W log_2(1 + SNR_{ij}) \tag{2}$$

where W is the system bandwidth assuming a frequency reuse factor of 1. Furthermore, in order to quantify the resource consumption of device i assigned to the cluster head j, we define a radio resource cost function, denoted as α_{ij}.

$$\alpha_{ij} = \frac{R_i^{min}}{u_{ij}} \tag{3}$$

where u_{ij} is the utility achieved by device i assigned to device j as a function of the transmission rate r_{ij} achieved by device i, and $\alpha_{ij} = 1$ would mean that the assignment of device i to device j requires all available radio resources to meet its rate requirement.

3.2   BS Assignment Problem

As illustrated in Fig. 1, the BS assignment problem aims to assign each IoT device to a given cluster head in order to optimize the system's throughput. We assume that IoT devices have a minimum downlink data rate requirement, whereas the cluster heads are assumed to have a limited amount of radio resources. Over such a basis, we define B as the assignment matrix of $D \times C$ elements, where each element b_{ij} is determined as follows:

$$
b_{ij} = \begin{cases} 1, \text{ if device } i \text{ is assigned to cluster head } j \\ 0, \text{ otherwise} \end{cases} \tag{4}
$$

Therefore, the optimization problem is defined as follows:

$$
\max_{b_{ij}} \sum_{j=1}^{C} \sum_{i=1}^{D} u_{ij} b_{ij} \tag{5a}
$$

$$
\text{s.t.} \sum_{i=1}^{M} \alpha_{ij} b_{ij} \leq 1, \ j = 1, \ldots, C \tag{5b}
$$

$$
\sum_{j=1}^{C} b_{ij} = 1, \ i = 1, \ldots, D \tag{5c}
$$

$$
R_i \geq R_i^{\min}, \ i = 1, 2, \ldots, D. \tag{5d}
$$

$$
b_{ij} \in \{0, 1\} \tag{5e}
$$

The BS assignment problem (5a) is a combinatorial problem due to the integer variables. Constraint (5b) works as a cost capacity for each cluster head, that also could be applied to denote the load condition of cluster head. Constraint 5c states that all IoT devices must be assigned to a single cluster head. Constraint 5d ensures that the minimum rate requirement of all devices is satisfied. Finally, constraint 5e indicates that the assignment variable only can take binary variables.

4   Clustering-Based BS Assignment Algorithm

In this section, we describe our clustering-based BS assignment algorithm. In what follows we firstly introduce the proposed device characterization.

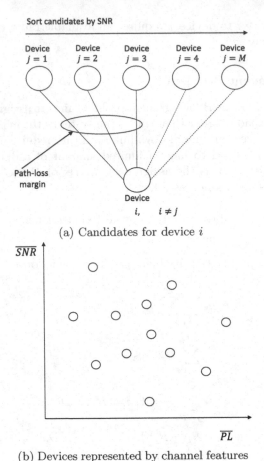

(a) Candidates for device i

(b) Devices represented by channel features

Fig. 2. Characterization process of IoT devices in cellular networks: (a) Candidate set of BSs for each user, and (b) each user characterized in terms of SNR and path loss attributes.

4.1 Clustering Characterization

In order to apply clustering algorithms over a set of objects, we need to firstly represent the objects by means a set of two or more attributes. Then, a measure of similarity is applied to group the objects that share the same attributes. Unlike related works, which resort on spatial attributes when addressing the BS assignment problem as a clustering problem, we define a representation that accounts for the SNR and path loss conditions observed between a given device and its potential BS candidates.

In order to cope with the problem stated before, we firstly compute for each device i the SNR, path-loss and cost observed to/from its candidates. The resulting metrics are represented in a vector denoted by $\overrightarrow{SNR_i}$, $\overrightarrow{PL_i}$, $\overrightarrow{\alpha_i}$. As showed in Fig. 2(a), the set of candidates for device i is determined by all devices that are between a path loss margin. Furthermore, in order to determine the attributes of each device according to its observed channel conditions, we compute a scalar value that represents the average metric between each device and its candidates, as follows:

$$\overline{SNR_i} = \frac{1}{|CS|} \sum_{j=1}^{|CS|} SNR_{ij} \tag{6}$$

where $\overline{SNR_i}$ denotes the average SNR observed between device i to/from its candidates. The same procedure is repeated to calculate the average path loss and cost between device i and each device on its candidate set. CS denotes the set of candidates of device i for each metric. As a result, devices are now represented by their attributes computed from channel conditions, as depicted in Fig. 2(b). The aim of the proposed representation is to account for the channel conditions observed by each device, which can be used by a given clustering algorithm to find the groups of devices belonging to each cluster head. In the following we detail our proposed clustering algorithm, which is an extension of the k-means algorithm.

The proposed clustering-based algorithm consists of two phases, namely *cluster heads searching* and *modified k-means algorithm*. The former follows a load based criterion to determine the number cluster heads, while the latter one is an extension of the well-known k-means algorithm to perform the clustering process. Firstly, the cost metric between each device and all devices in the system is computed. This is necessary since all devices could be selected as cluster heads. Then, k devices are randomly selected as the initial cluster heads (step 4), and the rest of devices are grouped with the cluster head j that satisfy the maximum SNR criterion (steps 5–8). After that, the total radio cost $\pi_j = \sum_{i=1}^{M} \alpha_{ij} b_{ij}$ of each cluster head j is computed. The total cost of each cluster head π_j could be seen as a measure of the load condition observed as a result of the grouping process. At step 13, if the cost capacity of each cluster head is not exceeded, the number of k is adequate to perform the clustering process. Otherwise, the algorithm continue with search for the number of cluster heads. Each cluster head exceeding cost capacity mark its associated devices with high cost as rejected devices, which is denoted by RD. That is, each cluster head accepts the devices to which its sum cost satisfy the condition $\pi_j < 1$. Also, the assignment variable is updated with $b_{ij} = 0$, and each device marks j as a visited cluster (step 17). Next, each device tries to be assigned to another cluster head that has not been visited, and the assignment variable is updated. This process is repeated (steps 14–26) until each device has tried to be associated with all the cluster heads, or the assignment does not exceed the cost capacity in any cluster head. At the end, it could be possible that some devices may not be assigned to any cluster head, so there is checked if the RD set is not empty (step 28). If there are devices not assigned, one new cluster head is determined by choosing randomly a device from the RD set. The device is added to the set of cluster heads and step 5 is repeated.

Once the number of k has been found in the first phase, the process continue to execute the k-means algorithm. Firstly, k devices are selected randomly to be the initial centroids. Then, devices are associated with the closest cluster head according to the maximum SNR (step 38). The centroids are updated by calculating the mean of the devices in each cluster (step 39). This process is repeated until no more changes are observed in the cluster centroids.

5   Simulation Experiments

In this section, we study the performance of the proposed clustering-based base station assignment algorithm. Firstly, we developed a custom made simulator in MATLAB to simulate the network scenario, which is composed of a single macro-BS at the center of the cell with a radius of 500 m. Then, IoT devices are uniformly distributed over the coverage area of the cell keeping a separation distance of 125 m between devices and the macro-BS. The maximum transmit power of the macro-BS is set to 47 dBm, whereas cluster heads have a transmit power of 18 dBm. A path-loss margin of 6 dbm is selected to define the candidate set of each device. Moreover, all devices are assumed to have the same downlink data rate requirement R_i^{min}. Log normal shadowing is accounted with standard deviation of 8 dB. The rest of simulation parameters are summarized in Table 1. We compare the proposed clustering-based approach with the traditional k-means algorithm. For the k-means, the spatial position of the IoT devices is considered as the attribute during the clustering process. Moreover, an arbitrary value of k selected as the number of clusters for the k-means algorithm. On the contrary, in our approach, we firstly determine the number of k in the first stage of the algorithm, and then the k-means algorithm performs the grouping process.

5.1   Simulation Results

Results are divided into clustering analysis and performance evaluation of the proposed clustering-based solution. The former consists in the analysis of the average number of cluster heads and devices per cluster head. The latter consist in a comparative between the proposed algorithm and the conventional k-means algorithm.

Tables 2 and 3 show the average number of clusters and the average number of device per clusters. The comparative was made for a variation of devices in the system and minimum data rate requirement ranging from 15 to 100 kbps. From the results there should be noted that as the rate requirement and the number of devices increases, the number of formed cluster heads also increases. In addition, there is observed that the average number of devices per cluster head remains equal for the variation in the number of devices and the rate requirement.

Algorithm 1. Cost-based clustering algorithm

Data: PL_{ij}, SNR_{ij}

Result: Set of CHs C, assignment matrix B

1 **Cluster heads searching**
2   **forall the** $i \in M$, $j \in M$ **do**
3 | Compute α_{ij}, and u_{ij}
4   **end**
5   Choose k devices randomly as CHs
6   **for** each device i find the most valuable CH j^* **do**
7 | j^*=arg max(SNR_{ij})
8 | $b_{ij^*} = 1$
9   **end**
10   **for** each CH j compute total radio resource cost **do**
11 | $\pi_j = \sum_{i=1}^{M} \alpha_{ij} b_{ij}$
12   **end**
13   **if** $\pi_c > 1$ for any h **then**
14   **while** CH not visited **do**
15   **for** each CH j with $\pi_j > 1$ **do**
16   Find devices exceeding cost capacity and mark them as rejected devices RD
17   For each device $i \in RD$ set $b_{ij} = 0$ and mark CH j as visited
18   **end**
19   **for** each device i in RD **do**
20   Select most valuable (not visited) CH j^*
21              $b_{ij^*} = 1$
22   **end**
23   **for** each CH j compute total radio resource cost **do**
24              $\pi_j = \sum_{i=1}^{M} \alpha_{ij} b_{ij}$
25   **end**
26   **end**
27   **end**
28   **if** RD not empty **then**
29   Choose randomly a device i' from RD to create a new CH
30        $i' \cup C$
31   Repeat step 5 until all devices are assigned
32   **end**
33 **end**
34 **Modified k-means algorithm**
35   Given the number of CHs previously found, set $k = |C|$
36   Choose randomly k devices from M as the initial centroids
37   **while** no change in centroids **do**
38   Assign device i to the closest CH j based on the SNR_{ij}
39   Recalculate the new centroid for each cluster
40   **end**
41 **end**

Table 1. Simulation parameters.

Parameter	Value
Cell radius	500 m
Operating frequency	2000 MHz
Bandwidth	Macro: 10 MHz
Macro Path-Loss	$128.1 + 37.6\log_{10}(\text{distance km})$
D2C Path-Loss	$148 + 40\log_{10}(\text{distance km})$
Macro-BS transmit power P_{BS}^{max}	46 dBm
Cluster head transmit power P_{C}^{max}	18 dBm

Table 2. Average number of cluster heads.

Devices	Rate requirement R^{min}							
	15 Kbps	20 Kbps	25 Kbps	30 Kbps	40 Kbps	60 Kbps	80 Kbps	100 Kbps
50	6.692	8.43	10.13	11.616	14.498	19.234	25.556	26.96
100	12.382	15.772	18.996	22.024	27.52	36.486	49.854	52.598
150	17.86	22.882	27.6	32.076	40.318	53.562	73.844	77.898
200	23.206	29.894	36.146	42.064	52.964	70.344	97.044	103.25
250	28.564	36.556	44.448	51.822	65.282	87.346	119.598	128.366

Table 3. Average number devices per cluster head.

Devices	Rate requirement R^{min}							
	15 Kbps	20 Kbps	25 Kbps	30 Kbps	40 Kbps	60 Kbps	80 Kbps	100 Kbps
50	6.522	4.955	3.955	3.320	2.461	1.607	0.958	0.857
100	7.101	5.357	4.275	3.549	2.640	1.744	1.006	0.902
150	7.418	5.569	4.444	3.682	2.724	1.802	1.032	0.926
200	7.635	5.702	4.542	3.760	2.778	1.844	1.062	0.937
250	7.769	5.849	4.632	3.829	2.831	1.863	1.093	0.947

Devices Distribution Between Cluster Heads: Figure 3 shows a graphical comparative in terms of the assignment found by our proposed clustering-based solution and the k-means algorithm. Initially, a value of $k = 5$ was set for both algorithms; however, as showed in Fig. 3(b) the number of cluster heads found by our proposed approach was of $k = 24$. This is because our approach follows a load balance criterion which creates a new cluster head when imbalance is observed. Moreover, there should be noted that the k-means algorithm groups the devices according to their spatial position then devices are assigned to the closest cluster head, whereas our proposed approach groups the devices according to the representative metrics of SNR and cost.

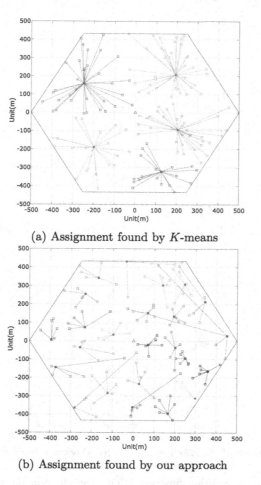

(a) Assignment found by K-means

(b) Assignment found by our approach

Fig. 3. Comparative of the assignment solution found by the k-means and our proposed clustering-based approach. The number of devices was set to 150 with a rate requirement of 25 Kbps.

Analysis of System Throughput: Figure 4 shows the cumulative distribution function of the achieved SNR by each algorithm for different minimum data rate requirements of devices. As shown in Fig. 4, our proposed clustering-based solution has a good performance as the percentage of devices achieving a good SNR value is greater than the achieved with the k-means. For instance, in Fig. 4(a) the 50% of the devices achieved an SNR value of 95 dBm with the k-means algorithm, while the achieved SNR with our clustering-based approach was of 105 dBm. A similar behavior is observed as the data rate requirement of devices is increased.

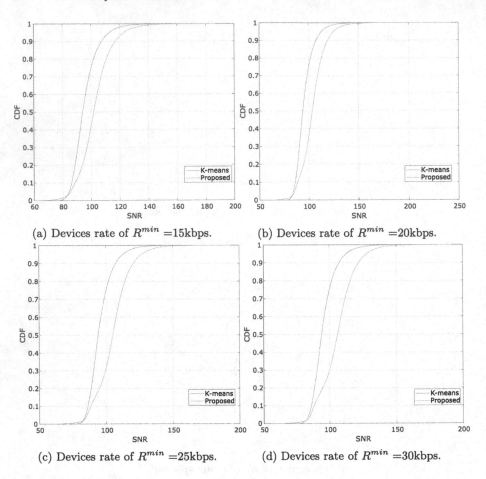

(a) Devices rate of R^{min} =15kbps.

(b) Devices rate of R^{min} =20kbps.

(c) Devices rate of R^{min} =25kbps.

(d) Devices rate of R^{min} =30kbps.

Fig. 4. Cumulative distribution function (CDF) for different data rate requirements. The number of devices is set to $M = 150$, and $k = 5$ for the k-means algorithm.

Analysis of the Average Sum Cost: Figure 5 shows the average sum cost per cluster head achieved by each algorithm under the variation of the number of devices. There should be noted that in our proposed approach, we have defined a cost constraint, which allows us to balance the load conditions between the cluster heads. From Fig. 5, the average sum cost of our proposed approach is below one, whereas the assignment solution found by the k-means algorithm always exceeds the maximum capacity. For instance, in the case of 250 devices, the k-means algorithm has an average cost of six times the maximum allowed capacity at each cluster head. The reason behind is that the k-means algorithm has a fixed value k which leads to overhead in clusters causing a cost increase.

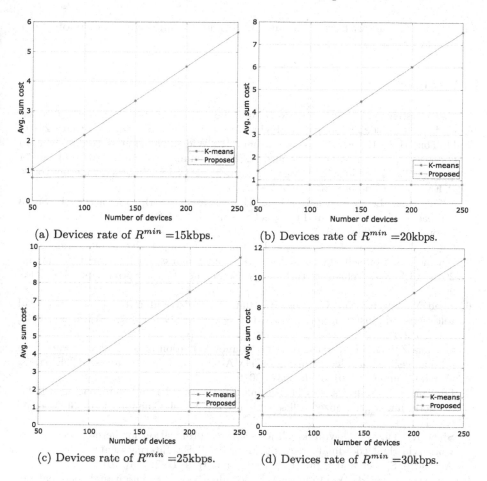

(a) Devices rate of R^{min} =15kbps.

(b) Devices rate of R^{min} =20kbps.

(c) Devices rate of R^{min} =25kbps.

(d) Devices rate of R^{min} =30kbps.

Fig. 5. Average sum cost for each cluster head as the number of devices is varied. The devices' data rate requirement is also varied ranging from 15 to 30 kbps.

6   Concluding Remarks

In this paper, a novel clustering-based base station assignment algorithm has been proposed to support the deployment of IoT devices under cellular communication systems. Unlike other clustering approaches, in our solution, we have developed a device representation that accounts for the channel conditions between the device and its potential candidates. We have shown through experiments that our proposed approach has significant gains in terms of the average sum throughput. Moreover, in terms of the average sum cost between the cluster heads, our approach has a better performance than the k-means algorithm. As future work, we aim to improve the process of the cluster heads discovery by exploring combinatorial approaches. In addition, we aim to study the behavior of other clustering algorithms from data mining for examining the behavior under the massive presence of IoT devices.

References

1. Cisco Systems: Cisco visual networking index: Global mobile data traffic forecast update, 2017–2022 white paper. Technical report, Cisco Systems, February 2019
2. Dhillon, H.S., Huang, H., Viswanathan, H.: Wide-area wireless communication challenges for the internet of things. IEEE Commun. Mag. **55**(2), 168–174 (2017)
3. Ge, X., Tu, S., Mao, G., Wang, C., Han, T.: 5G ultra-dense cellular networks. IEEE Wirel. Commun. **23**(1), 72–79 (2016)
4. Jafari, A.H., López-Pérez, D., Song, H., Claussen, H., Ho, L., Zhang, J.: Small cell backhaul: challenges and prospective solutions. EURASIP J. Wirel. Commun. Netw. **2015**(1), 206 (2015)
5. Cheng, L., Gao, Y., Li, Y., Yang, D., Liu, X.: A cooperative resource allocation scheme based on self-organized network in ultra-dense small cell deployment. In: 2015 IEEE 81st Vehicular Technology Conference (VTC Spring), pp. 1–6, May 2015
6. Zhao, Y., Liu, K., Xu, X., Yang, H., Huang, L.: Distributed dynamic cluster-head selection and clustering for massive IoT access in 5G networks. Appl. Sci. **9**(1), 132 (2019)
7. Galeana-Zapien, H., Ferrus, R.: Design and evaluation of a backhaul-aware base station assignment algorithm for OFDMA-based cellular networks. IEEE Trans. Wirel. Commun. **9**(10), 3226–3237 (2010)
8. Dhillon, H.S., Andrews, J.G.: Downlink rate distribution in heterogeneous cellular networks under generalized cell selection. IEEE Wirel. Commun. Lett. **3**(1), 42–45 (2014)
9. Shen, K., Yu, W.: Downlink cell association optimization for heterogeneous networks via dual coordinate descent. In: 2013 IEEE International Conference on Acoustics, Speech and Signal Processing, pp. 4779–4783, May 2013
10. Semiari, O., Saad, W., Bennis, M.: Downlink cell association and load balancing for joint millimeter wave-microwave cellular networks. In: 2016 IEEE Global Communications Conference (GLOBECOM), pp. 1–6, December 2016
11. Lai, W.K., Liu, J.: Cell selection and resource allocation in LTE-advanced heterogeneous networks. IEEE Access **6**, 72978–72991 (2018)
12. Hajjar, M., Aldabbagh, G., Dimitriou, N., Win, M.Z.: Hybrid clustering scheme for relaying in multi-cell LTE high user density networks. IEEE Access **5**, 4431–4438 (2017)
13. Kollias, G., Adelantado, F., Verikoukis, C.: Spectral efficient and energy aware clustering in cellular networks. IEEE Trans. Veh. Technol. **66**(10), 9263–9274 (2017)
14. Kazmi, S.M.A., Tran, N.H., Ho, T.M., Manzoor, A., Niyato, D., Hong, C.S.: Coordinated device-to-device communication with non-orthogonal multiple access in future wireless cellular networks. IEEE Access **6**, 39860–39875 (2018)
15. Tehrani, M.N., Uysal, M., Yanikomeroglu, H.: Device-to-device communication in 5G cellular networks: challenges, solutions, and future directions. IEEE Commun. Mag. **52**(5), 86–92 (2014)
16. Vlachos, C., Friderikos, V.: Optimal device-to-device cell association and load balancing. In: 2015 IEEE International Conference on Communications (ICC), pp. 5441–5447, June 2015

17. Xiao, S., Zhou, X., Feng, D., Yuan-Wu, Y., Li, G.Y., Guo, W.: Energy-efficient mobile association in heterogeneous networks with device-to-device communications. IEEE Trans. Wirel. Commun. **15**(8), 5260–5271 (2016)
18. Rostami, A.S., Badkoobe, M., Mohanna, F., Keshavarz, H., Hosseinabadi, A.A.R., Sangaiah, A.K.: Survey on clustering in heterogeneous and homogeneous wireless sensor networks. J. Supercomputing **74**(1), 277–323 (2018)
19. Sarkar, A., Murugan, T.S.: Cluster head selection for energy efficient and delay-less routing in wireless sensor network. Wirel. Netw. **25**(1), 303–320 (2019)
20. Tu, C., Ho, C., Huang, C.: Energy-efficient algorithms and evaluations for massive access management in cellular based machine to machine communications. In: 2011 IEEE Vehicular Technology Conference (VTC Fall), pp. 1–5, September 2011
21. Fodor, G., Parkvall, S., Sorrentino, S., Wallentin, P., Lu, Q., Brahmi, N.: Device-to-device communications for national security and public safety. IEEE Access **2**, 1510–1520 (2014)
22. Wang, L., Araniti, G., Cao, C., Wang, W., Liu, Y.: Device-to-device users clustering based on physical and social characteristics. Int. J. Distrib. Sens. Netw. **2015**(8), 1:1 (2015)
23. Koskela, T., Hakola, S., Chen, T., Lehtomaki, J.: Clustering concept using device-to-device communication in cellular system. In: 2010 IEEE Wireless Communication and Networking Conference, pp. 1–6, April 2010
24. El-Feshawy, S.A., Saad, W., Shokair, M., Dessouky, M.I.: An efficient clustering design for cellular based machine-to-machine communications. In: 2018 35th National Radio Science Conference (NRSC), pp. 177–186, March 2018

Fuzzy Logic Controller for Automation of an Autonomous Irrigation System Designed for Habanero Pepper (*Capsicum Chinense* Jacq.)

Jeni Molina-Puc, Mauricio Gabriel Orozco-del-Castillo[(✉)],
Dakar Fernando Villafaña-Gamboa, Romeo Alam Gómez-Buenfil,
José Misael Guzmán-Tolosa, and Humberto Sarabia-Osorio

Departamento de Sistemas y Computación,
Tecnológico Nacional de México/I.T. Mérida, Mérida, Mexico
{e15081607,mauricio.orozco,dakar.villafana,e15080988,
e15080844,e16080414}@itmerida.edu.mx

Abstract. Agriculture is a fundamental economic activity but implies a large consumption of water; in Mexico, the habanero pepper (*Capsicum chinense* Jacq.) is one of the main agricultural products. This work presents the design of a Sugeno based fuzzy controller with 18 if-then rules for an irrigation system that allows irrigation to be managed in a sustainable manner, reducing the loss of water giving habanero pepper plants a favorable environment for their growth. The controller consists of a set of rules designed to activate or deactivate the irrigation system based on four input variables.

Keywords: Fuzzy logic · Intelligent irrigation system · *Capsicum chinense* Jacq · Control systems

1 Introduction

The origin of irrigation systems goes back thousands of years when the rivers were used to irrigate the crops using a staircase design [1]. However, nowadays there is a water crisis due to the misuse that is made of it, causing the environment and millions of people to suffer the consequences [2]; according to the World Water Council, there are six major problems related to water: (1) scarcity, (2) lack of access, (3) decrease in quality, (4) decrease in the allocation of financial resources, (5) fragmentation in the administration and (6) the lack of awareness of the people when making an inadequate use of the water [3]. The Organization of the United Nations and Agriculture reports that 70% of the world's water is used mainly for activities such as agriculture [4].

Habanero pepper (*Capsicum chinense* Jacq.), after the tomato, is one of the main products of agriculture, grown in the states of Baja California Sur, San Luis Potosi, Sonora, Tabasco and in the states that form the Yucatan peninsula: Campeche, Quintana Roo and Yucatan, which have the denomination of origin of habanero pepper since 2010 [5]. The traditional cultivation techniques for this plant are obsolete, this is because the producers are limited in technology, income, among others [6]. According

M. F. Mata-Rivera et al. (Eds.): WITCOM 2019, CCIS 1053, pp. 284–293, 2019.
https://doi.org/10.1007/978-3-030-33229-7_24

to [7], the cultivation of habanero peppers is generally in the open field and with manual irrigation, which ends up affecting production by diverse environmental factors, capable of reducing the quality of the product, yield and profitability of the crop. Nowadays, the way to improve the crop has been sought using a controlled area where external factors are reduced [8].

Traditional farming techniques such as conventional irrigation systems have become obsolete due to limited technology and lack of income from producers. This is why irrigation systems have been updated to date by using automatic, autonomous and even intelligent controllers in order to improve the crop and reduce the physical work of farmers to a level where they only are required to perform a supervision of the system instead of a manual control of it [9].

Fuzzy logic is a branch of artificial intelligence that refers to the way people describe the environment that surrounds them, so it has turned out to be successful when applied to problems related to uncertainty and vagueness [10]. There are controllers based both on classic crisp sets and fuzzy sets. Crisp sets are sets with a discrete border and are an important tool for mathematics and science, however, when used in control applications, they do not demonstrate the thinking of the human being or the way in which he or she interprets the surrounding environment. Crisp sets are defined as a collection of objects or elements, which can belong to the set or not (true or false, respectively); there are no intermediate values [11]. On the contrary, a fuzzy set does not have a discrete border, so that belonging or not to some set occurs gradually [12]. The fuzzy set is an extension of the classical set, to which a defined membership function is added with a range between zero and one. A fuzzy set allows then to simulate the process of human reasoning to control systems based on their experience and solve problems using mathematical methods based on degrees of membership or belonging, associating them with linguistic values, defined with words or labels used naturally by a human being. When modeling information using statements that are not totally true or totally false, they are applied to expressions that can take a truth value from a set of values composed of two extremes and all their possible intermediate values. This modeling is carried out by using linguistic rules that approximate functions of inputs and outputs of the system [11].

Incorporating fuzzy logic with control systems results in fuzzy control systems or fuzzy inference mechanisms, which are responsible for determining what should be done to fulfill a process in the best possible way based on knowledge and experiences provided by a human being in charge of operating the system, since without the knowledge base it is impossible to develop a controller that works correctly [13]. A system based on fuzzy logic necessarily requires the use of different concepts such as fuzzy set, membership function, rules, linguistic variables and values [14]. The membership function is responsible for representing the degree of belonging of an element to a set, that is, represents the degree to which an element is part of such a set [14]. There are different ways to represent membership functions, among the most common are Gaussian, triangular, singleton, trapezoidal and sigmoidal. If-then rules are used and form a fundamental component in an inference system that can represent human experience in a specific process of a controller [14].

A fuzzy inference system (FIS) is a computational model based on fuzzy sets, rules and reasoning. To develop a FIS three conceptual components are required: (1) a set of rules with a selection of fuzzy rules, (2) a database in which the membership functions to be used in the fuzzy rules are defined, and (3) a reasoning mechanism. There are basic inference systems in which you can have fuzzy and discrete inputs, but the output must always be fuzzy, however, sometimes it is necessary to have a discrete output, as in the case of controllers. In these cases, it is necessary to have a defuzzification method to obtain a discrete value that best represents the fuzzy set. The different types of fuzzy inference systems are Mamdani, Sugeno and Tsukamoto; the type of system that should be used depends primarily on the nature of the output [11].

Currently, there are works that implement fuzzy logic in control modules, which logically determine the solutions to achieve the control objectives from the knowledge that is provided by the human being [11]. In [15] the operation of a fuzzy controller applied to an irrigation system is shown; the controller uses triangular and trapezoidal membership functions for the fuzzification of the variables and a rule base of the Mamdani type. In [16] a fuzzy logic controller is used, also based on the Mamdani model for the automation of a greenhouse irrigation system, taking into account as the input value the difference between the desired soil moisture and the actual soil moisture, and as output value a valve that allows to open and close the water passage; this is done to effectively estimate the amount of water avoiding that too much water is applied to the plants. In [17] an irrigation system based on the information provided by humidity, temperature and soil moisture sensors is proposed; considering the inputs, the output of the system determines the irrigation time for the crop while optimizing water use. In [18] and [19] climatic factors are used to determine the ignition of the irrigation pump of a greenhouse and then send the information obtained by the sensors by SMS and perform operations with a smartphone. In [20] an irrigation system is proposed that allows the optimization of water, using humidity, temperature sensors and a flow sensor in the field as inputs for a fuzzy Mamdani controller, while the outputs are the ignition of a lamp and an irrigation pump. Finally, in [21] an intelligent irrigation system is presented that uses an Android application to optimize water consumption in medium-scale gardens and fields using sensors that capture plant data and weather factors in real time. Fuzzy logic is used for decision making and activating the irrigation pump.

This paper presents the design and development of a controller for an automated irrigation system using fuzzy logic. The controller developed in this project uses sensors to measure soil moisture, ambient humidity, luminosity and ambient temperature to determine the activation of an irrigation pump. The soil moisture is periodically monitored to determine if the humidity needed to measure the other sensors is met and, if so, the data obtained from the sensors feeds a Sugeno FIS based on specific rules for habanero pepper plants; the system output activates or deactivates a pump for drip irrigation in a greenhouse.

2 System Design

The development of the controller consists of two subsystems, (1) detection and control by means of the sensors, and (2) the internal development of the controller. The development of these subsystems is described in more detail in the following subsections.

2.1   Sensing and Control

For the operation of the controller, three specific sensors are required: soil moisture sensor (FC 28), light sensor (LDR) and humidity and temperature sensor in the environment (DTH 11), which are connected to a Raspberry module, an electrovalve and finally to a power supply. The sensors perform readings that are sent to the controller to process the values of each of them and based on the fuzzy rules the activation of the solenoid valve is determined [22].

The operation of the controller is observed in Fig. 1. The controller performs a reading of the sensors every 10 min; the values thrown are verified by means of the fuzzy inference mechanism to determine if the rules to activate the irrigation system are met; once irrigation has started, a reading of the values of the sensors every 2 min is made to determine the moment in which the irrigation must be stopped.

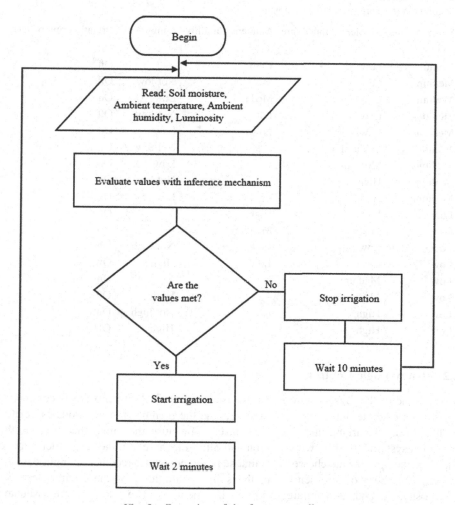

Fig. 1. Operation of the fuzzy controller.

A conventional solenoid valve is used to supply the water, since the irrigation system works only in two states: on and off. The solenoid valve is connected to a hose that works in conjunction with sprinklers and is activated by the fuzzy controller when complying with the rules presented in Table 1. These rules were defined by interviews with experts in the care of habanero pepper when presented with different scenarios with respect to the input variables. Soil moisture sensors are the ones that mainly determine if the activation of the system is necessary, because when the soil is completely humid, irrigation is not carried out regardless of the values of the other sensors, however, if the soil moisture sensors are in a "not wet" range (as described below), then the values of the other sensors are considered to determine the activation of the solenoid valve with the calculation of the rules.

Table 1. Rules to determine whether the irrigation pump should be turned on or off, according to experts in the care of habanero pepper.

Soil moisture	Ambient temperature	Ambient humidity	Luminosity	Irrigation pump state
High	–	–	–	Off
Medium	Low	High	–	Off
Medium	Low	Medium	Not low	Off
Medium	Low	Medium	Low	On
Medium	Low	Low	Not low	Off
Medium	Low	Low	Low	On
Medium	Medium	–	Not low	Off
Medium	Medium	–	Low	On
Medium	High	–	Not low	Off
Medium	High	–	Low	On
Low	Low	High	–	On
Low	Low	Medium	–	On
Low	Low	Low	Not high	On
Low	Low	Low	High	Off
Low	Medium	–	Not high	On
Low	Medium	–	High	Off
Low	High	–	Not high	On
Low	High	–	High	Off

2.2 Fuzzy Logic Control

The scheme of the fuzzy controller can be seen in Fig. 2. A Sugeno FIS is commonly used when discrete outputs are required because the membership functions associated with the output variable are linear or constant. Because the pump that controls the irrigation system has only two states, on and off, a FIS based on the zero-order Sugeno model is the appropriate choice. As a first step, the controller receives as input data the readings of the moisture sensors in the soil, s_1; humidity of the environment, s_2; luminosity, s_3; and temperature of the environment, s_4. The variables are evaluated (fuzzificated) according to the different rules on sigmoidal and Gaussian membership functions, whose parameters were defined empirically and, in the same way as the fuzzy rules, by means of interviews with experts in the care of habanero peppers. These values represent the input of the FIS, whose output determines the switching off or on of the irrigation pump. All the membership functions of the output variables in a Sugeno FIS are linear, and in our case, constants of the form $z = c$, where z represents the output variable and c a scalar value, in our case 0 (off) or 1 (on).

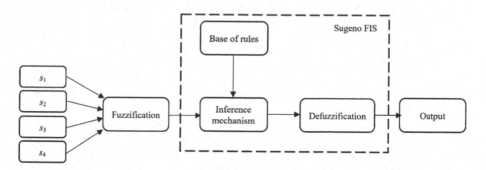

Fig. 2. Fuzzy controller scheme.

The membership functions are distributed according to the linguistic values established for each linguistic variable. Subsequently, the values are evaluated with the fuzzy inference mechanism, that is, the rules established in the base of rules are applied; the decision taken in each situation must take into account the fuzzification process, the result of the mechanism of inference with the minimum and maximum degree of belonging and the Sugeno base of rules. Finally, defuzzification is applied by calculating the weighted average so that the controller produces the desired output. The membership functions of the entries are shown in Fig. 3.

The operation of the system is briefly described below. For each rule, the data obtained from the sensors s_1, s_2, s_3 and s_4, are evaluated in their corresponding membership functions f_1, f_2, f_3 and f_4, and these results are used to calculate the firing strength of each rule. Because all the rules described in Table 1 use the logical conjunction (AND) and a Sugeno model is being used, the firing strength of rule i is calculated as

$$w_i = f_1(s_1)f_2(s_2)f_3(s_3)f_4(s_4). \tag{1}$$

The final output Z of the system is calculated (defuzzified) by means of the weighted average (based on the different firing strengths) of all the outputs for each rule, calculated as:

$$Z = \frac{\sum\limits_{i=1}^{18} w_i z_i}{\sum\limits_{i=1}^{18} w_i}. \tag{2}$$

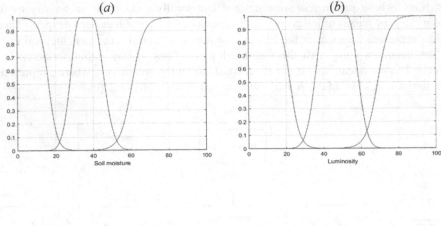

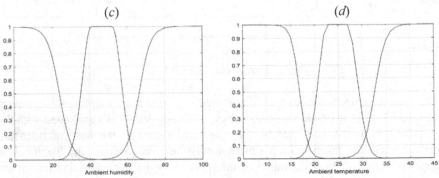

Fig. 3. The membership functions used in the FIS, (*a*) those for soil moisture, (*b*) luminosity, (*c*) ambient humidity and (*d*) ambient temperature.

A value of Z close to 1 turns on the irrigation system (or keeps it on, according to the situation), while a value close to 0 turns it off (or keeps it off).

3   Results

According to the input values of each sensor, the changes in the readings of the values obtained can be observed, therefore, compliance with the rules is evaluated to determine whether the solenoid valve should be turned on or off. Figure 4 graphically shows the operation of the system. Each row represents each of the 18 rules that regulate the behavior of the controller. The first four columns represent the different variables obtained from the sensor data: soil moisture, luminosity, ambient temperature and ambient humidity. The last column represents the activation (or not) of the irrigation pump based on each of the rules. The graph in the lower right corner represents the aggregation of the different outputs for each rule; it is this result that determines whether the irrigation pump is to be turned on or off.

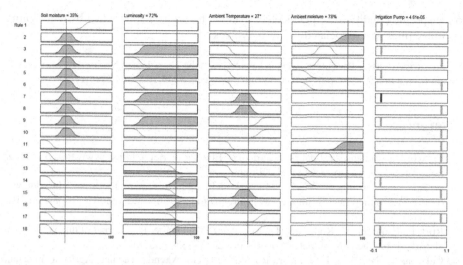

Fig. 4. Result of the operation of the FIS. Each row represents each of the 18 rules that regulate the behavior of the controller. The first four columns represent the different variables obtained from the sensor data. The last column represents the activation (or not) of the irrigation pump based on each of the rules. The graph in the lower right corner represents the aggregation of the different outputs for each rule. The graph shows a case of 35.3% moisture in the soil, 72.2% luminosity, 26.7 °C ambient temperature and 78.4% ambient humidity; the irrigation pump would be turned off in this case due to an aggregated value close to 0.

The operation of the fuzzy controller turns out to be as expected, since the irrigation system stays off when the soil is totally humid and there are high temperatures. In addition, the controller correctly complies with readings of the values of the sensors every 10 min when the pump is off and readings every 2 min when it is turned on.

4 Conclusions

In this work we describe the design of a fuzzy controller based on the Sugeno model for the control of an automatic irrigation system specifically designed for habanero pepper. Based on interviews with experts in the care of habanero pepper, 18 if-then fuzzy rules were established and the different membership functions corresponding to linguistic values of the four linguistic variables obtained from different sensors were designed: soil moisture, luminosity, ambient temperature and ambient humidity. These membership functions were designed with Gaussian and sigmoidal functions.

The implementation of fuzzy logic in a controller for an irrigation system implies a great impact and benefit for agriculture and the people who dedicate themselves to this activity, due to the automation of tasks that allows people to reduce time and processes that would normally need to be carried out by more than one person. It allows preserving the care of the water by having an automatic on/off control based on weather factors, in order to care for crops and thus help the farmer to increase productivity. The design of an irrigation system like the one proposed in this paper can also be extended to the specific conditions of plants other than the habanero pepper plant by redesigning the fuzzy rules and associated linguistic values.

Acknowledgements. The authors want to acknowledge the Tecnológico Nacional de México/I.T. Mérida for the financial support provided through projects 6449.19-P and 6714.19-P.

References

1. Traxco: Historia ancestral del riego agrícola - El agua de riego. https://www.traxco.es/blog/noticias-agricolas/historia-ancestral-del-riego
2. World Water Council: Visión Mundial del Agua-Resumen Ejecutivo. http://www.worldwatercouncil.org/fileadmin/wwc/Library/Publications_and_reports/Visions/Spanish ExSum.pdf
3. Ruiz, F., Esquivel, K., Rodríguez, D., Rodríguez, M., Duarte, R.: Internet of things (IoT), an alternative for the care of water, vol. 40, pp. 2318–2330 (2018)
4. Calzada, J., Narváez, J., Aguilar, R., Velasco, H.: Agenda Técnica Agrícola Yucatán, México (2015)
5. Narváez, M.: Chile habanero de Yucatán, único en el mundo. http://www.cienciamx.com/index.php/ciencia/mundo-vivo/22848-chile-habanero-yucatan
6. Andrade Rodríguez, M., Villegas Torres, O.G., Juárez López, P., López Gómez, J.D., Martínez Fernández, E., Sotelo Nava, H.: Rendimiento y calidad del chile habanero (Capsicum chinense Jacq.) por efecto del régimen nutrimental. Rev. Mex. Ciencias Agrícolas **8**, 1717 (2018). https://doi.org/10.29312/remexca.v8i8.699
7. Tun, J.: Chile habanero características y tecnología de producción. Secr. Agric. Ganad. Desarro. Rural. Pesca y Aliment. 79 (2001)
8. Ruiz, N., Medina, F., Martínez, M.: El chile habanero: su origen y usos (2011)
9. Scott, C., Banister, J.: The dilemma of water management "regionalization" in México under centralized resource allocation. Int. J. Water (2008). https://doi.org/10.1080/0790062070172 3083
10. Baum, B.A., Titlow, J., Vasanth, T., Welch, R.M.: Automated cloud classification of global AVHRR data using a fuzzy logic approach (1997)
11. Jang, J.-S.R., Sun, C.-T., Mizutani, E.: Neuro-Fuzzy and Soft Computing Jang: A Computational Approach to Learning and Machine Intelligence. Prentice-Hall Inc., Upper Saddle River (1997)
12. Zadeh, L.: Fuzzy sets, Berkeley, California (2013). https://doi.org/10.1007/978-1-4614-1800-9_73
13. Ying, H.: Fuzzy control and modeling : analytical foundations and applications. IEEE Press Series in Biomedical Engineering (2000)
14. Ying, H.: The simplest fuzzy controllers using different inference methods are different nonlinear proportional-integral controllers with variable gains. Automatica **29**, 1579–1589 (1993). https://doi.org/10.1016/0005-1098(93)90025-O
15. Touati, F., Al-Hitmi, M., Benhmed, K., Tabish, R.: A fuzzy logic based irrigation system enhanced with wireless data logging applied to the state of Qatar. Comput. Electron. Agric. **98**, 233–241 (2013). https://doi.org/10.1016/j.compag.2013.08.018
16. Hussain, M.H., Min, T.W., Siraj, S.F., Rahim, S.R.A., Hashim, N., Sulaiman, M.H.: Fuzzy logic controller for automation of greenhouse irrigation system (2011)

17. Suruthi, N., Saranya, R., Subashini, S., Shanthi, P., Umamakeswari, A.: Managing irrigation in Indian agriculture using fuzzy logic – a decision support system. Int. J. Eng. Technol. **7**, 321 (2018). https://doi.org/10.14419/ijet.v7i2.24.12075
18. Hilali, A., Alami, H., Rahali, A.: Control based on the temperature and moisture, using the fuzzy logic. Int. J. Eng. Res. Appl. **07**, 60–64 (2017). https://doi.org/10.9790/9622-0705036064
19. Parmar, B., Chokhalia, J., Desarda, S.: Terrace garden monitoring system using wireless sensor networks. Eng. Technol. Manag. **02**, 51–54 (2019)
20. Izzuddin, T., Johari, M., Rashid, M., Jali, M.: Smart irrigation using fuzzy logic method. ARPN J. Eng. Appl. Sci. **13**, 517–522 (2018)
21. Munir, M., Bajwa, I., Cheema, S.: An intelligent and secure smart watering system using fuzzy logic and blockchain. Comput. Electr. Eng. **77**, 109–119 (2019). https://doi.org/10.1016/J.COMPELECENG.2019.05.006
22. Boman, B., Smith, S., Tullos, B.: Control and Automation in Citrus Microirrigation Systems, Florida (2008)

Internet of Things for Irrigation System

J. M. Guzmán-Toloza, D. F. Villafaña-Gamboa$^{(\boxtimes)}$,
L. J. Peniche-Ruiz, R. A. Gómez-Buenfil,
J. K. Molina-Puc, and M. J. Rodríguez-Morayta

Departamento de Sistemas y Computación, Tecnológico Nacional de México,
I. T. de Mérida, Av. Tecnológico km. 4.5 S/N, 97118 Mérida, Yucatán, Mexico
{e15080844, dakar.villafana, larissa.peniche, e15080988,
e15081607, manuel.morayta}@itmerida.edu.mx

Abstract. Technological advances have impacted in recent years most of the economic sectors of the world, where they have managed to increase efficiency and profitability particularly with one of the fastest growing applications in this sector: the Internet of Things (IoT). Agriculture is not the exception. However, most farmers in Mexico still use traditional methods of control and monitoring, which prove to be inefficient, causing time and cost losses in today's globalized world.

The present design is an intelligent irrigation system, implemented under IoT principles and free hardware and software. There are soil moisture, luminosity, humidity and temperature sensors in the environment connected to a Raspberry Pi module; sensors detect values in real time while the Raspberry sends the data to be stored in the cloud. The control system is based on fuzzy logic rules that allow turning on and off a water pump. This design includes a mobile app where the system status is monitored. Tests show an appropriate behavior of the irrigation system.

Keywords: App mobile application · Internet of Things · Raspberry Pi · Irrigation system · Sensors

1 Introduction

In the last 100 years, the world's population has tripled, while water withdrawals have increased six fold, increasing the pressure on natural resources and specifically on water resources worldwide [1].

Agriculture is one of the main pillars of the Mexican economy, 76% of all available water is destined for agricultural use, while for public supply only 14.4%. In Mexico, most irrigation systems operate manually, which in practice ends up being of little use, promotes excessive use and even empirical use of water by not having a means to verify whether the plants have had optimal watering. Among the main difficulties for the technification of irrigation stand out: the high costs of conditioning the irrigation infrastructure, low efficiency of conduction and distribution due to filtration problems, excessive parceling of agricultural land, low efficiency of water application, due to ignorance of efficient irrigation methods and the requirement of water per crop; the weak organization of farmers and their low participation, so that innovation in irrigation

M. F. Mata-Rivera et al. (Eds.): WITCOM 2019, CCIS 1053, pp. 294–304, 2019.
https://doi.org/10.1007/978-3-030-33229-7_25

technology has become a priority in modern times, in order to make agricultural production more efficient and, at the same time, save the vital liquid [2].

Irrigation systems are composed of different elements such as hoses or pipes, as the case may be; step valves and motor pumps, which allow the flow of water through the system to the crop or land to be irrigated [3]. In recent years, technologies have been developed to automate or semi-automate irrigation, these technologies have come to replace the traditional agricultural irrigation mechanism [4]. At the end of the 90 s, the Internet was mainly used as a tool to search for information. In the last 10 years there has been a new way of using the Internet, where everything has become social, transactional and mobile [5]. Currently, society is immersed in what can be said in the second generation of the Internet, called IoT [6]. It is known as IoT to the ability to create connection between objects of the everyday world, allowing to share a lot of information and store it in a database that in most cases is in the cloud [7], thus having control and access to it information from wherever a person is, obviously with internet access [8].

A field of action of the IoT, is its application is the agricultural sector [9], thus creating precision agriculture, which consists in applying the tools offered today by information technology and communications together with different sensors and tools of IoT, in the administration, management of the crops and their land, taking into account the variables and properties that are important in order to improve crop yield, profitability and environmental quality.

Technology can be applied to monitor important characteristics of the plants that the farmers require to keep the crops in good growth condition. Agriculture is not an exact science and it depends on experience-based values; atmospheric conditions of plants in an outdoor field vary from place to place, which makes it difficult to maintain uniformity in all areas of the field [10]. This situation can be better approached from a fuzzy logic point of view, as it has been implemented in various investigations for both fields and greenhouses with efficient irrigation results on different crops.

It can be said that the technological universities of Ecuador, Colombia and Spain to name a few, have made similar designs where they use the Arduino card as the actuator node and the Raspberry module as the coordinating node or gateway, and they also use an app for system control. However, they still do not use fuzzy logic as a control system, which is an innovative branch of artificial intelligence for the present design.

This paper presents an intelligent irrigation system based on IoT [11] with an integrated system to monitor values in real-time using a Raspberry Pi microcontroller together with a number of sensors. The Raspberry Pi works as a gateway between the information collected by the sensors and a real-time database that constantly stores and updates the values of all sensors. It also has a mobile application through which it is possible to verify the state of the system, the eventualities and the values of the sensors in real time. This system offers an easy to implement wireless solution with water savings using technification as opposed to traditional irrigation systems.

2   System Architecture

The system architecture consists of 3 modules shown in Fig. 1: Sensors module, Embedded system module and Mobile application module. The following section contains a detailed description for each one.

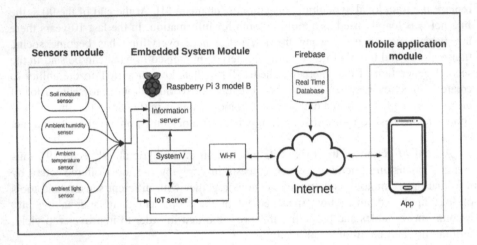

Fig. 1. Architecture for IoT-based monitoring.

2.1   Sensors Module

There are three sensors used according to the parameters: Luminosity, soil humidity and environmental humidity and temperature.

LDR. This sensor measures the luminosity in the environment. It is a resistor that varies its electrical resistance value depending on the amount of light that falls on it, it is also called photo resistor. The electrical resistance value is low when there is light affecting it and very high when it is in the dark. The variation of its resistive value has a certain delay, which is different if it goes from dark to lighted or from lighted to dark.

YL-69. This sensor was used to measure the humidity in the soil as it has the ability to measure soil moisture. It works applying a small voltage between the terminals of the module, a current passes depending on the resistance that is generated in the soil and it depends a lot on moisture. Therefore, when the humidity increases the current increases and when the current decreases it decreases [12].

DHT11. This sensor was used to measure the humidity and temperature in the environment. It is a digital sensor of temperature and relative humidity in the environment. It integrates a capacitive humidity sensor and a thermistor to measure the surrounding air; it displays the data by means of a digital signal on the data pin. This sensor is calibrated at the factory to obtain calibration coefficient recorded in its OTP memory, ensuring high stability and reliability over time. The communication protocol between the sensor and the microcontroller uses a single wire or cable [13].

2.2   Embedded System Module

This module is developed in the integrated Raspberry Pi 3 Model B system, which has the following main features: Cortex A53 quad-core with cache of 512 Kbyte L2 dedicated and 1.2 GHz, 1 GB of RAM, BCM43438 wireless LAN and operating system based on Linux, the kernel version used is 4.14 [14]. The integrated system has two servers: the data server and the IoT server, implemented in an integrated system based on a Linux distribution for Raspberry known as Raspbian. The data server is responsible for handling the requests and receiving the corresponding information from all the sensors that are being monitored. The IoT server is responsible for receiving the requests of the database in real time, sending the stored information of the sensors via Wi-Fi and storing it in the cloud. From the mobile application the corresponding requests are sent to get the updated information to be displayed on the device's screen.

2.3   Mobile Application Module

The mobile app allows displaying the real-time values collected on the database by means of the sensors constantly registering data. This application, developed on Android operating system with the Java programming language, can run on any mobile device or tablet with Android 5.0 Lollipop version onwards. Figure 2 shows the case of use with 3 main functions of the mobile application.

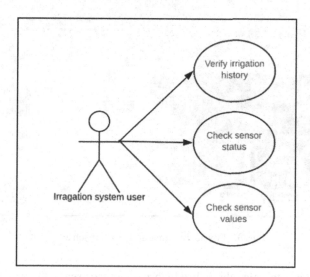

Fig. 2. Case of use of the mobile application.

The first two cases verify irrigation history and check sensor status; they provide a broad overview of the functionality of the system: the first one shows the user the exact date and time when irrigation started while the second shows the status of each sensor; this is useful to identify problems in the data collection or any malfunction. The last function, check sensor values, allows real time visualization of the values obtained by the installed sensors.

The V methodology was applied to develop the system [15], where tests for each module such as the data server and the IoT server, are first carried out. Next, hardware and software are integrated to verify the correct operation of both systems as a whole. Finally, the functionality tests of the system in general are carried out.

2.4   Sensors Tests

To verify the correct operation of each sensor (DHT11, LDR y YL-69), they were connected and tested one by one (see Fig. 3), until obtaining the data registered by the sensors for the server to process the information. The request is made from the Raspberry terminal by means of a Python code that lists the most recent information obtained by each sensor. To avoid information overlapping and to assure reliable information, a delay of 2 s between readings of one sensor and the next.

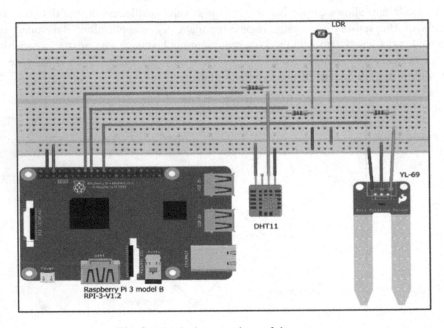

Fig. 3. Physical connections of the sensors.

Figure 3 shows the pins through which each sensor sends the recorded readings; each pin is connected in series with a resistance of 220 Ω to limit the current and thus avoid burning the Raspberry input terminal. The Raspberry Pi 3 module provides each sensor with a +5 Vdc supply to operate. The GPIO Raspberry terminals of the irrigation system electronic circuit are illustrated in more detail in the interconnection diagram in Fig. 4.

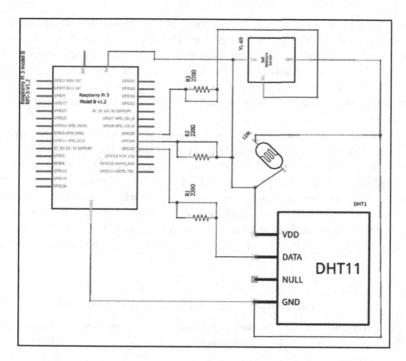

Fig. 4. Schematic diagram of the connections.

Once the information server has collected current data from all sensors, these are displayed in Raspberry terminal, so it is easy to visually verify that both the server and the sensors are working correctly, thus there is communication between them without interruptions or loss of information. Table 1 illustrates an example of the detected values.

Table 1. Example of sensor values in the CMD terminal.

Time delay	Environment temperature	Humidity in the environment	Soil moisture	Brightness
2 seg	33 °C	80%	30%	34%
4 seg	33 °C	79%	32%	35%
6 seg	33 °C	78%	31%	33%
8 seg	34 °C	79%	28%	35%
10 seg	34 °C	80%	29%	36%
12 seg	34 °C	79%	30%	37%

The information server sends the current data to the IoT server, which has the necessary configurations to make the connection through the internet with the database in real time.

In this project, the design and development of a controller for an automated irrigation system using fuzzy logic is carried out. The developed controller uses sensors for soil moisture, humidity in the environment, brightness and temperature in the environment to manage the activation of an irrigation pump; the moisture in the soil is monitored every 10 min to determine if the humidity necessary to read the other sensors is met and if each of the necessary factors is met, the irrigation system is activated.

A conventional solenoid valve is used to supply the water, since the irrigation system works only in two states: on and off. The solenoid valve is connected to a hose that works in conjunction with sprinklers and it is activated by the fuzzy controller when complying with the rules presented in Table 2. These rules were defined based on interviews with experts in the care of habanero pepper when presented with different scenarios with respect to the input variables. Soil moisture sensors are the ones that mainly determine if the activation of the system is necessary, because when the soil is completely humid, irrigation is not carried out regardless of the values of the other sensors.

Table 2. Rules to operate the irrigation system.

Soil moisture	Environment temperature	Humidity in the environment	Brightness	Irrigation pump state
High	–	–	–	Off
Medium	Low	High	–	Off
Medium	Low	Medium	Not low	Off
Medium	Low	Medium	Low	On
Medium	Low	Low	Not low	Off
Medium	Low	Low	Low	On
Medium	Medium	–	Not low	Off
Medium	Medium	–	Low	On
Medium	High	–	Not low	Off
Medium	High	–	Low	On
Low	Low	High	–	On
Low	Low	Medium	–	On
Low	Low	Low	Not high	On
Low	Low	Low	High	Off
Low	Medium	–	Not high	On
Low	Medium	–	High	Off
Low	High	–	Not high	On
Low	High	–	High	Off

2.5   Tests of the IoT Server

The IoT server (located in the Raspberry) waits for a request to obtain real time information from the database (located in the cloud), which in turn receives another similar request from the client of the mobile application module (located on the Smartphone) to obtain the latest information from the sensor module (located near the crop plants), represented as a block diagram in Fig. 1.

The IoT server has a established project address in the database, and the information destination nodes connected to it in order to send each value to the corresponding node. This ensures that the sensed data reaches the correct destination. Once the IoT server accepts a request, the data server makes a request for information to the sensors and then passes it to the IoT server to send it to the database in real time with an established format. The mobile application for its part makes a request to the database in real time to obtain the current information in the established nodes and then immediately displays it in the user interface for viewing (see Fig. 5).

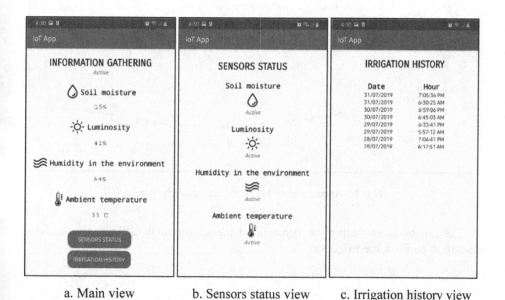

a. Main view   b. Sensors status view   c. Irrigation history view

Fig. 5. Views of the mobile application.

The mobile application allows representing the values obtained from each of the sensors through graphs due to the integration of a Microsoft Office Excel® plugin, which facilitates the analysis and understanding of the behavior of the data. Two graphs are shown in Figs. 6 and 7, corresponding to average values obtained from the luminescence and humidity sensors in the soil.

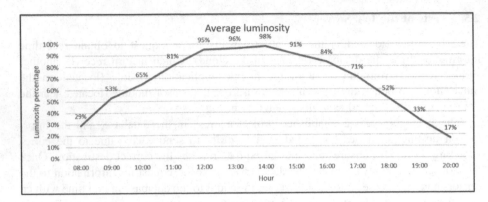

Fig. 6. Average luminosity graph.

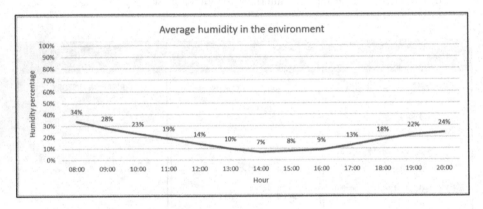

Fig. 7. Average humidity in the environment graph.

The graphs allow seeing the behavior of the sensors and facilitate the decision making to perform the irrigation.

3 Conclusions

There are already autonomous and automated irrigation systems in the market, but in most cases their costs are too high for the common farmer, making them inaccessible. This is why the proposed system considerably reduces the cost to make it available to rural people, who in most cases lack economic resources. Its operation is as simple as knowing the basics to manage applications and a smartphone or tablet with internet access. Furthermore, if we consider that the situation of water scarcity will worsen this kind of projects for the agricultural sector may contribute to solve this global problem and keep the vital liquid in optimal usage.

The architecture that makes up this project allows monitoring of parameters in the irrigation system, using a data server and an IoT server implemented in an integrated system based on a distribution of Linux for Raspberry known as Raspbian. The data server receives the information from the sensors every 2 s to avoid data overlapping and information loss. Therefore, the proposed architecture can perform real-time monitoring at low cost on the irrigation system. The IoT server sends the information of the sensors to a database in real time, which in turn provides the updated information to a mobile application implemented on a smartphone or tablet.

Implementing fuzzy logic in a controller for an irrigation system implies a great impact and benefit for agriculture and people who are engaged in such activity, due to the automation of tasks that allow people to reduce time and processes, based on weather factors, using water in an efficient way avoiding waste and providing the plants with sufficient quantity for optimum growth.

On a first stage, the irrigation system was developed and tested at laboratory level; it will subsequently be installed in a greenhouse to grow habanero pepper plants. In the future, more sections would be implemented within the mobile application, to have a greater amount of information for the irrigation system, with the advantage to be able to monitor real time data for better crops administration. It is also intended to integrate a digital image processing system with a neural network, for the prediction of crop pests and registration of plant growth, thus increasing the benefits of the intelligent irrigation system.

References

1. Comisión Nacional del Agua: Estadísticas del Agua en México, pp. 45–50 (2018)
2. Fereres, E., García-Vila, M.: Irrigation management for efficient crop production. In: Savin, R., Slafer, G. (eds.) Crop Science. ESSTS, pp. 345–360. Springer, New York (2019). https://doi.org/10.1007/978-1-4939-8621-7_162. https://link.springer.com/referenceworkentry/10.1007%2F978-1-4939-2493-6_162-3
3. IICA: Innovation and Water Management for Sustainable Development in Agriculture, pp. 20–29 (2015). http://repositorio.iica.int/bitstream/11324/3035/2/BVE17068948i.pdf
4. Organización de las Naciones Unidas para la Alimentación y la Agricultura: El estado mundial de la agricultura y la alimentación. Roma (2018)
5. Pastor, E.J.: Introducción al Internet de las Cosas, pp. 80–120 (2015)
6. Clúster ICT-Audiovisual de Madrid: Internet de las cosas: Objetos interconectados y dispositivos inteligentes, pp. 68–75 (2016). https://actualidad.madridnetwork.org/imgArticulos/Documentos/635294387380363206.pdf
7. Negrete, J.: Internet of things in Mexican agriculture; a technology to increase agricultural productivity and reduce rural poverty, pp. 46–47 (2018)
8. Alper Akkas, M.: An IoT-based greenhouse monitoring system with Micaz motes, pp. 604–608 (2017). https://www.sciencedirect.com/science/article/pii/S187705091731709X
9. World Water Vision Report: Visión Mundial del Agua, México (2017)
10. Karim, F., Karim, F.: Monitoring system using web of things in precision agriculture. In: The 12th International Conference on Future Networks and Communications (2017). https://reader.elsevier.com/reader/sd/pii/S1877050917312590

11. Shekhar, Y., Dagur, E., Mishra, S., Tom, R.J., Veeramanikandan, M., Sankaranarayanan, S.: Intelligent IoT based automated irrigation system. Int. J. Appl. Eng. Res. **12**(18), 7306–7320 (2017)
12. OBSoil-01: Octopus Soil Moisture Sensor Brick, p. 5 (2016)
13. D-Robotics: DHT11 Humidity & Temperature Sensor, Mouser Electronics. https://www.mouser.com/ds/2/758/DHT11-Technical-DataSheet-Translated-Version-1143054.pdf. Accessed 27 May 2019
14. Raspberry Pi Foundation: Raspberry Pi 3 Model B, Raspberry Pi Website, p. 137 (2016)
15. Perez, A., et al.: Una Metodología Para El Desarrollo De Hardware Y Software Embebidos En Sistemas Críticos De Seguridad. Sist. Cibernética e Informática **3**(2), 70–75 (2014)

Architecture Proposal for Low-Cost Hydroponic IoT Based Systems

Gutiérrez León Evelyn[1(✉)], Jorge Erik Montiel[1],
Carreto Arellano Chadwick[2], and Felipe Rolando Menchaca García[1]

[1] Escuela Superior de Ingeniería Mecánica y Eléctrica unidad Zacatenco,
Instituto Politécnico Nacional, Mexico City, Mexico
evelyngleon@hotmail.com, Jerikmontiel.isc@gmail.com,
fmenchac@gmail.com
[2] Escuela Superior de Cómputo, Instituto Politécnico Nacional,
Mexico City, Mexico
ccarretoa@ipn.mx

Abstract. This article proposes the design of an intelligent management system based on Internet of Things (IoT) for hydroponic crops, to bring farmers and marginalized sectors closer to the use of new technologies, increasing precision in agriculture according to the needs of the crop in "real time." On this work, we propose the development of prototypes based on the architecture and network topologies for IoT devices, as well as the technologies available in the market. All this, to acquire information about the environment of the crop and to help the user on the decision making. The premise of the project is to develop a modular solution, scalable, low cost, easy installation, management, and operation, to potentiate the technological update of the systems of crops already installed or projects to start.

Keywords: Internet of Things · Precision agriculture · Hydroponics systems · Smart farming

1 Introduction

Agriculture is the third economic activity in the country, about 22 million hectares are dedicated to the agriculture, of which, 75.67% implement some level of mechanization, and 64.92% of this is seasonal crop [1].

Of the agronomic population, approximately 35% of the farmers are in the micro, or small business sector with ties in the domestic market and 50% produce for self-consumption. Despite the existence of diverse imported solutions for the agro-food field, these are focused on intensive producers of the industrial scale. They require high initial investment and qualified personnel in the technology for its installation, operation, and maintenance. For this reason, its implementation has not been generalized for producers in the micro and small enterprise sectors as well as self-consumption orchards, who are more vulnerable to climate variability and change [2], generating a technological and economic gap between small farmers versus intensive producers.

© Springer Nature Switzerland AG 2019
M. F. Mata-Rivera et al. (Eds.): WITCOM 2019, CCIS 1053, pp. 305–322, 2019.
https://doi.org/10.1007/978-3-030-33229-7_26

Also, with the growing urban expansion, areas dedicated to agriculture have been reduced or displaced to forests and jungles, irremediably damaging the ecosystem by decreasing the participation of the population in agriculture.

According to this, the design of low-cost solutions based on alternative systems that potentiate the results of the agricultural campaign in small spaces, such as hydroponics, along with precision agriculture and the Internet of Things (IoT), allow the modernization of agriculture in the mentioned sectors without huge investments, obtaining better quality products, this with the aim of generating economic growth in the region.

1.1 Hydroponics Systems Characteristics

Hydroponics is the technique of production or cultivation without soil, in which water and nutrients are supplied to the plants through a complete nutritious solution (NS), providing the necessary conditions for its proper development [3].

Hydroponic systems are characterized by how the nutrient solution for the crop, the type of module, and the arrangement of the elements, as well as the size, space, and environmental conditions, are available. Therefore, a hydroponic system can vary from one farmer to another, or even within the same set of crops. Therefore, the design of the solution is focused on a series of devices to be placed in the hydroponic modules, regardless of their position, size or location, or if they are commercial or home modules.

1.2 Precision Agriculture

The Precision Agriculture (PA) also known as "Smart Farming" in the words of Patokar and Gohokar is "the technique of applying the appropriate amount of input (water, pesticides and fertilizers, among others) at the right time and place to improve production and increase crop yield" [4]. Its central premise is to obtain as much information as possible from the environment and the crop (in order to predict the changes and needs in the different stages of growth) to provide the stimuli and nutrients necessary for the proper development of the plant. where the use of IoT has been widely implemented [5]. The critical parameters of the hydroponics crops are the light intensity, ambient temperature and humidity, and the temperature of the NS [6, 7] cause affect the NS absorption directly. For the irrigation system, we are focused on the irrigation period and duration.

1.3 Internet of Things in the Agriculture

The use of networks of objects equipped with sensors (also called wireless sensor networks or WSN) has expanded in the agricultural field, due to the efficiency it has shown in obtaining information from it. Therefore, its study and implementation have increased in solutions based on the IoT communication paradigm [8].

The IEEE-SA Working Group has a project to develop an IoT standard: IEEE P2413. On the IEEE P2413 define an IoT architecture framework for the architectural needs of different IoT scenarios (see Fig. 1) [9].

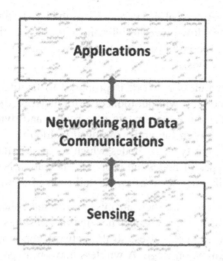

Fig. 1. Three-layer architecture for IoT proposed by the IEEE Working Group P2413.

The IoT solutions have many challenges to be facing [10–12]: Scalability, interoperability, mobility and adaptable solutions in order to provide evolved services. The edge computing and Fog architectures helps to stablish the IoT architectural definition and support its applications [13, 14] trough the implementation of different security mechanism stablished for Internet protocols and smart objects standards.

The first stage for the IoT solutions is about obtain all the behavior information of the study case, then analyze all the data collected in order to propose the algorithms for the decision making and finally the final solution needs to be tested and corrected to improve the results of the solution trough some advance control algorithms.

This article describes an architectural proposal for the development of a hydroponic management system using IoT technologies. In the following section, the analysis and design of the system are addressed, focusing on the development of two different networks, the intra-greenhouse network and the extra-greenhouse network which, in conjunction with sensors and actuators, monitors and control the greenhouse operation variables.

The third section shows the development of communication networks as well as the development of specific frames within the network, which allow optimizing the implemented communication. Subsequently, the implementation and the obtained results of the development of the system are briefly explained, and finally, we conclude with possible future improvements of the system.

2   Design

Between crop campaigns, the distribution and extension of crops is variable, for this reason, it's important design a network topology of the solution with the follow characteristics: modular in order to cover the needs of crop management at different scales; flexible and dynamic to allow variations in the geographical arrangement and configuration of the nodes; low power to offer the autonomy of the nodes; and tolerant to failures to ensure the operation of the network. According to this, the solution was divided into two action zones:

Intra-Greenhouse. A wireless network is proposed to facilitate the installation and communication of the modules without tools or extra material, the network is based on a mesh topology to meet the requirements of a robust and dynamic communication with enough coverage between the nodes arranged inside the greenhouse. Within this network can define different types of nodes which focus on different roles within the greenhouse, at least 3 types of nodes are proposed: Irrigation Node, Sensor Node and Master Node. In the following sections will detail each of them.

Extra-Greenhouse. It's required the transmission of data collected inside the greenhouse to the server for further processing. The solution considers the communication of the server to one or more greenhouses, so the network topology is defined as a star topology in this communication stage. A wireless network is proposed to facilitate the installation and communication of the modules without tools or extra material, the use of a mesh topology could satisfy the requirements of a robust and dynamic communication with enough coverage among the nodes arranged inside the greenhouse.

Subsequently, the mobile terminal requires obtaining the data stored on the server. To do so, it is necessary to consider the following cases:

Local network connection: The server will serve as a wireless access point to download the information collected in the mobile terminal.

Anywhere connection through the Internet: To achieve this, it is necessary to contract a service in the cloud for the exchange of data from the server to the mobile terminal through the Internet and the necessary infrastructure exists.

Finally, we can define a hybrid network architecture integrated by one or more "intra-greenhouse" networks which operate with a general "extra-greenhouse" network. These networks can be of different protocols if there is a node that works as middleware between both networks.

2.1 Network Architecture Model

The minimum case of the proposed architecture is observed when only one greenhouse is available (as in subsistence gardens, urban or backyard gardens), that is, where the coverage area is smaller. The Fig. 2 shows the use of sensor nodes with the function of capturing information about the crop environment; an irrigation node, which will collect information and control the status of the irrigation system, and a master node in charge of coordinating the network and concentrating the information provided by other nodes, repackaging the data and communicating them to the server through the Extra-network. Greenhouse. Subsequently, the server processes and stores the information to be displayed to the user through a graphical application interface for mobile devices.

This architecture can be replicated again based on the number of greenhouses that you want to manage within a location. This second case can be seen in the Fig. 3,

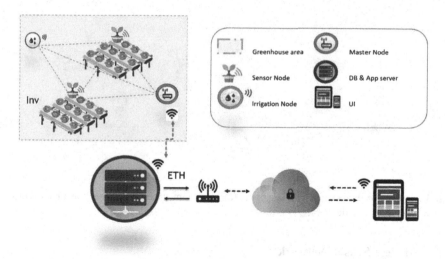

Fig. 2. The general architecture of the proposed network for the intelligent management system for hydroponic crops, minimum case.

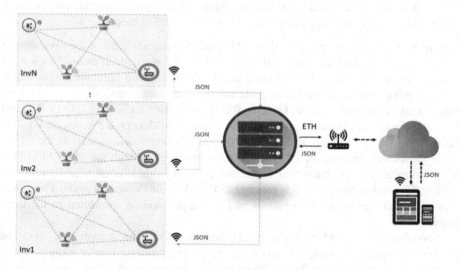

Fig. 3. Extra-greenhouse network diagram for multiple greenhouses

where we have multiple greenhouses, each one with its Intra-Greenhouse network connected to the same Extra-Greenhouse network and with it to the same server.

This modularity can be applied in the same way at the greenhouse level, so that we can have multiple greenhouses with different needs, in this case, it's the Intra-Greenhouse network that varies in the number of nodes, adjusting to the characteristics of each place, this can be visualized in the Fig. 4.

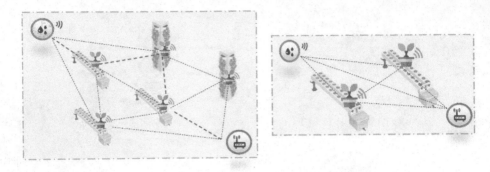

Fig. 4. Intra-Greenhouse network diagram: (a) minimum case, (b) expansion of the network after adding sensor nodes.

2.2 Wireless Sensor Network

Inside each greenhouse, three types of nodes are deployed that which works with specific tasks of capturing the information and activation of actuators depending on their role. The design of the nodes is made according to the coverage area, low cost, easy installation, spatial and connection independence, and compatibility between components. The block diagram of each sensor is specified below.

Sensor Node. These nodes are designed to obtain the current state of the environment in the hydroponic module. The block design of the sensor node is defined in 4 main blocks: Perception, Feeding, Processing and Control, and the communication block. The unit of perception in the sensor node has the necessary transducers to capture the information of the environment: Lighting (lx), Temperature (°C), Humidity (%RH) and Temperature of the nutrient solution (°C). These transducers are connected to the microcontroller unit through the I2C, UART and SPI interfaces, as well as the GPIO, while the wireless transceiver nRF24L01+ communicates through the inter - SPI of the microcontroller. By the characteristics of the previously mentioned requirements, the AtMega328p microcontroller was selected as the MCU of the sensor node. The power supply is made up by a Li-Po battery and a charger module connected to the main power.

Sampling time of 15 min was established to collect the information from the environment. Once the sample is taken, the data is pre-processed and packaged by the MCU to form the defined frame. Then the transmitter mode of the transceiver is enabled, of and the MCU sends the frame the to the master node directly or by the nearest node through the forwarding of packets. The transceiver changes to receiver mode and after a listening period is set to wait until it is activated again in the next reading of the environment (see the Fig. 5).

Irrigation Node. This type of node is responsible for obtaining information on the status of the nutrient solution through the pH and Temperature sensors. In besides to control the actuation and deactivation of the actuators involved in the irrigation action, consequently, the PCB shares the power lines with the power supply, it uses a standard

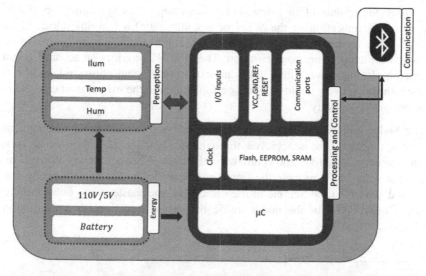

Fig. 5. Block diagram of the sensor node.

domestic power line (110V in México) to energize said actuators and control them through the change of state of optocoupled relays. The use of batteries for the irrigation node is added, to provide redundancy in power for the perception phase in case of disconnection in the electric supply. The processing unit is carried out (as with the sensor and master node) with the AtMega328p microcontroller and the wireless transceiver as the nRF24L01+ (see the Fig. 6).

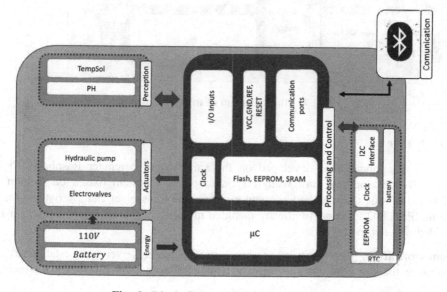

Fig. 6. Block diagram of the irrigation node.

To provide certainty in the irrigation task avoiding errors by duplication or desync (in case of disconnection of the WSN or a voltage dip) a real-time clock block is provided. This module is based on the DS3231 IC, which has an internal crystal oscillator with temperature compensation. The DS3231 provides an accurate count of time despite losing power since it has an extra battery that allows retains the time counting, this effectively avoids failures or duplication in the irrigation in case the node is not energized correctly.

Master Node. Finally, the master node is responsible for coordinating communication between the nodes; this is achieved through the dynamic allocation of the nodes, keeping the network active, and centralizing the data. When a frame is received in the master node, the MCU process the frame and shapes it to the corresponding format before and send it to the Server. In the same way, the master node obtains the configuration information of the nodes inside the greenhouse through consumption of REST services (see Fig. 7).

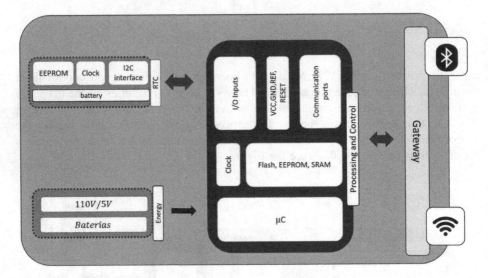

Fig. 7. Block diagram of the master node.

2.3   Server

The server application is developed on the single-board computer Raspberry Pi 3 model B+ development card with Raspbian operating system (based on Debian - GNU/Linux) due to its processor, memory and radio transceiver characteristics based on the IEEE 802.11 standard already included in the card. The design of the server is divided into two parts:

Communication. Two forms of communication with the server were established to guarantee the link, through the local area network using the Ethernet port, taking advantage of the user's infrastructure and through wireless communication provided by the server when is configured as an access point (WAP) (see Fig. 8).

Fig. 8. Communication lines of the master nodes and the mobile application with the server.

Functionality. For the development of the web server, we use Django which is a high-level application programming environment based on Python, Django allows us to create web servers in a friendly way and create the REST services necessary for the solution. The web application is constituted by Models, Uniform Resource Locators (URLs), and Views. The information is stored and managed by the database

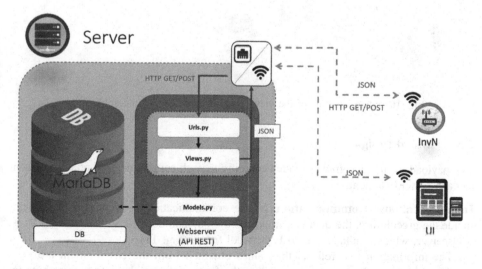

Fig. 9. Block diagram of server communication.

management system MariaDB, which offers the services of storage and control of the tables. The relational model is selected due to the need to link the data of different tables to establish the information of the crops, their belonging, and configuration (see Fig. 9).

2.4   Graphical User Interface

For the development of the graphics interface, we decided to use the framework for mobiles applications Xamarin.Forms through Microsoft Visual Studio IDE, which provides a programming environment in C# language to make applications using native resources, but with the option of sharing the code between the various mobile platforms (Android, iOS and Windows Phone).

The Fig. 10 shows the state machine diagram of the User Interface that provides the necessary views to add, configure, and eliminate the data of monitored crops, their configurations, and user and application information.

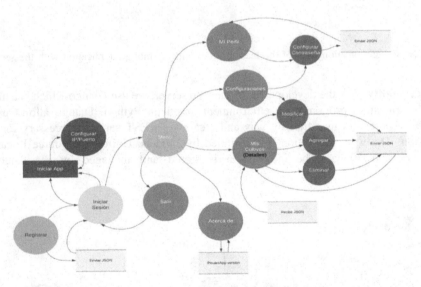

Fig. 10. State machine of the views (activities) of the mobile application.

2.5   Payload Design

The payload format design was made according to each communication phase between to each system element.

Intra-Greenhouse Communication. In the communication between the equipment inside the greenhouse, the data is sent within the payload defined by the NRF24L01 + transceiver, which emulates the BLE protocol frame (Fig. 11).

The information that reflects the values obtained from the environment are pre-processed in the node prior to constructing the frame defining the data type as byte to

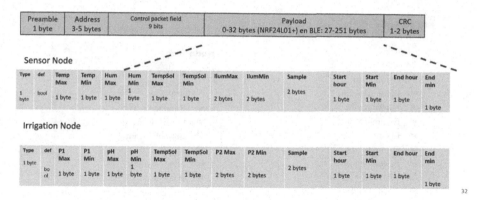

Fig. 11. Payload of the configuration message for irrigation node and sensor.

Table 1. Parameters included within the payload field of the nRF24L01+ frame.

Node type	Parameter	VMIN	VMAX	Precision	Steps	Data size
Sensor	Temp	2 °C	35 °C	0.2 °C	166	1 byte
	Hum	50%	85%	0.25%	141	1 byte
	Ilum	0	60 Klx	10 lx	6001	2 bytes
Irrigation	TempSol	10 °C	30 °C	0.1 °C	201	1 byte
	pH	5	7.5	0.1	26	1 byte

make the memory space per parameter more efficient, the Table 1 shows data size of the parameters monitored for hydroponic crops: Temperature (Temp), Humidity (Hum), Light intensity (Ilum), temperature of the Nutrient solution (TempSol) and pH level (Table 1).

For the communication of the message configuration by the master node to the sensor and irrigation nodes, it is necessary to add to the payload (Fig. 11) the maximum and minimum values of the parameters, their status (if enabled), the period in which the sensing sample will be taken. Also, the data about start and end time in which the configuration is valid, and in the case of the irrigation node, information referring to the irrigation activity (irrigation periods and duration), so 21 bytes of data was defined for data configuration message to be transmitted in this stage of design (see Fig. 12).

3 Development

This section briefly explains how the communication between the intra-greenhouse network and the extra-greenhouse network is developed, as well as the structure of the JSON (JavaScript Object Notation) messages that are used for the communication of the master node with the server.

Fig. 12. Data structure of the JSONs sent from the master node to the server

3.1   Extra-Greenhouse Communication

The data coming from the sensor and irrigation nodes are extracted from the BLE frame format by the master node and structured in a form for consumption of REST services of the Server. About the Nodes configuration message, the master node requests the data to the server and deserialize it to format in BLE frame structure to be sent to the sensor and irrigation nodes.

3.2   User Interface – Server Communication

After performing the actions defined in the Server Views and the information is stored in the database, it is required to request the data to the server to be showed in the user interface on the mobile device. This data is sent in JSON format through the consumption of the REST services. The Fig. 12 shows the data structure of the information sent from the nodes to the server.

3.3   BLE Mesh Network

To implement the BLE mesh network, the nodes are configured in the following roles: master node coordinates the routing configuration of the network allowing it to keep it enabled, including define the identifiers of the irrigation nodes and sensors and managing the retransmission of the frames among them. The Figs. 14 and 15 show the flow diagram of the intra-greenhouse BLE mesh network established.

After initializing the nRF24L01+ transceiver and the sensors installed in the nodes, the default range values are read from the internal MCU EEPROM; those values act as extreme values for the monitoring of the environment (Temperature, Humidity, Illumination, pH, Temperature of the nutrient solution). Likewise, the identification information of the node (node type and serial number) and the configuration of the control parameters of the system (sampling periods, times in which the configuration is valid and node status) are read.

The configuration and management of the mesh network begin as the master node dynamically assigns an identifier to the slave nodes (sensor node and irrigation node), promoting the dynamic registration (commissioning) of them and the joining and leaving of nodes to the network (see Fig. 13), thus allowing relocation of the nodes at any time. The connection between nodes is updated periodically to maintain the link between the nodes.

Finally, the operation of the slave nodes complies with the following steps: (see Fig. 14).

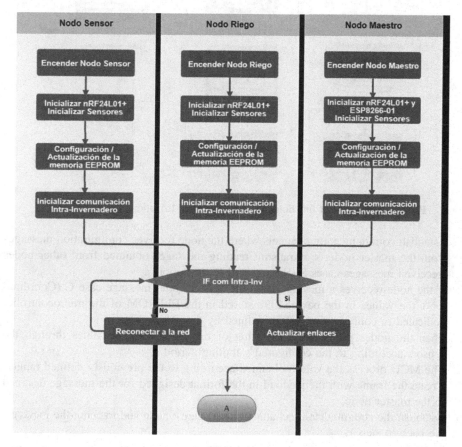

Fig. 13. Flowchart of the initialization of the nodes for the creation of the BLE network.

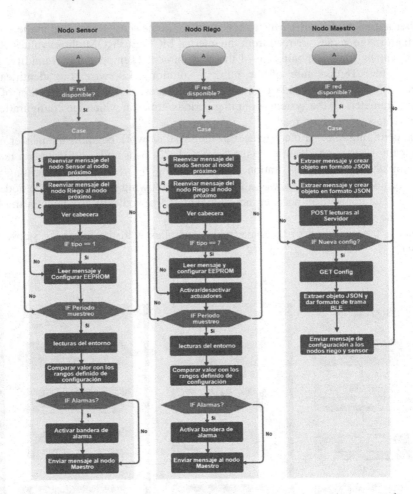

Fig. 14. Flowchart of functionality of the Sensors, Irrigation and master nodes

1. Establish communication channels where the node receives configuration messages from the master node or retransmit reading messages obtained from other nodes (received messages cases S (Sensor) and R (Irrigation)).
2. If the node receives a message from the master node (message case C (Coordinator)), the values in the payload are stored in the EEPROM of the microcontroller dedicated to configuration values defined by the user.
3. Then the nodes perform the sampling of the environmental values through the sensors according to the configured sampling period.
4. The MCU process the values obtained according to the previously defined ranges.
5. Create the frame with the payload in the format designed for the message destined to the master node.
6. Establish the communication channel to the nearest node and transmit the message.
7. Go back to step 1.

4 Implementation and Results

The development and implementation of the system were carried out between the facilities of the ESIME Zacatenco and a micro greenhouse in the town of Santa Isabel Tola, the network of nodes was developed with the proposed sensors, a master node, a server, and a prototype of the mobile application were developed (Fig. 15).

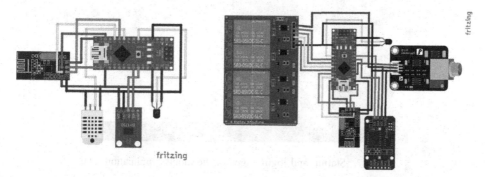

Fig. 15. Basic electronic diagram of Sensor Node and Irrigation Node

The configuration of the NRF24L01+ transceiver and behavior of the nodes to deploy the BLE mesh network within the greenhouse was defined, in the Fig. 16 shows the functionality of the nodes, in which the acquisition of the physical environmental data is shown.

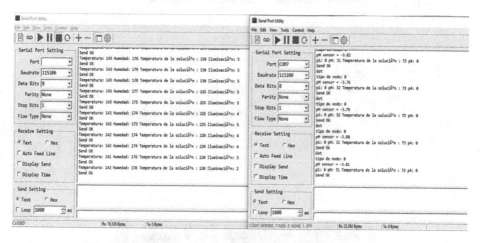

Fig. 16. Information capture of the sensor and irrigation nodes

The user utilizes the mobile application to enter the system to monitoring and configure the state of crop actuators in a friendly way (Fig. 17).

Fig. 17. Startup and login pages of the mobile application.

Then select a crop to visualize, and the application displays the information of the crop, its location, its assigned greenhouse, and the last recorded reading of the sensors in the location (see Fig. 18).

Fig. 18. List of registered crops and display of the details of a crop

5 Conclusions and Next Steps

This system is developed focusing on low-cost technologies that allow its implementation by independent farmers, self-consumption and micro and small businesses, which in most cases cannot acquire commercial systems due to its high cost. However, we have observed that the flexibility and modularity of the system allows it to be installed in many more places, for example, in urban and roof gardens or in indoor hydroponic systems, which can have a significant impact on the reduction of land used for traditional culture.

The above allows us to conclude that with minimal modifications this architecture could be implemented in massive hydroponic farms, improving the monitoring systems of these and with it the quality of the production. Finally, these types of modular IoT architectures can revolutionize the industry, lowering the cost of infrastructure and, soon, increasing the quality of life of the users.

The first stage of design was completed for the Intelligent system management for hydroponic crops, the intends of the solution pretend to be an easy tool for farmers and urban agricultures to improve their crops through the IoT technologies without high investments.

Currently, we are working on the implementation in a real hydroponic greenhouse to verify the correct functioning of the system. Based on the results of this implementation, the aim is to develop a machine-learning based algorithm that allows adjusting the monitoring ranges automatically, to optimize crop quality and yield.

It is also proposed to implement an LTE-M modem that allows monitoring remotely, as well as the sending of alerts by SMS, as an additional way of informing the user of possible ongoing problems.

Finally, we are working on a second version of the system focused on medium-scale crops, based on WSN, with greater coverage and flexibility, including a backup server in the cloud, so that this new system can be managed anywhere with an Internet connection.

References

1. Servicio de Información Agroalimentaria y Pesquera (SIAP). Uso de tecnología y servicios en el campo Cuadros tabulares (2016)
2. World Bank, CIAT, CATIE. Climate-smart agriculture in Mexico. CSA country profiles for Latin America Series. World Bank Gr (2014)
3. Oasis, S.: Manual de hidroponia, p. 32 (2002)
4. Patokar, A., Gohokar, V.: Precision agriculture system design using wireless sensor network, pp. 169–177 (2017). https://doi.org/10.1007/978-981-10-5508-9_16
5. Verdouw, C.: Internet of Things in agriculture. CAB Rev. Perspect. Agric. Vet. Sci. Nutr. Nat. Resour. 11 (2016). https://doi.org/10.1079/pavsnnr201611035
6. Azcón-Bieto, J., Talón, M.: Fundamentos de fisiología vegetal (2003)
7. Araceli, M.: Manual de hidroponia, Primera Ed. Instituto de Biología, Distrito Federal (2014)

8. Kiani, F., Seyyedabbasi, A.: Wireless sensor network and internet of things in precision agriculture. Int. J. Adv. Comput. Sci. Appl. **9**, 99–103 (2018). https://doi.org/10.14569/ijacsa.2018.090614

9. Minerva, R., Biru, A., Rotondi, D.: Towards a definition of the Internet of Things (IoT). IEEE Internet Things **86** (2015). https://doi.org/10.5120/19787-1571

10. Lin, J., Yu, W., Zhang, N., Yang, X., Zhang, H., Zhao, W.: A survey on Internet of Things: architecture. Enabling Technol. Secur. Priv. Appl. **4**, 1125–1142 (2017)

11. Chiang, M., Zhang, T.: Fog and IoT: an overview of research opportunities. IEEE Internet Things J. **3**, 854–864 (2016). https://doi.org/10.1109/JIOT.2016.2584538

12. Yang, Y., Wu, L., Yin, G., Li, L., Zhao, H.: A survey on security and privacy issues in Internet-of-Things. IEEE Internet of Things J. **4**, 1250–1258 (2017)

13. Shi, W., Cao, J., Member, S., Zhang, Q., Member, S.: Edge computing: vision and challenges. IEEE Internet Things J. **3**, 637–646 (2016). https://doi.org/10.1109/JIOT.2016.2579198

14. Razzaque, M.A., Milojevic-Jevric, M., Palade, A., Cla, S.: Middleware for internet of things: a survey. IEEE Internet Things J. **3**, 70–95 (2016). https://doi.org/10.1109/JIOT.2015.2498900

Informatics Security

Learning and Automatization of Searching in Digital Media, Based on Concurrency, Weighing and Decay

David Cordero Vidal$^{(\boxtimes)}$ and Cristian Barria Huidobro$^{(\boxtimes)}$

Vicerrectoría de Investigación, Centro de investigación en ciberseguridad CICS,
Universidad Mayor, Santiago, Chile
{david.cordero, cristian.barria}@mayor.cl

Abstract. The search for information of real interest for a particular topic has always been a challenge, especially when the source of this information is on the Internet, where there are many digital media, platforms, databases and from which you can explore data. Large companies such as Google or Yahoo help us find these sources of information through their search algorithms, but they are not very effective when filtering a particular information, so it is necessary to formulate a model that responds to this need, in the present The document proposes a model based on 3 components, using information filtering tools, word valorization techniques based on their concurrences, weights, anti-words and a proposal to apply a word decay log within the information, in order to maintain a "score" and avoid false weights (triggered weights) of the information.

Keywords: Search · Python · Feed · System · Automatization · Notification · Filtered out

1 Introduction

Information seeking through the network is a challenge nowadays. Internet has transformed in one of the main basic information sources for many systems, platforms and news media. Although there are tools which make easier to have access to information sources (Google, Yahoo, etc), these do not provide a precise solution when trying to find information of interest on specific topics. Some studies have researched on the way of filtering significant information employing neural networks, machine learning [1], IA [2], which solve, at a certain level, this issue.

The present investigation proposes a research method of digital information based on three components (obtainment, classification and acceptance). The objective is to filter interesting information for a person or organization, by determining the average time a key word appears within a piece of information based on a given dictionary. Later, to generate a proposal of key words which were not considered in order to define a filter drawn from each key word's weighted value within an information set.

© Springer Nature Switzerland AG 2019
M. F. Mata-Rivera et al. (Eds.): WITCOM 2019, CCIS 1053, pp. 325–334, 2019.
https://doi.org/10.1007/978-3-030-33229-7_27

2 Proposed Method for Information Searching

The investigation is based on a proposal of information searching and filtering drawn from three components: to know (1) information obtainment, (2) information classification, and (3) information acceptance. Each one needs tools and functionalities which are also determined by some variables.

2.1 Obtainment Information Component

This first component determines the digital informative media from which the information will be collected, by means of employing an algorithm drawn from the Universal Feed Parser library [3]. This is a Python module that works to download and analyze syndicated feeds; it supports RSS 0.90, Netscape RSS 0.91, Userland RSS 0.91, RSS 0.92, RSS 0.93, RSS 0.94, RSS 1.0, RSS 2.0, Atom 0.3, Atom 1.0, and CDF feeds. This library will allows us to base this investigation on a single algorithm, as the data delivery is structural and unchangeable, independently of the information source (shown on Fig. 1).

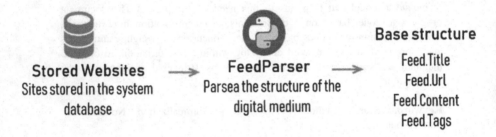

Stored Websites → **FeedParser** → **Base structure**

Stored Websites	FeedParser	Base structure
Sites stored in the system database	Parsea the structure of the digital medium	Feed.Title Feed.Url Feed.Content Feed.Tags

Fig. 1. FeedParser functionality.

In this way, it is possible to determine the variables that define the obtainment process. These are found on all digital media which fulfils the condition of delivering information in the Feed RSS format (Really Simple Syndication) [4].

- Obtainment Variables: RSS Feed Structure: From this RSS structure taken from the FeedParser library, we will base the information searching on collecting the data now shown. These will change their content as the information source feeds update, but the structure always remains unchangeable.
    - feed.tittle
    - feed.url
    - feed.content
    - feed.tags
- Information Digital Media: The Information Digital Media (news websites, blogs, etc) will deliver the information requested by the model. These could be classified by topics, and the collecting condition will be given by the information delivery format (Feed RSS).

- Feed Update Time: The different information digital media update their feeds when modifying the information. For example, every time a digital newspaper publishes a news, the feed changes and generates new information captured by the model.
- Collecting Cycle Time: This refers to the time the model will last to collect all the digital information media before starting again.
- Total Collecting Time: The total time employed to collect the information (Table 1).

Table 1. Variables of the information obtainment.

Variable	Measure unit
Feed	Text (it changes according to the information digital media) tittle, tags and information body
Information digital media	Number of websites registered
Collecting cycle time	Minutes
Total collecting time	Days
Feeds update time	Minutes

2.2 Classification Information Component

Once the information has been provided by the obtaining component, it is necessary to classify and filter by key words; this determines two filters: the first is by tittle and tags, the second is by the information body reading. From this, the following variables are determined.

Classification Variables, words: These are found within the tittle, tags and information body. They have a semantic meaning, and it is possible to determine their topic of discussion through their study.

Stopword: The term Stopword [5] refers to words that lack meaning, also known as empty words. Usually they refer to articles, pronouns, conjunctions, prepositions, among others. Likewise, to eliminate these from titles, tags and information body optimizes the algorithm route when looking for key words.

Key Words: These correspond to words related to the topic of interest. Google, one of the leading sources of information searching on Internet, puts at people's disposal tools that help them on their searches. If we focus on these searching tools, the first that comes to our minds is the browser [6], which its algorithm is secret (private source code). Nonetheless, one of its revealed characteristics is the key word searching, which is determined by the frequency or location these have within a website. Key words will be defined by means of the topic of interest itself or by the person's own judgement [7].

It is important not to define words that are considered to be "Stopwords", as these will not be considering when filtering the information. This is because these words are considered meaningless by itself.

Concurrency: The concurrent value will be given by the time a key word shows on the information (Table 2).

Table 2. Variables from the information-collecting component.

Variable	Measure unit
Words	Number of words
Key words	Number of key words
Stopword	Number of Stopwords
Concurrency	Number of times

Classification Tools: To classify the information is necessary to employ tools that make easier the component's process. In this investigation, the following will be employed.

Dictionaries: Repository of related words. Each dictionary contains its own key words [8]. The weighted value (the importance of a word within a dictionary) of each word will be given by the topic of interest, as the same word can have another relevance within other context.

For example, the word "boy" could appear in many dictionaries or categories. If this is found on a dictionary of children's games, its weighted value will be higher than if it is found on one of table games. In this way, the model works finding information by means of organized word groups that have a closeness of meaning with the topic of interest.

Natural Language Toolkit (NLTK): The use of the library NLTK [9] that incorporates a support for thousands of lexical corpuses and trained modules, such as wordnet. Also, it includes tools to process, derive, label and conduct semantic analyses, which clean the text from Stopwords and vectorize only those that give meaning to the information. This finally optimizes the vector's final route over which the model is based.

2.3   Acceptance Information Component

Once the information has been classified, the model has two acceptance criteria. The first is the key words' weighing in the information body, which refers to the average of the weighted sum drawn from the filtered information plus the expert's judgment. The second is the concurrency of key words about the given information. For this, the acceptance procedure is conditioned to the following variables.

Acceptance Criteria Based on Concurrency: To define the acceptance criteria is necessary to define the quantity of key words that will be shown on the title, tags and information body. From this, a dictionary will be prepared based on the topic of interest and the words related to it. Under this condition, the information will be filtered, and for the purpose of this study, two filtering conditions were defined. The first is based on the concurrency of key words in the title and tags; the second on the information body (Table 3).

Table 3. Variables of the weighing component

Variable	Measure unit
Acceptance criteria	Number of key words

3   Component Metrics

The sample taking is conducted to register the metrics of each component, in which the values of the identified variables are obtained. This is conducted by a determined hardware and software, which are mentioned as following:

Hardware:

- Intel I5 8th Generation
- 8 GB Ram
- 256 GB SSD

The software. Libraries employed:

- Linux Kubuntu 16
- Python 3.6
- Framework Django 2.1
- Virtualenv 17.0
- PostgreSQL 11.2
- NLTK library, Text Blob
- FeedParser 5.2.0

3.1   Metrics of the Obtainment Information Component

The samples are obtained from a hundred information digital media (website URL, which provides the Feed information). These media are categorized as informative (national and international news). For example, if the topic is "Armed Forces", the dictionary will have the same topic. In this way, we find 120 key words that relate to the Armed Forces (Table 4).

Table 4. Variables of the obtainment component

Variable	Measure
Feed	It changes depending on the collected fee (Title, Tags, and Body)
Information media	100 URLs
Collecting cycle time	11 min
Feed update time	15 times average

Each collected fee changes from the news media (the news title, the body and the related tags). The update average time of these 100 media is of 15 min. This is variable because it changes depending on the news' contingency. At the moment of this study, the contingency developed normally, without existing a high number of interesting news in the news media. The model lasts approximately 11 min to track all the registered websites. From these metrics, 17.000 feeds were collected and these will sustain the information classification component.

3.2   Metrics of the Classification Information Component

The obtained metrics come from the number of key words in the information titles and tags. In the following table, it is shown that the more key words are found in the first filter, less news are registered. However, it is also shown the loss of many candidates news (example: news that can be of interest for the topic proposed). From now on, the filter of 01 key words was chosen to be worked with as first filter (Table 5).

Table 5. Filter of key words over 17.000 news from a 100 information media

Number of key words	Number of candidate news	Percentage of total news
01	4.320	25,41%
02	338	1,98%
03	44	0,25%

3.3   Metrics of the Acceptance Information Component

The present investigation based its information acceptance logic on the representation procedure of Bag-of-Words texts [10], using the NLTK library. In this way, the information corpus selected is narrowed and represented as a vector of constant length, which reflects the onset of each term in the text.

Two forms are proposed for accepting a candidate piece of information: (1) under the criteria of the sum of total concurrency of key words of the dictionary in the information body, and (2) the total weighted value of the information body. The last is only a proposal, and object of future study that is further explained in the further studies section.

Acceptance Criteria based on Concurrency: As it is shown in the following table, the more number of key words are found in an information body, the percentage of successes increases (example: interesting news about the topic), and as counterbalance, less news are declared to be candidates. The loss of news is relevant to understand the model leaves out information that could be of interest as from the acceptance criteria of 04, 05, 06 and 07 key words in the information body (from a basis of 120 key words in the dictionary). As conclusion, it could be said that from 6 key words on, the degree of success is higher than the filter loss (Table 6).

Table 6. Information acceptance over 4.320 news

Number of Key Words in the information corpus	Number of filtered news	News of Interest	Number of filtered news from the total information	Percentage of Interest about filtered news
04	1344	413	7,90%	30,72%
05	763	411	17,66%	56,22%
06	466	405	10,7%	86,10%
07	287	264	6,64%	91,98%

4   Model Proposal

From the components described previously, we propose the following model based on three components (Fig. 2), and a flow chart which explains the model's addressing (Fig. 3).

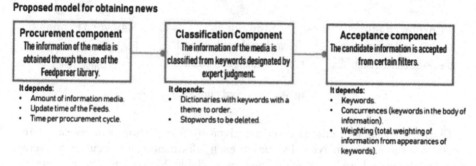

Fig. 2. Proposed model based on three components

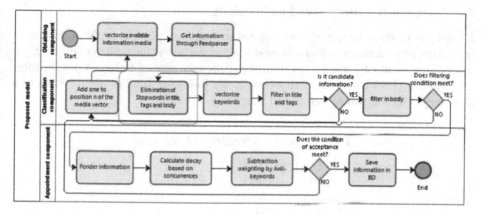

Fig. 3. Processes of the proposed model

5 Continuous Learning

Once the system has been sustained with the information of interest, it is possible to automatically determine new key words, example: words not considered by the expert's judgement at the beginning of the procedure. With the library NLTK (Natural Language Toolkit), all corpuses available can be vectorized, stopwords erased and significant words are selected. Likewise, it can be determined which words are more concurrent so to propose them to the dictionary indexation.

Consideration: It is the value or importance a key word has within a dictionary, and it relates to the topic of interest. In this way, the words are prioritized according to their importance in the topic. The same logic is employed by the procedure based on representation of Bag-of-Words' text [10], and used by the NLTK library to assign the relevance meaningless or too repetitive words could have (Fig. 4).

Corpus reading ⟶ **Stopwords** ⟶ **Keyword Proposal**
Reading of all information bodies extracted through RSS | Elimination of words without proper meaning of the corpus | Proposal of keywords from concurrency

Fig. 4. Key words proposal

Even the acceptance criteria could be given by a collection of news of interest, which allows to get the individual values of each information and calculate an average result that defines a base line from the samples available. Mathematically speaking, this logic is represented for the following equation:

5.1 Acceptance Criteria Based on Weighing

By the use of these weightings, we can reduce the false positive in the collection of feed. This procedure applied as a second filter to the acceptance criteria will be given by the sum of words' weightings from the dictionary applied to the corpus or information body (RSS content). As an example, the following table shows the basis of a dictionary with the words' values and weightings (Table 7).

Table 7. Value and weighting of key words

Key word	Value	Weighting
Boy	High	0.4
Park	Medium	0.2
Bicycle	Medium	0.2
Boat	Low	0.1
Ball	Low	0.1

The total weighing dictionary has to be equal to 100% in the amount of words registered to define the correct prioritization. The value of each word depends on topic, as the same word in different topics could have different weighing values (importance). The weighing value could be assigned by the expert's judgement.

Decay Logarithm: If there are repeated words within the body information, a logarithm of decay will be applied [11]. The value for this logarithm will be obtained from the number of manifestations shown in the vector. This procedure is conducted because a single key word can alter the acceptance criteria, as many concurrencies can show a high weighing followed by a value decay within the total sum of words found.

If the vector of the frequency (repetitions) of the dictionary words $f^\wedge(t)$ in a given text t, then to calculate the score of the text it would be enough to calculate the next sum:

$$\text{sum\_}\{\text{word i of the dictionary}\}\, d\_i(f\_i^\wedge(t))$$

where $f\_i^\wedge(t)$ is the number of times the word number i in the dictionary appears in the text t and d_i are functions of the form:

$$d\_i(f\_i^\wedge(t)) = 0 \qquad \text{when } f\_i^\wedge(t) = 0 \tag{1}$$

$$d\_i(f\_i^\wedge(t)) = a\_i + b\_i * \log(f\_i^\wedge(t)) \qquad \text{when } f\_i^\wedge(t) \geq 1 \tag{2}$$

where a_i and b_i are parameters that can be calibrated.

Anti-Key Words: A dictionary of anti-key words is also defined; that is to say, words that were not considered within the information context. For example: if the topic of search is Politics, the word Football, considering the information corpus, will reduce total sum of key words and their total weighing.

6 Conclusions and Future Work

Nowadays, it is fundamental to obtain information from different digital media. The necessity of maintaining oneself informed determines the opportunities in the digital area or 4th generation [14]. For this reason, blogs, social networks, online newspapers become the main information sources and are the ones which valorize the same.

We think it is crucial to develop a model that allows getting information of real interest in no time, but this is only possible if we have a data source that has been filtered correctly.

We believe that some information could be crucial for people or organizations in particular, and certainly, it is possible to narrow these search processes when pre-existing tools are employed correctly.

From the collection of massive information pieces of real interest on a defined topic, with the support of NLTK and Text Bob, it is possible to obtain useful information, determine sub-topics or tendencies not previously considered, in order to relate this information to future events. Keeping the logic of the proposed model, we could even conduct this search towards social networks.

An example will be Twitter [12], which provides an API with which we can look for Tweets related to a topic. Another will be the tools of Google, particularly Google alerts, which provide information available on the website through sides that have not been registered in the system (digital information media).

The integration of a system that connects to any API and sends real-time notifications at the moment of finding a piece of information is crucial. Libraries such as Telebot (Telegram) allows to manage these notifications directly from the source code. It is necessary to create only a BOT from Telegram [13], to include the application token key directly to the source code in order to send the messages with the results.

References

1. Dua, S., Du, X.: Data Mining and Machine Learning in Cybersecurity. Auerbach Publications, New York (2016). 9780429063756
2. Fawaz, S., AbuZeina, D.: Toward an enhanced Arabic text classification using cosine similarity and Latent Semantic Indexing. J. King Saud Univ. – Comput. Inf. Sci. 29(2), 189–195 (2017)
3. Feedparser. https://pythonhosted.org/feedparser/. Accessed 06 May 2019
4. Bharathi, S., Geetha, A., Sathiynarayanan, R.: Sentiment analysis of twitter and RSS news feeds and its impact on stock market prediction. Int. J. Intell. Eng. Syst. (2017). https://doi.org/10.22266/ijies2017.1231.08
5. Saif, H., Fernández, M., Yulan, H., Harith, A.: On stopwords, filtering and data sparsity for sentiment analysis of Twitter. In: Proceedings of the Ninth International Conference on Language Resources and Evaluation, LREC 2014, pp. 810–817 (2014)
6. Prat, M.: Posicionamiento web: estrategias de SEO: Google y otros buscadores. s.l.: Eni (2016). 2409004903
7. Cabero, J., Llorente, M.: The expert's judgment application as a technic evaluate information and communication technology (ict), Revista de Tecnología de Información y Comunicación en Educación, vol. 7, no. 2 (2013)
8. Díaz, I., Suárez, S., Sidorov, G.: Creation and evaluation of a dictionary tagged with emotions and weighted for Spanish, Onomázein: Revista de lingüística, filología y traducción de la Pontificia Universidad Católica de Chile, no. 29, pp. 31–46 (2014). ISSN-e 0717-1285
9. Perkins, J.: Python 3 Text Processing with Nltk 3 Cookbook (2014). ISBN-10: 1782167854
10. Hasan, K.S., Ng, V.: Stance classification of ideological debates: data, models, features, and constraints. In: Proceedings of the Sixth International Joint Conference on Natural Language Processing, pp. 1693–1701 (2015)
11. Kumar, S., Morstatter, F., Liu, H.: Twitter Data Analytics. Springer, Heidelberg (2013). https://doi.org/10.1007/978-1-4614-9372-3. ISBN 1461493722
12. Setiaji, H., Paputungan, I.: Design of telegram bots for campus information sharing. In: IOP Conference Series: Materials Science and Engineering, vol. 325, p. 012005 (2018). https://doi.org/10.1088/1757-899x/325/1/012005
13. Salas Alvarez, D.: Revolución 4.0, RII, vol. 4, no. 2 (2016)

Security Hierarchy for the NDN Network: Description and Experimentation

P. David Arjona-Villicaña[(✉)] and Alejandra G. Silva-Trujillo

Facultad de Ingeniería, UASLP, San Luis Potosí, Mexico
{david.arjona,asilva}@uaslp.mx

Abstract. Information centric-networks propose a new architecture for the Internet where IP addresses are replaced by names that represent the information or service that users request. The Named Data Networking (NDN) project is seeking to implement and experiment one type of these networks. A fundamental principle of NDN is that all the information needs to travel through the network using a secure hierarchical infrastructure. This article describes this security hierarchy and, using experiments, shows its implementation in two test networks.

Keywords: Information centric networks · Distributed systems · Network security

1 Introduction

The Internet is a worldwide data network whose main objective is to allow pairs of computers to exchange information. In order to identify each computer, it becomes necessary to employ a unique number, the IP address. However, most users do not need to know their own devices' address, nor the procedures required to exchange information in this network. These procedures are relegated to different protocols, like TCP and UDP. Since what it is important to the Internet's users is to obtain information and services, there are currently proposals to implement new network architectures that are oriented to obtain, transmit and deliver information, instead of establishing a connection between two computers. This shift of the main architectural objective of the Internet has been named *Information-Centric Networking* or ICN [1,2].

The main objective of ICNs is to implement a network infrastructure that is better suited on how users currently employ the Internet, which are more interested in accessing information, rather than its physical location. Special attention is given to content distribution, security and mobility support. There have been different proposals to implement ICNs. Examples of these are Data-Oriented Network Architecture (DONA) [3], Publish-Subscribe Internet Technology (PURSUIT) [4], Scalable and Adaptive Internet Solutions (SAIL) [5] and Named Data Networking (NDN) [6].

Named Data Networking or NDN is a type of ICN that is currently being developed and implemented by the *NDN Project*. This project is a team effort

© Springer Nature Switzerland AG 2019
M. F. Mata-Rivera et al. (Eds.): WITCOM 2019, CCIS 1053, pp. 335–344, 2019.
https://doi.org/10.1007/978-3-030-33229-7_28

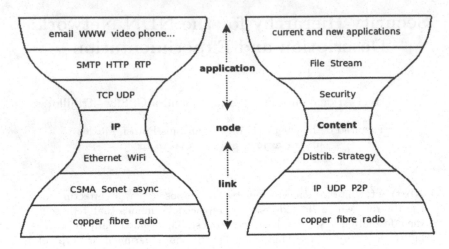

Fig. 1. The main functional elements of the current Internet and NDN.

by many universities and research laboratories around the world, including the Universidad Autónoma de San Luis Potosí (UASLP) [7]. Currently, participants to this project are trying to implement the main functionalities of an NDN node, for example: hierarchical name structure, security methods and procedures, routing, forwarding and in-network storage [6]. Others are working on applications that need to employ some of the functionalities described before. The main idea behind these developments is to prove NDN functionality by testing it in a setting that is as close to a real network as possible. Therefore, the NDN project is also implementing a global network to test the protocols, services and applications under development [8]. This network includes a node at UASLP.

Another of the main objectives of NDN is to maintain a structure that is as simple as the one currently implemented for the Internet. This has been called the thin waist model (Fig. 1). For today's Internet, the simplest (thinnest) functional element is the IP packet; for the case of NDN, is the Content or the name of the information, which is sent through two different types of packets, Interest and Data.

Addresses in an NDN network are the name of the information or service that the user requests [6]. These addresses follow a hierarchy which enables names that are more specific to have priority over more generic ones. For example, a name like /uaslp/ingenieria/computacion has precedence over /uaslp or /uaslp/ingenieria. This is similar to how current routing protocols work, where a network using a /24 mask (a set of specific IP addresses) has priority over another using a /20 mask (a less specific set of addresses). NDN employs only two types of packets: Interest and Data. *Interest* packets are used to request information and *Data* packets are used to answer each Interest packet. Neither of these packets is associated with the computer that originally requested the information or the one that generated the Data packet.

In an NDN network, routers maintain a database which temporarily stores the received Interest and Data packets. Each Data packet must satisfy an Interest packet that has been previously received. Since no packet is associated to the computer that originally generated it, it is possible for a router to receive requests for the same Interest from different devices or network interfaces, which the router satisfies by sending the same Data packet that has been temporarily stored in its database. Following this procedure, a router may send the same information which is requested by different users in a short period of time. This will reduce the traffic in the network since the router only needs to receive one Data packet to satisfy many Interest packets. This also means that NDN is not connection-oriented and that the network has a built-in memory that allows it to distribute information that is constantly or simultaneously being requested.

Since NDN introduces a new paradigm for the architecture of the Internet, it becomes necessary to define the other elements that form this network, for example, security. The Internet was originally based on trust and security mechanisms were added as needed [9]. NDN follows the opposite approach: it is a network that requires security mechanisms to prevent that Interest and Data packets are modified as they travel through the network [10].

Because security is a requisite to exchange messages between nodes in an NDN network, it becomes necessary to understand and being able to set up security before other applications and protocols can be used or tested. Therefore, the main contribution of this paper is to provide two experiments that show how to configure security in an NDN network. These experiments are described at Sect. 2.

Other elements that need to be defined for NDN are routing protocols. Currently, a protocol based on Dijkstra's algorithm [11], the Named Data Link State Routing Protocol (NLSR) [12], is being used. However, before this or any other protocol exchanges routing information in an NDN network, it is necessary to define and configure a security infrastructure. This article describes how to configure this infrastructure (Sect. 2.1) and includes a pair of experiments that show how to perform these configurations (Sects. 2.3 and 2.4). After describing these experiments, the article provides conclusions at Sect. 3.

2   NDN Security

This section first describes the NDN security hierarchy (Subsect. 2.1). Followed by a description of the software needed for implementing the experiments (Subsect. 2.2). Finally, two experiments are described in Subsects. 2.3 and 2.4.

2.1   NDN Security Hierarchy

NDN follows a hierarchical security structure (see Fig. 2). A *root* is at the top of this hierarchy and is the entity in charge of certifying each *site* in the network. Then, each site certifies one or more *operators* which, in turn, certify each *router* in the network. Each one of these different entities must be defined and certified

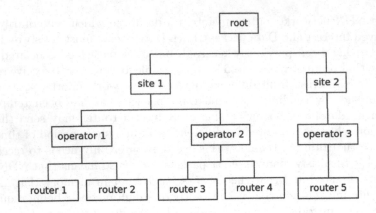

Fig. 2. Example of NDN's hierarchical security structure.

in an NDN network. For networks that have few nodes, it is possible that one router simultaneously assumes the function of more than one of these entities. It is important to consider that this security hierarchy needs to be defined and configured before any other protocol or application can exchange messages. This includes even routing protocols, like NLSR.

Figure 2 shows an example of a security structure for and NDN network with two sites. Site 1 employs two operators: operator 1 is responsible for router 1 and router 2, while operator 2 is responsible for router 3 and router 4. Site 2 has a simpler configuration since it only has one operator (operator 3) which only handles router 5. This hierarchy is independent of how the routers are connected between themselves and, as it was said before, more than one entity could be defined in a single router or node.

In order to implement this hierarchy, it is necessary to exchange keys and certificates using the following procedure: The dependent entity (the one that is below in the hierarchy) generates a key which is then copied to the parent entity (the one that is above). The parent entity employs the key as an input to generate a certificate, which is then copied back to the dependent entity. Finally, the dependent entity installs the certificate. This procedure is shown in Fig. 3. The only exception to this procedure is the root, which is the only entity allowed to self-certify its key.

2.2 Previous Work to the Experiment

Before performing the experiments described in Sects. 2.3 and 2.4, it is necessary to install ndn-cxx and NFD in each node in the test network. The *ndn-cxx* library is a set of programs developed in C++ that implement different NDN support applications. The NDN website [13] includes information and instructions on how to install this application's library. *NFD* is an application that implements an NDN forwarder node that supports the NDN protocol and is able to receive and send Interest and Data packets. The NDN site [14] includes instructions on

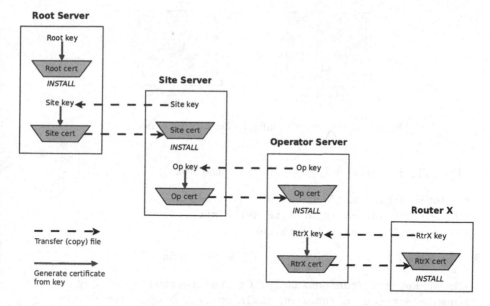

Fig. 3. Generating and installing keys and certificates in NDN.

how to install this application and a description of NFD's architecture may be found at its Developer's Guide [15].

To verify that the security hierarchy has been successfully configured, it is necessary to execute an application that employs this hierarchy. The NLSR protocol is an example of these applications. But before installing NLSR, the Chronosync and Psync applications must also be installed. More information about installing NLSR, Chronosync and Psync may be found at [16].

It is also recommended to review the beginners' installation guide [17] which includes all the necessary steps to install ndn-cxx, NFD and NLSR in a computer running the Linux Fedora operating system.

2.3 Experiment 1

This experiment shows how to configure the security hierarchy for the simplest NDN network: two routers communicating between themselves (see Fig. 4). This network has two routers, R1 and R2, which connect to each other using a crossover Ethernet cable. R1 is configured to be the root, site, operator 1 and R1, while the other computer is only configured to be R2. The commands needed to configure R1 are included below.

1. The following commands configure R1 as the root:

```
ndnsec-key-gen /ndn/ > root.key
ndnsec-cert-dump -i /ndn/ > root.cert
ndnsec-cert-install -f root.cert
```

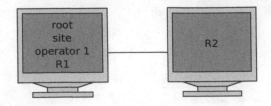

Fig. 4. Topology and configuration for first experiment.

2. The following commands configure R1 as the site:

```
ndnsec-key-gen /ndn/edu/uaslp > site.key
ndnsec-cert-gen -s /ndn/ site.key > site.cert
ndnsec-cert-install -f site.cert
```

3. The following commands configure R1 as the operator 1:

```
ndnsec-key-gen /ndn/edu/uaslp/%C1.Operator/op1 > op1.key
ndnsec-cert-gen -s /ndn/edu/uaslp op1.key > op1.cert
ndnsec-cert-install -f op1.cert
```

4. The following commands configure R1 as a router:

```
ndnsec-key-gen /ndn/edu/uaslp/%C1.Router/R1 > R1.key
ndnsec-cert-gen -s /ndn/edu/uaslp/%C1.Operator/op1 R1.key
    > R1.cert
ndnsec-cert-install -f R1.cert
```

Since R1 is already configured as the root, site and operator 1, R2 only needs to be configured as a router whose parent entity is the same operator (operator 1). The commands included below need to be executed in R2 and R1 to perform this configuration.

1. R2 generates its own key:

```
ndnsec-key-gen /ndn/edu/uaslp/%C1.Router/R2 > R2.key
```

2. The key is copied to operator 1 (R1) and it is then certified using the following command:

```
ndnsec-cert-gen -s /ndn/edu/uaslp/%C1.Operator/op1 R2.key
    > R2.cert
```

3. The certificate is copied back to R2 and then it is installed using the following command:

```
ndnsec-cert-install -f R2.cert
```

```
1565189850.423914 DEBUG: [nlsr.Nlsr] Successfully enabled incoming face id indicationfor face id 267
1565189850.423977 DEBUG: [nlsr.Nlsr] Successfully registered prefix: /localhop/ndn/nlsr/LSA
1565189850.424041 DEBUG: [nlsr.Nlsr] KEY prefix: /ndn/edu/uaslp/%C1.Router/R1/nlsr/KEY registration is successful.
1565189850.424206 DEBUG: [nlsr.Nlsr] KEY prefix: /ndn/edu/uaslp/%C1.Router/R1/KEY registration is successful.
1565189850.424266 DEBUG: [nlsr.Nlsr] KEY prefix: /ndn/edu/uaslp/%C1.Operator registration is successful.
1565189850.424315 DEBUG: [nlsr.Nlsr] KEY prefix: /ndn/edu/uaslp/KEY registration is successful.
1565189850.424359 DEBUG: [nlsr.Nlsr] Successfully registered prefix: /localhost/nlsr
1565189850.424400 DEBUG: [nlsr.Nlsr] Successfully registered prefix: /ndn/edu/uaslp/%C1.Router/R1/nlsr
1565189850.424835 DEBUG: [nlsr.route.Fib] Successful in name registration: /ndn/edu/uaslp/%C1.Router/R2 Face Uri:
udp4://148.224.94.100:6363 faceId: 264
1565189850.424869 DEBUG: [nlsr.route.FaceMap] ------- Face Map----------
1565189850.424883 DEBUG: [nlsr.route.FaceMap] Face Map Entry (FaceUri: udp4://148.224.94.100:6363 Face Id: 264)
1565189850.425211 DEBUG: [nlsr.route.Fib] Successful in name registration: /localhop/ndn/nlsr/sync/%FD%06 Face Uri:
udp4://148.224.94.100:6363 faceId: 264
1565189850.425236 DEBUG: [nlsr.route.FaceMap] ------- Face Map----------
1565189850.425244 DEBUG: [nlsr.route.FaceMap] Face Map Entry (FaceUri: udp4://148.224.94.100:6363 Face Id: 264)
1565189850.425453 DEBUG: [nlsr.route.Fib] Successful in name registration: /localhop/ndn/nlsr/LSA Face Uri:
udp4://148.224.94.100:6363 faceId: 264
1565189850.425474 DEBUG: [nlsr.route.FaceMap] ------- Face Map----------
1565189850.425479 DEBUG: [nlsr.route.FaceMap] Face Map Entry (FaceUri: udp4://148.224.94.100:6363 Face Id: 264)
1565189860.415270 DEBUG: [nlsr.HelloProtocol] Expressing Interest :/ndn/edu/uaslp/%C1.Router/R2/nlsr/INFO/
%07%24%08%03ndn%08%03edu%08%05uaslp%08%08%C1.Router%08%07R1
1565189860.415349 DEBUG: [nlsr.HelloProtocol] Sending scheduled interest: /ndn/edu/uaslp/%C1.Router/R2/nlsr/INFO/
%07%24%08%03ndn%08%03edu%08%05uaslp%08%08%C1.Router%08%07R1
1565189860.415368 DEBUG: [nlsr.HelloProtocol] Scheduling HELLO Interests in 60 seconds
1565189860.426140 DEBUG: [nlsr.HelloProtocol] Received data for INFO(name): /ndn/edu/uaslp/%C1.Router/R2/nlsr/INFO/
%07%24%08%03ndn%08%03edu%08%05uaslp%08%08%C1.Router%08%07R1/%FD%00%00%01l1%98%3D%E9
1565189860.426208 DEBUG: [nlsr.HelloProtocol] Data signed with: /ndn/edu/uaslp/%C1.Router/R2/nlsr/KEY/
d%2B%F2zP%EF%9D%C7
1565189860.429535 DEBUG: [nlsr.HelloProtocol] Interest Received for Name: /ndn/edu/uaslp/%C1.Router/R1/nlsr/INFO/
%07%24%08%03ndn%08%03edu%08%05uaslp%08%08%C1.Router%08%07R2
1565189860.429600 DEBUG: [nlsr.HelloProtocol] Neighbor: /ndn/edu/uaslp/%C1.Router/R2
1565189860.429978 DEBUG: [nlsr.HelloProtocol] Sending out data for name: /ndn/edu/uaslp/%C1.Router/R1/nlsr/INFO/
%07%24%08%03ndn%08%03edu%08%05uaslp%08%08%C1.Router%08%07R2
1565189860.430077 DEBUG: [nlsr.HelloProtocol] Expressing Interest :/ndn/edu/uaslp/%C1.Router/R2/nlsr/INFO/
%07%24%08%03ndn%08%03edu%08%05uaslp%08%08%C1.Router%08%07R1
1565189860.430840 DEBUG: [nlsr.HelloProtocol] Received data for INFO(name): /ndn/edu/uaslp/%C1.Router/R2/nlsr/INFO/
%07%24%08%03ndn%08%03edu%08%05uaslp%08%08%C1.Router%08%07R1/%FD%00%00%01l1%98%3D%E9
1565189860.430878 DEBUG: [nlsr.HelloProtocol] Data signed with: /ndn/edu/uaslp/%C1.Router/R2/nlsr/KEY/
d%2B%F2zP%EF%9D%C7
```

Fig. 5. Extract of NLSR log showing successful key registration and message exchange.

After finishing the previous procedure, it is necessary to execute NLSR and verify that the configuration has been successful. Setting up and running this routing protocol is beyond the topics covered by this article, hence, readers may refer to the NLSR web page [16]. However, Fig. 5 shows an extract of a log generated by this application, where it is possible to read that the different keys have been successfully registered and that messages have been exchanged using NLSR's Hello protocol. Since the logs at Fig. 5 do not show error messages related to key registration and is able to exchange packets, the security hierarchy has been set up correctly.

2.4   Experiment 2

To verify the robustness and generality of Experiment 1, a second experiment with a more complex structure and network topology was performed. The topology and structure for this experiment is shown in Fig. 6. This topology includes five routers which will perform the following roles: R1 is configured to be the root, site, operator 1 and R1; R2 is configured to be operator 2 and router R2; R3 is configured as a router whose parent is operator 2; R4 and R5 are configured to be routers whose parent is operator 1.

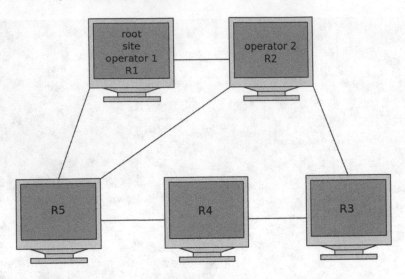

Fig. 6. Topology and configuration for second experiment.

To configure the security hierarchy for R1, it is only necessary to repeat the same steps that were shown at Sect. 2.3 for R1.

The commands included below may be used to configure security for R2.

1. Operator 2 generates its own key:

   ```
   ndnsec-key-gen /ndn/edu/uaslp/%C1.Operator/op2 > op2.key
   ```

2. The key is copied to the site (R1) and it is then certified using the following command:

   ```
   ndnsec-cert-gen -s /ndn/edu/uaslp op2.key > op2.cert
   ```

3. The certificate is copied back to R2 and it is then installed using the following command:

   ```
   ndnsec-cert-install -f op2.cert
   ```

4. The following commands configure R2 as a router:

   ```
   ndnsec-key-gen /ndn/edu/uaslp/%C1.Router/R2 > R2.key
   ndnsec-cert-gen -s /ndn/edu/uaslp/%C1.Operator/op2 R2.key
      > R2.cert
   ndnsec-cert-install -f R2.cert
   ```

To configure R3, R4 and R5 it is necessary to repeat the same steps that were used at Sect. 2.3 for R2. However, these instructions need to be adjusted to consider that R3's parent is operator 1, while the parent for R4 and R5 is operator 2.

After performing the security configuration for the five nodes in this network, NLSR was executed again and it was verified that all the computers exchanged messages and were able to generate a routing table.

3   Conclusions

ICNs are a proposal to redefine the Internet from a network that allows to establish communication between two computers, to an infrastructure whose main objective is to obtain information from the network. This, in turn provides the opportunity to examine new ideas and to reflect on the fundamental principles that allowed to construct today's network.

For the specific case of NDN networks, security mechanisms are required to guarantee that Interest and Data packets are not modified as they travel through the network. This paper has shown how to properly configure this security using two different test networks. This correct configuration allows the implementation of an Internet which should be safer by definition.

Besides the topic of security, there is a large number of protocols and applications under development and experimentation for NDN. These developments represent an opportunity to contribute to a project which may have a significant impact in the design of new architectures for the Internet. However, engineers interested in contributing to the NDN project, first need to understand its security hierarchy. The experiments included in this article are a first step to understand this hierarchy and its main concepts.

The authors of this article are trying to propose new routing strategies for NDN and this article shows the path that may be followed in the next stages of research.

Acknowledgments. The authors would like to thank Lan Wang and Ashlesh Gawande form the University of Memphis which helped to understand and clarify many of the concepts exposed in this article.

References

1. Ahlgren, B., Dannewitzh, C., Imbrenda, C., Kutscher, D., Ohlman, B.: A survey of information-centric networking. IEEE Commun. Mag. **50**(7), 26–36 (2012)
2. Xylomenos, G., et al.: A survey of information-centric networking research. IEEE Commun. Surv. Tutor. **16**(2) (2014)
3. Koponen, T., et al.: A data-oriented (and beyond) network architecture. In: ACM SIGCOMM, pp. 181–192 (2007)
4. FP7 PURSUIT project. http://www.fp7-pursuit.eu/
5. FP7 SAIL project. http://www.sail-project.eu/
6. Zhang, L., et al.: Named data networking. ACM SIGCOMM Comput. Commun. Rev. **44**(3), 66–73 (2014)
7. NDN Testbed Status. http://ndndemo.arl.wustl.edu/
8. NDN Traffic Map. http://ndnmap.arl.wustl.edu/
9. Bellovin, S., Schiller, J., Kaufman, C.: Security Mechanisms for the Internet, RFC 3631 (2003)
10. Zhang, Z., et al.: An overview of security support in named data networking, NDN, Technical report NDN-0057 (2018)
11. Dijkstra, E.: A note on two problems in connection with graphs. Numerische Mathematik **1**(1), 269–271 (1959)

12. Lehman, V., Mahmudul Hoque, A., Yu, Y., Wang, L., Zhang, B., Zhang, L.: A secure link state routing protocol for NDN, NDN, Technical report NDN-0037 (2016)
13. ndn-cxx: NDN C++ library with eXperimental eXtensions. http://named-data.net/doc/ndn-cxx/current/
14. NFD: NDN Forwarding Daemon. http://named-data.net/doc/NFD/current/
15. NDN Project Team, NFD Developer's Guide, Technical report NDN-0021 (2016)
16. NLSR, Named Data Link State Routing. http://named-data.net/doc/NLSR/current/
17. Arjona-Villicaña, P., Rentería-Vidales, O., Gawande, A.: A beginner's guide to installing and testing NLSR in Fedora. http://named-data.net/doc/NLSR/current/beginners-guide.html

Methodology for Malware Scripting Analysis in Controlled Environments Based on Open Source Tools

Diego Muñoz[(⊠)], David Cordero[(⊠)],
and Cristian Barría Huidobro[(⊠)]

Centro de Investigación en Ciberseguridad, Universidad Mayor, Santiago, Chile
diego.munoze@mayor.clm,
{david.cordero, cristian.barria}@mayor.cl

Abstract. In today's interconnected world, there is a latent threat called malware or malicious software. Different variations of these polymorphic and metamorphic malware continue to evolve, even becoming large industries called Malware as a Service (MaaS) [1]. This combined with the large number of new technologies has evolved along with different threats, which can seriously damage from a workstation, to large network architectures [2]. In order to face it, it is necessary to be able to analyze and understand its operation, for this reason to carry out this task a defined methodology is necessary. This paper proposes a methodological structure for working with malware scripting, for which a detailed example of practical application in a controlled environment is illustrated. After the analysis of the results obtained, a concept map is offered with the stages and activities related to the proposed methodology.

The present investigation provides an adequate look for the rapid analysis of malicious scripts, which allows decisions to be made during situations of IT crisis, which in turn will be the basis for a thorough further analysis.

In order to start with any type of analysis, it is important to establish a working methodology or framework to be able to carry out a sample study of some type of malware scripting, also considering identifying its classification, based on "Malware Analysis and Classification: A Survey" [3].

Keywords: Malware scripting · Static analysis · Dynamic analysis · Methodology

1 Introduction

To take advantage of different security flaws or breaches of some system, cybercriminals focus on the end user, as Jorge Mieres points out in his whitepaper about computer attacks, demonstrating how cybercriminals take advantage of exploiting any weaknesses or failures in the systems [4] also considering use social engineering, as Kevin Mitnick details in his book "The Art of Invisibility" [5], applying different techniques so that victims can provide the necessary data for a future attack, which is a

M. F. Mata-Rivera et al. (Eds.): WITCOM 2019, CCIS 1053, pp. 345–354, 2019.
https://doi.org/10.1007/978-3-030-33229-7_29

cause of concern for cybersecurity managers who must generate computer security awareness instances or culture.

Many of the attacks that occur today are based on malicious software and the different variations that may arise from a single threat, it is for this reason that the need for malware analysis is born, which in definition could be considered as the art of dissecting malicious software, to understand how it works, how to identify it and thus be able to defeat it.

Malicious codes or scripts will continue to be one of the main threats to the modern world, becoming an endless battle between those who write new scripting malware and those who seek to detect their execution in time and avoid all types of fraud through cyberspace. The exploitation of systems through the infection of scripting malware also propagated by phishing, are the perfect mix to continue deceiving the end user and to penetrate even the most sensitive information we store.

2 Proposed Method Analysis

Currently there are different methods to perform different activities framed within the field of cybersecurity and cyber defense, one of these disciplines is malware analysis.

As a way to help researchers and analysts on this matter, the present analysis of malicious software is focused on malware scripting, that is very simple code sequences that automate malicious tasks in real time and that do not need to be compiled as is the case with files executables (.EXE). These can infect, download, redirect or slow down a computer, in addition to not being discovered developers obfuscate the code to make them undetectable and thus not be discovered by antivirus engines.

Some languages to perform this type of malware can be used different programming languages, such as Visual Basic Script (VBS), Java Script (JS) or Python (PY).To carry out this type of methodology, the following 5 stages are proposed:

2.1 Stage 1: Sample Identification

Every time we face a sample it is necessary to know what kind of file we are analyzing, some try to deceive the victim by posing as images, folders or any other extension that a normal user would consider harmless.

Upon receiving a sample of the malicious software we can rely on utilities such as the "file" command that brings most of the GNU/Linux operating systems, which is responsible for testing the file we want to evaluate and returns the information of both its type and its format.

Already knowing the file type it is necessary to obtain its metadata, identifying the size in bytes, date of creation, date of modification, among other characteristics, as can be evidenced in the following (Table 1):

Table 1. Data that must be identified

Data	Example	Note
Type	Executable	Can also be scripts
Format	.EXE	.AVI, .MP4, .PDF, .JPG, etc.
Weight	285.13 KB	Can also be defined as MB, GB, etc.
Hash	8d357c0f0cc37dd573a2ba57b8	Can also be used for online analysis
Date	02-jun-2019	Creation and/or modification date

2.2 Stage 2: Static Analysis

Having the sample relevant background, we proceed to perform a static analysis of the malicious code. The static analysis allows us to examine the sample code in a safe environment, without the need to execute it, so we can generate hypotheses of what its effects are or will be once executed.

In order to carry out this activity, reverse engineering is performed, that is, the process to determine the operation by disassembling each component if necessary. For this reason it is important that the analyst understands both high and low level language, in order to carry out an analysis that allows conclusions to be drawn while advancing in the study of malicious code, especially on low level language since it is precisely this with which reverse engineering is performed, understanding in the same way that both levels of language are interpreted by the CPU in a machine language. For this reason it is essential for an analyst to know different types of programming languages [7, 8], which helps to better understand how the developer built the scripting malware (Fig. 1).

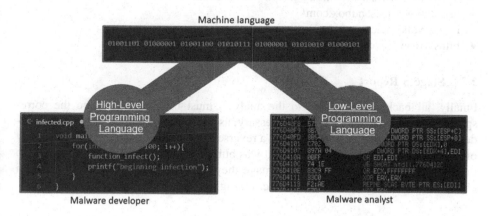

Fig. 1. Levels of abstraction to interpret.

This type of analysis happens when it is necessary to calculate the different hashes that the sample can have, such as its MD5 hash, SHA1, among others, it is also possible to rely on integrated development environments (IDE), or it can even be studied quickly with any text editor, since they do not need to be compiled for execution.

After the background or data obtained, it is important to look for information in open sources, in order to know if this threat has already been studied by other researchers.

2.3   Stage 3 Dynamic Analysis

With the collection of static analysis, it is already possible to identify certain characteristics of the malware, which leads us to the next phase that is dynamic analysis. This type of analysis is to execute the sample to demonstrate its behavior and what capabilities it has by being able to execute it. We can in some cases visualize what types of changes are made in a computer, such as file modifications, file deletion, creation of keys, among others.

Many of the tools that can be used for analysis are available on the Internet, there is even a detailed guide called Practical Malware Analysis: The Hands-On Guide to Dissecting Malicious Software, by the writer Michael Sikorski [8] which we will be guided to know What tools to use.

2.4   Stage 4 Dynamic Analysis Support Tools

There is a considerable amount of online tools to support our analysis, for this reason after the manual study of the sample it is possible to rely on the following websites that have the ability to analyze malicious files [9].

- https://any.run/
- http://www.virustotal.com
- https://metadefender.opswat.com
- http://www.intezer.com/
- https://go.crowdstrike.com/try-falcon-prevent.html
- https://www.joesandbox.com/
- https://valkyrie.comodo.com
- https://www.reverse.it/

2.5   Stage 5 Report

Finally, all background related to the analysis must be used to prepare the corresponding final documentation, or if necessary, use this background for another more in-depth analysis phase, such as executing a reverse engineering process, that is, the study of a sample in order to determine how it was built, disassembling its code to be able to understand what it can do or what damage they cause, in short, to discover what an object is made of, sample, software, etc. through conjectures that arise in the study.

3   Applied Example

3.1   Setting up a Work Environment

In order to work safely, it is necessary to configure a laboratory that has certain restrictions to avoid damaging other computational assets, this is possible thanks to virtualization software [6], which allow us to install and configure different operating systems to perform analysis, but when configuring them it is necessary to consider at least the following:

- Before working make a snapshot or clone of the machine.
- Once the sample is loaded on the machine, disable USB to prevent infections that use this technology to spread.
- Once the sample is loaded on the machine, disable any network card in the device.
- Not having or creating shared folders on the network, there should be no connection to the host computer.
- It is very likely that depending on the tools or capacity of the scripting malware that needs to be analyzed, it is necessary to use different operating systems such as Windows or one based on GNU/Linux. Therefore, it is advisable to configure at least 2 different laboratories with the same sample, in this way it is possible to use different tools or functionalities of each environment.

3.2   Stage 1 Identification of a Sample

We begin by identifying the sample that we will analyze, in this case a Java Script called "hmskerx.js". We will use the Kali Linux distribution and the "md5sum" tool to perform an MD5 hash of the sample, using the following command (Fig. 2):

```
root@kali:~/Desktop# md5sum hmskerx.js
1c767d9d6391c9c0ac9e68ffb9ff914e  hmskerx.js
```

Fig. 2. Sample MD5.

Once the MD5 hash is obtained, we proceed to extract the metadata contained in the sample, this may vary with each case (Fig. 3):

```
root@kali:~/Desktop# exiftool hmskerx.js
ExifTool Version Number         : 11.16
File Name                       : hmskerx.js
Directory                       : .
File Size                       : 80 kB
File Modification Date/Time     : 2018:01:11 13:17:56-06:00
File Access Date/Time           : 2019:06:15 12:52:07-06:00
File Inode Change Date/Time     : 2019:06:15 12:51:19-06:00
File Permissions                : rw--------
Error                           : Unknown file type
```

Fig. 3. Sample metadata.

When extracting the metadata and realizing that the type of file is unknown, we use the "File" utility that comes by default in Kali Linux to obtain more data, as shown below (Fig. 4):

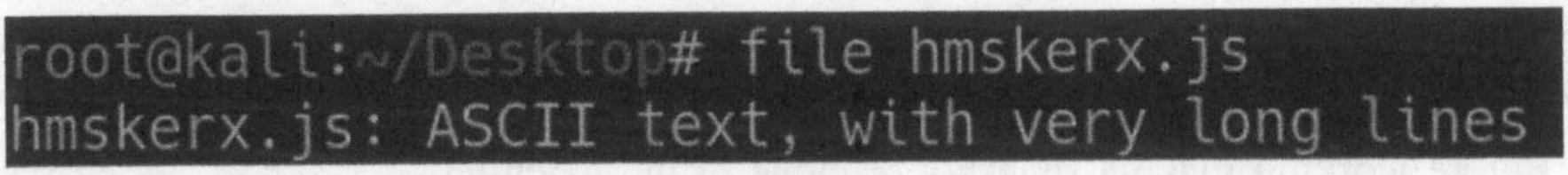
root@kali:~/Desktop# file hmskerx.js
hmskerx.js: ASCII text, with very long lines

Fig. 4. File type

This gives us an indication that the sample has ASCII characters and that it is also composed of large lines of code.

3.3 Stage 2 Static Analysis of a Sample

In order to work with the information that the sample possesses, it is important to be able to extract the hash that it contains in all its formats, for them we can use the "hashcalc" tool and calculate not only the MD5 of this sample, this information could be useful When you need to search through open sources for information on the sample under analysis (Fig. 5).

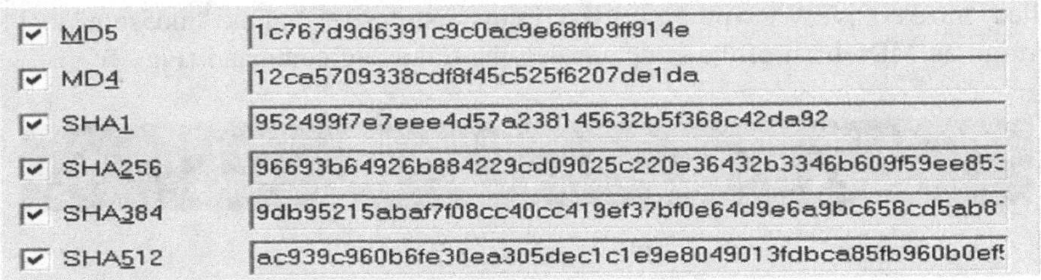
MD5
1c767d9d6391c9c0ac9e68ffb9ff914e
MD4
12ca5709338cdf8f45c525f6207de1da
SHA1
952499f7e7eee4d57a238145632b5f368c42da92
SHA256
96693b64926b884229cd09025c220e36432b3346b609f59ee85
SHA384
9db95215abaf7f08cc40cc419ef37bf0e64d9e6a9bc658cd5ab8
SHA512
ac939c960b6fe30ea305dec1c1e9e804901 3fdbca85fb960b0ef

Fig. 5. File type.

If we open an editor to analyze the sample, we come across what appears to be obfuscation of the code, this to prevent antivirus detects the threat and can run without problems, this is also possible to observe using the tool "strings" that shows us information regarding the characters that can be printable per console as evidenced in the following image (Fig. 6):

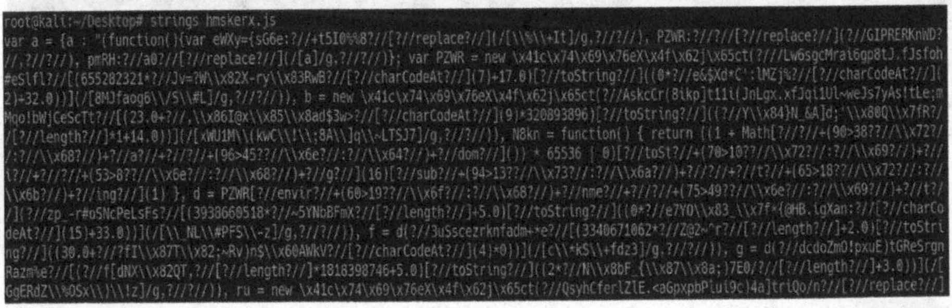
root@kali:~/Desktop# strings hmskerx.js

Fig. 6. Sample printable characters.

If we go to the end of the result we can observe the following (Fig. 7):

```
try {
with(WScript) FullName = "";
} catch (e) {}
if (typeof ActiveXObject == "function" && typeof WScript.FullName == "string") {
var b = {a : [typeof document]};
var c = {a : b, b : a};
String.prototype.a = function() {return eval(a)};
b = c.a.a[0].charCodeAt(!0);
if (b == 110) a = c.b.a.replace(/\?\/\//g, "\"");
Number.constructor("".a())();
```

Fig. 7. Sample printable characters.

We already have some data regarding how the obfuscation of this script works, which by the way uses WScript, an environment developed by Windows for the execution of scripts in its operating system.

Now, with the background information obtained, it is possible to perform searches in open sources, using tools such as "total virus" to analyze, for example, some of the hashes of the sample, as it is possible to observe in the following image:

3.4   Stage 3: Dynamic Analysis of a Sample

3.4.1   Evidence Taking

In order to be able to show or understand the changes that a computer undergoes when executing malicious script, it is necessary to identify what are the normal processes that must be running before executing the sample (Fig. 8).

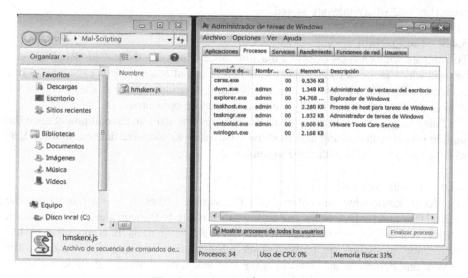

Fig. 8. Process evidence taking.

3.4.2   Sample Execution, Review and Process Comparison

At this point it is necessary to identify what processes were created after execution, it is also important to visually inspect if there is any change in the environment such as unknown extensions, file deletion, file duplication, etc. (Fig. 9).

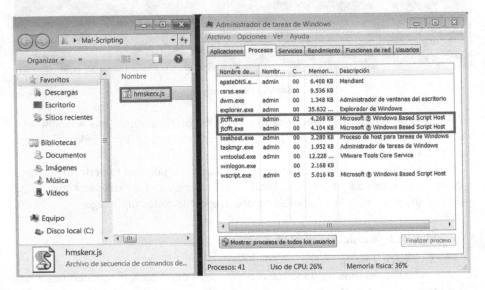

Fig. 9. Taking evidence of new processes generated.

A good activity now is to review each of the processes generated to identify their properties and where they are stored.

3.4.3   Comparison

To compare what changes exist in a machine once infected, a tool called "Regshot" can be used which makes a comparison of the before and after a sample is executed, as can be seen in Fig. 10, a "shot" to a clean machine, then the sample is executed, then a second shot" is taken and finally the results must be compared.

This will give us a text file with all the changes that arose in the equipment once the sample was executed, being able to show how many values were deleted, modified, as well as folders or keys within the system.

3.4.4   Traffic Analysis

In order to know what kind of requests the sample makes, it is possible to use the "ApateDNS" tool which helps answering DNS requests through the malicious script without connecting to the Internet, and as with these tools it is possible to use "Wireshark" to analyze the traffic and see what requests or requests are made on the network and determine any malicious domain that tries to download some malicious software once connected to the Internet.

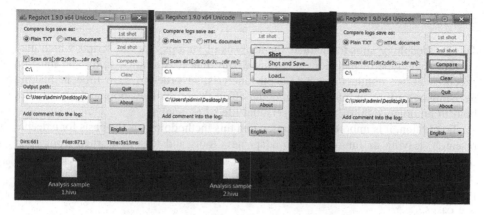

Fig. 10. Tool for comparing changes in the system logs.

3.5   Stage 4 and 5: Dynamic Analysis Support Tools and Report

It is also possible to rely on online tools such as "Valkyrie" (https://valkyrie.comodo.
com) or "Any run" (https://any.run/) which are platforms that allow you to load
samples to be analyzed automatically and manual depending on the interest of the
analyst and once obtained the greatest amount of background the analyst must process
the information and draw from it a conclusion regarding the study, the report must be
ordered and in phases as proposed in this investigation.

4   Model Proposal

Based on the above, the following malware scripting analysis methodology is proposed
(Fig. 11):

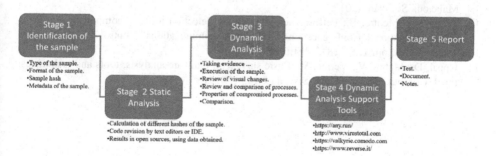

Fig. 11. Proposal methodology on based 5 stage.

5 Conclusions and Future Work

This methodology aims to facilitate the analysis of various types of scripts which may contain some type of malicious use, considering that it is a quick study and must be executed before conducting an in-depth analysis, in order to save time in making decisions regarding an infection that could affect the normal development of activities both in an organization and in the personal life of an analyst.

In addition, it is important to mention that this methodology is the basis for a deeper research, leaving as future work to adapt new tools and lessons learned from other disciplines [10], such as computer forensics, in terms of custody and recognition of evidence. Thus, this paper is intended as a first approach to the issue at hand, in order to provide the foundations for a thorough methodology proposal, tested against real-life use cases.

References

1. Gutmann, P.: The commercial malware industry. In: DEFCON Conference (2007)
2. Baltimore, B.: Baltimore's out-of-date and underfunded IT system was ripe for ransomware attack (2019)
3. Baltimorebrew classification homepage. https://www.baltimorebrew.com/2019/05/21/baltimores-out-of-date-and-underfunded-it-system-was-ripe-for-a-ransomware-attack/. Accessed 21 May 2019
4. Gandotra, E., et al.: Malware analysis and classification: a survey. J. Inf. Secur. 5, 56–64 (2014). https://doi.org/10.4236/jis.2014.52006
5. Mieres, J.: Ataques informáticos. Debilidades de seguridad comúnmente explotadas. Recuperado (2009). http://proton.ucting.udg.mx/tutorial/hackers/hacking.pdf
6. Mitnick, K.: The Art of Invisibility: The World's Most Famous Hacker Teaches You How to be Safe in the Age of Big Brother and Big Data. Hachette, UK (2017)
7. Gómez, J., Villar, E.: Introducción a la virtualización (2018)
8. Fedorenko, E., Ivanova, A., Dhamala, R., Bers, M.U. The Language of Programming: A Cognitive Perspective. Trends in cognitive sciences (2019)
9. Sikorski, M., Honig, A.: Practical Malware Analysis: The Hands-On Guide to Dissecting Malicious Software (2012)
10. Pandey, S., Mehtre, B.: Performance of malware detection tools: a comparison. In: 2014 IEEE International Conference on Advanced Communications, Control and Computing Technologies, pp. 1811–1817. IEEE (2012)
11. Uppal, D., Mehra, V., Verma, V.: Basic survey on malware analysis, tools and techniques. Int. J. Comput. Sci. Appl. (IJCSA) 4(1), 103 (2014)

Validation of ICS Vulnerability Related to TCP/IP Protocol Implementation in Allen-Bradley Compact Logix PLC Controller

Jaime Pavesi[1]([⊠]), Thamara Villegas[1], Alexey Perepechko[2],
Eleazar Aguirre[3], and Lorena Galeazzi[4]

[1] Facultad de Ciencias, Universidad Mayor, Santiago, Chile
{jaime.pavesi, thamara.villegas}@umayor.cl
[2] Independent IOT/IIOT Security Researcher and Security Architect,
Amsterdam, The Netherlands
alexey.perepechko@gmail.com
[3] Instituto Politécnico Nacional, Mexico City, Mexico
eaguirre@cic.ipn.mx
[4] Centro de Investigación en Ciberseguridad CICS, Universidad Mayor,
Santiago, Chile
lorena.galeazzi@mayor.cl

Abstract. Industrial Control Systems (ICS) research and testing process was implemented to validate the existence of a well known security vulnerability in a Rockwell Automation Allen-Bradley Compact Logix PLC controller. The study was conducted considering a public advisory from the manufacturer, which includes a large list of families of affected products by the vulnerability. The established hypothesis of the study considered the existence of the vulnerability in a specific available PLC model, included by Rockwell Automation manufacturer in the list of affected products. An exploit was developed and multiple testing was performed to trigger the vulnerability.

Testing methodology and results indicates there is sufficient evidence to establish that Rockwell Automation Allen-Bradley Compact Logix 5370 L2 controllers, are not affected by the same type of Improper Input Validation vulnerability, than the Compact Logix 5370 L3 controllers, as it was stated by the manufacturer in a public advisory.

Keywords: ICS · PLC · TCP/IP · Security · Vulnerability · Exploit

1 Introduction

Industrial Control Systems (ICS) play a very important role in world economy and current way of living. ICS became highly automated and network connected, introducing benefits but also new security vulnerabilities. This is particularly important in Critical Infrastructure ICS such as energy, water, transportation, etc. [12].

Automation components of ICS include sensors, actuators, PLCs and SCADA systems, among others components [8]. New ICS vulnerabilities are discovered every

M. F. Mata-Rivera et al. (Eds.): WITCOM 2019, CCIS 1053, pp. 355–364, 2019.
https://doi.org/10.1007/978-3-030-33229-7_30

year. In several countries, regulation forces manufacturers to recognize and inform ICS vulnerabilities in public advisories, which usually include mitigation procedures and recommendations to their customers, such as software or firmware upgrades, ICS network isolation, traffic block, renew equipment, etc.

Such mitigations actions may have an <u>important</u> cost for the companies and are also time consuming. Most of the companies rely on the information provided by ICS world class manufacturers, such as Rockwell Automation, Siemens, etc.

When an ICS vulnerability become public, including a list of ICS affected products, companies currently using those products feels they are at risk of being attacked. This is particularly important in the case of critical infrastructure companies, whose operation depends on ICS systems that are supposed to be vulnerable [9].

Those companies don't hesitate to follow the risk mitigation recommendations of their provider/manufacturer, assuming the involved costs. But, what if the information provided by manufacturers, related to ICS vulnerabilities, is not enough accurate?

What if ICS manufacturers decide to include families of products supposedly affected by a vulnerability, in their public advisories, to prevent a possible damage, without having complete demonstrated confirmation of the vulnerability, in some of the products?

Looking for an answer to all these questions, this study focuses on technical validation of PLC vulnerability in Rockwell Automation Allen-Bradley Compact Logix PLC affected products, declared in NCICC Advisory ICSA-18-172-02 [1].

That specific PLC was selected for this research, because the research team has full access to a Lab with 4 of those PLCs and also has access to the PLC configuration and communication licensed software, which are needed for the purpose of the study.

2   Problem Definition and Hypothesis

In June 2018, researcher Alexey Perepechko from Applied Risk company based in the Netherlands, discovered a PLC vulnerability and sent an Advisory Report [2] to Rockwell Automation manufacturer. The report include the following main information:

"A vulnerability in the Rockwell Automation Allen-Bradley CompactLogix 5370 Controller 1769-L30ERMS could allow an unauthenticated, remote threat actor to reboot the device and switch the device to the "Major Non-Recoverable Fault" mode, resulting in a Denial of Service ("DoS") condition" [2].

"Vulnerability Details. The vulnerability is due to incorrect processing of TCP ACK packet additional options by the listener at Ethernet/IP TCP port (default 44818). An incorrect order on the NOP option leads to a immediate device reboot and enters a "Major Fault" mode which must be resolved manually. To trigger the vulnerability, the NOP option must be put first and the number of options must be more than one" [2].

The vulnerability discovered and reported, was recognized by the PLC manufacturer. Rockwell Automation determined there were additional products affected by the vulnerability and reported this information to NCCIC [3], which result in NCICC Advisory ICSA-18-172-02 [1]. List of affected products by the vulnerability, according to Rockwell Automation [1, 13]:

1. Allen-Bradley CompactLogix 5370 L1 controllers, Versions 30.014 and prior,
2. Allen-Bradley CompactLogix 5370 L2 controllers, Versions 30.014 and prior,
3. Allen-Bradley CompactLogix 5370 L3 controllers, Versions 30.014 and prior,
4. Allen-Bradley Armor CompactLogix 5370 L3 controllers, Versions 30.014 and prior,
5. Allen-Bradley Compact GuardLogix 5370 controllers, Versions 30.014 and prior, and
6. Allen-Bradley Armor Compact GuardLogix 5370 controllers, Versions 30.014 and prior.

CVE-2017-9312 [14] and CWE-20 "Improper Input Validation" were assigned to this vulnerability by NIST [4, 15] and MITRE [5] organizations. The specific controller already mentioned, used to discover this vulnerability, belong to family number 3 of affected products in the above list.

Universidad Mayor in Santiago, Chile, has an Automation Lab equipped with Rockwell Automation controllers included in the list of affected products. The controllers belong to family number 2 of affected products in the above list. The specific PLC model is CompactLogix 5370 L24ER-QB1B. Based on the indicated vulnerability information, a research was initiated with the following hypothesis.

Hypothesis: "Rockwell Automation Allen-Bradley CompactLogix 5370 L2 controllers, have the Improper Input Validation vulnerability as stated by the manufacturer. The vulnerability can be exploited, resulting in a Denial of Service condition of the PLC".

3   Methodology Design

The methodology to prove the stated hypothesis was based on the "vulnerability details" contained in Sect. 2 of this paper, plus the analysis and definition of all the elements that had to be considered. Several components needed to be defined:

- Confirmation of available controller with affected firmware version
- Confirmation of required conditions to trigger the vulnerability
- Define platform to perform testing
- TCP/IP protocol details study
- TCP packet Option Field details study
- TCP/IP network protocol analyzer
- TCP Parameters and Options for specific PLC model available
- Exploit method
- Restore procedure of the PLC system, in case of successful exploitation.

3.1   Confirmation of Available Controller with Affected Firmware Version

Available Rockwell Automation PLC has firmware 21.01 and belongs to the list of affected products, indicated in Sect. 2. All controllers with firmware version 30.014 or prior are supposed to be affected, according to the manufacturer.

3.2 Confirmation of Required Conditions to Trigger the Vulnerability

As indicated in Sect. 2 in "Vulnerabilty Details", the PLC must use Ethernet/IP protocol communication and have TCP port 44818 open (or other similar TCP port open). Using NMAP scan tool, it was confirmed that TCP port 44818 is open in the PLC and it's used for Ethernet service. Therefore, these required conditions are ok (Fig. 1).

Scan Summary

Nmap 7.70 was initiated at Mon Mar 25 13:51:34 2019 with these arguments:
nmap -p 1-65535 -T4 -A -v 130.130.130.1

Verbosity: 1; Debug level 0

130.130.130.1 / vctr-01-67.admin.uow.edu.au

Address

- 130.130.130.1 - (ipv4)
- E4:90:69:9C:3D:94 - Rockwell Automation (mac)

Hostnames

- vctr-01-67.admin.uow.edu.au (PTR)

Ports

The 65533 ports scanned but not shown below are in state: **closed**

Port		State (toggle closed [0] | filtered [0])	Service
80	tcp	open	http
44818	tcp	open	EtherNet-IP-2

Fig. 1. Nmap scan confirms TCP port 44818 open for Ethernet-IP service

3.3 Defining a Platform to Perform the Tests

The Automation Lab at Universidad Mayor has an SMC FMS-200 manufacture plant, with 4 PLCs connected to Ethernet network and 2 Desktops running Controller Communication and Configuration software (Logix Designer software) over Windows 10 (Fig. 2).

Fig. 2. SMC FMS-200 manufacture plant with 4 PLCs

Logix Designer is already running on Windows in the Automation Lab. Logix Designer was used to get the appropriate communication parameters with the PLC.

Research for available TCP/IP packets injection tools on windows was done, as it will be explained in section "Exploit Method" of this paper.

The selected platform for TCP/IP packets injection was Linux. Specific platform was Kali Linux version 2018.2 over VMWare virtual machine workstation version 15, running over Windows 10, in a desktop connected to the PLCs network.

3.4 TCP/IP Protocol Details Study

TCP protocol is defined in RFC 793 [6] and IP protocol is defined in RFC 791 [7].

One of the main important concepts to understand regarding this protocol is the 3 Way Handshake (3WHS), which is used to establish a connection and also to finish a connection.

3WHS consist in a sequence of three specific packets between a client and a server.

To establish a connection, the correct sequence is:

1. SYN packet
2. SYN + ACK packet
3. ACK packet

In this study, the Kali Linux environment is the Client and the PLC is the Server or Host (Fig. 3).

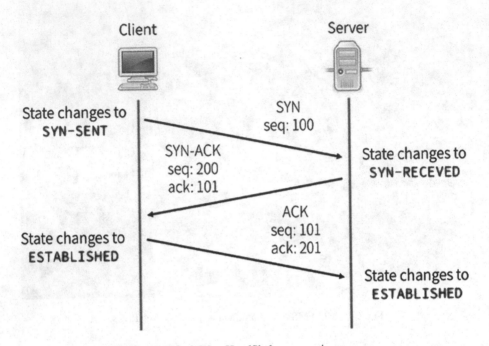

Fig. 3. 3WHS: 3 Way HandShake connection sequence

The above figure allow to understand the 3WHS sequence needed to establish a connection. It's also important to notice that proper handle of sequence and acknowledge numbering in TCP protocol, is required.

3.5 TCP Packet Options Field Details Study

TCP packet format must comply with RFC 793. Proper manipulation of TCP Options field is key for the testing to trigger/exploit the known vulnerability, due to the vulnerability details already explained in Sect. 2 (Fig. 4).

3.6 TCP/IP Network Protocol Analyzer

To have network traffic visibility during the exploit testing process and to capture the appropriate TCP parameters for valid communication with the PLC, it is mandatory to have a network protocol analyzer tool. Wireshark tool was the preferred choice for this purpose. It runs on Windows and Linux.

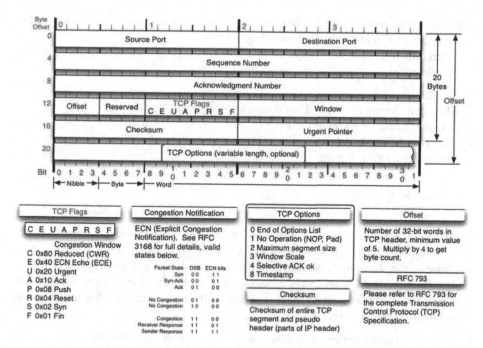

Fig. 4. Valid TCP packet format with multiple TCP options field

3.7 TCP Parameters and Options for Specific PLC Model Available

Each Rockwell Automation PLC model has specific communication parameters over TCP/IP network protocol, with the communication and configuration software Logix Designer. Those same parameters were used in the exploit code, to establish

No.	Time	Source	Destination	Protocol	Length	Info
137	53.994568	130.130.130.11	130.130.130.5	TCP	66	7626 → 44818 [SYN] Seq=0 Win=2300 Len=0 MSS=1460 WS=4 SACK_PERM=1
153	58.235124	130.130.130.11	130.130.130.5	TCP	62	[TCP Retransmission] 7626 → 44818 [SYN] Seq=0 Win=2300 Len=0 MSS=1460 SACK_PERM=1
154	58.237127	130.130.130.5	130.130.130.11	TCP	82	44818 → 7626 [SYN, ACK] Seq=0 Ack=1 Win=10000 Len=0 MSS=1426 SACK_PERM=1
155	58.237177	130.130.130.11	130.130.130.5	TCP	54	7626 → 44818 [ACK] Seq=1 Ack=1 Win=2300 Len=0
156	58.251635	130.130.130.11	130.130.130.5	ENIP	78	Unknown Command (0x0001) (Req)
157	58.251603	130.130.130.11	130.130.130.5	ENIP	78	List Services (Req)

```
▷ Frame 137: 66 bytes on wire (528 bits), 66 bytes captured (528 bits) on interface 0
▷ Ethernet II, Src: D-LinkIn_71:0e:ca (84:c9:b2:71:0e:ca), Dst: Rockwell_9c:3d:91 (e4:90:69:9c:3d:91)
▷ Internet Protocol Version 4, Src: 130.130.130.11, Dst: 130.130.130.5
▲ Transmission Control Protocol, Src Port: 7626, Dst Port: 44818, Seq: 0, Len: 0
    Source Port: 7626
    Destination Port: 44818
    [Stream index: 0]
    [TCP Segment Len: 0]
    Sequence number: 0    (relative sequence number)
    [Next sequence number: 0    (relative sequence number)]
    Acknowledgment number: 0
    1000 .... = Header Length: 32 bytes (8)
  ▷ Flags: 0x002 (SYN)
    Window size value: 2300
    [Calculated window size: 2300]
    Checksum: 0x0537 [unverified]
    [Checksum Status: Unverified]
    Urgent pointer: 0
  ▲ Options: (12 bytes), Maximum segment size, No-Operation (NOP), Window scale, No-Operation (NOP), No-Operation (NOP), SACK permitted
    ▷ TCP Option - Maximum segment size: 1460 bytes
    ▷ TCP Option - No-Operation (NOP)
    ▷ TCP Option - Window scale: 2 (multiply by 4)
    ▷ TCP Option - No-Operation (NOP)
    ▷ TCP Option - No-Operation (NOP)
    ▷ TCP Option - SACK permitted
  ▲ [Timestamps]
      [Time since first frame in this TCP stream: 0.000000000 seconds]
      [Time since previous frame in this TCP stream: 0.000000000 seconds]
```

Fig. 5. Wireshark capture showing valid communication parameters with the PLC

communication with the PLC. Wireshark was used to capture valid 3WHS traffic between the PLC and Logix Designer (Fig. 5).

Therefore, for Compact Logix 5370 L24ER-QB1B specific available controller model, the valid parameters and options are:

- Window = 2300
- Maximum Segment Size (MSS) option = 1460
- Window Scale (WS) option = 2
- Selective ACK ok (SAok) option = Yes
- Timestamp option = none.

3.8   Exploit Method

The options were basically two: finding a suitable and available TCP/IP packets injection tool for Windows or Linux, or a customized software development. Several tools were tried: Packet Sender, NetScanTools Pro, Trex, OpenStego, Nmap, Warp.

None of the above tools is capable to properly handling the Options Field of a TCP packet, for suitable ACK and SYN injections. Therefore, the alternative was a software development, which require to select a proper software language. After research, the main language options were two:

1. C++ with Libnet library, a specific library for network applications
2. Python with Scapy library, also a specific library for network applications

Python with Scapy library was selected, because that was the same language and library used by researcher Alexey Perepechko to successfully exploit the vulnerability in the other PLC model, the Rockwell Automation Allen-Bradley Compact Logix 5370 L30ERMS.

3.9   Restore Procedure of the PLC System, in Case of Successful Exploitation

Before starting the exploit testing, it was confirmed that in case of a major fault and a Denial of Service condition of the PLC, we were capable of restoring the PLC to normal operation, by reloading a backup of the firmware and the application software, with the Logix Designer tool provided by the manufacturer.

4   Experimental Testing and Results

The testing consisted on running multiple exploit versions, while monitoring and capturing network traffic with Wireshark. Valid parameters and options previously shown were used, for Compact Logix 5370 L24ER-QB1B PLC model.

A total of 90 tests were done, changing the python exploit code to achieve the following combinations:

- SYN crafted packet with 1 NOP option first and then MSS, WS and SAok options
- SYN crafted packet with 2 NOP option first and then MSS, WS and SAok options

- SYN crafted packet with 1 NOP option first and 1 NOP between MSS, WS, SAok
- Same previous one, but changing the location of the 2nd NOP in the Options
- ACK crafted packet with 1 NOP option first and then MSS, WS and SAok options
- ACK crafted packet with 2 NOP option first and then MSS, WS and SAok options
- ACK crafted packet with 1 NOP option first and 1 NOP between MSS, WS, SAok
- Same previous one, but changing the location of the 2nd NOP in the Options
- SYN & ACK crafted packets with 1 NOP option first and then MSS, WS and SAok options
- SYN & ACK crafted packets with 2 NOP option first and then MSS, WS and SAok options
- SYN & ACK crafted packets with 1 NOP option first and 1 NOP between other options
- Same previous one, but changing the location of the 2nd NOP in the Options
- Additional tests, suppressing a RESET (RST) packet that was automatically sent by Linux Kernel to the PLC, after receiving a SYN + ACK packet from the PLC
- Tests ended using the exact same python exploit code, with valid parameters, that was capable of exploiting the vulnerability in the Compact Logix 5370 L30ERMS PLC model [10, 11].

In all these tests, communication with the Compact Logix 5370 L24ER-QB1B PLC was established and confirmed, always having the 3 packets of the 3 Way Handshake, always getting the SYN + ACK reply from the PLC. Multiple Wireshark network traffic captures were saved for documentation purpose.

However, the Improper Input Validation vulnerability was never triggered for this PLC model. There was no major fault of the controller and no denial of service condition.

5   Conclusions

It's important to notice that Alexey Perepechko, the same researcher that discovered and exploited the vulnerability in the Rockwell Automation Allen-Bradley Compact Logix 5370 L30ERMS PLC model, participated in this research to trigger/exploit the same vulnerability in the Compact Logix 5370 L24ER-QB1B PLC model. Both PLC models are supposed to be affected products by the tested vulnerability, according to Rockwell Automation manufacturer.

Multiple exploit tests were done, including the exact same python exploit code, with valid parameters, that was used in successful exploitation when this vulnerability was discovered. Considering the experimental testing and results shown in Sect. 4, the hypothesis of this research was false.

However, there is sufficient test evidence to establish that Allen-Bradley Compact Logix 5370 L2 controllers, are not affected by the same type of Improper Input Validation vulnerability, than the Compact Logix 5370 L3 controllers. This evidence is opposed to the statement of the manufacturer, which informed NCICC that both controllers are affected products by the same CWE-20 Improper Input Validation vulnerability.

References

1. ICS CERT US Homepage. https://ics-cert.us-cert.gov/advisories/ICSA-18-172-02. Accessed 15 June 2019
2. APPLIED RISK Homepage. https://www.applied-risk.com/resources/ar-2018-002. Accessed 15 June 2019
3. NCICC Homepage. https://www.us-cert.gov/. Accessed 15 June 2019
4. NIST Homepage. https://nvd.nist.gov/vuln/detail/CVE-2017-9312. Accessed 15 June 2019
5. MITRE Homepage. http://cwe.mitre.org/data/definitions/20.html. Accessed 15 June 2019
6. RFC Homepage. https://www.rfc-editor.org/info/rfc793. Accessed 15 June 2019
7. RFC Homepage. https://www.rfc-editor.org/info/rfc791. Accessed 15 June 2019
8. Serhane, A., Raad, M. Raad, R., Susilo, W.: PLC Code-level vulnerabilities. In: 3rd International Conference on Computer and Applications (ICCA), Beirut, Lebanon, pp 348–352. IEEE (2018)
9. Lee, R., Assante, M., Conway, T.: Analysis of the cyber attack on the Ukrainian power grid. Technical report, E-ISAC, Washington, DC (2016)
10. Echeverri, D.: Hacking with Python. Zeroxword Computing, Madrid (2015)
11. Echeverri, D.: Python for Pentesters. Zeroxword Computing, Madrid (2014)
12. Krotofil, M., Gollmann, D.: Industrial control systems security - what is happening? In: 11th International Conference on Industrial Informatics (INDIN), Bochum, Germany, pp 664–669. IEEE (2013)
13. Milinkovic, S., Lazic, Ljubomir.: Industrial PLC security issues. In: 20th Telecommunications Forum (TELFOR), Belgrade, Serbia, pp. 1536–1539. IEEE (2012)
14. CVE Details Homepage. https://www.cvedetails.com/cve/CVE-2016-9343. Accessed 15 June 2019
15. NIST Homepage. https://nvd.nist.gov/vuln/detail/CVE-2016-9343. Accessed 15 June 2019

Identifying Components Belonging to Wireless Connectivity Security

Lorena Galeazzi Avalos[1]([⊠]), Cristian Barría Huidobro[1],
and Thamara Villegas Berbesi[2]

[1] Vicerrectoría de Investigación, Centro de Investigación en Ciberseguridad
CICS, Universidad Mayor, 7500628 Santiago, Chile
{lorena.galeazzi, cristian.barria}@mayor.cl
[2] Vicerrectoría de Investigación, Facultad de Ciencias, Escuela Ingeniería
Electrónica, Universidad Mayor, 7500628 Santiago, Chile
thamara.villegas@umayor.cl

Abstract. Information systems security has been a need for people and enterprises. This paper presents a review about the different variables studied in the literature affecting normal operations in Wi-Fi, these variables can change or affect the normal scenario, conditions, even vulnerabilities, hindering or facilitating attack by a third party. According to variables number identified, they are grouped and related into four categories components. All of this in support of to achieve a higher level of physical and information security.

Keywords: Components security wireless · Communications devices · Transmition system · Security of the environmental · Variable

1 Introduction

Currently, data security has an important role for enterprises and people. Different institutions have been trying to unify standards for risks evaluation linked to information handling, creating criteria to guarantee data security, integrity and confidentiality. This paper delivers base analysis to establish security level for WiFi networks, focused on the way the different instructions are performed by the different programs algorithms and their interaction and, the process management required to coordinate the different components needed to build the communication up.

The study objective is identifying components belonging to wireless connectivity security considering the variables that directly connect the physic and data link layers from OSI model or the access layer from the TCP/IP model (see Fig. 1).

© Springer Nature Switzerland AG 2019
M. F. Mata-Rivera et al. (Eds.): WITCOM 2019, CCIS 1053, pp. 365–373, 2019.
https://doi.org/10.1007/978-3-030-33229-7_31

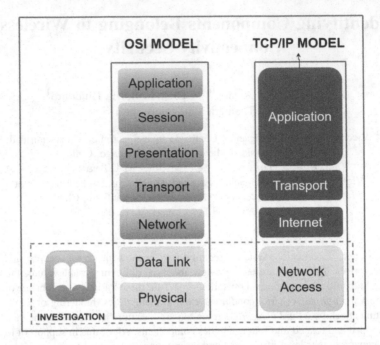

Fig. 1. A figure OSI model, physical and data link layers (Source: prepared)

2 Development

A wireless network, as defined by 802.11x standard, radiofrequency technology, is used as an alternative of using wired cable. This investigation is based on the wireless transmission media and the identification of the variables from the different components involved in the Wi-Fi security according to OSI and TCP/IP models, specifically in the first layers [1].

Wireless networks are defined by the radio waves modulation and data transmitting signaling [2]. Because of their nature, wireless networks are exposed and easily identified or monitored. Hence, importance to have clearly identified the variables and components belonging to the wireless network.

Components are catalogued according to the element characteristics, behavior and effects on the Information System. Variables are the component elements that change and impact the risk test results. Different components and associated variables can be identified (see Fig. 2).

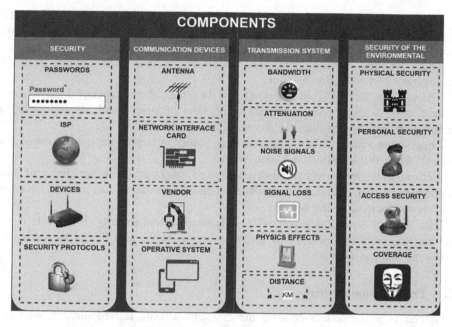

Fig. 2. Variables grouped by components (Source: prepared)

2.1 Security

This component groups the variables in the protection level (see Fig. 3).

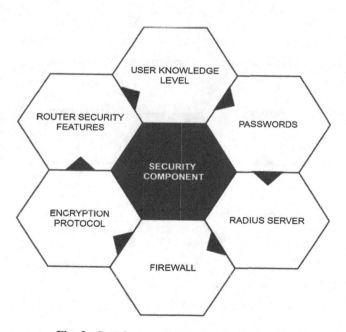

Fig. 3. Security component (Source: prepared)

The "User Knowledge Level", refers to the knowledge level the user has to detect a security fault or to configure the system to avoid the security issue. Users with knowledge are able to apply security and use support tools like software and apps.

There are three types of "Password", according to user level: device, technical administrator and web administrator.

The variable "Router Security Feature", as there are different types of devices, some of them with defense incorporated for some kind of attacks and are considered a security part and the first filter for any suspicious activity.

"Encryption Protocol", are a first security barrier as cypher the data transmission through WEP, WPA, WPA2 and soon WPA3.

Because of device variety and different kind of attacks available, the "Firewall" is a containment barrier considered a variable. In case of an attack, can mitigate attacker chances and increase router security.

The "Radius Server" is accountable of network access security. It controls if the user and password are valid, gives access to servers to the user that is attempting to access the wireless network.

2.2 Transmission System

Cataloged as a component because the elements amount related directly with the transmission process. In the case of wireless networks, this transmission type corresponds to a non-guided medium, as the electromagnetic waves are transmitted without combination through the air. The radiofrequency signal are electromagnetic waves that transport information [3].

The variables or elements part of this component are related to (see Fig. 4).

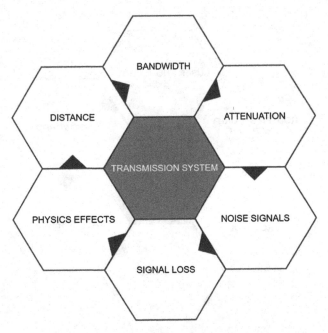

Fig. 4. Security transmission system (Source: prepared)

Effective **"bandwidth"** is the frequency band where is concentrated the most part of the signal, which is limited by the transmission speed. Therefore, there is a direct relation between transmission speed and bandwidth: the higher the transmission speed of a signal, the greater the effective bandwidth [4].

The **"attenuation"** described as factors, like distance and atmospheric, are conditions affect the transmission energy level and consequently the receiver errors level.

"Noise Signals" are present in the transmission media, non-wanted signals affect between the transmitter and receiver, distorting the information signal. The noise can be classified in four categories: Thermal noise, Intermodulation noise, Crosstalk and Impulsive noise.

"Signal Loss" is consequence of different effects [5], like atmospheric absorption, and absorption through the interaction with the matter like walls, glass, concrete, marble, wood, stone, etc. that can be defined as signal absorbers.

The **"Physics Effects"**, such as diffraction, is energy redistribution in a wave front when goes at the border of an object; allows wave propagation through the corners [6]. Reflection, when the electromagnetic wave pass through the border between two mediums, a part of the wave is reflected in the opposite direction [6]. Refraction, changes the signal direction by passing in an oblique direction from a medium to another, with different propagation velocity [6].

The **"Distance"**, defined as the range of space or time that mediates between two things or events [7]. In wireless transmissions, the signal is dispersed by distance, therefore the greater the distance from the transmitter, the transmission power range will be considerably reduced [8].

2.3 Communication Devices

These are the devices needed for a wireless network connection and operation (see Fig. 5).

"Antenna" is an electric conductor used for transmitting or receiving electromagnetic signals from bi-directional communications. The antenna converts the electrical energy from the transmitter to electromagnetic energy and then is radiated to the atmosphere, space or water [4]. By the other side, the antenna converts the electromagnetic signal to electric energy and is sent to the receiver [4].

The antennas are designed to transmit and receive in a specific frequency [9]. Antennas are designed considering distance to reach, radiation intensity, beam width and power. The radiation intensity, is the three dimensional radiation pattern, and shows the direction the antenna radiates the signal [9]. This investigation only will treat the antennas used for transmitting and receiving Wi-Fi wireless networks. The antennas are classified as omnidirectional and directional, the most of devices used in wireless networks use omnidirectional antennas. Directional antennas are used mainly for long distance connection or to cover a specific area.

The variable "Network Interface Card" is an essential part when penetration test tools are used [10]. Network interface cards should have the monitor mode enabled to make the penetration test. Network interface cards have a chipset used for penetration testing, but not all chipsets allow monitor mode, therefore, is important to know which chipset [12] can be enabled to monitor mode [11].

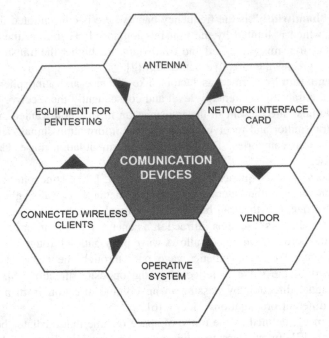

Fig. 5. Communication devices (Source: prepared)

This variable considers the differences that wireless device manufacturer, in this case described like "Vendor", have according to their policies, production schemes, support and updates. hat the first paragraph of a section or subsection is not indented.

According to the vendor, it is the degree of security at the administration level and protection barriers that can be estimated as preliminary data to consider, at the time of performing a pentesting.

Updates are a characteristic associated with the manufacturer, it defines whether the device is vulnerable or not. It is also possible to mention, the location installed device, normally they are not installed according to what the installation manual says, It may not be installed as recommended by the manufacturer's manual, for ignorance or changes made without considering the initial implementation, This is an advantage for any attacker, since the power varies and change the emitted signal direction by the transmitter. Facilitating detection attacker activity, where the attacker can detect a signal wireless networks, from any vulnerable place for any of penetration attack.

To pentesting level process, the amount "Connected wireless clients" to the devices, it is considered a variable. Mainly in the process attack, there are different types, depend of traffic users generated when navigate on the network, for be used by a software exploitation execution.

The Operative System of the endpoint, wireless router, and any tools of pentesting software, are considered as an important variable for vulnerability level. The configuration systems and applications installed by operative systems, influence bad practices adopted by users and administrators, for simple carelessness.

In process of the activities to be carried out, the "Equipment for Penetration Test", it is considered like a variable, considering different stages or phases of process, such as recognition, attack, among others. The activities depend on different devices such as a cell phone, notebook or tablet, among others. An interesting example is a notebook or mobile used from a car in motion to detect wireless networks (wardriving) [13].

2.4 Environmental Safety

Internal and external environment where a wireless network is operating defines the security requirements and vulnerability options. The access level in the neighborhoods as well as the security personal presence can modify this component. That is the reason to consider following variables (see Fig. 6).

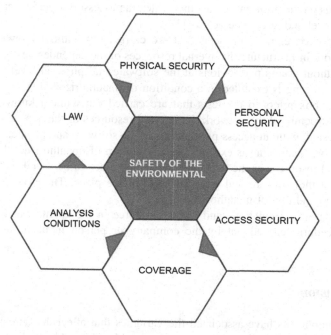

Fig. 6. Safety of the environmental (Source: prepared)

The "Physical Security" is determined by the physical difficulties of location and infrastructure of the unit, important features, to decide the level of network security by the user and by the attacker to make a malicious activity.

People presence around the site to difficulting access attacker, determined like variable "Personal security", which directly affects on any activity to be carried out, both in the process of pentesting, as the physical security network.

"Access security" is determined as the set of physical elements that allow you to control access to the network. These elements are related to technology, focused on the function of the company or organization, in support of control and information security.

The first paragraphs that follows a table, figure, equation etc. does not have an indent, either.

The "coverage" variable is related to the previous ones, allows the preparation and use of masking tools, any type of activity associated with violating security without being detected. Coverage is the way to penetrate the place with high security without being detected.

This is directly related to conditions analysis, the way in which the safety tests will be carried out is considered, and the conditions of access to information, two models can be defined like "white box" or "black boxes" models.

The white box refers to the test procedures that use information on internal performance and the source code in the case of transparent software testing, this type of test has a focus on the information that the pentesting assessor or performer has, both at the systems level and at the site access [13].

The black box refers to the tests that are carried out without knowledge of the internal network infrastructure, its internal resources or the dependencies of the place to be tested, without access permissions at the software and physical level of the place. Therefore, pentesting is executed in a condition of unauthorized [13].

The black box refers to the tests that are carried out without knowledge of the internal infrastructure of the network, its internal resources or the dependencies of the place to be tested, without access permissions at the software and physical level of the place. Therefore, pentesting is executed in a condition of unauthorized [13].

Its internal resources or the dependencies of the place to be tested, without access permissions at the software and physical level of the place. Therefore, pentesting is executed in a condition of unauthorized [13].

The regulations, regulations and "laws" in force in the country, and the internal security procedures carried out by the company or person in its network must be considered.

3   Conclusion

Identified components have associated the variables that affect the wireless transmission medium. Some of these variables are not considered in other studies or have been considered on an isolated way. As result of this paper, these variables have been grouped to find a relationship between them and define a real scenario affecting the pentesting procedures. Penetration tests fail to achieve their objectives as only use ideal environment parameters leaving aside other key parameters.

Therefore, each component variables compilation offers a new transmission medium vision, providing decision making support to feasible attacks and make wireless network security improvements.

This investigation defines future works on a guide design to evaluate wireless network security level according to identified components.

References

1. International Organization for Standardization (ISO homepage) (2019). https://www.iso.org/standard/20269.html
2. Pacio, G.: Data Center hoy. Buenos Aires - Argentina, año, Editorial Alfaomega (2014)
3. Stallings, W.: Comunicaciones Redes de Computadores. 7ma Edición (2004)
4. Hi, Y., Boile, K.: Antennas from Theory to Practice. Wiley, United Kingdom (2008)
5. Morán, J.: Efectos de interferencia sobre redes basadas en el estándar IEEE 802.11 en el espectro de 2.4 GHz (2012)
6. Eleftheriades, G.V., Balmain, K.G.: Negative Refraction Metamaterials: Fundamental Principles and Applications. Wiley-IEEE Press, Hoboken (2005)
7. https://dle.rae.es/?id=Dy4u4UW
8. Barclay, L.W.: Propagation of Radio Wave. IEE (2003)
9. Beard, C.: Wireless Communication Networks and Systems, William Stallings. Pearson, London (2016)
10. Joshua, W., Cache, J.: Hacking Exposed Wireless: Wireless Security Secrets & Solutions. McGraw-Hill Osborne Media, New York (2014)
11. Aircrack-ng Homepage, June 2019. https://www.aircrack-ng.org/doku.php?id=compatibility_drivers
12. Ron, S., et al.: Analytic Methods in Systems and Software Testing. Institute, Technion, Israel Fabrizio Ruggeri CNR-IMATI, Italy Frederick W. Faltin The Faltin Group and Virginia Tech, USA (2018)
13. Hurley, C., et al.: WarDriving & Wireless penetration Testing. Syngress Publishing, Inc. Rockland, Canada (2007)

Author Index

Printed in the United States
By Bookmasters